Serial Murderers and Their Victims

Third Edition

ERIC W. HICKEY
California State University, Fresno

WADSWORTH
THOMSON LEARNING

Australia • Canada • Mexico • Singapore • Spain
United Kingdom • United States

WADSWORTH
THOMSON LEARNING™

Executive Editor, Criminal Justice: Sabra Horne
Development Editor: Terri Edwards
Assistant Editor: Dawn Mesa
Editorial Assistant: Lee McCracken
Technology Project Manager: Susan DeVanna
Marketing Manager: Jennifer Somerville
Marketing Assistant: Neena Chandra
Advertising Project Manager: Bryan Vann
Project Manager, Editorial Production: Jennie Redwitz
Print/Media Buyer: Karen Hunt
Permissions Editor: Bob Kauser
Production Service: Shepherd, Inc.
Copy Editor: Julie Kennedy
Cover Designer: Yvo Riezebos
Cover Image: © EyeWire
Cover Printer: Webcom Limited
Compositor: Shepherd, Inc.
Printer: Webcom Limited

Printed in Canada
10 9 8 7 6 5 4 3

ISBN 0-534-54569-6

Wadsworth/Thomson Learning
10 Davis Drive
Belmont, CA 94002-3098
USA

For more information about our products, contact us:
Thomson Learning Academic Resource Center
1-800-423-0563
http://www.wadsworth.com

International Headquarters
Thomson Learning
International Division
290 Harbor Drive, 2nd Floor
Stamford, CT 06902-7477
USA

UK/Europe/Middle East/South Africa
Thomson Learning
Berkshire House
168-173 High Holborn
London WC1V 7AA
United Kingdom

Asia
Thomson Learning
60 Albert Street, #15-01
Albert Complex
Singapore 189969

Canada
Nelson Thomson Learning
1120 Birchmount Road
Toronto, Ontario M1K 5G4
Canada

To the victims, both the living and the dead—
may their suffering not be ignored nor forgotten.

And to every person who has a passion for the study of forensics.

And to my children, Trevor, Erin, Alicen, and Chad.

About the Author

Eric W. Hickey, earned a Ph.D. in social psychology from Brigham Young University and taught sociology and criminology course at West Georgia College and at Ball State University. In 1990 he became a member of the criminology department at California State University, Fresno, where he currently teaches criminal psychology, patterns in homicide, and sex crimes. Dr. Hickey also serves as an adjunct professor for Fresno City College and the California School of Professional Psychology. He has considerable field experience working with the criminally insane, psychopaths, sex offenders and other habitual criminals. Internationally recognized for his research on multiple homicide offenders, Dr. Hickey has published and lectured extensively in the etiology of violence and serial crime. This book, *Serial Murderers and Their Victims,* Third Edition, is used as a teaching tool in colleges and universities and by law enforcement personnel in studying the nature of violence, criminal personalities, and victim-offender relationships.

Dr. Hickey's research is often the subject of newspaper, radio, and television interviews including *National Public Radio, Larry King Live, 20/20, A&E, BBC, Good Morning America, Court TV,* and Discovery Channel and Learning Channel documentaries. He frequently speaks to school and community organizations and provides training seminars for administrators, school psychologists, and counselors in addressing crime and the deterrence of violence.

A former consultant to the UNABOM Task Force, Dr. Hickey assists various law enforcement and private agencies and testifies as an expert witness in both criminal and civil cases. He conducts training seminars for government agencies involving the profiling and investigating of sex crimes, arson, and homicide, as well as stalking and workplace violence. Dr. Hickey has travelled to Israel and trained VIP protection specialists from around the world in profiling and deterring stalkers. He assisted in developing a cyber-stalking training course for the National District Attorney's Association and the American Prosecutor's Research Institute. His latest research, a study of 220 victims of stalking, examines the psychology and classification of stalkers, victim-offender relationships, intervention, and deterrence strategies for potential offenders and modes of victim assistance.

Contents

Foreword

As editor of the Wadsworth Contemporary Issues in Crime and Justice Series, I am delighted to introduce the Third Edition of *Serial Murderers and Their Victims* by Eric W. Hickey. The series is dedicated to the exploration of important issues in crime and justice that receive limited attention in textbooks, but deserve closer study. Books appearing in this series are used by students to deepen their understanding of important questions facing the fields of criminology and criminal justice, and we are proud to say that the series has, over the years, published some of the most important books on current topics of interest to the field. This book is one of them.

Serial murders are a bit like natural disasters: In the scheme of things they are quite rare, but when they happen they demand our attention. They interest us for several reasons, but especially because they are so dramatically threatening, and they profoundly challenge our sense of our own everyday safety. But unlike natural disasters, which happen according to an age-old, semistable rhythm, there is solid evidence that the number of serial murders in American society is rapidly increasing. So the phenomenon challenges us to think about contemporary society. We ask, "Why?" It also challenges us to think about the human condition. We wonder, "What could make someone commit such horrible crimes?"

Professor Hickey shows that this question opens the door to a stunning world of issues and provokes a whole new set of questions. Though rare in number, serial murders seem to mirror our larger society in ways both fascinating and troubling. It is easy to get overly emotional about the topic as well. But Professor Hickey shows us, with his careful and thorough analysis of these events in contemporary history, that replacing unfocused emotion with detached investigation can yield a richness of insight that fully rewards those who will devote themselves to a deeper foray into the topic.

Mastery of several different scientific fields is required for a thorough understanding of the social significance of serial murders. Forensic psychology, social pathology, and sociobiology help us to understand the etiology of the serial murderer's behavior. Sociology and anthropology help us to gain a deeper insight about the social meaning of the apparent rise in serial killing. Political science and public administration give us the basis for more informed public policy regarding serial violence. And forensic criminology gives us insights into effective actions regarding this problem.

Professor Hickey has crossed a variety of disciplines in order to give us not just part of the story, but a full and rich understanding of this distressing phenomenon. We learn about the variety of serial killing incidents over recent history, and how serial killing seems to be changing in current times. We also learn that there are important controversies regarding the definition of serial murder, and that these controversies tell us something about modern society as well. And we learn that no single theory or explanation will suffice to fully reveal the causes and consequences of serial killing.

Perhaps the most affecting parts of this book are the profiles Professor Hickey provides. The stories of the offenders are arresting, and we find ourselves drawn into the appalling reality of what they have done and how they came to do it. Even more upsetting are the stories of the victims, whose experiences in too many criminological studies remain shrouded in secrecy. In one thoroughly jolting part of this book, we read the words of a serial killer in an interview, and we get a remarkable glimpse into the thinking and relaxed emotionality that must accompany what are shocking acts.

What emerges is a moving study of a subject that turns out to be astonishing in its complexity. We come to see how serial murder, while socially extreme, can only be understood within the contemporary social context. We also come to see how it is through a better understanding of this disturbing phenomenon that we can build a plan of social action to help prevent serial murders from happening—or at least reduce the damage to victims and society when the serial killer starts to work.

Thus the Third Edition of *Serial Murderers and Their Victims* is the most important study of serial killing yet published. Professor Hickey gives us a superbly thorough and detailed treatment of the subject of serial murder, and gives us the tools for a more profound understanding of this social phenomenon. This book ably illustrates the goal of the Wadsworth Contemporary Issues in Crime and Justice Series: to advance our understanding of important questions in the fields of criminology and criminal justice. I commend this book to you. Once you are finished reading this text, your understanding of the awesome reality of serial killing will be deeper and more effective, and you will be a more informed and capable citizen for having read it.

Todd R. Clear, Series Editor
Florida State University

Preface

Serial Murderers and Their Victims, First Edition, was the first scholarly, comprehensive, empirical examination of serial murder in the United States. The Second Edition expanded the exploration of serial murderers by providing a thorough analysis of the lives of serial killers through the examination of individual cases, typology construction, and models. The extensive data examined not only provided insights into individual killers but revealed factors common to 399 serial killers—including male solo offenders, female offenders, and those who murder with accomplices. The Third Edition is an extensive revision that brings to the reader some of the latest cases in serial and mass murder. Included are amazing interviews with a serial killer, a paraphilic serial arsonist, and a psychopathic stalker. This edition provides close examination of the maladaptive behaviors of disturbed children, including cruelty to animals, fire setting, and enuresis. A complete new classification system for understanding stalking and its role in violent behavior will cause the reader to think about crime from radically new perspectives. An entire chapter is dedicated to examining serial murder from a global perspective, which helps readers redefine traditional definitions of serial killing. Finally, this new edition explores the effectiveness of profiling criminals, especially serial killers, and examines a new and horrifying form of serial murder that increases the accessibility of serial murderers to certain target populations.

Serial Murderers and Their Victims debunks the myths and stereotypes that have evolved from public efforts to find easy explanations for the relatively rare yet horrifying phenomenon of serial murder. It also raises many questions about serial killers and their behavior. The research for this book has included visits to prisons, police departments, and numerous university libraries across the United States, as well as extensive computer searches, and interviews with several serial murderers, their spouses, ex-spouses, lovers, and friends. I explored the lives of dead victims and victims who survived the attacks, and I communicated with families and relatives of the victims. Despite the extensive social, psychological, physiological, and financial devastation inflicted by serial murderers on their victims and the victims' families, the victims are often reduced to little more than crime statistics. The etiology of victimization and the continued suffering of survivors must not be forgotten or neglected.

ORGANIZATION

This book explores five aspects of serial murder. Chapter 1 examines the emergence of serial and mass killing in the United States and the many problems involved in adequately defining the phenomenon. Readers are introduced to the role of paraphilia in serial murder. Chapters 2, 3, and 4 explore cultural, biological, psychological, and sociological frameworks as explanations for serial murder and present a model for understanding serial killing as a process. The role of stalking in serial murder is examined and placed into a classification system. Chapters 5, 6, and 7 sort out the demographic, social, and behavioral characteristics of male and female offenders and those who murder with accomplices. Chapter 8 examines the victims and prospective victims of serial murderers: prostitutes, young women, gay people, children, and the elderly. Chapter 9 includes an in-depth interview with an incarcerated serial killer. Chapter 10 explores serial killing around the world and compares serial murder in the United States to its occurrences in other countries. Finally, Chapter 11 addresses current issues faced by law enforcement officials, such as detection and apprehension of offenders using a variety of emerging profiling techniques. The role and utility of forensics is explored as a science in studying and investigating serial crime. The chapter concludes by presenting sentencing, punishment, treatment, and prevention tactics in cases of serial murder.

This book is intended for students interested in understanding the nature of serial killing, the offenders, and their victims. It is designed to supplement a variety of college and university courses—including criminology, criminal justice, deviant behavior, victimology, abnormal psychology, and penology. Students using this book will be exposed to concepts and information that will help prepare them to understand society's most dangerous criminals. For those currently working in law enforcement, this book should serve as a useful reference and in-service tool.

ACKNOWLEDGMENTS

I wish to recognize and thank the many people who helped during the course of my research and publication of this Third Edition. I want to thank Brad Gorby for his passion in researching serial murder, and my "Charlie's Angels," Dr. Catherine Purcell, Dr. Janna Oddie, Dr. Laura White, and Dr. Alexa Wasserman for their friendship and expertise. I thank Dr. Debra Margulies for her encouragement and loyal assistance in compiling stalking data, as well as Dr. Rocky Underwood, Stephanie Petrucci, and Dr. Nicole Mott for their loyalty and support. Their enthusiasm was contagious. In addition, my profound gratitude goes to my colleagues Dr. Otto Schweizer, Harvey Wallace, Dr. Thomas Dull, and my lifelong friends Dr. John R. Fuller, Steve Opager, and Lloyd A. Mackenzie, whose counsel, encouragement and true friendship will never be forgotten. I also wish to thank Joan Jeffries and Elizabeth Swift, our departmental secretaries, for their patience and support throughout this project, as well as Mary Ellen Pistalu for her technical assistance. In addition, I want to express my gratitude to Mr. Phil Bethier, of London, England, for all the clippings and correspondence. Finally, I want to thank my dear friend, Holly Peacock, for her contributions, encouragement and assistance on my behalf. Your patience and insights were valuable beyond measure.

A special thanks to California State University–Fresno for their financial support in helping me complete the data collection for the Second Edition and to Roberta Roper of the Stephanie Roper Committee and Ruth and John Kuzmaak of Victim's Voices United for their willingness to share their personal tragedies and their efforts to be more than mere survivors. I also want to thank those who reviewed the manuscript for their helpful comments. They are Joseph Davis, Institute of Law, Psychology and Public Policy Studies and Center for Forensic Behavioral Sciences; Steven Egger, University of Illinois at Springfield; Rhonda DeLong, Indiana University, South Bend; John Evans, Walter State Community College; and D. Kim Rossmo, Simon Fraser University. In addition, my appreciation goes to the entire Wadsworth team, especially to my editor Sabra Horne (who never gave up on me) and to the series editor, Todd Clear. I deeply appreciate their support and guidance. Never could an author expect to find a more competent, professional team of editors than those at Wadsworth.

And to my four beautiful children, Trevor, Erin, Alicen, and Chad, who, as they journey through life might think of their dad with kindness and always know that I will love them forever and ever. And to my dear mother, Shirley Hickey, for her constant wit, devotion, and support. I love you, Mom.

Eric W. Hickey

Now ask yourself this question and see if by the time you have finished reading this most horrifying book, you have discerned the answer:

What is required to live the life of one's own image?

The answer is within . . .

1

Introduction

The Phenomenon of Serial Murder

Multiple homicide is undoubtedly one of the most terrifying and fascinating phenomena of modern-day crime. It is also one of the most sensationalized areas of research within the fields of criminology, psychology, and sociology. Getting down to the "real facts" of a case rather than getting caught up in the inevitable media barrage has become a task difficult for even the most stringent, reputable researchers. The problems are many and interrelated. Philip Jenkins (1994), in his book *Using Murder: The Social Construction of Serial Homicide,* provides a scholarly examination of how serial killing has been dealt with by the media, law enforcement, and the public. His findings are consistent with this author's: Much of what we "know" about serial murder is based on misinformation and myth construction. As a result of the sensational nature of this form of murder, the aura surrounding it has assumed a life of its own as it filters throughout both the public and private sectors of society.

In the summer of 1981 the present author relocated to the Atlanta, Georgia, area. Coincidentally, Wayne Williams, a young African American male believed to one of the nation's more prolific serial killers, was arrested at that time in the same area. This case brought to the forefront the fact that not all serial killers were white nor were the victims. Technology, specifically hair/fiber evidence, became a critical factor in convicting Williams, and forensic science became prominent in explaining why such evidence ultimately played a key role in linking Williams to the crimes. Over 20 homicides were attributed to Williams, most of them children, although he was actually convicted of murdering just two of his victims. The horror and fascination of this case focused media attention on Atlanta both during the homicides and after Williams's capture. Within the next three years several more accounts of serial murder appeared in newspapers around the country. The American public had been invaded by a new criminal type, the serial murderer. Lurking in our communities, preying upon hapless victims, serial murderers had suddenly emerged from the criminal underground—perhaps a product of the Vietnam War or possibly a byproduct of technology and the moral decay of our society. Most citizens simply assumed serial killers must be insane. No one knew for sure. The cases of serial murder increased as did the body counts. Eventually, the ever-growing reality of multiple murders began to obtrude on public awareness. Something had to be done to stem the tide of homicides with no apparent motive.

In 1984 the Federal Bureau of Investigation (FBI, 1984a, 1984b; Ninety-eighth Congress, 1984) appeared before the United States Senate to seek funding for the development of a program specifically targeting violent criminals. According to news accounts of the hearing, as many as 5,000 people per year were believed to be killed by serial murderers. Indeed, the numbers used to describe the victims in all categories of violent crime were shocking and incredible. The public and public officals alike were horrified, and funding was procured for the program. For the next several years the incidence of serial murder was considered by the public to be pervasive in our society, though in fact this was far from the truth. No one knew how many serial killers actually existed at any one time, but it was clear that the number of victims killed by such offenders did not even begin to approach 5,000. Where that inflated figure first originated was a mystery. Perhaps a piece of information exchanged during an interview between the media and law enforcement had been misinterpreted. In any event the number appeared and immediately sparked media attention. What is important is not who started the rumors but that they were so quickly disseminated without ever being verified.

Such forms of disinformation are not new or uncommon. For example, when marijuana came into public view during the 1940s, a film, *Reefer Madness,* was distributed, depicting the powerfully destructive forces of the illegal substance. Clean, upstanding young men and women, on experiencing the effects of just one reefer, were transformed into raving, sex-crazed lunatics. Though amusing to us now, such exaggeration is disturbing in light of the film's original purpose and effects.

Much of the proliferation of disinformation is a result of public pressure to know more about a specific subject. In some respects, a symbiotic relationship has developed among law enforcement, the media, and the public that serves in fact to encourage disinformation in regard to certain sorts of issues. Realizing this, some researchers, such as Jenkins, the present author, and others, began questioning the actual extent of serial murder. We do not question that serial murder occurs, but to what quantifiable and qualitative extent. This is the role of the social scientist: to objectively examine phenomena to determine their origin, nature, and impact on society.

SERIAL MURDER: FACT AND FICTION

The apparent increase in the modern serial, or multiple, murder has incited interest among social scientists in several areas. Researchers have begun to explore the social, psychological, and biological makeup of the offenders in order to establish accurate profiles. In spite of their efforts, during the 1980s the body of knowledge about serial murders remained small compared to the number of unanswered questions—especially about the extent of the phenomenon. In more recent years law enforcement personnel and academicians have come closer to understanding the dynamics of serial killing and its etiology, or causation.

The pure sensationalism and horror of serial murder has also spawned a plethora of novels about such murders, and the figure of the "cold-blooded, senseless" serial killer has been exploited by the media: for example, in television documentaries and prime-time shows—such as those that depicted California's Hillside Strangler case and the infamous Ted Bundy (*The Deliberate Stranger*)—and in various box office thrillers. Because of the wide publicity given to serial murderers, a stereotype of this type of killer has formed in the mind of American society. The offender is a ruthless, blood-thirsty sex monster who lives a Jekyll-and-Hyde existence—probably next door to you. Increasingly, crime novels and movies have focused on multiple-homicide offenders. Consider the steady proliferation of multiple-homicide films, noted by Main (1997), in which serial killing is the primary agenda (see Table 1.1).

Although this list is not exhaustive, it is representative of each decade. It does not include films involving mass murder (the killing of a number of people all at one time) or horror films depicting vampires and murderous zombies, but only films portraying real people murdering other people. Notice the explosion of serial-murder themes during the 1990s. At least half of those never made it to theaters but went straight to videos. In the privacy of one's home viewers are bombarded with graphic killings, mutilations, and sexual torture. Clearly, this cinematic emphasis has added credibility to the notion of high body counts at the hands of ubiquitous serial-killer monsters.

Table 1.1 Increase in Films with Serial Killing, 1920s–1990s

Decade	Number of Serial-Murder Theme Films
1920s	2
1930s	3
1940s	3
1950s	4
1960s	12
1970s	20
1980s	23
1990s	117

In his 1987 book, *The Red Dragon,* Harris gave a fictional account of a serial killer who took great pleasure in annihilating entire families. Later his work was made into the movie *Manhunter,* an engrossing drama of psychopathology, blood, and carnage. At that time Hollywood was only beginning to realize the huge market for multiple-murder movies. Some years later, the next book by Tom Harris and the derivative movie, both titled *Silence of the Lambs,* caught the American imagination. By 2001 movies such as *Copycat, Kiss the Girls,* the *Scream* trilogy, *Along Came a Spider,* and *Hannibal,* continued to exploit the public's fascination with serial murder without yielding much insight about the offender. Filmmakers unable to adequately navigate the minds of serial offenders resorted to technology and special effects to draw in viewers as seen in *The Cell.* Other films, such as *Seven,* a dark, disturbing movie, attempted to offer some understanding of the murdering mind but confused viewers with the concepts of psychopathy, psychosis, and murder.

Novelists such as Easton Ellis, with his exploration of psychopathy, narcissism, sadism, and murder in *American Psycho* (later made into a movie by the same name) and Carr's acclaimed serial-murder thriller *The Alienist,* clearly indicate that writers are familiarizing themselves with the topic of serial murder and have begun to inject some insightful and historical perspectives into their narratives. The fictional accounts of serial killing, however, often fail to surpass the horror described in nonfictional accounts of serial murder by writers such as Ann Rule, a former acquaintance of the serial killer Ted Bundy, who was executed in January 1989. Besides her work on Bundy (*The Stranger Beside Me,* 1980), she has written about Randy Woodfield (*The I-5 Killer,* 1984), Jerry Brudos (*Lust Killer,* 1983), and Harvey Carnigan (*The Want-Ad Killer,* 1988).

Throughout the 1990s dozens of novels and nonfiction accounts of multiple homicide have been published for the entertainment and sometimes enlightenment of the general public. Amid this proliferation, female serial killers have been given increased attention, in true crime accounts of "black widows" (women who, for various reasons, kill their husbands, then remarry only to carry out the cycle of homicide again and again); nurses who kill their elderly, young, or otherwise helpless patients; mothers who murder their children; females who assist men in serial killing; and a few women who have stalked and murdered men.

The researchers who have been examining the phenomenon of serial murder to promote greater understanding—and, they hope, develop intervention strategies—have also been busy. Case study analysis of serial murder has begun to provide researchers with insightful information, however tenuous. For example, Elliot Leyton (1986a) in his book *Hunting Humans* provides in-depth examinations of the lives and minds of a few contemporary U.S. serial killers and their relationships with their victims. In *Mass Murder: The Growing Menace* (1985) and *Overkill* (1994), Jack Levin and James Fox assess some of the dynamics of serial and mass murder. Ronald Holmes and James DeBurger, in their work *Serial Murder* (1988), formulate typologies based on material gathered from interviews with serial murderers. Holmes's second work, *Profiling*

Violent Crimes (1990), has become a useful tool in the investigation of serial murder. Steve Egger's work *Serial Murder: An Elusive Phenomenon* (1990) and his *The Killers Among Us* (1998) underscore several critical problems encountered by researchers and law enforcement investigations of serial murder. Robert Keppel, who as a law enforcement officer has investigated several cases of serial killing, published his observations in *Serial Murder: Future Implications for Police Investigations* (1989). Jenkins (1994) has examined societal forces such as law enforcement, the media, and public interest, which have acted as catalysts in the emergence of the serial-murder phenomenon as a social construct. Also in recent years, a number of documentaries, such as CNN's *Murder by Number,* have critically examined the extent and impact of serial murder. In 1994 British television produced an award-winning documentary *To Kill and Kill Again* (Optomen Television, 1994). As a result of the case of Jeffrey Dahmer and the writing of this book, serial murder began to be explored not merely as an act, but as a *process.* In 1996, several books examining serial murder, including *Serial Murderers and Their Victims,* were placed on the compact disk entitled *Mind of a Killer.* This "serial-murder library" allows researchers, students, and law enforcement to access a vast amount of information, including biographies, photographs, and the investigative tools used to track serial killers. By 2001, other scholarly television documentaries including *Understanding Murder* (the Learning Channel), aired, which examined the roles of psychology and biology in serial murder.

Many other people associated with research on serial murder have also contributed to the body of knowledge on the subject. For instance, Harold Smith, past editor of *Criminal Justice International* at the University of Chicago, has collected data on transnational serial killers—that is, killers whose victims are from different countries. Philip Jenkins, at Pennsylvania State University, has explored the social environments of serial murderers, whereas Candice Skrapec, a forensic psychologist in the Department of Criminology, California State University–Fresno, has gathered data on the psychogenic status of serial offenders. Al Carlisle, a psychologist at the Utah State Prison and Provo Canyon Boys School, has explored dissociative states and other forces that may affect the mind of a serial killer. David Canter of Liverpool, England, has organized an investigative psychology program that, among other things, emphasizes the geographic profiling of crimes and offenders. D. Kim Rossmo, formerly of the Vancouver Police Department, in his 1995 dissertation made a substantial contribution to the field of forensics through his geographic profiling of serial murderers. He is now considered to be one of the top geographic profilers in the world. Increasingly, both academicians and law enforcement are becoming involved in the study and exploration of violent serial crime.

Law enforcement officials have been dealing with serial murders for many, many years. By the 1990s, however, the nature and sophistication of investigation techniques changed. Computer technology, especially the development of the Internet, expedited data collection and analysis. During the mid-1980s, the Federal Bureau of Investigation established, at their Behavioral Science Unit in Quantico, Virginia (now referred to as the Investigative Support Unit), the Violent Criminal Apprehension Program (VICAP). The VICAP program is designed to collect detailed information on homicides throughout the United States. Investigators like former FBI agents Robert Ressler and John Douglas, who have interviewed several serial killers in the United States, have made considerable progress in understanding certain types of serial offenders. Ressler and colleagues published their findings in *Sexual Homicide* (1988). In addition, the U.S. government continues to develop programs such as the National Center for the Analysis of Violent Crime (NCAVC) to focus specifically on repetitive offenders, including serial murderers.

NUMBERS AND TYPES OF MASS MURDERS AND SERIAL KILLINGS IN THE UNITED STATES

The number of murders in the United States fluctuated around 25,000 per year by the early 1990s. By that time we had witnessed a 20-year period of murder and manslaughter rates increasing 300% while police clearance rates for these crimes had declined from 93% in 1962 to 74% in 1982 and to about 65% by 1995 (Federal Bureau of Investigation, 1995). Homicide rates in the United States appeared to be one of the highest of any westernized nation. In recent years, however, we have seen a remarkable decline in violent crime. The last several years have seen fewer violent and property crimes. By 2000 the United States was reporting 30-year lows in crime rates (see Table 1.2). The Center for Disease Control (2001) found that in 1997, of the 5,285 workplace deaths, 14% were homicides, far behind deaths caused by mining and agriculture accidents.

The drop in violent crimes, especially murder, is explained by several contributing factors. First, the U.S. economy, bolstered by new advances in technology, has been in a strong growth for the past eight years. Unemployment is at an all time low and demand for skilled labor is high. Second, the Victim's Movement has been the catalyst for many new legal reforms. For example, Mike Reynolds, father of Kimberly who was gunned down while leaving a

Table 1.2 United States Homicide Rates, 1988–1999

Year	Number of Murders	Rate per 100,000 Population
1987	20,096	8.3
1989	21,500	8.7
1991	24,703	9.8
1993	24,536	9.5
1995	21,597	8.2
1997	18,209	6.8
1999	15,533	6.0

SOURCE: Uniform Crime Reports, 2000

restaurant in Fresno, California, became the father of Three Strikes laws along with many other laws requiring harsher punishments for repeat offenders. Some states like New York have seen a dramatic increase in the numbers of police officers on duty. Some argue that violent offenders eventually age out because they become too old to commit violent crimes. For whatever reasons, crime has dropped dramatically and steadily. Behind the statistics is the reality that crime rates will inevitably rise again. Although Eitzen and Timmer report that the majority of murders result from domestic and community conflicts, they also suggest that perhaps as many as one-third of all murders are perpetrated by strangers (1985, pp. 130–131). By 2000 this trend of increasing numbers of stranger homicides was clearly established. Because of a marked increase in stranger-to-stranger homicides, in some cities such as Los Angeles, as many as 60% of all murders go without being prosecuted each year. The increasing number of serial murders is believed by some experts to account for some of these unsolved cases (Holmes & DeBurger, 1988, pp. 19–20). Ressler and his colleagues (1988) have also documented a dramatic rise of stranger-to-stranger homicides, or murders with no apparent motive. According to their research, these murders represented 8.5% of all murders in 1976, 17.8% in 1981, 22.1% in 1984, and 22.5% in 1985 (p. 2).

Serial murders, however, may not be the only type of killings attracting considerable public attention. Mass murders, in which several victims are killed within a few moments or hours, seem to be occurring with greater frequency. The current frequency of mass murder in the United States has increased from approximately one case per month to approximately one case every five to six days (author's files). Part of the increase can be attributed to how we define mass murder. Although mass murders were once considered to involve public displays of violence (post office attacks, for instance), we now must include frequent domestic mass murders (the killing of some or all of one's family members). Some cases of mass murder involve offenders walking into shopping malls, restaurants, or government offices and randomly shooting bystanders—as in April 1990, when a man released only the day before from a psychiatric institution walked into a crowded shopping mall in Atlanta, Georgia, and began shooting everyone in his path. In other cases a troubled parent or sibling has annihilated entire families. In recent years there have also been several instances of assailants walking into elementary or secondary schools, or sometimes just standing by the playground, and randomly shooting children.

Still another type of mass murder includes the killing of family members. Based on the number of victims in each case, some domestic mass murders are viewed as *mini-mass murders* because relatively few victims (3–4) are killed. When combining all mass murders, mini-mass murders, and attempted mass murders, the incidence of such murders is at an all time high. This trend is opposite of the noticeable, steady decline of homicides in general in the United States. Although the reality for murder is that we are experiencing relatively low homicide rates (the actual number of murders per 100,000 population), public perception, fueled by highly publicized mass murders, leads us to feel that murder is more common than ever. (See Profile 1.1.)

PROFILE 1.1 Columbine High School Massacre, 1999

"Good wombs hath borne bad sons." Shakespeare.

"They're going to be put through Hell once we do this," Eric Harris said of his parents. Indeed, it has been Hell and immeasurable, unbearable sorrow, untold grief, and devastating repercussions that will affect not only his parents, family, and friends but the United States as a nation for many years to come.

On April 20, 1999 (or "Judgment Day" as the killers called it), Eric Harris and Dylan Klebold, donned in black trenchcoats and draped with 95 explosive devices and ammunition, walked through their high school at Columbine, Colorado, and gunned down 12 of their fellow students and a teacher. Their goal was to kill hundreds but the bombs, left earlier throughout the school, failed them. Driven by revenge and hatred, the boys had plotted for a year to kill and injure as many as they could. Klebold said, "niggers, spics, Jews, gays, fucking whites, I hope we kill 250 of you." Five secret videotapes the boys made prior to the massacre reveal the depths of their scorn and their plans to punish those who had dispossessed them—the athletes and socialites. The social climate in Columbine, like so many schools, can foster a culture that is cruel, elitist, and relentless in its deprecation of those who don't fit into the "jock culture." As one athlete confirmed: "Columbine is a clean, good place except for those rejects. Most kids didn't want them there. They were into witchcraft. They were into voodoo dolls. Sure, we teased them. But what do you expect with kids who come to school with weird hairdos and horns on their hats? It's not just jocks; the whole school's disgusted with them. They're a bunch of homos, grabbing each other's private parts. If you want to get rid of someone, usually you tease 'em. So the whole school would call them homos, and when they did something sick, we'd tell them. 'You're sick and that's wrong.' "

Harris and Klebold, rejected and alone, found each other and became friends. Their synergism became their catalyst for violence. Harris said, "People constantly make fun of my face, my hair, my shirts." One parent whose son was killed said, "jocks could get away with anything. If they wanted to punch a kid in the mouth and walk away, they could. Had I known this, my son wouldn't have been there." About the school he said, "They did nothing to protect students from each other."

But others viewed the boys simply as "bad seed," angry and fueled by a thirst for notoriety and not loners who acted desperately to seek reprieve from their persecutors. If that were the case, then they might have taken their guns and pipe bombs to the locker room and aimed at anything wearing a sports uniform (*Time,* 1999, p. 42). Both Harris and Klebold were involved in school events and activities like everyone, including attending the prom and participating in sports.

But they did suffer humiliation and found support in each other. Their anger became generalized and with distorted motives sought not only retribution, but also celebrity and infamy. They even contemplated which movie producer would be suitable to carry their torch, to immortalize their revolution: Steven

Spielberg or Quentin Tarantino. Klebold said, "Directors will be fighting over this story."

Surely there were "red flags," harbingers of volatility, evidence of deep and abiding resentment, signs of callous and truncated emotion. The purpose of the secret tapes was to have the "last word" with their oppressors, their parents, and those paid to theorize causation. On one tape Klebold blamed his extended family. He said, "You made me what I am. You added to the rage." Blaming day care and the snobs attending he said, "Being shy didn't help. I'm going to kill you all. You've been giving us shit for years." *Time* (1999) reported, "Klebold and Harris were completely soaked in violence: movies like *Reservoir Dogs* and gory video games they tailored to their imaginations. Harris liked to call himself 'Reb,' short for rebel. Klebold's nickname was VoDKa (his favorite liquor, with the capital DK for his initials). On pipe bombs used in the massacre he wrote 'VoDKa Vengeance.' "

Klebold anticipated his parent's thoughts, "If only we could have reached them sooner or found this tape." Harris added, "If only we would have searched their room. If only we would have asked the right questions." The boys left journals and Web sites and secret tapes, all that could have been found by a parent desperate to reconnect to their child. As clever as the boys wanted everyone to believe they were, they were not undetectable. At one point, Harris recalls how his mother watched him walk out of the house with a gun sticking out of his gym bag. She assumed it was his BB gun and asked no questions. Mr. Harris allegedly found a pipe bomb Eric had made and together took it outside to detonate it. What's more, a clerk from Green Mountain Guns had called the Harris home to say the clips that had been ordered had arrived. Mr. Harris said he didn't order any clips and hung up. No questions asked. Eric said of this conversation, "If either one had asked just one question, we would've been fucked." Klebold said, "We wouldn't be able to do what we're going to do." But what of the emotions and attitudes attending such virulent aspirations? It is difficult to fathom that a healthy relationship between child and parent could thrive under such concealment. Indeed, it does not.

Investigators insist that the parents were fooled like everyone else. Of the Klebolds they said, "They were not absentee parents. They are normal people who seem to care for their children and were involved in their life" (*Time,* 1999, p. 50). The Klebolds now realize they never knew their son. They search every interaction for clues to their son's unhappiness. In one video tape Dylan thanked his parents for teaching him "self-awareness, self-reliance . . . I always appreciated that." He said, "I'm sorry I have so much rage."

Later, a parent of one of the victims committed suicide and two more teenagers from Columbine High School would be shot and killed. The killer(s) remains unknown. The couple was found dead in the local sandwich shop where one of them worked. The sadness and weeping for their lost friends and continuing tragedy turns to despair that the pain will never stop, that they are cursed—with no hope, no future, and destined to suffer.

Several mass murderer typologies developed by Holmes and Holmes (2000) at the University of Louisville are presented here including three from other authors. Their thorough classification of mass murderers identifies behavioral and psychological characteristics of these offenders:

1. **Family Slayer or Annihilator—**a person who kills his family and commits suicide.
2. **Murder for Profit—**a person(s) who kills in order to profit materially. They may kill their family or other groups of people such as coworkers or friends. In 2000 Joseph Kibwetere, leader of the Ugandan cult group, Members of the Movement for the Restoration of the Ten Commandments of God, murdered over 700 followers in order to avoid having to return money and possessions they had entrusted to him.
3. **Murder for Sex—**a rare form of mass murder with the primary goal to sexually torture, rape, and murder the victims. Richard Speck forced his way into a nurse's residence and raped and tortured eight nurses to death (Levin & Fox, 1985).
4. **Pseudo-Commando—**a person with an obsession for guns and fantasy for murder. James Huberty walked into a McDonald's restaurant, shot 21 persons to death, and wounded another 19 victims (Dietz, 1986).
5. **Set-and-Run Killers—**individuals who plan an escape route for themselves following the killing aftermath. An example is the bombing of the Federal Building in Oklahoma City, Oklahoma, where 168 persons, including 19 children, perished. Other set-and-run killers may use poisons or set fires.
6. **Psychotic Killers—**persons suffering from acute or chronic psychosis who are considered to be legally insane.
7. **Disgruntled Employees—**persons who seek revenge for real or imagined wrongs at the hands of their coworkers or employers. During the 1990s several incidents of postal workers killing coworkers and supervisors spawned the phrase *going postal.*
8. **Disciple-Type Killer—**a person(s) commits murder at the behest of a charismatic leader such as Charles Manson.
9. **Ideological Mass Murderers—**persons, especially cult leaders, who are able to persuade others to kill themselves or each other as in the cases of Jim Jones (Jonestown Massacre), Herff Applewhite (Heaven's Gate), and David Koresh (Waco Massacre).
10. **Institutional Mass Murderers—**persons who commit mass murder as a crime of obedience when ordered to by their leader. This often is manifested in the form of genocide, "ethnic cleansing," and religious bigotry as occurred in the Kosovo region, the Stalin farm collectivization, Armenian and Nazi Holocausts, and the Crusades (Hickey, 2000).

Although researchers have barely begun to collect data on such crimes, certain commonalities have emerged from their findings: The offenders are primarily white, male, and encompass a wide age range. Invariably, handguns, semiautomatic guns, and rifles are the weapons used to kill suddenly and swiftly. Although victims are often intentionally selected by the killer (for example, a former boss, an ex-wife, or a friend), other persons who happen to be in the area often also become prey. Some offenders, simply frustrated by perceived injustices and inequities, lash out at groups of victims who bear no relationship to them. Table 1.3 gives a brief listing of modern-day mass murderers.

Unlike serial killers, the mass murderer appears to give little thought or concern to his or her inevitable capture or death. Some are killed by police during the attack, whereas others kill themselves once they have completed the massacre. In some cases offenders surrender to police and offer no resistance. With the exception of those who murder their families, most appear to commit their crimes in public places. In cases in which families are murdered, the killer usually leaves ample evidence to lead to his or her arrest.

As stated earlier, some mass murders appear to be premeditated—as in the case of Charles Whitman, who fired on unsuspecting victims from the bell tower at the University of Texas at Austin. He carried a footlocker full of supplies, including food and ammunition, to the top of the tower in preparation for his attack. Conversely, some cases of multiple homicide may be sparked by what could be viewed as a trivial remark, simply a minor insult or provocation. However, in both cases those who engaged in multiple homicide appear to do so in an effort to regain, even for a brief moment, a degree of control over their lives. To the observer this motivation may not appear rational. To the killer, however, it may make perfect sense, given his or her psychological disorientation.

It would appear that not all mass murderers are motivated by similar circumstances, yet the final outcome is the same. Feelings of rejection, failure, and loss of autonomy create frustrations that inevitably overwhelm them, and they experience a need to strike back. And for many killers the best way to lash out against a cold, forbidding society is to destroy its children. Gunning down children on a schoolyard not only provides the needed sense of power and control but is also a way of wreaking vengeance where it hurts the community the most. According to a *New York Times* study in 2000 of 100 "rampage" mass murderers where 425 people were killed and 510 injured, the killers:* (Fessenden, 2000).

1. Often have serious mental health issues
2. Are not usually motivated by exposure to videos, movies, or television
3. Are not using alcohol or other drugs at the time of the attacks
4. Are often unemployed
5. Are sometimes female
6. Are not usually Satanists or racists
7. Are most often white males although a few are Asian or African American

*These murders were generally not domestic, robbery, or gang related.

Table 1.3 A Sampling of Modern Mass Murderers

Year	State	Offender	Death Toll
1949	New Jersey	Howard B. Unruh	Shot neighbors—13 dead
1966	Illinois	Richard F. Speck	Stabbed/strangled nurses—8 dead
1966	Texas	Charles Whitman	Shot students and bystanders—16 dead
1966	Arizona	Robert B. Smith	Shot women in beauty salon—5 dead
1974	Louisiana	Mark Essex	Shot police officers—9 dead
1975	Ohio	James Ruppert	Shot family members—11 dead
1976	California	Edward Allaway	Shot coworkers—7 dead
1977	New York	Fred W. Cowan	Shot coworkers—6 dead
1982	Penn.	George Banks	Shot family and acquaintances—13 dead
1984	California	James O. Huberty	Shot patrons at McDonald's—21 dead
1985	Pennsylvania	Sylvia Selgrist	Shot several in mall—2 dead
1986	Oklahoma	Patrick Sherrill	Shot coworkers—14 dead
1987	Florida	William B. Cruse	Shot persons at a mall—6 dead
1987	Arkansas	Ronald G. Simmons	Shot family—16 dead
1988	California	Richard Farley	Shot workers in a computer company—9 dead
1988	Minnesota	David Brown	Axed family—4 dead
1988	Illinois	Laurie Dann	Shot, poisoned many—1 dead
1988	N. Carolina	Michael C. Hayes	Shot neighbors—4 dead
1989	California	Patrick Purdy	Shot several children on school yard—5 dead
1990	Florida	James E. Pough	Shot 13 in an auto loan company—8 dead
1990	New York	Julio Gonzalez	Set fire to a nightclub—87 dead
1991	Michigan	Thomas McIlvane	Shot 9 at post office—4 dead
1991	Iowa	Gang Lu	Shot 6 people at the University of Iowa—5 dead
1991	Texas	George Hennard	Shot 45 people in Luby's restaurant—23 dead
1992	California	Eric Houston	Shot 14 at high school—4 dead
1993	Texas	David Koresh	Fire/shooting, murder/suicide pact—101 dead
1993	California	Gian L. Ferri	Shot 14 at a law firm—8 dead

8. Sometimes have college degrees or some years of college
9. Often have military experience
10. Give lots of pre-attack warning signals
11. Often carry semiautomatic weapons obtained legally
12. Often do not attempt escape

Year	State	Offender	Death Toll
1993	New York	Colin Ferguson	Shot 25 in commuter train—6 dead
1993	Arizona	Jonathan Doody	Shot several in Buddhist Temple—9 dead
1995	New York	Michael Vernon	Shot 8 in a store—5 dead
1996	California	Joshua Jenkins	15-year-old allegedly beats/stabs family—5 dead
1997	Kentucky	Michael Carneal	14-year-old shoots students—3 dead
1997	S. Carolina	Arthur Wise	Shot several workers in a parts plant—4 dead
1997	California	Daniel Marsden	Shot two coworkers, wounds 4 and kills himself
1997	California	Arturo Torres	Shot ex-boss and 3 others—killed by police
1998	Arkansas	Mitchell Johnson	13-year-old and
		Andrew Golden	11-year-old shot students—5 dead
1998	Connecticut	Matthew Beck	Shot 3 supervisors and president of Connecticut Lottery Corp., then kills himself—4 dead
1998	Oregon	Kip Kinkel	15-year-old shoots 28 students—2 dead after killing his parents
1999	Georgia	Mark Barton	Shot 22 at stock trading companies—9 dead after beating his wife and two children to death
1999	Hawaii	Bryan Uyesugi	Shot and killed 7 coworkers at Xerox office
1999	Colorado	Eric Harris Dylan Klebold	Two seniors at Columbine High School shoot and kill 12 students, 1 teacher in deadliest school massacre in U.S. history. Killers committed suicide.
2000	Florida	Dexter Levingston	Mildly retarded man kills 4 relatives and a 12-year-old girl by shooting and stabbing them with machete and screwdriver
2000	Pennsylvania	Richard Baumhammers	A former immigration lawyer, who hated non-whites, shoots and kills 5 men in Pittsburgh: 1 Jew, 2 Asians, 1 African American, and 1 man of Indian descent

13. Half commit suicide or are killed by others
14. Most have a death wish

White (2000), in her study of mass murderers, found that most offenders who kill in the workplace do not attempt suicide and do not force authorities to kill them or try to evade arrest. These findings contradict the observations of

PROFILE 1.2 Mark Barton, Portrait of a Mass Murderer, 1999

He was a stock day trader at the All-Tech Investment Group in Atlanta, Georgia. On July 29th 1999 Barton armed himself with over 200 rounds of ammunition and with his Glock 9-mm and Colt .45 went to Momentum Securities, a brokerage firm. After some small talk he shot and killed four people. He then calmly drove over to All-Tech and killed five more people. As he left he was overheard saying, "I hope this won't ruin your trading day." Barton would later shoot himself in the head as police cornered him in Atlanta. He was angry over the loss of $100,000 in day trading in recent weeks. The money he was investing had been collected from a life insurance policy that he had taken out on his first wife, Debra, in 1993. Only a month after the policy was in force, Debra and her mother Eloise Spivey were found chopped to death with a hatchet. Police believed that Barton was the killer but lacked evidence to arrest him. Barton eventually was given $450,000 of the life insurance money, but by then he had already found his new wife, Leigh Ann, a woman with whom he was having an affair while still married to Debra. His new life, however, was far from peaceful. Barton, once suspected of molesting Mychelle as a small child, underwent a court-ordered evaluation. The psychologist noted during testing that Barton was capable of committing homicide. More insightful words would be hard to find. In one of his final notes he wrote, "I don't plan to live very much longer, just long enough to kill as many of the people that greedily sought my destruction."

Just prior to the mass murder in Atlanta, Mark Barton, 44, murdered his second wife, Leigh Ann, 27, his son, Matthew, 12, and daughter Mychelle, 8. Barton would later write on his suicide note that his sweetheart (Mychelle) and buddy (Matthew) died "with little pain." Each of the children died from hammer blows to the head while they slept, then were placed under water in the bathtub to be sure they were dead. He wrapped sheets and towels around each of the three bodies to only allow their faces to show and placed a teddy bear on Mychelle and a video game on Matthew.

Hickey (1997) and Holmes and Holmes (1992, 1994). This may be explained by noting that White, in her thorough examination of mass murderers, delineated various subcategories of mass murder, whereas other researchers examined them as a whole. It is the author's opinion that the single most salient factor in such rampage mass murders is mental disorder. Some mass murderers, so deeply depressed, become schizophrenic or psychotic. Others suffer with severe anxiety and personality disorders. These are not rational people at the time of the murders, even when their behaviors are calculated and decisive. Many of them are not legally insane but suffer from severe psychological dysfunctioning as a result of both chronic and acute stress. (See Profile 1.2.)

The social impact of mass murders tends to be restricted to the communities in which they occurred. Increased security at schools, office buildings, and shopping malls is the usual response, including improved social services to better identify potentially dangerous individuals. However, the track record in predicting criminal behavior thus far has been dismal. Recognizing potential mass murderers is usually a matter of hindsight; we are quick to attach motivating factors and personality defects to offenders once they have vented themselves on their victims. The fact remains, however, that mass murders, in relation to other crimes—even other forms of homicide—are relatively rare, and they appear to occur as randomly as serial killings do.

Differences among Mass Murderers, Serial Killers, and Spree Murderers

In both mass and serial murder cases, victims die as the offender momentarily gains control of his or her life by controlling others. But the differences between these two types of offenders far outweigh the similarities. First, mass murderers are generally apprehended or killed by police, commit suicide, or turn themselves in to authorities. Serial killers, by contrast, usually make special efforts to elude detection. Indeed, they may continue to kill for weeks, months, and often years before they are found and stopped—if they are found at all. In the case of the California Zodiac killer, the homicides appeared to have stopped, but an offender was never apprehended for those crimes. Perhaps the offender was incarcerated for only one murder and never linked to the others, or perhaps he or she was imprisoned for other crimes. Or the Zodiac killer may have just decided to stop killing or to move to a new location and kill under a new *modus operandi,* or method of committing the crime. The killer may even have become immobilized because of an accident or an illness or may have died without his or her story ever being told. Speculation exists that the Zodiac killer has stalked victims in the New York City area. The Zodiac case is only one example of unsolved serial murders, many of which will never be solved.

Second, although both types of killers evoke fear and anxiety in the community, the reaction to a mass murder will be much more focused and locally limited than that to serial killing. People generally perceive the mass killer as one suffering from mental illnesses. This immediately creates a "they"/"us" dichotomy in which "they" are different from "us" because of mental problems. We can somehow accept the fact that a few people go "crazy" sometimes and start shooting others. However, it is more disconcerting to learn that some of the "nicest" people one meets lead a Jekyll-and-Hyde life: a student by day, a killer of coeds by night; a caring, attentive nurse who secretly murders sick children, the handicapped, or the elderly; a building contractor and politician who enjoys sexually torturing and killing young men and burying them under his home. When we discover that people exist who are not considered to be insane or crazy but who enjoy killing others for "recreation," this indeed gives new meaning to the word "stranger." Although the mass murderer is viewed as a deranged soul, a product of a stressful environment who is just going to "explode" now and then (but of course somewhere else), the serial murderer is seen as much more sinister and is more capable of producing fear.

Third, the mass murderer kills groups of people at once, whereas the serial killer individualizes his or her murders. The serial killer continues to hurt and

Table 1.4 Differences among Mass, Serial, and Spree Murders

	Mass	Serial	Spree
Murder is means of control over life	✓	✓	✓
Usually arrested or killed at crime scene	✓		✓
Often commits suicide after the crime	✓		✓
Eludes arrest and detection		✓	
Likely to travel and seek out victims		✓	✓
Evokes long-term media/public attention		✓	
Kills individuals		✓	
Kills several in short period of time	✓		✓
Murders viewed as single incident	✓		✓
Minimum number of victims agreed upon by researchers	4	4	4
Murderer is usually white male	✓	✓	✓
Motivated primarily by material gain or revenge	✓		✓
Victims usually female		✓	
Firearms are the common choice of weapon	✓		✓
Kills in spontaneous rage	✓		✓

murder victims, whereas the mass murderer makes his or her "final statement" in or about life through the medium of abrupt and final violence. We rarely, if ever, hear of a mass murderer who has the opportunity to enact a second mass murder or to become a serial killer. Similarly, we rarely, if ever, hear of a serial killer who also enacts a mass murder.

The mass murderer and the serial killer are quantitatively and qualitatively different, and disagreement continues about their characteristics just as it does about the types of mass and serial offenders that appear to have emerged in recent years. Researchers have distinguished *spree* murders from mass and serial murder as being three or more victims killed by a single perpetrator within a period of hours or days in different locations. They often act in a frenzy, make little effort to avoid detection, and kill in several sequences. Offenders may kill more than one victim in one location and travel to another location. There appears to be no cooling-off period even though the murders occur at different places (Greswell & Hollin, 1994).

These murders, sometimes called *cluster killings,* tend to last a few days, weeks, or even months. In 1997, Andrew Cunanan, a 27-year-old from San Diego, California, went on a four state killing spree that culminated in the murder of fashion designer Gianni Versace in Florida. Cunanan feared that he might be infected with the AIDS virus and vowed revenge on whomever was responsible. Some of the five men he murdered were gay and some were not. Upon killing them with guns, knives, and blunt objects, Cunanan would steal cars and money from his victims. He continued to kill as he journeyed southeastward toward his final murder and suicide. White (2000) thoroughly examined the differences among mass, serial, and spree murders and summarized the differences as shown in Table 1.4.

Perhaps the single most critical stumbling block that today stands in the way of understanding serial murder is the disagreement among researchers and law enforcement about how to define the phenomenon.

DEFINING HOMICIDE, MURDER, AND SERIAL MURDER

The reader should be clear about how we define the taking of a person's life. Each state has very specific criteria for defining murder. In California, for example, to receive a death sentence an offender must be "death eligible," which means that the person must have committed a homicide. The term *homicide* can be defined as "that most extraordinary of crimes: the theft of a human life." All homicides are not illegal, however. In some cases, such as self-defense or when the state holds an execution, the killings are viewed as homicides, and are not considered illegal killings. The author noted the cause of death on the death certificate of a man executed in California as being a homicide. Indeed, a *murder* requires an illegal taking of another's life. From a judicial point of view the most serious of murders are those that are *capital* cases. Such cases may qualify a person, if convicted, for a death sentence. However, most persons convicted of *first-degree* murder find their way into lengthy prison terms rather than a death sentence. First-degree murder usually includes *felony murder,* or murder committed while in the course of committing another felony, such as killing someone while robbing a bank. Other forms of first-degree murder may involve poisoning, lying in wait, torture, use of explosives, and in some states like California using armor-piercing bullets or doing a "drive-by" killing.

Usually for a sentence of death the offender must have willfully, deliberately, and with premeditation murdered another with *special circumstances.* These special or aggravating circumstances in first-degree murder may include a prior murder by the offender; multiple murders; killing of a peace officer, witness, prosecutor, or judge; lying in wait; torture with intent to kill; murder due to race, ethnicity, religion, or nationality; felony murder; and use of poison. Even when an offender does receive a death sentence, the likelihood of actually being executed is minimal. In California the average length of time for an appeals process to be completed is 14 years and 9 months. Most of the condemned in California die of natural causes or commit suicide.

Serial murder, one of those special circumstance categories, draws a lot of media attention. In February, 1989, the Associated Press released a story about a serial killer who preyed on prostitutes in the same area of Los Angeles that harbored the Southside Slayer.* He was believed to have killed at least

---

*Identity unknown; killed 12–20 victims between September 1983 and May 1987. Offender believed to be black and to have enjoyed mutilating his young female victims.

12 women, all with a small handgun. The news story referred to the victims as "strawberries"—young women who sold sex for drugs. Farther north, the Green River Task Force in Seattle, Washington, continued to investigate a series of murders of at least 45 young women over an eight-year span. When the corpses of boys and young men began appearing along the banks of the Chattahoochee River in Atlanta, Georgia, during the early 1980s, police became convinced a serial killer was at work in the area.

The preceding cases are typical of murders one might envision when characterizing victims of serial killers. The media quickly and eagerly focus attention on serial killings because they appear to be so bizarre and extraordinary. They engender the kind of headlines that sell newspapers: "The Atlanta Child Killer," "The Stocking Strangler," "The Hillside Strangler," "The Sunday Morning Slasher," "The Boston Strangler," ad infinitum. The media focus not only on how many victims were killed but also on how they died. Thus they feed morbid curiosity and at the same time create a stereotype of the typical serial killer: Ted Bundy, Ed Kemper, Albert Desalvo, and a host of other young white males attacking unsuspecting women powerless to defend themselves from the savage sexual attacks and degradations by these monsters.

Egger's (1984) global definition of serial murder attempts to create parameters for the behavior:

> Serial murder occurs when one or more individuals . . . commits a second murder and/or subsequent murder; is relationshipless (victim and attacker are strangers); occurs at a different time and has no connection to the initial (and subsequent) murder; and is frequently committed in a different geographic location. Further, the motive is generally not for material gain but is usually a compulsive act specifically for gratification based on fantasies. The key element is that the series of murders do not share in the events surrounding one another. Victims share in common characteristics of what are perceived to be prestigeless, powerless, and/or lower socioeconomic groups (that is, vagrants, prostitutes, migrant workers, homosexuals, missing children, and single and often elderly women).

But is this definition too restrictive? For those in law enforcement, serial killing generally means the sexual attack and murder of young women, men, and children by a male who follows a pattern, physical or psychological. However, this definition fails to include many offenders and victims. For example, in 1988 in Sacramento, California, several bodies of older or handicapped adults were exhumed from the backyard of a house where they were supposed to have been living. Investigators discovered the victims had been killed for their Social Security checks. It was apparent the killer had premeditated the murders, had selected the victims, and had killed at least six over a period of several months. Most law enforcement agencies would naturally classify this case as a serial killing—except for the fact that the killer was female. Because of rather narrow definitions of serial killing, females are generally not classified as serial killers even though they meet the requirements for such a label. One explanation may simply be that we rarely, if ever, hear of a female "Jack the Ripper." Women who kill serially generally use poisons to dispose of their victims and are not associated with the sexual attacks, tortures, and violence of their male counterparts.

Although many offenders actually fall into the serial killer classification, they are excluded because they fail to meet law enforcement definitions or media-generated stereotypes of brutal, bloodthirsty monsters. The "angels of death" who work in hospitals and kill patients, or nursing-home staff who kill the elderly, or the "black widows" who kill their family and relatives also meet the general criteria for serial killing except for the stereotypic element of violence. These men and women do not slash and torture their victims nor do they sexually attack them; they are the quiet killers. They are also the kinds of people who could be married, hold steady jobs, or simply be the nice man or woman who lives next door. They are rare among serial killers, just as serial murders are rare compared with other types of homicide.

To include all types of serial killers, the definition of serial murder must clearly be as broad as possible. For instance, Hickey (1986), by simply including all offenders who through premeditation killed three or more victims over a period of days, weeks, months, or years, was able to identify several women as serial killers. However, there exists such confusion in defining serial killing that findings can also easily be distorted. In addition, current research presents some narrow operational definitions of serial murder without any documented assurances that the focus does not exclude pertinent data. To suggest, for example, that all victims of serial murder are strangers, that the killers operate primarily in pairs, or that they do not kill for financial gain is derived more from speculation than verifiable evidence, given the current state of serial-murder research.

In essence *serial murderers* should include any offenders, male or female, who kill over time. Most researchers agree that serial killers have a minimum of three to four victims. Usually there is a pattern in their killing that can be associated with the types of victims selected or the method or motives for the killing. This includes murderers who, on a repeated basis, kill within the confines of their own home, such as a woman who poisons several husbands, children, or elderly people in order to collect insurance. In addition, serial murderers include those men and women who operate within the confines of a city or a state or even travel through several states as they seek out victims. Consequently, some victims have a personal relationship with their killers and others do not, and some victims are killed for pleasure and some merely for gain. Of greatest importance from a research perspective is the linkage of common factors among the victims—for example, as Egger (1985) observed, the "victims' place or status within their immediate surroundings" (p. 3). Commonality among those murdered may include several factors, any of which can prove heuristic in better understanding victimization.

TYPOLOGIES OF MURDER

Much of our information and misinformation about criminal offenders is based on taxonomies, or classification systems. Megargee and Bohn (1979) noted that researchers usually created typologies based on the criminal offense. This invariably became problematic because often the offense comprised one or more subgroups. Researchers then examined repetitive crime patterns, which in turn created new complexities and problems. Megargee and Bohn further noted that, depending on the authority one chooses to read, one will find between two and eleven different types of murderers (pp. 29–32). Although serial murder is believed to represent a relatively small portion of all homicides in the United States, already researchers have begun the difficult task of classifying serial killers. Consequently, various typologies of serial killers and patterns of homicides have emerged. Not surprisingly, some of these typologies and patterns conflict with one another. Some are descriptions of causation, whereas others are diagnostic in nature. In addition, some researchers focus primarily on individual case studies of serial killers, whereas others create group taxonomies that accommodate several kinds of murderers.

Wille (1974) identified ten different types of murderers covering a broad range of bio-socio-psychological categories:

1. Depressive
2. Psychotic
3. Afflicted with organic brain disorder
4. Psychopathic
5. Passive aggressive
6. Alcoholic
7. Hysterical
8. Juvenile (a child is the killer)
9. Mentally retarded
10. Sex killers

Lee (1988) also created a variety of labels to differentiate killers according to motive, including:

1. Profit
2. Passion
3. Hatred
4. Power or domination
5. Revenge
6. Opportunism
7. Fear
8. Contract killing

9. Desperation
10. Compassion
11. Ritual

Even before American society became aware, in the early 1980s, of serial murder as anything more than an anomaly, researchers had begun to classify multiple killers and assign particular characteristics and labels to them. Guttmacher (1973) described the sadistic serial murderer as one who derives sexual gratification from killing and who often establishes a pattern, such as the manner in which they kill or the types of victims they select, such as prostitutes, children, or the elderly. Motivated by fantasies, the offender appears to derive pleasure from dehumanizing his or her victims. Lunde (1976) recognized and noted distinctions between the mass killer and the serial killer, notably that the mass killer appears to suffer from psychosis and should be considered insane. By contrast he found little evidence of mental illness among serial killers. Danto (1982) noted that most serial murderers might be described as obsessive-compulsive because they normally kill according to a particular style and pattern.

Researchers have been attempting to create profiles of the "typical" serial killer from the rapidly accumulating statistics on offenders and victims in the United States. The most stereotypic of all serial murderers are those who in some way are involved sexually with their victims. It is this type of killer who generates such public interest and alarm. Stories of young women being abducted, raped, tortured, and strangled appear more and more frequently in the newspapers.

Sexual Homicides

Most serial killers known widely to the public have usually been involved sexually with their victims. This may include rape, sodomy, and an array of sexual tortures and deviations. Indeed it is a shared belief among most law enforcement officials and many clinicians that most serial murders are sexual in nature (Lunde, 1976; Ressler et al., 1985, 1988; Revitch, 1965). There have been serial killings that appear to have no sexual connotations; however, not all sex murders *overtly* express sexual needs. In other words, some serial killing that may appear to be motivated by factors such as financial gain or cult-related goals may actually have sexual motives. In one instance a multiple murderer who had been killing patients for financial gain later admitted she also became aroused watching her victims die.

Some researchers differentiate sex murderers from lust murderers. The sex murderer kills often out of fear and a desire to silence his victim, whereas the lust murderer appears to harbor deep-seated fantasies. This certainly does not exclude the possibility that some rapists may also premeditate their killings and experience deep-seated fantasies. For killers such as Albert Desalvo, the Boston Strangler, rapes are only a continuation of progressive sexual fantasies and behaviors that finally lead to murder. Revitch and Schlesinger (1981) noted that women, although in fewer numbers than men, also are capable of developing homicidal fantasies and becoming involved in sadistic murders and mass killings.

In recent years researchers have continued to note differences between rape murders and lust killings (Prentky et al., 1986; Ressler et al., 1985; Scully & Marolla, 1985). Special agents from the FBI examined a sample of 36 sexual murderers, 29 of whom were convicted of killing several victims. Specifically they were interested in the general characteristics of sexual murderers across the United States. They explored the dynamics of offenders' sexual fantasies, sadistic behaviors, and rape and mutilation murders. These investigators noted several deviant sexual behaviors practiced before, during, or after the victim has been killed. The act of rape, whether it be the actual physical act or a symbolic rape during which an object is inserted into the vagina, was found to be common among serial killers in this study. For some offenders the act of rape served as only one form of sexual assault; they engaged in a variety of mutilations, sexual perversions, and desecrations of the victim's corpse (Ressler et al., 1988, pp. 33–44).

Paraphilia and Other Sexual Misconduct

Of course, sexual deviations have influenced our perceptions and definitions of those who kill. "Sex maniac" becomes the layperson's term for anyone capable of performing acts of sexual perversion on his or her victims. Each of the following categories listed below describes a type of sexual behavior engaged in by one or more serial killers in this study, behavior that was believed to be in some way linked to the killings. In some cases the offenders as children were subjected to one or more of these sexual activities. In each case the sexual abuse was deeply traumatizing. The list is not exhaustive nor does it imply cause and effect. What is important to understand is how these categories of sexual behavior influence the typecasting of offenders.

According to the *Diagnostic and Statistical Manual of Mental Disorders,* fourth edition (DSM-IV), published by the American Psychiatric Association (1994), many of the terms listed describe various forms of *paraphilia.** Common almost exclusively to males, paraphilia involves sexual arousal through deviant or bizarre images or activities. The DSM-IV identifies such repetitive sexual activities as paraphilia once a pattern has been established linked to a time frame of at least six months. Multiple paraphilia are also commonly found in one person but usually one paraphilia becomes dominant until replaced by another. For example, a pedophile, or someone who is sexually attracted to children, may also succumb to fetishes, such as being aroused by a child's hair, rubber gloves, or self-administered enemas. Most psychosexual disorders are a

*According to Money and Werlas (1982) a paraphilia is an erotosexual condition involving an obsessive dependence on an unusual stimulus, physical or fantasy, in order to achieve or maintain sexual arousal and/or orgasm. The DSM-IV also adds that such a condition covers a time frame of at least 6 months.

result of an aberrant fantasy system fueled by traumatic childhood and adolescent experiences. Many of the offenders in this study fit into the extreme end of the paraphilic continuum because they engage in *erotophonophilia,* or lust/sexual murder. This involves the acting out of sadistic behaviors in the course of brutally torturing and murdering their victims.

Fantasies can be reinforced by powerful sex drives that, in turn, facilitate some unusual behaviors. During World War II England was decimated by repeated German bombing attacks. Always lingering was the fear of poison-gas attack. Today, one has only to read the personal advertisements in British newspapers to see some of the long-term results. Gas-mask fetishes are common. People seek partners interested in sexual activity using gas masks and slickers (rubberized raincoats) (Dietz, 1994). Purcell (2000) in her insightful research on paraphilia examines the etiology and development of paraphilic behavior through the use of fantasy and masturbation. She provides an integrative model for understanding paraphilia through case study analysis. The following discussion of sexual behaviors is not intended to be exhaustive but rather specific to serial offenders in this research of 399 offenders. Fantasy is a key component in facilitating most of these behaviors.

1. **Animal Torture**—stabbing or chopping animals to death, especially cats, and dissecting them. One offender admitted killing several puppies in order to relive the experience of killing his first child victim. Persons who become multiple-homicide offenders have often reported being cruel to animals when they were children. Certainly there are serial killers who do not harm animals or express a morbid interest in animal viscera. In children, such behavior may be explained as part of a DSM-IV conduct disorder that involves repetitive, persistent patterns of violating societal norms or the basic rights of others. Several serial killers as children have exhibited conduct disorders, which include animal torture or evisceration of dead or dying animals. These offenders were also found to exhibit aggression toward other people, destruction of property (fire-setting, vandalism), or theft.
2. **Anthropophagy**—eating the victim's flesh or slicing off parts of flesh from the body. Several of the offenders included in the present study practiced this form of cannibalism. Some are known to have eaten the breasts of victims, another cooked portions of his victim's thighs in casseroles, whereas another delighted in a main diet of children.
3. **Autoeroticism**—sexual arousal and gratification through self-stimulation. The most common form involves masturbation to pornography, fantasies, or images. Other forms of autoeroticism include erotic and aqua-erotic asphyxiation. Erotic asphyxiation or "scarfing" involves using devices or material such as scarves, ropes, and plastic bags to cut off one's oxygen supply to the brain in order to enhance sexual gratification. Several hundred deaths each year can be attributed to erotic hanging. Often the person cross-dresses, uses pornography, and masturbates to his fantasies while slowly hanging himself. Generally the same elements apply to aqua-erotic

asphyxiation except that the paraphilic uses partial drowning to induce increased sexual excitation. A few serial offenders have reported engaging in a variety of autoerotic activities.

4. **Coprophilia**—an interest in feces whereby the offender may receive some sexual gratification from touching or eating excrement and/or urine. Although rare among serial killers, at least one is known to have eaten his own excrement.
5. **Exhibitionism**—deliberate exposing of one's genitals (usually male) to an unsuspecting stranger. According to the DSM-IV, such behavior must be recurring over at least a six-month period to be considered paraphilia. The exposure, followed by masturbation, serves to reinforce the behavior and in turn the behavior is repeated. Exhibitionism provides the offender with a momentary sense of power and control. Exhibitionists who are caught often express sincere embarrassment and remorse for their crimes but on release quickly recidivate. Exhibitionists generally are not considered to be dangerous offenders. However, some of these paraphiliacs have escalated to more serious crimes, including rape and homicide.
6. **Fetishisms**—finding sexual gratification by substituting objects for the sexual partner. In one case a person (although not a serial killer) had been breaking into several homes in a city in Georgia. A voyeur, this person also enjoyed collecting women's underwear, and on his arrest police discovered over 400 pairs of women's underwear in his possession. In October of 1988 in Riverside, California, a man known as the "panty bandit" was arrested after a series of robberies. During the course of his robberies this man would often order the female clerks to remove their underwear and then would engage in sexual acts in front of his captive audience.

   Serial killers have also been known to engage in a variety of fetishes. Some offenders have been known to remove the breasts of their victims for later use; another saved sex organs by placing them in containers; and yet another removed the skin of his victims, out of which he fashioned articles of clothing, ornaments, and even purses. Others have saved victims' teeth or hair as part of their "souvenir fetish." In one case the offender enjoyed decapitating his victims. Later, after shampooing their hair and applying makeup, including lipstick, he would have sex with the heads, sometimes while showering. A final example was the offender who cut off the foot of at least one of his victims. He kept the foot in his refrigerator so he could dress it up in red spiked heels for his personal gratification.
7. **Gerontophilia**—seeking out elderly persons of the opposite sex for sexual purposes. Those serial killers who seek out elderly persons are often believed to harbor hatred toward them. Some of these offenders reported sexual gratification from raping elderly women, some of whom have been in their eighties and nineties. One offender raped and killed several elderly tenants of an apartment complex, whereas another, referred to as the Boston Strangler, sought out elderly widows who lived alone.

8. **Klismaphilia—**sexual arousal through the administration of enemas. A klismaphiliac will substitute enemas for genital intercourse. While some enjoy receiving the enemas, others prefer to administer enemas to others. Sometimes children become the unsuspecting victims of klismaphiliacs who use enemas as a form of sexual abuse.
9. **Infibulation—**self-torture. Involves piercing one's own nipples, labia, clitoris, scrotum, or penis with sharp objects such as needles, pins, and rings. Albert Fish, a man who murdered children, cannibalized them, and wrote letters to victims' families telling them how much he enjoyed eating their children, was an infibulator who derived sexual gratification by jabbing sewing needles into his scrotum and penis. After his execution an autopsy revealed nearly two dozen needles in his genitals.
10. **Lust Murder—**murdering sadistically and brutally, including the mutilation of body parts, especially the genitalia. One offender who chopped off the penis of a young boy with a pair of wire cutters still expresses a strong desire to mutilate sexual organs. Another would sometimes shoot his victims in the head while they performed oral sex, and another enjoyed crushing his victims' nipples with pliers and mutilating their breasts. Others have torn off the nipples of their victims with their teeth. On several occasions offenders have completely dismembered their victims' bodies, then tossed the parts onto highways or into wooded areas, shallow graves, or sometimes left them for animals to consume. One offender was discovered with several pounds of body parts stashed in his refrigerator. A few offenders drank the blood of their victims. Sex murderers may perform similar acts but often are more spontaneous and react more out of fear of detection than lust murderers do.
11. **Necrophilia—**having sexual relations with dead bodies. This form of deviation is common among offenders who are involved sexually with their victims. Generally necrophilia is thought to be practiced only by males, but Gallagher (1987) notes that in 1983 a California woman confessed to having sex with dead people. This woman, a mortuary employee, said she would often climb into coffins to have sex with the corpse or drive corpses in a hearse up to the mountains where her "love making" would not be disturbed. Apparently she had been sexually "involved" with at least 40 corpses. In another case of serial killing, the offender had sex with the corpse of a child, then placed her body under his bed so that he could repeat the experience. Several occurrences of necrophilia have been recorded among serial killers. One offender decapitated his victims and, while showering, had sex with the heads. Another offender robbed graves to have sex with the corpses and, as he noted, to have someone for company. In some cases the necrophile wants not only to have sex with a corpse but also to keep them nearby, as in a closet or under the bed.

    Necrofetishism is having a fetish for dead bodies. Some offenders actually enjoy keeping cadavers in their homes. In one case police found six decomposing corpses in the bedroom of one offender. Another offender liked to share his bed with various corpses, some of which had been decapitated. Jeffrey Dahmer was one of the most prolific necrophiles in the modern U.S. annals of crime.

Necrophilia can be described as typologies or as process, depending on interpretation. Some necrophiles use fantasy to experience sex with a corpse. Some prostitutes cater to paraphiliacs and for the right price will ice themselves down, dust on white powder, and lay motionless with eyes closed in a casket, while her "john" acts out his fantasies. Other necrophiles seek out real corpses from funeral parlors, cemeteries, morgues, and hospitals. Serial killers such as Dennis Nilsen and Ed Gein both fulfilled some of their fantasies by grave robbing. Similar to these forms of behavior is *pygmalionism,* or the sexual involvement of a person with dolls or mannequins. Both pygmalionists and necrophiles avoid rejection by having sex with inanimate objects (dolls) or corpses. In both forms of behavior the paraphiliac exercises total control over his environment. The paraphiliac can do whatever he or she wants with the object or body and then dispose of it. Finally, a few necrophiles will kill people in order to use their corpse for sexual gratification. These three types of necrophilia may also be viewed as escalation in fantasy fulfillment. Both Nilsen and Gein eventually went on to kill people in order to sexually abuse the corpses.

12. **Pedophilia**—having a sexual preference for children. A 16-year-old boy who had been arrested for sexual assault on children admitted to me that his favorite places to pick up children were the toy centers in department stores. Knowing that some parents are willing to leave their small children to look at toys while they go shopping for a few minutes, he easily found victims. He would simply select the youngest or most vulnerable-looking children and take them to the washrooms, where he would molest them. It was not uncommon for this young man to find three or four victims in one evening. Although most pedophiles have no intention of violence toward their victims, some serial killers destroy their victims as a way of destroying the evidence against them. One serial killer who sexually assaulted several young boys admitted he killed them to cover up his sexual misconduct. Some serial killers have themselves as children been victimized by pedophiles and later, as adults, act out on children in the same manner in which they were abused. Pedophiles range in aggressiveness from very passive to extremely violent, depending on their fantasy development and orientation. The three major pedophile organizations today are: North American Man/Boy Love Association (NAMBLA), a group primarily comprised of homosexuals who prefer sex with young boys, which is well organized, with offices in several major cities such as New York (headquarters); the Rene Guyon Society, also nationally organized, whose motto is "Sex Before Eight or Else It's Too Late"; and the Childhood Sensuality Circle (CSC) of San Diego, California.

13. **Pederasty—**adults having anal intercourse with children (anal intercourse in general is called sodomy). This is a common act among serial killers who target children as victims. In some cases various "instruments" have been used to sodomize the child, including baseball bats shaped in the form of a penis.
14. **Pornography and Obscene Material—**using sexually explicit literature and photographs. Even among serial killers pornography tends to be used only by certain types of offenders. However, trying to determine how much and to what degree pornography affects an offender is nearly impossible to measure. Some offenders admit to occasional or frequent use of pornography, sometimes violent material involving bondage and the torture of women and children. The advent of our computer era and the Internet has provided fertile ground for the production and distribution of pornography and obscene material such as "kiddie porn" or pictures sexually exploiting children.
15. **Pyromania—**intentional setting of fires on more than one occasion by a person experiencing tension or affective arousal. These persons often report a fascination with or curiosity about fire-setting. Offenders express feelings of gratification or relief when watching fires in progress and the individual or community response fires often command. Some adult offenders the author has spoken with find the sound of emergency-response vehicles coming to the scene of the fire to be exhilarating. Occasionally pyromaniacs report sexual gratification (e.g., masturbation) in setting or watching fire scenes, but the role of sexuality in fire-setting does not appear as the primary reason for such behavior. In children, pyromania is often explained as a DSM-IV conduct disorder, which also requires other criteria, such as aggression toward people or animals and deceitfulness or theft. Fire-setting by children may be a response to severe stressors in the family, such as child abuse, drug and alcohol abuse, and family violence. Children sometimes report fires as being magical or that they feel better when they set fires. Children who are chronic fire-setters often report that such behavior provides a sense of control. Some serial murderers as children were fire-setters. However, as they age, serial offenders tend to cease fire-setting behaviors in favor of more controlling, focused acts of violence.
16. **Rape—**having forced sexual intercourse with another person. This appears to be the most common of all sexual behaviors among serial killers in this study. Often the rapes involve beatings and torture. One offender enjoyed taking his victims out into the desert, where he would lash them to the front of his car, tear off their clothing, rape them, and then strangle them to death. Some serial killers are paraphilic rapists who are driven more by specific fantasies of rape and domination than the terror experienced by the victim. For example, the offender may desire the victim to wear specific clothing or repeat certain words while being attacked.

17. **Sadomasochism**—inflicting mental/physical pain on others (sadism) or oneself (masochism). Although masochism is not particularly common among serial killers, one offender over the years had inserted dozens of needles into his genital area, occasionally burned himself, and eagerly anticipated the experience of his own execution.
18. **Scatophilia**—sexual gratification through the making of obscene phone calls. While callers seem to vary in their levels of sexual references, tone of voice, and desire to shock or frighten, the offender is often conditioning himself through masturbation to fantasies of control over his victims. Offenders calling the same victims repeatedly are engaging in stalking behavior, which has, in a few cases, led to violent confrontations.
19. **Scoptophilia (Voyeurism)**—receiving sexual gratification by peeping through windows and so forth to watch people. Several offenders in this study had at one time or another peeped through windows. One offender explained how he first began as a voyeur, then graduated to raping women, and finally practiced necrophilia. The connection between voyeurism and homicide is not automatic. Most "peeping Toms" never progress past this deviant stage, whereas some may later attempt rape or other violent sexual behaviors.

    One subcategory of voyeurism is *mixoscopia* or *triolism,* or the sexual arousal from seeing oneself in sexual scenes. This includes taking photographs of nude victims, which sometimes include the offender. A few sexual predators whose crimes have escalated to serial murder have utilized equipment such as ceiling mirrors, video cameras, and cameras with self-developing film. Triolism can also involve sexual gratification by sharing a sexual partner with another person, allowing the triolist to become the observer. Sometimes serial killers who work in groups have engaged in triolistic behaviors. One offender took snapshots of his nude victims, then enlarged the photographs and mounted them on his bedroom walls. Another offender took photographs of victims performing oral sex on his partner. Still other offenders used tape recorders to reproduce the screams and terror of dying victims as they were sexually mutilated. Offenders (both male and female) have admitted to watching while another offender raped or sodomized a victim. One female offender voluntarily watched while her male counterpart raped a child.
20. **Torture**—resorting to a large variety of sadistic acts, including burning victims' breasts, dismembering living victims, placing victims in water and electrocuting them, and touching bare electrical wires to victims' arms, face, breasts, or genitals. Often those who engage in these acts will also be involved in other "lust murder" behaviors.

Serial-Murder Typologies

Creating sexual taxonomies to categorize serial killers represents one of several ways by which offenders have been classified by researchers. For some investigators, the sexual nature of the crime may be viewed as a subtype of one or

PROFILE 1.3 Charles Albright, the Case of the Paraphilic Serial Killer, 1990–1991

Consider the case of Charles Albright, a serial killer in Texas, who between 1990 and 1991 murdered several female prostitutes. Charles was a white, 57-year-old married male with children, with a history of juvenile delinquency, property crimes, and prior incarcerations. As a child he experienced mental and emotional abuse as well as rejection by his parents. A product of an unstable home, Charles developed an intense hatred for women. He derived great satisfaction in bludgeoning and shooting his victims.

Charles was no ordinary man. Very intelligent, he was fluent in Latin, Spanish, and French, or at least he promoted himself in that light. He became a biology teacher and a skilled taxidermist. Charles was a skillful painter and musician and was adored by women. He had a great sense of humor and was portrayed as the class clown in college. He was a ladies' man and enjoyed impressing them with his varied artistic talents. He was athletic and enjoyed coaching football and later playing slow-pitch softball. He was affable and mingled well in groups.

Yet there was a disturbing side to him seldom any could see. He could not hold a job more than a few months. Charles portrayed himself as a faithful family man, but he frequented prostitutes. He developed some masochistic attitudes. He carefully concealed his history of thefts. He forged his college transcripts, making it appear that he had graduated. He once referred to his biological mother as a prostitute, although there was no proof of his accusation. He raped a 13-year-old girl when he was 51 years old but managed to minimize the incident. He became increasingly sexually aggressive with women. He was a consummate liar and con man, a true Jekyll-and-Hyde personality. Along the path of adolescence Charles also developed a fascination and obsession for eyes. He was always trying to paint perfect eyes. He would paint portraits without eyes because he felt he could not do the eyes justice. When the autopsies were performed on his victims, the staff discovered the eyeballs of each victim had been surgically removed without damaging the eyelids. The eyeballs were never recovered. Now incarcerated in a state prison, Charles continues his obsession with eyes. He subscribes to a magazine devoted to iridology and has the first issue of *Omni* magazine (October 1978), which displays on the cover an eyeball, as if it is floating in the air (Hollandsworth, 1993; Matthews, 1996).

more general taxonomies. In certain serial killings the sexual attack is an integral part of the murder both psychologically and physiologically for the offender. For other offenders the sexual attack may represent the best way to degrade, subjugate, and ultimately destroy their victim but have little connection to the actual motive(s) for the killing. (See Profile 1.3.)

Holmes and DeBurger (1988, pp. 55–60) have characterized four types of serial murderers and examined the motives reported to have influenced the offenders. The formation of these typologies is based on specific assumptions about the phenomenon of serial killers. These assumptions include the belief that such crimes are nearly always psychogenic, meaning that such behavior is usually stimulated not by insanity or economic circumstances but by "behavioral rewards and penalties." The "patterns of learning" are in some way related to "significant others" who in some way reinforce homicidal behavior. A second assumption involves an "intrinsic locus of motives," whereby motives are explained as something only the offender can appreciate because they exist entirely in his or her own mind. Most "normal" people have great difficulty in fathoming why someone would want to kill other people. However, in the mind of the killer the motivations are often very meaningful. In a final assumption, Holmes and DeBurger explain that the reward for killing is generally psychological even though some killers may benefit materially from their crimes. According to these "core characteristics" Holmes and DeBurger (1988) identify the following four types of serial killers:

1. **Visionary Type**—such murderers kill in response to the commands of voices or visions usually emanating from the forces of good or evil. These offenders are often believed to be suffering from some form of psychosis.
2. **Mission-Oriented Type**—these offenders believe it is their mission in life to rid the community or society of certain groups of people. Some killers may target the elderly, whereas others may seek out prostitutes, children, or a particular racial/ethnic group.
3. **Hedonistic Type**—offenders in this category are usually stereotyped as "thrill seekers," those who derive some form of satisfaction from the murders. Holmes and DeBurger also identified subcategories in this typology, including those who kill for "creature comforts" or "pleasure of life." This would include individuals such as Dorothea Montalvo Puente of Sacramento, California, who was arrested in November 1988 for allegedly poisoning to death at least seven destitute elderly victims in order to cash their Social Security checks. Another subcategory Holmes and DeBurger refer to is "lust murderers," which include offenders who become sexually involved with the victims and often perform postmortem mutilations.
4. **Power/Control-Oriented Type**—in this typology Holmes and DeBurger contend that the primary source of pleasure is not sexual, but the killer's ability to control and exert power over his helpless victim. Some offenders enjoy watching their victims cower, cringe, and beg for mercy. In one case an offender killed his young victims only after he had been able to break their will to survive. Once the victim had acquiesced, the offender would complete his task and slaughter him or her.

These general classifications of serial killers are useful in organizing existing data. Such motivational taxonomies help us to understand why certain offenders take the lives of their victims. Levin and Fox (1985) have also constructed types of serial murders including sexual or sadistic killings that appear to mirror Holmes and DeBurger's subcategory of "lust murders." Another typology similar to Holmes and DeBurger's hedonistic subtypes is described by Levin and Fox as murders of expediency or for profit (1985, pp. 99–105). Their third typology identifies "family slayings" as a major category of murder. This "type" does not appear to be particularly consistent with their prior two categories, which are constructed from motivational dynamics. Although family killers could be motivated by sadism or expediency, with few exceptions they are generally blood related to their victims and kill them all in a relatively short period of time. However, the noting of this inconsistency should not be viewed as a criticism of Levin and Fox's work.* Instead we are obliged to recognize the need for other typologies that may not be constructed solely on the basis of apparent motivations.

The Federal Bureau of Investigation, through extensive application of profiling techniques, has identified the characteristics of "organized" and "disorganized" murders (Ressler et al., 1988, Chapter 8). Using information gathered at the scene of the crime and examining the nature of the crime itself, agents constructed profiles of the offenders, which in turn were categorized as "organized" or "disorganized." For example, an organized murderer is often profiled as having good intelligence and being socially competent, whereas the disorganized offender is viewed as being of average intelligence and socially immature. Similarly, some crime investigators often find that organized offenders plan their murders, target strangers, and demand victims to be submissive, whereas disorganized killers may know their victims, inflict sudden violence on them, and spontaneously carry out their killings (pp. 121–123).

More specifically, organized killers profiled as lust murderers (an offender sexually involved with his victim) by the FBI possess many of the following personal characteristics:

1. Highly intelligent
2. High birth-order status
3. Masculine image
4. Charismatic
5. Socially capable
6. Sexually capable
7. Occupationally mobile
8. Lives with partner
9. Geographically mobile
10. Experienced harsh discipline
11. Controlled emotions during crime
12. High interest in media response to crime
13. Model inmate

*In the data set constructed by Levin and Fox, 33 cases are identified involving 42 offenders, including those who had been involved in simultaneous incidents of murder and cases of serial killing. Little differentiation is noted between simultaneous and serial murder.

The organized lust killer also exhibits fairly predictable behaviors after the crime, including a return to the crime scene, a need to volunteer information, enjoys being friendly with police, expects to be interrogated by investigators, sometimes moves the victim's body to a new location, or exposes the body to draw attention to the crime. The disorganized offender is characterized as follows:

1. Below-average intelligence
2. Low birth-order status
3. Socially immature
4. Seldom dates
5. High school dropout
6. Father often under- or unemployed
7. Lives alone
8. Has secret hiding places
9. Nocturnal
10. Lives/works near crime scene
11. Engages in unskilled work
12. Significant behavioral changes
13. Low interest in media attention
14. Limited alcohol consumption
15. High anxiety during crime

According to the FBI, the disorganized lust killer also exhibits a variety of predictable behaviors following a murder, including: will return to the crime scene, possibly will attend the funeral or burial of victim, keep a diary, change employment, become religious, experience changes in personality, and submit personal advertisements in newspapers regarding his victims (FBI, 1985). Although such profiles have proven helpful in understanding offender behavior, we have only begun to delve inside the minds of serial murderers. Indeed, many of the behaviors listed give us clues about the psychological mind-sets of offenders. To understand such offenders can help to curb their behavior both through efforts of law enforcement and most importantly by addressing the etiological roots of the crimes.

In the quest to comprehend why serial murderers treat the lives of others so callously, research usually focuses on the perceived overt motivations of the offenders. Did they kill for money? Thrills? Were they focusing on hatred, revenge, sexual pleasures, or other likely motivations? We erroneously assume that if we stare long and intently enough at a perceived motivation for homicidal behavior we will be able to comprehend the dynamics of its etiology. What we must not forget is that the amount of research to date in the area of multiple homicide is limited. Recognizing this handicap, researchers, whether they are involved with the technical forensics of a case or responsible for clas-

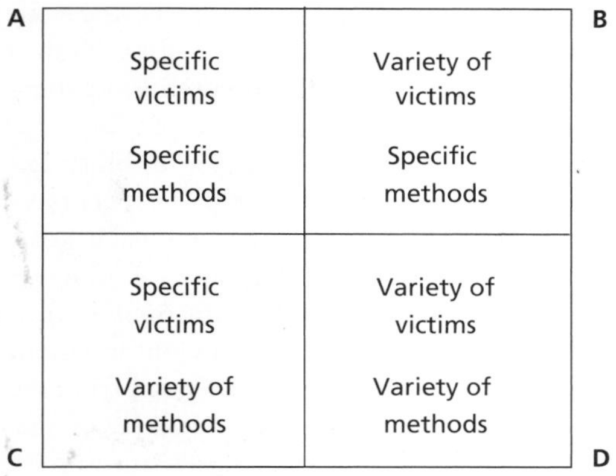

FIGURE 1.1 Factors for Constructing Typologies

sifying or typing offenders, must be willing to explore other factors that may contribute to motivations or to the construction of typologies. To say a serial killer murdered as a result of greed, hatred, or fantasy may easily obscure other important variables. For example, the types of victims or the methods used to kill may point to other reasons why the murders occurred.

Figure 1.1 illustrates just one of the many possible combinations of factors that may assist researchers in the construction of typologies. Because we have only begun to explore serial murder in an organized manner, we may find that matching variables may generate new ways of conceptualizing offenders' behavior or victimization patterns. In Figure 1.1 each cell refers to victims and methods of killing victims. Theodore Bundy, for example, sought out young, attractive females whom he bludgeoned and tortured to death. He was particularly specific in both victim selection and method of killing. David Bullock of New York was suspected in 1982 of killing at least six victims, including a prostitute, his roommate, and several strangers, by shooting each one. In this case the killer sought out a variety of victims but used a specific method to kill them. In the case of Richard Cottingham, also known as "The Ripper," the killer hunted prostitutes in New Jersey and New York. Even though he went after specific targets, he varied his methods of killing. Finally, Herbert Mullin, of California, is believed to have killed 13 victims, including campers, hitchhikers, friends, and people in their homes, using a variety of methods. Why is it that some offenders have no specific victims as targets whereas others are extremely particular in whom they choose to murder? And why do some offenders always follow a ritualistic pattern of killing but others use different methods of killing their victims?

Some serial killers such as Ted Bundy always go hunting for their victims and, once they find a suitable person, kill and dispose of the body in remote areas. Conversely, some serial killers wait at home for their victims to walk into their traps, similar to the spider awaiting the fly. In some cases the victims are killed and buried on the offender's property. John Wayne Gacy is believed to have killed 33 young males, most of whom became buried trophies under the offender's home. In other cases offenders advertise in the newspapers for offers of employment, marriage, and so on, waiting for unsuspecting victims to ring their doorbell. Each of these modus operandi may be useful in generating particular typologies of serial killers.

Hickey (1986), in noting specific variations in the degree of mobility exercised by offenders, has delineated three distinct groups of offenders: (1) traveling serial killers, who often cover many thousands of miles each year, murdering victims in several states as they go; (2) local serial killers, who never leave the state in which they start killing in order to find additional victims (Wayne Williams, for example, operated in several different law enforcement jurisdictions in and around Atlanta, Georgia, but never had a need to move elsewhere); and (3) serial killers, who never leave their homes or places of employment, whose victims already reside in the same physical structure or are lured each time to the same location. These "place-specific" killers include nurses (male and female), housewives, offenders who are self-employed, and other individuals or accomplices who prefer to stay at home rather than go out hunting.

Each new typology raises the issues of motivation and etiology. We may find sometimes that typologies overlap one another or that one generates more explanations and understanding than do others. For the present, researchers continue to examine the phenomenon of serial killing from a multitude of perspectives. Different perspectives will continue to generate a variety of typologies and operational definitions of serial murder. Which typologies seem the most appropriate depends on who is applying them. What is important to remember is that the limited research done so far on serial murder leaves considerable room for new ideas.

METHODOLOGY USED IN THIS BOOK

The data for the present study were gathered through biographical case study analysis of serial murderers and their victims. As Glaser and Strauss (1967) have convincingly argued, there are systematic methods in conducting qualitative research that may point toward theoretical explanations for social behavior. Their notion of "grounded" theory as a methodology includes what they refer to in their work as "constant comparisons." By examining different groups or individuals experiencing the same process, we learn to identify structural uniformities. Grounded theory stresses a systematic, qualitative field method for research. The present study is based on cases of serial murder within the specified time frame of 1800–1995. The cases were identified through as many avenues as possible, including interviews, newspapers, journals, bibliographies, biographies, computer searches of social science abstracts, and of course, the data set from the first edition of this book, until the process became repetitive or redundant and new information ceased to be found.

Unfortunately, one can never be sure of the precise moment the data collection should be halted. Depending on one's range of definitions for serial murder, one technically could include in one's research killings committed by individuals who work as enforcers within the realm of organized crime, political and/or religious terrorists who kill repeatedly, and members of street gangs. One might also include those who repeatedly tamper with food and medicinal products, bringing death to persons who ingest them; those who practice euthanasia; or—based on certain people's perspective—those who carry out abortions in clinics. From a historical perspective one might also include the gunslingers of the Old West who frequently killed in order to promote themselves and their lifestyles.

Although each of these typologies and perspectives might be worth attention, this study excluded them from its overall operational definition of serial murder. Instead, only cases appearing in a text or a news report in which an offender had been charged with killing three or more individuals over a period of days, weeks, months, or years, were included. In addition, patterns of conduct and victim-offender relationships were examined to determine offenders' motivations for homicide.

A few exceptional cases were also included in which offenders were reported to have killed only two victims but were suspect in other slayings or in which evidence indicated their intent to kill others. To justify inclusion, the homicides had to be deliberate, premeditated acts whereby the offender selected his or her own victims and acted under his or her own volition. Often a distinct pattern emerged in the method of killing or in the apparent motives for the murders. Usually the murders were to some degree motivated by sex, money, vengeance, hatred, or an unidentifiable impulse to kill. Each case was analyzed for specific data, including the time frame and the geographic locations of the criminal behavior, the number of victims, the relationship of victim to offender, age and gender of particular victims, and the degree of victim facilitation (responsibility of the victim for his or her own death).

This third edition of *Serial Murderers and Their Victims* provides more scientific analysis of offender behavior and updated coverage of serial-murder cases. Spanning the time frame between 1800 and 1995, the data represent the victims of approximately 62 women and 337 men in the United States. They are responsible for a minimum of 2,526 homicides and a maximum of 3,860 homicides. This victim range is specified because a few serial murderers killed so many people that only close approximations of the actual number can be ascertained. Difficulty occurs in accurately determining the number of victims of serial murderers, especially when one is dealing with a few offenders who have allegedly killed over a hundred people. Indeed the majority of these particular cases occurred in the nineteenth century, when recordkeeping was not as accurate or efficient as it is today. Often data sources are not consistent in reporting figures for these "super" serial killers. In addition, some of the data on victims may have been exaggerated because of the sensational nature of the crimes. Consequently, the killers in these cases were excluded from our study as were the killers in unsolved cases of homicide in which serial murder was suspect. Although the data do not represent an exhaustive study of serial murderers, they do form one of the largest and most varied assortments of multiple killers ever studied. (The total number of serial murders will, in all probability, never be known.)

In tandem with the increasing number of serial-murder typologies is the expanding literature that attempts to sort out and explain why such a phenomenon occurs with such regularity. The next two chapters will examine a plethora of literature, including medical, biological, psychological, sociological, structural, philosophical, religious, and environmental perspectives.

2

Cultural Development of Monsters, Demons, and Evil

Halloween, Friday the 13th, Nightmare on Elm Street, and other "splatter" movies remind us that evil, dangerous beings reside in our communities. The notion of evil monsters, demons, ghouls, vampires, werewolves, and zombies roaming the earth can be traced back to early civilization. In the past, explanations for mass and serial murders were often derived from demonology or the belief that life events were controlled by external forces or spirits. The notion that life on earth was primarily controlled by forces of good and evil has its origins in the belief in the existence of gods and devils.

In many past cultures—and in some modern ones—mental illness was generally viewed as a distinct form of possession, the controlling of a human by an evil spirit. The Gospel of St. Matthew in the Bible refers to two persons possessed with devils who were "exceedingly fierce," and when Christ bade them come out, they went immediately and entered the bodies of swine. In turn the "swine ran violently" to the sea and perished in the waters (Matthew 8:28–32). In the Gospel of St. Mark a similar experience occurs except the man is described as a lunatic possessed with a devil. The devil, discovered to be many devils, was thus called Legion and consequently cast out into a herd of swine. In turn, the swine again "ran violently" into the sea and perished (Mark 5:1–14). In the modern-day world, David Richard Berkowitz, the "Son of Sam" or "44-Caliber Killer," who hunted 13 victims over a period of 13 months in New York City, first claimed he did the killings because his neighbor's demonically possessed dogs commanded him to do so. Later he admitted he concocted the story to get back at his neighbor and his noisy dogs.

There seems to have been some confusion in the past in distinguishing insane persons from those who were "possessed." Sometimes those who were mentally ill were identified as being possessed and vice versa, at least in the Middle East, and sometimes mentally ill or possessed people were revered as the oracles of a deity or a soothsayer. In other times and places, similarly afflicted people were stoned to death or subjected to trephining, an early form of treatment of illnesses whereby holes were drilled in the skull to allow the evil spirits to leave (Suinn, 1984, p. 32).

Some cultures also believed that a person could be "invaded" by more than one spirit at a time. In modern days we might call such a manifestation a case of "multiple personalities," as described in Thigpen and Cleckley's *The Three Faces of Eve* (1957) and Flora Schreiber's *Sybil* (1973). The notion of multiple personalities has been sometimes used as a defense by serial killers. For example, Kenneth Bianchi, one of the "Hillside Stranglers" in California and also Washington, claimed that he was involved in killing 12 women because he was controlled by multiple personalities. Convincing for a while, Bianchi's defense finally came apart under close scrutiny by psychiatric experts.

People have also believed that evil spirits can inhabit the bodies of animals, causing them to act wildly. Just as many cultures have long entertained the notion that criminals can be possessed by demons, they have identified particular animals that are most likely to be possessed as well. In many legends and much folklore wolves are singled out as being the most likely animal to have dealings with the devil. The natural enmity between wolf and man has existed for centuries, and consequently wolves have been hunted relentlessly. Given the belief that humans and animals can be demonically possessed, it is not surprising the belief also exists that a possessed human could become a wolf. A person able to command such a metamorphosis became known as a werewolf (*were* was an old English term for *man*). The belief in "lycanthropy," or the transformation of persons into wolves, can be traced back to at least 600 B.C., when King Nebuchadnezzar believed he suffered from such an affliction. Jean Fernal (1497–1558) of France, a physician, believed lycanthropy to be a valid medical phenomenon. Many societies around the world have a term for "werewolf": France, *loup-garou;* Germany, *Werwolf;* Portugal, *lob omen;* Italy, *Lupo mannaro.* In Africa stories abound of "were-leopards" and "were-jackals," whereas "were-tigers" are common in India (Hill & Williams, 1967, p. 185).

To those living in the sixteenth and seventeenth centuries witches were similar to werewolves in that one was able to experience the transformation only if a pact was made with the Prince of Darkness, or Satan. In the sixteenth century, Paracelsus wrote that violent, wicked men may have the opportunity to return after death as an animal, usually a wolf. The purpose of this human-to-wolf transformation was the inevitable killing of humans, particularly children, in order to eat their flesh. Recurrent throughout werewolf literature is the theme of anthropophagy, or the enjoyment of eating human flesh. Jean Grenier, a young seventeenth-century Frenchman, claimed to be a werewolf and confessed that he had devoured the flesh of many young girls. Another notorious werewolf was Germany's Peter Stubb, or Stump, of the sixteenth century. After completing a "pact" with the devil he simply donned a wolf-skin belt and was able to transform himself whenever he had the urge to kill. Naturally he murdered those who offended him along with several women and girls, whom he raped and sexually tortured before cannibalizing. Stubbs, who fathered a child by his daughter and then ate his own son, managed to murder 13 young children and two expectant mothers by some of the most perverse and cruel methods imaginable (Hill & Williams, 1967, pp. 189–190).

Lycanthropy was also viewed as a form of madness in which a person believed him- or herself to be an animal, usually a wolf, and expressed a desire to eat raw meat, experienced a change in voice, and had a desire to run on all fours. To ensure the perpetuation of werewolf lore, stories of those possessed usually included reminders of how difficult it was to destroy such monsters. The werewolves were believed to be extraordinarily powerful creatures who could change back to human form at will or at the break of day. Belief in these terrifying creatures was often fueled by the occasional discovery of a mutilated corpse along a highway or brought in with the tide. Consider the story of the Sawney Beane family and how their behavior may have reinforced the belief in werewolves and other similar monsters.

> Born under the reign of James I of Scotland, in east Lothian near Edinburgh, Sawney Beane, described as idle and vicious, took up with a woman of equally disreputable character. They relocated to a large cave that was difficult to detect because the sea tide covered the entrance. Sawney and his wife took shelter in this cave and began robbing and murdering unsuspecting travelers. To avoid detection they murdered every person they robbed, and to satisfy their need for food they resorted to cannibalism. Each time they killed someone they carried him or her to their den, quartered the victim, and salted the limbs and dried them for later consumption. Each family member played a specific role in capturing and killing their victims. To ensure that no one escaped, precautions were taken to attack no more than six people on foot or two on horses. This arrangement lasted several years, during which time they sired six sons and six daughters, eighteen grandsons and fourteen granddaughters, most the offspring of incest.
>
> Frequently the Beane family would dispose of surplus legs and arms by throwing them into the sea. In due course many of these body parts were carried by the tides to other shores, where they were discovered by townspeople. Search parties failed to uncover any new information; they just cast suspicion on innocent travelers and innkeepers. Although dozens of persons were arrested, people continued to disappear regularly. Following several years of searching, soldiers finally discovered the cave, but they were not prepared for what they found inside. Aside from many boxes of jewels and other valuables, arms, legs, and thighs of men, women, and children hung in rows while other body parts were soaking in pickling.

> The family was arrested and executed without trial, the men suffering death by extreme mutilation and the women burned at the stake (Kerman, 1962, pp. 11–15).

Vampires also took their place in the showcase of horror but not until they received the attention of writers in the nineteenth century. Bram Stoker's *Dracula* (1897) was modeled on the fifteenth-century Wallachian nobleman Vlad Tepes, also known as "Vlad the Impaler" and "Drakul" (Dragon). He was particularly known to be a "vicious and depraved sadist" who enjoyed torturing and murdering peasants who lived within his jurisdiction. Stories circulated about the secret horror chambers in the depths of his castle and how he was believed to be the devil or at least one of his emissaries (Hill & Williams, 1967, p. 195). Tales evolved suggesting that some vampires could also transform themselves into werewolves. However, vampires usually had but one goal—to drink human blood—whereas werewolves mutilated and cannibalized. Vampires were also believed to be sexually involved with their victims, albeit discreetly, because of (for some people) the erotic nature of sucking human blood. In his book *Man Into Wolf* (1951), Robert Eisler described a British "vampire" who in 1949 murdered nine victims and drank blood from each of them. By 1995, any erotic subtleties in vampirism had been replaced with direct expressions of sexual arousal, gratification, and their fusion with violence and death. In the film *Interview with a Vampire: The Vampire Chronicles,* vampires dine upon the blood of female victims, who experience orgasmic arousal and, immediately following, terror and death. Thus, the repeated implications of sexual mania in the role-creation of the vampire throughout history are clear.

Werewolves and vampires are joined by a host of other sinister monsters all bent on the destruction of humankind, especially young women and children. Among them are zombies, or walking "corpses," and ghouls who reportedly feast on both live and dead bodies. The sexual connotation of these acts is pervasive.

Some of the early European serial killers who were thought to have been vampires or other "creatures of the night" in reality were nothing more than depraved murderers. Following are brief descriptions of two such people:

> *Gilles de Rais,* born in 1404, became heir to the greatest fortune in the whole of France. After fighting alongside Joan of Arc and being awarded the title Marshall of France, his beloved Joan of Arc was captured and put to death. Apparently he never recovered from the loss and soon lost his great wealth. Convinced that he needed to make a pact with the Devil himself in order to regain his fortunes, he murdered a young boy by slitting his throat, severing his wrist, cutting out his heart, and ripping out his eyes from their sockets. He then saved the boy's blood to write out his pact with the Devil. Having discovered his enjoyment for torturing and killing children, he began to recruit them in large numbers for his own murdering pleasure. Although documentation is not available, it is believed he killed several hundred children, drinking their blood and engag-

ing in necrophilia. One of his many perverted pleasures was to have the heads of his child victims stuck on upright rods. De Rais would then have their hair curled by a professional beautician and have their lips and cheeks made up with rouge. A beauty contest was then held, and the "winner" was used for sexual purposes.

Countess Elizabeth Bathory of fifteenth-century Hungary became heavily involved in sorcery, witchcraft, and devil worship. Although she married and bore children, she maintained a predilection for young girls. With her husband off to the wars, she began to indulge herself in the torture and slaying of young girls and women. Stimulated by sado-eroticism, the countess bathed in the blood of her victims in order to maintain her fair complexion. She was believed to have been responsible for the deaths of more than a hundred victims.

Such people appear to be the forerunners of the modern serial killer. Their acts are no more disgusting or cruel than those of their twentieth-century counterparts. We have kept their legends alive by scapegoating the wolf and perpetuating the tales of vampires, witches, ghouls, and zombies.

A function of the early European church was to find ways to eradicate the problems attributed to witchcraft and sorcery. Under guidance from Pope Innocent VIII, two Dominicans, Heinrich Institor (Kramer) and Jakob Sprenger produced the first encyclopedia of demonology, the *Malleus Maleficarum* (*Witch's Hammer*), in 1486. This compendium of mythology would be used for centuries to identify and destroy witches, wizards, and sorcerers. Thousands of people were "identified" through torturous means and then promptly burned at the stake (Marwick, 1970, pp. 369–377). The latent or unintended function of the great witch hunt, or the Grand Inquisition, was the creation of a witch "craze" that cost many innocent lives. Sanctioned by government, the witch hunt took on new meaning, and practically overnight witches were to be found everywhere. The efforts of the church and state probably did more to perpetuate the belief in sorcerers, werewolves, vampires, witches, and so on, than any other single force in society.

One more type of historical "monster" bears mentioning: In Jewish medieval legend a *golem* was a robot, or an artificial person (*golem* means a "clay figure supernaturally brought to life"). Golems were given "life" by means of a charm; occasionally they ran amok and had to be destroyed. Dr. Joshua Bierer (1976) uses the term *golem* to describe a case in which a man and his wife were having serious marital problems due primarily to his inability to develop any kind of meaningful relationship. His extramarital affairs were frequent, always in search of something he could not find. His mistresses did not sense that he was actually without love, commitment, or a desire for meaningful relationships. In reality he hated all women and wanted to kill them. To avoid this psychological truth he moved quickly from one affair to another. Dr. Bierer explained that this client had had a difficult childhood during which his mother was incapable of showing him any affection. Both parents were absent for long periods of time, leaving him to the whims of a cruel nanny who apparently forced him into frequent, emotionally stressful situations. Dr. Bierer concluded that everybody needs love, affection, and attention. Without these one can become emotionally truncated and run the risk of developing into a golem (1976, pp. 197–199).

Although we cannot assume that people suffering from the "golem syndrome" will become murderers, the golem profile does appear to capture the essence of many serial killers. A person who can orchestrate the destruction of another human being and have no remorse, no feeling for his or her victim or external need to defend his or her actions exemplifies the term golem.

For example, the present author had the opportunity of working with a patient during the late 1970s who was confined to a state mental hospital for the criminally insane. As a young man, rather alienated from others, he had dropped out of school but was still living with other students. His feelings of inferiority and fear of others fueled his journey into loneliness. Fantasy replaced reality, and soon he began indulging himself in morbid literature while his disdain intensified for those around him. He began reading a work by Dr. David Abrahamsen, *The Murdering Mind,* and quickly identified with the main character. He also began to fantasize about death and how it might feel to kill another person. One night after quarreling with a roommate over a box of detergent, this young man drifted into his fantasy world. He decided it was now time to realize his ultimate fantasy. He went to a closet and removed and loaded a shotgun and then went into his roommate's bedroom. He carefully placed the shotgun next to the head of his intended victim, and a moment later another roommate across the hall was jolted awake by the blast. The killer calmly propped the shotgun against the wall, called the police, and informed them that he had just killed his roommate and that he would be waiting for them to come and get him. People were appalled by his "coolness," his lack of remorse, his lack of feeling for what had taken place. He appeared to be void of emotions entirely. He was finally found guilty but mentally ill and confined to the state hospital.

Although the monsters we have discussed have their origins in demonology, witchcraft, belief in the supernatural, and folklore, modern "monsters," of course, are no longer attributed to transcendental sources. The mutilated corpses strewn in pieces along highways in California and the bodies left to rot in secluded wooded areas of Washington state or secreted under the floorboards of someone's home in Chicago are not the victims of fictional beings. Instead, they are the victims of the David Hills, the Ted Bundys, and the John Gacys of our society. Monsters in their own right, but the monster lives within and is unleashed only when the intended victim has entered his or her area of control. Are the men and women who commit such atrocities today possessed of the devil, or are they simply evil people, devils unto themselves who make their conscious choice for evil, just as others choose good? The answer may become difficult and complicated as we explore the possible explanations for serial murder.

SERIAL MURDER, CULTS, AND THE OCCULT

Closely tied to the notions of evil and demonology are cult-related activities. In the United States it is not a crime to belong to a cult—the term means "a system of religious worship; devotion or homage to person or thing." Nor is it a crime to practice beliefs of the occult—things that are "kept secret, esoteric, mysterious, beyond the range of ordinary knowledge; involving the supernatural, mystical, magical" (Sykes, 1976, pp. 249, 755)—provided those practices occur within an accepted legal framework.

Satanic cults in the United States appear to have attracted a growing number of followers interested in the worship of Satan. The problem does not stem from the fact that people join satanic organizations but from the belief that such cults may indeed practice human sacrifices. Anton LaVey, a one-time rock musician and actor consultant for the movie *Rosemary's Baby,* founded the Church of Satan on the witches' feast day of Walpurgis Night (Walpurgisnacht), April 30, 1966, which reportedly has a membership of 20,000 (Holmes, 1990). LaVey wrote *The Complete Witch, The Satanic Rituals,* and *The Satanic Bible.* According to LaVey's bible (1969), members worship the trinity of the devil—Lucifer, Satan, and the Devil—including the nine pronouncements of the devil:

1. Satan represents indulgence, instead of abstinence!
2. Satan represents vital existence, instead of spiritual pipe dreams!
3. Satan represents undefiled wisdom instead of hypocritical self-deceit!
4. Satan represents kindness to those who deserve it, instead of love wasted on ingrates!
5. Satan represents vengeance, instead of turning the other cheek!
6. Satan represents responsibility, instead of concern for the psychic vampires!
7. Satan represents man as just another animal, sometimes better, more often worse, than those who walk on all fours, who because of his divine and intellectual development has become the most vicious of all!
8. Satan represents all of the so-called sins, as they lead to physical, mental or emotional gratification.
9. Satan has been the best friend the church has ever had, as he has kept it in business all these years! (LaVey, 1969, p. 25)

Holmes (1990), who interviewed two high priests and several coven members of satanic cults, noted that members are encouraged to fulfill their potential by advancing through different levels of "actualization" via magic, spells, rituals, and so on. They progress by holding membership in the Church of Satan and participating in traditional worship services similar to the rituals, hierarchy, and organization of other churches. They may then progress to other levels within the church. Members learn from their Satanic Bible various "invocations," including the Invocations Employed toward the Conjuration of Lust and Destruction. One chapter carries the title "On the Choice of a Human Sacrifice." Those who are proven devotees and have advanced in the levels of "personal affiliation" are invited to participate in human and animal sacrifices that include the use of various devices and rituals. It is important to understand that membership involvement in satanic churches depends on factors common to any church, including loyalty, knowledge, and understanding of doctrines and oaths and the degree of commitment to these covenants. Indeed, many satanic cults operate independently of the main church. For example, in 1971 the Satanic Orthodox Church of Nethilum Rite was established in Chicago in an occult bookshop. As a competitor to LaVey's church, members of the Chicago church believe in God as the creator of the universe and that Satan, as the holder of all knowledge, created God.

In the late 1960s, Charles Manson and his followers gave new meaning to the word *cult*. Each member was believed to have paid homage to Manson and to have carried out his ritualistic death sentences. Allegedly, Manson was affiliated with the Process, or Church of the Final Judgement, a satanic cult. In the late 1980s a voodoo cult in Matamoros, Mexico, heavily involved in drug smuggling into the United States, was believed to have killed 15 to 20 victims, executing them with machetes, guns, and knives. The group had come to believe that through certain forms of witchcraft the drug smugglers could gain protection from police, bullets, and other threats to their drug trade. By cutting out and burning the brains of a victim and then mixing them with blood, herbs, rooster feet, goat heads, and turtles, the cult members believed they could operate with impunity (Associated Press, 1989).

Voodooism predates La Vey's Church of Satan by hundreds if not thousands of years and varies considerably in rituals, spells, and hoaxes. Rather than a formal organization, voodoo is the use of or belief in religious witchcraft. Persons trained in the practice of voodoo cast spells on or bewitch others as a means of protection, vengeance, and so forth. In this particular case the secret charms and hoaxes of voodoo were practiced to meet the "special" needs of the smugglers. The group, led by a "godfather" and a female witch, killed and mutilated anyone for their own reasons, including greed and vengeance.

Most serial murderers who are involved in cult-related homicides do not appear to be particularly advanced in satan worship. Several appear to be self-styled satanists who dabble in the occult, but the extent of their involvement is difficult to measure. Donald Harvey, believed to have methodically murdered 58 victims in at least three different hospitals, had books on satan worship in his possession but refused to comment about the material. Richard Ramirez, the Night Stalker in California, ardently proclaimed his ties to satanism by displaying his pentagram* tattooed on his left palm, shouting "hail Satan!" when leaving court, and listening incessantly to the AC/DC *Highway*

*A five-pointed star formed by intersecting lines, used as a mystical symbol.

to Hell album. Part of his ritualistic attacks included inscribing satanic symbols in the homes of victims. Henry Lucas, a serial killer who roamed the southern states and killed hitchhikers, confessed his involvement with satan worship. Allegedly he and his partner Otis Toole were paid to kidnap children to be used for human sacrifices, prostitution, and black-market sales. The duo were believed to be members of the satanic group Hand of Death. Robin Gecht and three other young men terrorized Chicago in the early 1980s by abducting, mutilating, and killing several young women. In a form of satan worship they were believed to have cut up animal and human body parts for sacrifice on a makeshift altar and then cannibalized some of the remains. Robert Berdella of Kansas City publicly admitted in 1989 to the ritual tortures and homosexual murders of several young men but denied any connection to satan worship even though evidence indicated otherwise.

Steve Daniels (1989), a specialist in ritual/cult groups, reasons that

> one can see that if a serial killer picks and chooses beliefs that fit his aberrant needs, mixes this with signs, symbols, and machinations of satanism, conceives personal rituals and adds to all of this a liberal use of drugs, a frightening picture emerges: an evil, drug-lubricated butchering machine who justifies his behavior by exalting Satan.

Assessing the degree of influence of satanic worship among serial killers has begun to attract both law enforcement and academic researchers. It is premature to state that serial killers in general have ties to satanic cults even though what the offenders *do* is satanic in nature. The fact remains that many serial killers have had no ties to satan worship before or during their murder careers. Perhaps offenders mention satanism when they are captured simply to add to the already sensational nature of the homicides. Perhaps the police and the media overreact and refer to satanism when they are confronted by the work of a serial killer. Perhaps there are certain types of serial killers who can be described as cult-driven, whereas others are influenced only superficially by satanism. In the cases of those who do become involved in satanic worship and serial killing, we should determine which behavior started first. Does satanic worship stimulate individuals or groups of people to kill, or were they already murderers when they found satanism to be attractive? For whatever reasons, it appears that reports of cult-related homicides continue to persist—which may provide researchers with useful research data.

THE NOTION OF EVIL

Levin and Fox (1985) refer to multiple murderers as evil people (p. 210). In the "hard sciences" such as chemistry and physics, exactness and quantification are necessary requirements; however, the notion of evil is intangible and unmeasurable, and it is often used as a misnomer for inappropriate behavior. In Western culture the closest we come to quantifying good or evil is by observing that someone is a really good person or a really bad person. We have a tendency to judge people in terms of their goodness or badness, but seldom do we refer to others as being "evil." Instead, evil is a label we reserve for those worse than bad. "Badness" we expect to find in many people, but evil relegates individuals to a special classification that suggests some form of satanic affiliation. Interestingly, both bad and evil persons may engage in similar types of undesirable behaviors yet be categorized with different labels. Part of the problem in assigning such labels is determining exactly what constitutes good or evil. Some people believe that gambling is "of the devil," whereas others see it more as a benign form of entertainment or recreation. The same can be said of drinking alcohol, committing fornication, or illegal use of drugs.

But homicide is another matter. Killing for recreation is not only unacceptable, it elicits some of our deepest anxieties about being alone and meeting strangers. We can understand to some degree the typical "domestic" homicide—a husband and wife, or other family members, find themselves in altercations that end in someone being killed. One can even understand why a person with a grudge may finally lash out at his or her tormentor or why an individual dying of an incurable disease is killed by a friend or a family member to halt the suffering. We may not agree in any way with the act of killing—most people believe that killing another human being is wrong. We do, however, understand to some degree the reason for killing and are able to place such homicides in context with everyday life. We consider them to be domestic, "crimes of passion" or situational killings that can be explained away as marital problems, family disputes, or acts of mercy. These types of crimes are illegal and wrong in the eyes of society. However, we know that most of these offenders will not kill again. They have freed themselves from their intimate entanglements and most then want, at some point, to get on with their lives. Domestic homicides, however, are in stark contrast to serial murder.

Multiple-homicide offenders, especially serial murderers, are incomprehensible to society. If someone has murdered children because he enjoys killing, that raises serious questions about the offender's rationality. Surely no one in his or her "right" mind could rape and murder a dozen children simply for recreation. We find it disgusting to imagine such crimes and disturbing to hear words such as "enjoyment" and "recreation" associated with the taking of human life. For many, evil then becomes the appropriate label for those who apparently enjoy controlling and destroying human life. What greater crime exists than to deny another person his or her free agency, the right of self-determination?

The quest for power and control over the lives of others is exemplified by the case of Josef Mengele (Profile 2.1), a physician and geneticist recruited into the Nazi ranks to direct the processing of concentration camp prisoners at Birkenow and Auschwitz during World War II. While Hitler stepped up his campaign for his "Final Solution," Mengele also promoted his own bizarre agenda for thousands of camp victims. Posner and Ware (1986), in their book *Mengele,* examine the depths to which one person is willing and able to descend, once given unbridled control over the lives of others.

PROFILE 2.1 Josef Mengele, 1911–1979

One of Adolph Hitler's most insidious goals was his Final Solution: genocide, the killing of all Jews in Europe and inevitably throughout the world. Genocide involves people killing large numbers of victims while at the same time remaining emotionally detached from the operation. Special techniques were routinely used to neutralize any guilt associated with the wholesale slaughter of humans. Large rations of alcohol were distributed regularly to many of the executioners; they were also provided with better food and housing than their peers. To professionalize the killing, special terminology, such as *human material* and *subjects,* was used to identify intended victims.

Physicians usually supervised the incoming trains at the death camps such as Auschwitz and Treblinka. Their job was to identify which prisoners would or would not be immediately sent to the gas chambers. For some of the doctors this was a very stressful task that evoked severe anxiety. This was not true of Dr. Josef Mengele; indeed he regularly volunteered for selection duty. At 32 Dr. Mengele was an aspiring geneticist who held a passion for fame and notoriety. Disturbed by the lack of warmth between him and his parents, Mengele was determined to raise himself up in their eyes through a successful career in medicine. He easily accepted the Nazi philosophy that it was possible through selection, refinement, and genetic engineering to create the ultimate "pure" race. At the camps he had an endless supply of human material on which to experiment. Those who were not deemed fit for experimentation were usually gassed and cremated shortly after their arrival, except those prisoners who were forced to labor.

Mengele set himself apart from the other physicians and soon became known as the most feared man in Auschwitz. His "experiments" turned out to be ruthless, diabolical acts of torture that nearly always ended in death. Unlike many who simply followed orders, Mengele undertook his work with a passion. Witnesses reported having seen tables and walls in his laboratory lined with pairs of eyes from his experiments on dozens of victims. His obsession was to conduct comparative research on children, especially twins. He was constantly in search of identical twins. He often performed surgery on the children without anesthetics. In one case he took two children, one of them a hunchback, and surgically sewed them back to back.

Mengele never tired of his work and killed hundreds of children simply to dissect them. In one instance he had a hunchback father and his 15-year-old son, who had a deformed foot, executed, then had all the flesh boiled off their frames. After bleaching their skeletons, Mengele displayed the victims' bones for his colleagues to see. He also ordered several adult female prisoners to be shot and their breasts and muscles from their thighs extracted to be used as "cultivating material" for future experiments. According to the West German indictment, Mengele was reported to have jumped on pregnant women's stomachs until the fetuses were expelled and even dissected a 1-year-old child while it was still alive.

His indifference to suffering was immense. He was charged with having 300 children, most under the age of 5 years, burned alive. Witnesses recount the night when several dump trucks arrived and parked near a large pit fire that had been started earlier by soldiers. One by one the trucks backed up and emptied their load

(continued)

PROFILE 2.1 Continued

of screaming children into the roaring fire. Some of the burning children managed to crawl up to the top of the inferno. Under the direct supervision of Mengele, soldiers with sticks pushed the little girls and boys back into the pit.

Mengele went to great lengths to care for children who developed various diseases. Once they were cured, he sent them to be gassed. His goal was not to relieve misery but to succeed at his task. One survivor reported how sometimes he would calm frightened children whom he had ordered killed by making their last walk into a game he called "on the way to the chimney."

Mengele was an intelligent, articulate individual who appeared dedicated to his work. Married, with a family, he managed to compartmentalize his life in and out of the camps. Under the guise of science he masqueraded as a medical researcher, but his rationalizations could not hide the truth. But do all people have such propensities? What, if anything, keeps most of humanity from such diabolical practices? Martin Buber, a noted Jewish theologian, examined the myths and notions of evil and found that some people are in a process of moving toward evil whereas others have been consumed by it. This may be analogous to a continuum along which we are constantly moving toward increasing degrees of goodness or increasing degrees of badness or, ultimately, evil. Some religions, such as Christianity, refer to the temptations people must endure and overcome in order to achieve a state of goodness; those who succumb become slaves to their own vices and passions. The ultimate notion of evil may be defined by those individuals who appear to have progressed past worldly temptations and have become devils unto themselves, completely without guilt, remorse, or compassion for their victims.

Erich Fromm (1973) refers to human evil as a process that includes the principle of agency or choice.

> Our capacity to choose changes constantly with our practice of life. The longer we continue to make the wrong decisions, the more our heart hardens; the more often we make the right decision, the more our heart softens—or better perhaps, comes alive. . . . Each step in life which increases my self-confidence, my integrity, my courage, my conviction also increases my capacity to choose the desirable alternative, until eventually it becomes more difficult for me to choose the undesirable rather than the desirable action. On the other hand, each act of surrender and cowardice weakens me, opens the path for more acts of surrender, and eventually freedom is lost. Between the extreme when I can no longer do a wrong act and the extreme when I have lost my freedom to right action, there are innumerable degrees of freedom of choice. In the practice of life the degree of freedom to choose is different at any given moment. If the degree of freedom to choose the good is great, it needs less effort to

choose the good. If it is small, it takes a great effort, help from others, and favorable circumstances (pp. 173–178).

Dr. M. Scott Peck refers to evil people as the "people of the lie": They are constantly engaged in self-deception and the deception of others. He goes on to say that "the lie is designed not so much to deceive others as to deceive themselves. They cannot or will not tolerate the pain of self-reproach. The decorum with which they lead their lives is maintained as a mirror in which they can see themselves reflected righteously" (1983, pp. 66–75). Peck observed that although it might be difficult to define evil people by the illegality of their actions, we can define them by the "consistency of their sins" (p. 71).

The notion of evil may best be understood if one perceives evil to be both a characteristic of an individual and a behavior. Men and women who commit evil acts are often perceived to possess evil characteristics. Thus serial killers not only *do* evil, but they also possess various developmental characteristics that may contribute to the evil. This differentiation between behavior and characteristics may depend on the type of serial killer. For example, some serial murderers possess highly developed narcissistic, or self-centered qualities. Fromm (1973), discussing the pathology of narcissism, refers to people who exhibit "malignant narcissism." Many of these offenders display an unrelenting will to promote their own wants and needs over everyone else's. As Peck (1983) observes, "they are men and women of obviously strong will, determined to have their own way. There is remarkable power in the manner in which they attempt to control others" (p. 78). The epitome of narcissism may well be the total domination of others. (See Profile 2.2.)

For example, the present author researched a case in which the offender is believed to have murdered 12 to 14 victims during a series of robberies on the West Coast. He usually stalked and attacked dark-haired, attractive women working in stores and other places of business. After robbing his victims he would bind them with tape and force them to engage in sexual acts. This entailed the victim assuming a kneeling position and being forced to perform fellatio on her attacker. During these encounters he held a gun to the victim's head. Sometimes he forced the woman to look him in the eyes until he climaxed, at which point he fired a bullet into her brain. Usually those whom he executed were victims who became hysterical, cried, and begged for mercy. Those who survived had complied with his demands but remained calm, some even joking with their assailant. The killer sought total domination and submission over his victims before pulling the trigger. The victim's death symbolized the attacker's signature on a completed act of total control over another human being.* In 1996, this author contacted one of the victims who had survived being attacked. A prominent magazine in England wanted to do a story on a female survivor. I was impressed with the inner strength possessed by this woman determined not only to survive, but to live without fear.

*Some of this information was gathered from interviews with the offender and surviving victims in December 1988.

PROFILE 2.2 Gerard Schaefer, Jr., Evil for Evil's Sake

Gerard Schaefer, Jr., graduated from Florida Atlantic University in Boca Raton at 22 with a degree in geography. He worked as a security guard, fishing guide, and deputy sheriff. He was refused a position as a police officer because he failed the psychological examination, but later became a police officer at a small police department until he was fired six months later for not having "common sense." A few days after being hired as a police officer he abducted two 18-year-old girls and took them, gagged and blindfolded, to a secluded area in the woods and told them he was about to hang them from the trees. The girls managed to escape and Schaefer was arrested and served six months in jail for assault. By then he had already disposed of two other teenage girls and two women in their twenties. In 1973 Schaefer was convicted of two murders and received two concurrent life sentences at Florida State prison. Investigators linked him to eleven other murders of women and girls. He will be eligible for parole in 2016. The following is from one of several stories written by the killer and found in his trunk after his arrest for the murders:

> I walk into the bar and look around. There is something special that I am looking for, or should I say, someone special. A woman with that look about her, that look of wildness, uncaring, a willingness to do anything for a price, a whore or someone like one. I have to be sure she is the right one because one blunder could be the end for me. When I find the one that I am looking for, I have to be sure through conversation. I'll make sure that no one notices me and then I'll make my offer. And if she accepts she has signed her death warrant. Everything has been arranged long before in preparation of this event. I take her for a ride. I am cordial enough and make no threatening motions. I give her no reason to become alarmed. I drive out to the place that I am going to leave my car, a place I have left it many times before, so as not to draw suspicion. I could be an ordinary traveler out

When Evil Embraces Good

The notion of evil becomes complicated by the generally accepted belief that those who commit sins can repent and virtually turn their lives around. The Christian Bible is replete with exhortations to repent. Whether or not we accept the Christian principle of repentance, the fact remains that people can and do stop committing sins and crimes. This "change of heart" may precipitate in some a desire to correct the wrong they have done and to become productive rather than destructive members of society. Prisons seem to breed religious conversions, which sometimes do appear to effect a change in attitude and behavior.

Is it possible for convicted and incarcerated serial killers to experience this "change of heart," experience remorse for their crimes, and never engage in them again? The scope of this research does not provide concrete answers to this question, but a few brief observations can be made.

of gas or taking a nap on the side of the road. Nobody would think differently, not even the police. That is important.

I pull over and casually say that we are here, and for her to get out. This is the place I seek. I have been there many times before, only those times it was in rehearsal and there was no victim, only the fantasy of it all. But I do know what will be done and how to do it step by step.

The woman is by this time very frightened. This is good because the more frightened she is, the greater the thrill for me. I tell her to strip, but I let her leave her underwear on. I tie her to a branch and gag her if she is too noisy while I go about the business at hand. I bring over the white sheet and pillowcase to go over her head. I explain that I am going to hang her and she might as well accept the fact and cooperate. The gun is persuasive and there is always hope, so she cooperates. The limbs are arranged perfectly for the deed, all the right height and distance apart. It has taken a long time to find the right tree and the right person, but I finally did it. I arrange the rope and noose and I dress the woman in a white shroud, place the pillowcase over her head, and then if I feel like it, sit down and entertain her with a bit of my conversation. Terrorize her. Give her my ideas on what she will look like while she is hanging there, fighting the rope that is slowly choking the life out of her. Make it as real as possible for her, so that she is petrified with fear. Make her know that she is going to die.

The noose is arranged so that she will strangle slowly. I will leave and then return so it will be unbelievable to myself that I did the deed. I will not be able to remember doing it. Funny isn't it? Then I will dispose of the body, and it will soon rot away in the tropical heat, with the help of the bugs and vermin, the rats and raccoons that abound here. This is what I intend to do, but I do not know why (King, 1996).

Frequently in the processing of offenders a judge is influenced in sentencing by the display of remorse. The general public is incensed when a convicted criminal displays no remorse for his or her crimes. Many people do not or cannot fathom homicide beyond the realm of television and expect those who commit such crimes to have some degree of remorse. We tend to equate remorse with the recognition that a terrible wrong has been committed and that the offender, recognizing his or her wrong, feels sorrow.

Recognizing words such as "sorrow" and "remorse" as qualitative terms and difficult to quantify, we are faced with the task of determining sincerity. Many serial murderers, some who have killed dozens of victims and are now in prison, profess a sincere conversion and deep commitment to God and/or Christian principles.

In one case an offender killed at least 12 victims. Some of those murdered were children whom he tortured and sexually attacked for hours before finally taking their lives. He recalled during an interview that on one occasion a young woman he attacked died too quickly. He was outraged that she had not lived longer for him to torture. In his anger he hung her from a ceiling and for several minutes bludgeoned and kicked the corpse. Later that day he found another young woman, who died much more slowly. This killer is now a converted Christian who is confident that God has forgiven him for his crimes and that he eventually will be set free.

Another offender killed 11 children over a period of one and one-half years in the early 1980s. Seven of the eleven boys and girls were raped or sodomized. Some he bludgeoned to death with a hammer, others he strangled or stabbed to death. Apprehended for only the last missing child, he made a deal with the authorities. In return for money he would be willing to take authorities to the grave sites of other missing children, but without the money there would be no bodies. The parents of the missing children in the area naturally wanted to know if it was their son or daughter killed by this mass murderer or whether their child was still alive somewhere. The authorities, without public knowledge, agreed to the exchange, and the killer began locating the dead children. Each time a body was recovered, $10,000 was placed in an account bearing the offender's wife's name. After ten bodies had been exchanged, the offender terminated the deal. He now resides in an isolation unit in a maximum-security facility and as a result of public outrage, his wife was forced to return the $100,000.

This author has corresponded and spoken with the offender on several occasions. He clearly understands what he has done is wrong, but now claims no remorse for his deeds. When asked about his victims, he responded, "I have put this whole matter behind me now. They are my brothers and sisters in Christ. All the children are with our Lord Jesus Christ now, and some day I shall be there with them." Claiming to have always been a Christian, the offender enrolled at a divinity college, where he pursued coursework in religious studies. He has written essays condemning abortion and capital punishment (a reversal of his previous stance) and supporting the power and importance of prayer.

A third offender sodomized and murdered five young boys over the course of several months. Once caught and sentenced to die, he expressed great remorse for his actions. He desperately wanted the families of his victims to forgive him. He sought forgiveness from God. He wrote letters to the victims' families. He cried bitterly over his crimes and to prove his remorse he stopped his appeals process. He stated that he deserved to die for what he had done. However, he also stated that despite his deep remorse, he knew that if he was ever again returned to society that he would start killing again because he had been consumed by powerful urges to destroy children.

These are only three of many cases of serial killers who ardently embrace God. Whether the embracing of God and/or Christianity will inevitably lead to productive rather than destructive lives remains to be seen. The prognosis, in this author's opinion, is not good.

When Good Embraces Evil

The more perversely and obscenely some murderers tend to behave or are depicted by the media to have acted, the greater the interest by the general public. Most persons are simply fascinated and shocked with the innovative destructiveness of multiple murderers. Most serial killers, especially those males viewed as attractive and charming, quickly draw a following of women, mostly young. These women attend the trial, write letters, and send photographs of themselves hoping to receive some attention from the killer. Some wish to help the offender recover from his aberrant behavior or are simply interested in having contact with someone so dangerous, but from a safe distance. We have yet to adequately explore the impact of media and public attention on serial killers and future offenders. We do know serial murders elicit an immediate response from some people who otherwise would in all probability never have contact with the offender. The relationship between the public and the offender is shaped to some degree by the amount of publicity, the types of victims, and the personality of the offender.

Inevitably some people are drawn to the offender because they have a desire to befriend and understand the person. Every serial killer whom this author has known always has a group of followers. They are, themselves, a most fascinating group of people. They come from a variety of backgrounds, but most are female. In one instance a woman met an offender after he had been convicted and sentenced to prison for killing children. She came to believe that it was God's will that she devote herself to the betterment of this man's life and has every intention of remaining faithful to him. She understands the nature and the extent of his crimes but is convinced that the offender is salvageable. After 15 years of devotion, she married the offender, who is never expected to be released. This type of involvement by a convicted killer with morally "straight" members of the community raises several questions. What influence, if any, do such offenders have over members of the community? What factors create attraction between someone who has ritualistically killed children and another person who abhors violence? Is there an attraction between people who strive to do good and those who commit acts of evil? It is easy to ascribe naiveté to those who align themselves with offenders, but we fall short in understanding the dynamics of such relationships.

3

Biology and Psychology in Serial Murder

The early schools of thought addressing biogenic explanations for homicide included the notion of "inheritance," or the belief that criminality is an inherited trait. For example, research included the case study of the offspring of Martin Kallikak and Ada Jukes. Among 2,000 descendants researchers identified 450 paupers, 258 criminals, 428 prostitutes, and a variety of other socially unacceptable types (Dugdale, 1910; Estabrook, 1916, pp. 60–61). The inheritance school of thought is discounted by most researchers today because it is impossible to determine if the criminal behavior is a product of inherited or acquired traits. Clearly, the propensity for homicide cannot be explained away by simply knowing the identity of a killer's parents.

PSYCHOBIOLOGY AND BIOCHEMICAL THEORIES OF VIOLENT BEHAVIOR

The earliest biocriminologists studied the shape of the head and the body, including facial features and bumps on the skull. *Phrenologists* were believed at the time to be able to detect criminal predisposition by examining bumps and abnormalities on the surface of the skull. Cesare Lombroso (1835–1909), often referred to as the "father of criminology," studied physical characteristics of criminals. He believed that people born with traits that lead them to commit crimes have particular atavistic anomalies—that is, physical characteristics typical of distant ancestors. These anomalies, or crimogenic physical traits, were believed to be inherited from degenerate family types and sometimes tempered by environmental factors. Lombroso believed born criminals (those biologically predisposed) were cold and cruel, showed no remorse, retained no close friends, and were prone to sell out their accomplices. The notion of born criminals provided the impetus for the eugenics movement of the early 1930s. Based on the belief that many criminal traits and mental illnesses were inherited, 27 states allowed the forced sterilization of the "feeble-minded," chronic offenders, and the insane. However, the work of Lombroso and those supporting "body-build theories" have yet to be proven as valuable in understanding criminal behavior. What is important rests in more scientifically sound research.

Today efforts are being made to study the naturally occurring "lumps" on heads but from a different vantage point. Scientists are very concerned about the role of brain injury in subsequent violent behavior. Considering that abuse is a common theme in the childhoods of serial killers, we must also be concerned with those who received head trauma. Although head trauma may not directly cause violent behavior, the persistent correlation must not be ignored.

Modern research now supports a variety of biochemical factors involved in criminal behavior, such as allergies, environmental conditions, and diet. For example, lithium has been used for many years to treat patients who have chemical imbalances and who are sometimes prone to schizophrenia and episodes of violent behavior. Psychotropic medications continue to be used to control certain violent individuals. Also, vitamin deficiency and use of vitamin supplements continue to receive attention as factors in violent, aggressive behavior, but because of limited testing and methodological problems in sampling, little credible evidence of the connection currently exists (Gray, 1986). Hypoglycemia, a state of low blood sugar that affects the functioning of the brain, has been connected to antisocial behavior, including homicide and habitual violence (Hill & Sargent, 1943; Podolsky, 1964; Virkkunen, 1986). Other research has begun to focus on contaminants in our ecosystem—including metals such as copper and lead, food additives such as artificial dyes and colors, and radiation from artificial lighting, television sets, and computer screens—that may negatively influence behavior (Ott, 1984).

Considerable attention has also been given to chromosome studies attempting to link an abnormal number of Y chromosomes (XYY) in men to violent behavior, but findings always remain tenuous (Mednick & Volavka, 1980). Even as late as the 1960s screening was being performed to identify babies with an extra Y chromosome because research had indicated that the condition was conducive to criminal behavior. Other research involving adopted twins has been more concrete, but much more evidence is needed to establish a relationship among heredity, environment, and criminality (Mednick et al., 1983; Rowe, 1986). In reviewing biogenic literature we must proceed with extreme caution to avoid confusing factors that may correlate with violent behavior and those that address causality. The argument that biological factors determine aggressive behavior remains premature, with little substantiating data. When Charles Whitman fired on dozens of students from the bell tower at the University of Texas, speculation arose that his violent behavior may have occurred as a result of a brain tumor later discovered during his autopsy.

However, studies continue in the area of hormones and their relationship to violent behavior. Hormone research has ineffectively attempted to link the principal male sex hormone, testosterone, to aggressive and violent behavior (Rada, 1983; Rada et al., 1976; Rubin, 1987). Review of premenstrual syndrome (PMS) research by Horney (1978) found little support in connecting increased amounts of estrogen and progesterone with aggressive behavior in females. Indeed, Johns Hopkins University provides sex offenders estrogen and progesterone therapy to lower their testosterone levels. Some states, such as Texas, Michigan, and California, are recommending the use of hormones to perform chemical castration on convicted rapists. The movement toward biological definitions for explaining violent behavior may be gaining momentum. In Indiana a bill was introduced in the legislature in 1989 to allow sex offenders the opportunity to be surgically castrated in exchange for reduced time in prison. The bill was defeated.

By 1995 increasing focus came to bear on psychiatrists, neurologists, biochemists, and geneticists to identify criminality and to forge links between brain chemistry, hormones, heredity, physiology, and violent behavior. Biological factors do not appear to explain single-handedly criminal causation but increasingly provide greater insights. In physically aggressive males the sex hormone testosterone can be found in higher levels. Exactly how that makes someone more likely to be aggressive is unclear. Everyone with higher testosterone levels does not become violent, but those who do must also be studied for social risk factors such as child abuse, divorce, and drug abuse. Other research has examined pulse, pupil dilation, vocal tension, and blood levels of norepinephrine, a neurotransmitter, and of cortisol, a stress-regulating hormone, and their relationship to temperament. Reiss and Roth (1993), in their research on inhibition, suggest that inhibited children are less prone to aggressiveness and violence, whereas uninhibited children are more prone to violence. Still, temperament must also be measured with other social and psychological factors in forging strong correlates to criminal behavior. Consider the case of Arthur Shawcross, a typical serial lust killer (Profile 3.1). What links can be made, if any, between Shawcross's biological composition and his violent behavior?

The role of neurobiology in violent crime is of growing importance in understanding the dynamics of the interactions among the forces of biology, psychological factors, and our environment. Some of the most recent research centers on the role of serotonin, a chemical that inhibits the secretion of stomach acid and stimulates smooth muscle and acts as a neurotransmitter in brain functioning. Connections between serotonin and aggression in animals have been studied for several years. The effect of serotonin on the central nervous system may well assist in studying violent behavior. Serotonin binds itself to various neural receptors, which in turn affect brain functioning. Jeffery (1993) suggests that serotonin has a "calming effect on behavior by reducing the level of violence." Increasing the level of serotonin may then reduce violent behavior. Volavka and colleagues (1991) suggest that serotonergic transmission may be impaired in some violent offenders, a defect that may serve to reduce impulse control. Virkkunen (Virkkunen et al., 1987) and Linnoila (Linnoila et al., 1983) and their associates examined both Finnish homicide offenders and arsonists. The subjects were classified according to their impulsivity in committing the crime. Where there was little or no provocation, the victim was unknown to the offender, or the attack was not motivated by money or property, those who murdered were classified as impulsive. Conversely, the nonimpulsive classification was given to offenders who attempted robbery, knew the victim, or otherwise premeditated the crime. The researchers found that the impulsive group reported lower levels of CSF 5-HIAA (5-hydroxyindoleacetic acid, a principal serotonine metabolite) than the nonimpulsive group. Lower levels were also found in the recidivist group or those reporting a history of suicide attempts. Those who set fires were all considered to be impulsive and all had lower CSF 5-HIAA levels than either the violent offender or nonoffender control groups. However, more research using larger pools of subjects with stricter methodologies will be needed to address the affects of serotonin. Also, serotonin can fluctuate within the brain, depending on location and time sequence. Administering Prozac, a serotonin booster and antidepressant to control mood and behavior, may be at the expense of ignoring environmental factors that can exacerbate already predisposing genetic influences (Gibbs, 1995, pp. 101–107).

Hans Eysenck (1977), from a biosocial perspective, argued that criminal behavior, including homicide, stems from both interactions of environmental conditions and inherited personality traits. In addition he concluded that the combinations of interactions of biological, environmental, and personality factors determine different types of crimes. Unlike those who believe in the "born" criminal, who is genetically programmed for criminal activity, Eysenck attributed criminality to persons born with nervous system characteristics that are distinct from "normal" people. In turn, these characteristics interfere with their ability to conform to the rules, values, and laws of society. He contends that most people are not criminals because as children they were classically conditioned to obey the rules and laws of society—much like the dogs in Pavlov's experiments. According to Eysenck, most people avoid antisocial behavior because they have been trained to recognize the negative consequences.

In addition, Eysenck believes that *extroverts* are more likely than *introverts,* because of the biological differences in their nervous systems, to be involved in antisocial behavior. Serial killers are often viewed as charismatic, thrill-seeking types of individuals (Ted Bundy, Randy Woodfield, Clifford Olson), although cases exist in which serial murderers are found to be quiet, introverted types

PROFILE 3.1 Arthur John Shawcross, 1972–1990

Arthur Shawcross, born in 1945 in Maine, was arrested in the state of New York, January 3, 1990, and confessed to the murders of 11 women. Shawcross, like some other serial killers, felt a need to return to the crime scene to relive the killing moments. Most of his victims he had sexually assaulted and mutilated. He had cannibalized some of his later victims; he had retrieved body parts of others as trophies of his fantasies. He returned to the crime scene of one victim three days after killing her in order to eviscerate and consume her genitals. He had already served nearly 15 years for raping and murdering an 8-year-old girl and confessed to sexually assaulting and murdering a 10-year-old boy. He blamed his compulsion to kill on childhood trauma and posttraumatic stress disorder from serving in the Vietnam War. Nothing in Shawcross's military papers indicates he did anything more than process papers in a support company office.

His physical conditions and childhood experiences, however, may well have predisposed Shawcross to kill. He possesses an extra male chromosome, sometimes found in persons inclined to violent behavior. His IQ tests indicate below-average intelligence. Shawcross also suffers from kryptopyroluria, a disorder that allows high levels of bile or uric acid in the bloodstream. The disorder can affect short-term memory, temperament, and tolerance for stress. The indications are that Shawcross had 10 times the normal bile/uric level. Shawcross also suffered head injuries both as a child and as an adult. As a child he was knocked unconscious when struck by a rock and again as an adult when he fell off a ladder and struck his head. On another occasion he was diagnosed as a child with inflammation of the brain.

Childhood events must also be considered in connection with his physical condition. Shawcross claims he experienced a very unhappy life as a child. His dysfunctional family life included frequent parental conflicts, beatings, and sexual abuse. By age 11 he had his first homosexual experience as well as sexual relations with animals. His youth was marked by bouts of stealing, vandalism, assaults on peers, and enuresis (chronic bed-wetting). He was given the moniker of "Oddie" by his peers because he had a difficult time fitting in anywhere. His impulsiveness contributed to a series of failed relationships. He was constantly dissatisfied with his marriages and other relationships because his growing deviant sexual fantasies were demanding more and more of

(Richard Angelo, Donald Harvey). Certainly, this is one perspective that has yet to receive much attention by researchers.

Occasionally, when examined, serial killers and other violent offenders display abnormalities in their genetic composition. Such findings should stimulate further research rather than hasty conclusions of causality. Certainly, biological research is not without merit, and, in future explanations for homicide, particularly multiple-homicide offenders, new findings may well prove to be helpful. However, given the current state of biogenic research, it is unlikely that in the foreseeable future biological factors will be established as the sole link between humans and violent behavior.

Arthur Shawcross's Victims

DATE	NAME	AGE	OCCUPATION	METHOD*	SEXUAL ABUSE OR MUTILATION
Apr. 1972	Jack Blake	10	Student	Bludgeoned	Yes
Sep. 1972	Karen Hill	8	Student	Suffocated	Yes
Mar. 1988	Dorothy Blackburn	27	Prostitute	Strangled	Yes
Jul. 1989	Anna Steffen	27	Prostitute	Strangled	Probable
Jul. 1989	Dorothy Keeler	59	Bag lady	Unknown	Yes
Oct. 1989	Patricia Ives	25	Prostitute	Strangled	Probable
Oct. 1989	June Stott	30	Prostitute	Unknown	Yes
Nov. 1989	Frances Brown	22	Prostitute	Unknown	Probable
Nov. 1989	Maria Welch	22	Prostitute	Unknown	Probable
Nov. 1989	Elizabeth Gibson	?	Unknown	Strangled	Probable
Dec. 1989	Darlene Trippi	32	Prostitute	Unknown	Probable
Dec. 1989	June Cicero	34	Prostitute	Unknown	Yes
Dec. 1989	Felicia Stephens	19	Prostitute	Strangled	Probable

*Mode of death was difficult to determine in some cases as a result of decomposition. Shawcross's typical pattern as a serial murderer was death by strangulation/suffocation followed by postmortem mutilation. He seldom varied in his methods but did appear to be escalating in degree of mutilation.

him. In tandem with his fantasies were his variety of property and violent crimes. As a young adult his frequent setting of fires eventually placed him in prison for five years, where he claims to have been gang-raped. By the time he was released and married again for the second time, Shawcross, now 27 years old, had murdered his first victim.

INSANITY: WHAT IS IT?

Most people's immediate response on learning that someone has murdered several persons is that he or she must be crazy. This is especially common when an individual enters a school yard, a shopping mall, or a restaurant and begins shooting randomly. Many such killers are found to have a history of mental problems, drug usage, and encounters with the law. For example, in Stockton, California, in January, 1989, an intruder entered the Cleveland Elementary School yard and began firing rounds from a Russian-made AK-47 assault rifle. Five children were killed and at least 30 other children wounded, many seriously, from the

110 expended rounds. The attacker then fired a bullet into his own head, killing himself instantly. Police and psychologists who investigated the case believed that something "snapped" in him and he reacted violently. The man's history indicated a life of drug abuse, arrests, and isolation. In this particular case the attacker appeared unable to cope any longer with an intolerable existence. He could not accept the fact that others around him were becoming successful. The feelings of inadequacy, loss of self-esteem, perceived rejection by others, and failure to achieve can become too much for some individuals to bear. They finally respond by lashing back at society. In this case the killer may have been exacting the greatest possible revenge on society by killing children.

Confronted with such cases, we sometimes employ terms that may blur the distinction between legal and medical definitions of mental disorders. Once an offender is charged with multiple murders, the "not-guilty-by-reason-of-insanity" defense (NGRI) may be used as the defense strategy. However, as far as the criminal courts are concerned, insanity is a legal term, not a psychiatric distinction.

The courts usually determine the state of mind of the accused before a trial commences. During the trial the courts must then determine if the offender was insane at the time of the crime and to what extent he or she is responsible for the crime. Thus the legal system uses the term *insanity* to define the state of mind of an offender *at the time of the offense;* offenders may be deemed insane at the moment of the crime and *only* for that period of time. Insanity pleas have been commonly used by offenders charged with serious crimes such as homicide, especially when the defense team sees little hope of acquitting their client by any other means. Most legal jurisdictions ensure that NGRI offenders are automatically placed in psychiatric facilities, regardless of their present state of mind. In *Jones* v. *United States* (1983) the Supreme Court ruled that insanity may continue after the criminal act, and therefore the offender could be placed in a psychiatric facility until such time when he or she is determined to have recovered from his or her afflictions. For some offenders confinement in a mental institution is tantamount to a life sentence because they must be clinically evaluated and deemed no longer to be a threat to society before they can be released.

Less than 1% of all criminal cases use the insanity defense, and most of those are unsuccessful. Those who do plead insanity generally are nonviolent offenders. Contrary to popular opinion, most serial killers do not use the insanity plea, although one might expect such a defense. Legal determination of insanity usually stems from specific tests for criminal responsibility. American courts usually apply rules patterned after British law. In the United States, courts generally follow the M'Naughten Rule, the Brawner Rule, or the Durham Rule.

The M'Naughten Rule

The M'Naughten Rule is often used to define insanity because of its simplicity:

> To establish a defense on the ground of insanity, it must be proved that at the time of the committing of the act the party accused was laboring under such a defect of reason from disease of the mind as not to know the

> nature and quality of the act he was doing; or, if he did know, that he did not know he was doing what was wrong (M'Naughten, 1843, p. 718).

The M'Naughten Rule is used in about 16 states to determine if the offender was unable to distinguish between right and wrong as a result of mental disability. Critics of the rule feel it fails to include situations in which offenders can distinguish between right and wrong but are simply unable to control their behavior. Some states used to supplement the M'Naughten Rule with the Irresistible Impulse Test, which allows an insanity defense when it can be determined that the offender understands the difference between right and wrong yet succumbs to uncontrollable impulses (Kadish & Paulsen, 1981). The defense then had to prove only that the offender could not control him- or herself during commission of the crime.

The Brawner Rule

Today the Brawner Rule, or Substantial Capacity Test, is commonly used in the United States to test for insanity because it combines the intents of the M'Naughten Rule and the Irresistible Impulse Test. It states in part:

> A person is not responsible for criminal conduct if at the time of such conduct as a result of mental disease or defect he lacks substantial capacity either to appreciate the criminality (wrongfulness) of his conduct or to conform his conduct to the requirement of the law (*United States* v. *Brawner,* 1972).

Under this test, or rule, the accused need only show a lack of substantial capacity instead of total impairment. This partial incapacity, however, excludes repeated criminal behavior, such as acts committed by sociopaths or acts determined to have been committed by people with antisocial personality disorders.

The Durham Rule

Finally, the Durham Rule, known also as the Products Test, held in *Durham* v. *United States* (1954) that "An accused is not criminally responsible if his unlawful act was the product of mental disease or defect." Controversy arose over establishing "mental disease" or "defect" and defining the term *product.* Essentially, in such cases the jury has no standards to follow but instead must rely heavily on psychiatrists' decisions about defendants' mental faculties. Consequently nearly all states have discontinued use of the Durham Rule.

Incompetency

Another important issue from a legal perspective is that some defendants are incompetent to stand trial. This has nothing to do with the court's determination of criminal responsibility, because anyone determined to be incompetent does not stand trial and thus has not been found guilty of a crime. The defendant's state of mind at the time of the crime may differ greatly from his or her state of mind later in court. If a person is found incompetent, he or she is usually placed in a mental institution until such time as he or she is considered competent by medical experts, after which the person must stand trial. Few serial murderers are found to be incompetent.

In recent years considerable public pressure has swayed some states to change their use of the insanity defense. For example, Alaska, Delaware, Georgia, Illinois, Indiana, Michigan, and New Mexico have created a guilty-but-insane defense. Under this plea, offenders are confined to psychiatric facilities until their mental states improve. They are then transferred to prisons to finish out their sentences. Another reason for some states to revise their rules for determining insanity is the federal government's 1984 revision of the criminal code, which abolished the Irresistible Impulse Test.

Public pressure does affect the judicial system. The extremely high visibility of serial murderers, although they are relatively few in number, draws increasing attention to offenders who to some extent have "beaten the system"—for example, by going to a psychiatric institution instead of to prison. The public is becoming frustrated with lengthy appeals, insanity defenses, and competency hearings and is anxious to see the application of swift and certain punishment. However, in our haste for reform we must not remove adequate protection under the law for those who were legally insane when they committed the offense.

Mental Disorders and Personality Disorders

We are inclined to believe that persons capable of random homicides must indeed be mentally ill or sick. In many cases the term *mental illness* is a misnomer and is better stated as *mental disorder.* The differentiation is more than semantical. Illness implies some form of degenerative state that may possibly be cured given the appropriate psychotropic medications, electroconvulsive therapy, or, in some cases, psychosurgery. Mental disorders, on the other hand, often are states of mind that are neither degenerative nor curable. Instead, they may remain constant or simply controlled by medication. Much of the treatment is directly related to the severity of the disorder. The DSM-IV provides descriptions of diagnostic categories to assist clinicians in diagnosing, treating, and studying mental disorders.

As a society, we have long harbored feelings of fear and loathing toward those who appear to be mentally unbalanced. Defining states of mind according to behavior, our society has long felt a need to protect itself from mentally deranged individuals by confining them in a variety of institutions. Those who were particularly violent found themselves in institutions for the criminally insane and referred to as homicidal maniacs, a label still used by the general public. The following discussion of mental disorders identifies the most relevant states of mind as we explore the thought processes and behaviors of violent offenders.

Psychosis Attaining a clinical consensus on an exact description of psychotic behavior is often difficult. Psychosis has generally been viewed as a severe form of mental disease in which the individual suffers from a severe break with reality and may exhibit dangerous behavior. However, movies such as *Halloween,* depicting escaped mental patients slaughtering unsuspecting victims, create an unwarranted distortion of people suffering from psychosis. According to the DSM-IV, psychotic disorders include one or more of the following symptoms: delusions, hallucinations, disorganized speech, or grossly disorganized or catatonic behavior. Some psychotic episodes are brief whereas others may linger. They can be induced by physiological malfunctioning, environmental stressors, or substance use. Most of the psychotic patients this present author has encountered generally were not violent. Those who became dangerously violent were usually at a much greater risk of hurting themselves than anyone else. In one instance a young woman who was believed to be in a psychotic state was admitted to a hospital. The day after her arrival she sat quietly by herself, staring off into space. Suddenly she jabbed an index finger in behind her right eyeball, partially tearing it from the eye socket. She proceeded to nearly sever two fingers with her teeth before attendants were able to stop her. The woman appeared to have experienced no pain during the self-mutilation and probably would have chewed off all her fingers had there been no intervention. In another case a female patient in moments of psychosis would seek out the edge of a door casing on which to split open her skull. The poor woman would thrust her forehead against the casing until the front of her head began to split open. In such a state she also appeared to have no feeling of pain.

It is exactly these types of images of mental disease that are held and perpetuated by our communities. It becomes easy to believe that "psychotic" people are prone to kill others. However, empirically based research literature discounts notions that psychotics are particularly dangerous people. Henn and colleagues (1976) examined the psychiatric assessments of nearly 2,000 persons arrested for homicide between 1964 and 1973 and noted that only 1% were considered to be psychotic. Similar results were also reported in other studies (Hafner & Boker, 1973; Zitrin et al., 1975).

Until recently, persons determined to be psychotic were routinely transferred into institutions for the criminally insane without ever having committed a criminal act—even though, as mentioned earlier, psychotics are more likely to hurt themselves than others. Psychotics are perceived by the public as dangerous to others. By contrast, people who are called "criminally insane" often display few, if any, overt signs of mental illness. "Criminal insanity" is more of a contradiction in terms, an oxymoron of sorts. Most people who commit crimes are sane, whereas those who truly are insane commit few crimes. Serial killers are rarely found to be suffering from psychotic states. Joseph Kallinger, who now resides in a psychiatric institution, is clearly psychotic. Suffering from delusions and hallucinations, Kallinger managed to murder his own son and others in his community. He claims that a large, floating head with tentacles, whom he refers to as "Charlie," instructed him to kill millions of people and cut up their genitals. The fact that he began carrying out those orders prior to his incarceration and still has strong urges to kill again will likely require permanent hospitalization. The U.S. Supreme Court ruled in *Vitek* v. *Jones* (1980) that administrative hearings are mandatory prior to transferring psychotic individuals to institutions for the criminally insane. Given the deplorable and limited facilities for the severely mentally disordered, it is unlikely that this ruling will significantly alter the flow of psychotic patients to such institutions.

Neurosis *Neurotic* behavior generally has been defined as a variety of forms of mental disorders of less violent nature than occur in cases of psychotic behavior. As with psychosis, the term *neurosis* has remained vague and nebulous, including persons afflicted with high anxieties and compulsive and obsessive behaviors, to name but a few disorders.

The latest revision of the DSM has provided much clarification and reordering of the categories of disorders. For example, anxiety disorders include panic attacks, agoraphobia (fear of being in a crowd, being outside the home alone, or traveling on public transportation), obsessive-compulsive disorders, posttraumatic stress disorder, acute stress, and substance-abuse disorders.

Research efforts have failed to substantiate claims that what was formerly referred to as neurotic behavior is common among criminals. Brodsky (1973) in his review of nine studies of prisoner populations found only 1–2% psychotic types and only 4–6% neurotic types among the inmates. Monahan and Steadman (1984) in their exhaustive review on the relationship between mental disorder and crime found little evidence that the mentally disordered are more inclined to criminal activity than anyone else. By contrast, many inmates are diagnosed as having a variety of personality disorders. Currently some research points toward offenders reporting dissociative disorders and their influence on criminal behavior.

Dissociative Disorders

Researchers have recently begun to explore dissociative disorders and their relationships to serial killers. Such disorders include abrupt, temporary changes in consciousness, identity, and motor activity. Gallagher (1987) identifies different forms of dissociation, including dissociative identity disorder, formerly known as multiple personality, the most widely known dissociative disorder. He noted that only a few hundred cases have been reported, and by 1978 approximately 100 cases were being treated in the United States (pp. 117–119). By 1996, dissociative identity disorder had become more common as a diagnosis but continues to be a rare disorder.

Dissociative Identity Disorder The 1994 DSM-IV defines dissociative identity disorder (DID) as "the existence within the person of two or more distinct personalities or personality states." More commonly known as multiple-personality disorder (MPD) and sometimes referred to as the "UFO of psychiatry" because of the debate as to its actual existence, little evidence has been produced to support multiple personalities as a true disorder (Ondrovik & Hamilton, 1991). Some argue that in most cases the disorder is actually *ia-*

trogenic, meaning that practitioners and clinicians are responsible for its occurrence. In effect, we find what we want to find. Multiple symptoms can easily be interpreted as more than one disorder as well as the result of the power of suggestion to patients during hypnosis (Orne et al., 1984). Hale (1983) found fewer than 300 documented cases of multiple personality, whereas Sizemore (1982), herself a case of multiple personality, believes there are no more than 100 to 200 cases of true multiple personalities. However, by 1989 the number of cases of dissociative identity rose from 300 to over 6,000 primarily as a result of the American Psychiatric Association officially classifying "multiple personality" as a disorder. To date the disorder has yet to have much impact as a defense in criminal trials (Slovenko, 1989).

Prince (1908) documented the classical case of Christine Beauchamp, a Radcliffe student who appeared to have three distinct personalities. Thigpen and Cleckley (1957), in their book *Three Faces of Eve,* observed that their patient Eve White experienced at least 22 completely different personalities. Chris Sizemore, who eventually revealed herself publicly as Eve, is not sure of the origins of her personalities but observed that "it was a defense and a unique coping mechanism which created satellite persons to cope with conflicts that were unbearable" (Suinn, 1984, p. 180).

Having more than one personality may be an attempt to suppress or deny severe traumatizations as a child. Gallagher (1987) describes the highly acclaimed multiple personality case of Sybil, who was initially believed to be controlled by three personalities—thirteen others became manifest during treatment. Sybil appeared to have begun developing these personalities at age 3 1/2. An only child born to a mother determined by psychiatrists to be paranoid schizophrenic, Sybil was forced to watch her parents engage in sexual activities and became the target of her own mother's bizarre fantasies. Each morning Sybil was strapped to the kitchen table, and, following a prescribed ritual, objects including knife handles, flashlights, a buttonhook, and bottles were inserted into her vagina. Frequently her mother administered enemas and forced Sybil to retain the contents while the mother played melodies on the piano. If the child soiled herself, she immediately received a vicious beating. There were times when Sybil was burned, had bones broken, was locked in trunks and other confined spaces, and hung upside down.

Sybil's psychoanalyst would later explain that Sybil's personality had split or divided into several selves as a mode of self-preservation from the nightmares to which she was subjected. The "new" personalities denied the existence of Sybil's mother as their mother, thus allowing Sybil to cope with the immeasurable amount of stress and pain placed on her (pp. 118–199). Schreiber (1973) suggested that Sybil was traumatized by her mother's attitude toward being a woman. When Sybil first menstruated, her mother jabbed her in the abdomen and remarked, "It's simply awful. The curse of women. It hurts you here, doesn't it" (p. 118).

Multiple personality as a dissociative disorder may be one way in which some people avoid or escape stressful or painful experiences. Much more common among females, those with dissociative identity are particularly impressionable, highly suggestible, and can be readily hypnotized. One plausible explanation for dissociative identity is that we all possess subpersonalities that reflect our moods and attitudes. Thus, a change in personality is little more than a shift in moods (Bartol, 1995, p. 167). Wilbur (1978) in her studies of MPD argues that all personalities diagnosed as dissociative had been battered as children. Stress that fuels anxieties may trigger a dissociative response to adapt to intolerable situations. Without such a defense mechanism the individual may be subject to a psychotic break with reality that inevitably could become self-destructive.

Using multiple personalities disorder to explain serial murder behavior is a rare but usually highly publicized event. In the case of the Hillside Strangler, one of the killers, Kenneth Bianchi, while under hypnosis, suddenly revealed another personality whom he called Steve Walker. Initially, the explanation of MPD was eagerly embraced by many observers. Although on the one hand there was Ken, the kind, loving father and responsible individual, on the other hand there was Steve, the other personality, the cold, vicious killer. Psychiatrists postulated that Ken had deeply resented his mother and had repressed these feelings only to have them surface in the form of Steve Walker. Dr. Ralph Allison, an expert on multiple personalities, interviewed "Steve Walker" under hypnosis.

> "I fuckin' killed those broads . . . those two fuckin' cunts, that blond-haired cunt and the brunette cunt. . . ."
>
> "Why?"
>
> "'Cause I hate fuckin' cunts" (Schwarz, 1981).

Bianchi explained to Allison during the hypnosis that he had met Steve while being abused by his mother. Allison recommended to the court that Bianchi was incompetent to stand trial as a result of his dual personality. Dr. Martin Orne of the Department of Psychiatry of the University of Pennsylvania Medical School was brought in to examine Bianchi to see if perhaps he could be faking the multiple personalities. Just before placing Bianchi under hypnosis, Orne mentioned to him that it was rare to find a case of MPD with only two personalities. Within moments after being hypnotized, "Billy" emerged as a third personality. Several people questioned Bianchi's disorder, including the police and the detectives involved in the case. Further investigation uncovered an academic transcript from Los Angeles Valley College that Bianchi had stolen from another student and then altered. The original owner of the transcript was Thomas Steven Walker. Bianchi, always the manipulator, had successfully deceived at least two experts. Before his capture he had easily conned a North Hollywood psychologist into allowing him to use some of his office space while he launched his counseling practice. Producing a phony master's degree in psychology from Columbia University, he deftly talked his way into a professional career, albeit short-lived. Bianchi, now under attack for faking MPD, dropped his plea of insanity and admitted guilt for the murders of several young women.

There do not appear to be any well-documented cases of MPD in serial killing. Even in single homicides, MPD is more likely to be used as a decoy defense than to be valid. Coons (1988), in his review of eight one-time murderers who used MPD as an insanity defense, noted that five were found guilty, one not guilty by reason of insanity (NGRI), and two people's guilt was never mentioned. In none of these cases in which MPD was claimed was the defendant ever described properly enough to substantiate an unequivocal diagnosis of MPD.

Dissociative Amnesia Although MPD has yet to be empirically proved in cases of serial murder, other forms of dissociative disorders that may play a role are only now beginning to receive attention. Dissociative amnesia, formerly referred to as psychogenic amnesia, is a loss of memory due to psychological reasons rather than organic problems. It is considered to be rare and can be triggered by highly stressful events such as war and natural disasters (Frederick, 1981; Hirst, 1982). Frequently, those afflicted display anterograde amnesia, or loss of memory after a traumatic experience (Golden et al., 1983).

Dissociative Fugue Another dissociative disorder, dissociative fugue, formerly known as psychogenic fugue, is described by the DSM-IV as "sudden, unexpected travel away from home or one's customary place of work, with inability to recall one's past" (pp. 229–230). Those afflicted may engage in partial or complete identity change triggered by their loss of self-identity or confusion about their identity. Fugues are still considered rare among dissociative disorders. Kirshner (1973) noted that only 7 out of 1,795 cases of admissions to a medical facility were diagnosed as fugue states.

Depersonalization Disorder This dissociative disorder involves persons feeling detached from one's mental processes or physical body. Sometimes referred to as an out-of-body experience, these experiences also cause significant impairment in social or occupational functioning (DSM-IV, p. 231). In one case, a man claimed that while having such an experience he got out of bed in the middle of the night, drove 30 miles to his father-in-law's home and shot him to death.

What we are beginning to learn from studies of dissociative disorders is that memories can be terrifyingly painful for some individuals. Splitting off, blocking out, or not remembering anything may all serve as vehicles to thwart undesirable memories. Indeed, we all to some degree repress certain memories that cause discomfort. Memories of failure, divorce, death(s), rejection, even of always being the last child chosen for a ball team, all can cause that psychological "wincing" that most people prefer not to discuss in detail. Suinn (1984) found that individuals report poor memory of uncompleted tasks that imply a sense of failure. He suggested that memory can be very selective when dealing with threatening information, even in the mildest forms (p. 175).

Psychoanalytic Factors

The notion of repression of feelings and thoughts was promoted by Sigmund Freud in linking abnormal behavior to mental problems induced by early childhood trauma. According to Freud, the mind is constantly engaged in balancing the three-part personality structure of id, ego, and superego. The id represents the primal component of a person's mental state, the driving force for the necessities to sustain life, including food, water, and sex. The ego develops from birth and serves to guide individuals' behavior to conform to rules, laws, and community standards. It is the pragmatic component of the mental state. The superego is the composite of moral standards and values learned within the family and community, which to some degree have been internalized. The superego sits in judgment of a person's behavior. The id and the superego generally oppose each other: The id seeks pure pleasure and the superego strives for morality and acceptable ethics. The ego, the arbitrator of the personality triad, constantly seeks to mediate between these two forces and generally provides a compromise. To illustrate the psychoanalytic concept, imagine someone being taunted by racial slurs. His immediate feelings (id) might be to strike the offending party in retaliation, but the superego senses that such behavior would be not only an overreaction but inherently dangerous behavior. Torn between the two forces, the ego guides the individual to a compromise. The individual may discount the event as meaningless and choose to ignore the situation or perhaps file harassment charges against the offender.

From the psychoanalytic perspective, violent persons appear to give little attention to morality, ethics, or standards when their id functions have been aroused. For example, Henry Lucas, a confessed serial killer of dozens of victims throughout the southern states, described himself as sometimes quick-tempered. On one occasion the 42-year-old Lucas became involved in a dispute with his 15-year-old lover and confidante. In anger the girl reached over and slapped Lucas, who responded by stabbing her repeatedly until she was dead.

Gallagher (1987), in describing the conflict between the id and the superego, concludes that abnormal behavior is the product of a conflict between innate human needs and societal norms (p. 47). Such conflicts usually stem from traumatic experiences during childhood that place tremendous stress on an individual. Most often the stress is generated by a conflicted parent-child relationship; the personality of the individual may become fixated or halted as a result of the unresolved conflict.

Such psychological scarring can be devastating to a young person. For instance, Edmund Kemper experienced significant childhood conflict with his mother, which left him with intense feelings of love and hate for her. At age 15 he killed both his grandparents because he was angry and wanted to know what it would be like to kill someone. After a few years of treatment Kemper was released into the care of his mother, which only escalated his feelings of rage toward her. He quietly went on a wild and terrifying homicidal rampage. Picking up female hitchhikers from the University of California at Santa Cruz campus where his mother worked, he sexually attacked and then butchered his victims. During this time Kemper was also fulfilling the terms of his parole and regularly attended sessions with his psychiatrist. During one of Kemper's visits the psychiatrist told Kemper how much better he appeared to be functioning and that he was pleased with his progress. During that particular visit, even as they spoke with each other, the head of one of Ed's latest victims lay in the trunk of his car. In this case, as in the cases of many serial killers, appearances were not only deceiving, but costly. Kemper eventually murdered several young female students before finally killing his mother and decapitating her. Kemper believed that once he had "resolved" the conflict with his mother his rages would subside, and he would not feel compelled to kill more victims. This seems to contradict the fact that a couple of days after eviscerating his mother, Kemper invited her best friend over for dinner. On her arrival, Kemper murdered her and violated the corpse. Kemper was arrested again and is now eligible for parole. He feels he no longer is a threat to society.

According to psychoanalytic theory, there are several paths to fixation besides harsh treatment of a child and anxiety-producing infantile experiences. Various forms of sexual assault on a child, including parental abuse, exposure of a child to sexual activities, and acts of incest by older siblings, can also contribute to early childhood traumatizations (Nunberg, 1955). The efficacy of the emphasis on disrupted sexual development of the child is not the focus of this research, but the fact that some serial killers demonstrate symptoms of psychosexual dysfunctioning should be a point for future investigation.

August Aichorn (1934), a psychoanalyst associated with Freudian analysis, studied delinquent youths and concluded that societal stress alone could not explain a life of crime. He noted that a predisposition was also prerequisite for a youth to engage in antisocial behavior. *Latent delinquency,* a term he coined to describe a state in which a youth constantly seeks immediate gratification while neglecting the feelings or needs of others, centers on a lack of remorse or sense of guilt in satisfying instinctive urges.

Indeed, there now exists considerable literature that lends support to the belief that most seriously violent offenders (excluding serial killers) suffer from various forms of personality disturbances. Lewis and colleagues (1985) studied a group of nine youths who had been examined prior to their homicidal attacks. They found that all nine had manifested "extreme violence" as children and as adolescents. They also noted that factors that were associated with the violence clustered around neuropsychiatric and family factors. The boys were found to be the offspring of psychotic households filled with violent behavior and physical abuse. Most of the boys were found to have suffered neurological damage as a result of head injuries or seizure disorders.

Smith (1965), based on his studies of eight adolescent murderers, reported that each boy had experienced various forms of deprivation in his life that interrupted his ego development and facilitated violent aggression. Similarly, McCarthy (1978) found a tendency for homicidal behavior among young men who had experienced early deprivation and, in a study of ten killers, noted complex feelings of low self-esteem and deep-seated anger. Sendi and Blomgren (1975) found that sexual abuse of a child by a parent was associated with homicidal behavior. Corder and associates (1976) found psychosis, chronic alcoholism, and criminal behavior among the parents of adolescent murderers. Malmquist (1971), commenting on the function of homicide, asserted that it "can serve the illusory function of saving one's self and ego from destruction by displacing onto someone else the focus of aggressive discharge." Pfeffer

PROFILE 3.2 Eric Smith

Eric Smith, age 13, appeared to be a very well-adjusted boy who was loved and cared for by his family. He was not an aggressive child and seemed to be outwardly happy. Unfortunately, outward signs can be misleading. One day while riding his bike in a local park he noticed Derrick, a blond-haired, 4-year-old boy walking alone. Approaching the boy, Eric offered to show him a shortcut through a wooded area leading to his destination. Leaving his bike, Eric escorted Derrick a short distance into the woods. Without saying a word, Eric stepped up behind Derrick and strangled him. A short struggle ensued, followed by Eric smashing the little boy's head with large rocks until he was dead. Opening the child's lunch pail, he poured Kool Aid onto the corpse, making special effort to put the liquid into the wounds. He then pulled the child's pants down and sodomized him with pieces of a tree branch.

A few days after the body was found, Eric admitted seeing Derrick in the park the day he was killed. He claimed never having seen the boy before. After several conflicting stories, Eric confessed to his family that he had killed Derrick. He stated that he did not know why he had killed the child.

What was it that made Eric kill? Perhaps he possessed some genetic makeup that predisposed or influenced him. Perhaps he was driven by some conscious or subconscious urge to destroy brought on by his environment. Let us now consider some additional information that may help the reader form some tentative ideas as to the etiology of Eric's violence.

Biologically, Eric was considered normal in most areas. He did possess deformed ears, an early childhood speech impediment, wore thick glasses, and had very bright red hair. Although none of these has any connection to violent behavior, each did provide a source of frequent embarrassment at school when other children would tease him. Eric was also diagnosed as having attention deficit hyperactivity disorder (ADHD), which appears to have affected his academic success.

(1980) concluded that young men who victimize and murder others do so in an effort to neutralize early childhood traumatization. Dutton and Hart (1992, pp. 129–137) examined the institutional files of 604 federal inmates to determine the impact of childhood abuse and neglect on violent behavior as adults. Men abused as children were three times more likely than nonabused men to act out violently as adults. In addition, men who were physically abused were also the most likely to be violent, whereas those sexually abused were most likely to be sexually violent. Dutton and Hart note their results are consistent with the cycle-of-violence hypothesis: Abused children are more likely as adults to abuse others or even other children.

Consider the true story of Eric Smith (Profile 3.2).

David Abrahamsen (1973) in *The Murdering Mind* found one common characteristic among people who murder. He observed that all murderers are intensely tormented and are constantly beset by inner conflict:

> The prime marks of the murderer are a sense of helplessness, impotence, and nagging revenge carried over from early childhood. Intertwined with

Environmentally, Eric experienced many problems. His poor school performance had necessitated keeping him back two years. He had difficulty fitting in with children two years his junior. On one occasion he remarked: "My life is junk, kids treat me like trash." His grandmother, whom he loved dearly, had recently passed away. He had also lost a friend killed in a car accident. His family life was disturbing. He had lived much of his life with his grandparents because of his parents' divorce. His stepfather was very authoritarian and controlling. His 16-year-old sister Amy moved out under claims that the stepfather had sexually molested her. There were claims, but never substantiated, that Eric had been sexually abused. Perhaps this was the explanation for Eric's sexual assault on the child he killed.

Psychologically, Eric was a very angry youth. His self-esteem was nonexistent. He deeply resented the ridicule of his peers. When Eric confessed to authorities about the murder, he found himself really enjoying their attention. He joked and smiled as if oblivious to his situation. Eventually, Eric admitted that he had seen Derrick before. The little boy received lots of attention from his parents. Eric could tell that Derrick was very cute and very popular.

So, why did Eric kill? Do we have enough information to determine causation? Probably not, but we can talk about the correlation of predisposition, family dysfunctioning, abuse, low self-esteem, anger, fantasy, frustration, and rejection. Did he kill Derrick because of envy, because Derrick symbolized everything Eric was not going to be? Did he internally suffer from the effects of his parents' divorce and the continual feelings of failure at school? Was he influenced by the nightmare of child sexual abuse, his feelings of shame, disgust, and helplessness becoming fuel for violence? These become pieces of the puzzle. Perhaps there are more pieces to make the puzzle complete. What do you think?

this core of emotions which color and distort his view of life and all his actions are his irrational hatred for others, his suspiciousness, and his hypersensitivity to injustices or rejection. Hand in hand with these go his self-centeredness and his inability to withstand frustration. Overpowered by frequent uncontrollable emotional outbursts, he has a need to retaliate, to destroy, to tear down by killing (p. 13).

Abrahamsen, as well as several others who subscribe to the Freudian perspective of psychoanalytic theory, places a considerable emphasis on psychosexual factors. Indeed, many childhood trauma experiences are sexual in nature. It is these sexual traumatizations that may later surface as aggressive, sometimes homicidal, behavior. Abrahamsen also noted an intimate connection between the offender and the victim as the "intertwining of our murderous and self-murderous impulses. . . . Every homicide is unconsciously a suicide and every suicide is, in a sense, a psychological homicide. Typically, the killer is afraid of killing himself, afraid of dying, and therefore he murders someone else" (p. 38). This effort to assert himself, to show that he is indeed capable and not a weakling, is an attempt to restore his "narcissistic" masculine self-esteem. Violence is an ego defense mechanism against intense inner pain and loss of self-esteem. Asserts Abrahamsen, "Frustration is the wet nurse of violence" (pp. 42–43).

For most, if not all, serial killers, frustration appears as a common theme from one homicide to the next. For many, the homicidal act is preceded by sexual torture. In one case, a serial killer in Michigan ritualistically rammed broken branches from trees and bushes into his victim's vagina. Sex as a vehicle to vent the killer's frustration, anger, hate, and fear becomes a powerful destructive tool. By contrast, there are various cases of serial killers who derive sexual gratification from watching their victims suffer and die without sexually assaulting them or overtly using sex in any way to harm or degrade them. One offender reported how he would administer poison to prostitutes and immediately leave, even before the chemical began taking effect. As he walked home he would revel in and fantasize about the agony his victim was now going through.

One might argue, however, that even in the last case the offender may have been vicariously experiencing sexual pleasure. Although some cases of serial murder appear to involve absolutely no sexual motivations, one may argue that latent sexual motivations exist unknown even to the offender. Psychoanalytic literature is replete with examples of defense mechanisms that serve to reduce anxiety states. Freud identified several, including denial, the conscious refusal to admit a factual event; repression, an unconscious exclusion from consciousness of anxiety-producing material or events; suppression, the conscious exclusion of anxiety-producing material; projection, the initial repression of a trait and subsequent attachment of it to others; displacement, the venting of unacceptable impulse(s) toward a substitute target; and sublimation, directing unacceptable impulse(s) into socially acceptable channels (Suinn, 1984). Each of these mechanisms appears at one time or another in the personality profiles of various serial killers. A tendency does exist for serial offenders to engage in a process of blocking out past experiences too painful or stressful to accommodate. The magnitude of the role these and other psychoanalytic factors play in the mind of the serial murderer is only now beginning to be explored.

Personality Disorders

The DSM-IV indicates that personality disorders have an "enduring pattern of inner experience and behavior that deviates markedly from the expectations of the individual's culture." Patterns are generally manifested in two or more of the following ways:

1. Cognition (perception and interpretation of self, other people, and events)
2. Affectivity (range, intensity, and appropriateness of emotional response)
3. Interpersonal functioning
4. Impulse control

The DSM-IV notes that the enduring pattern is inflexible and pervasive across a wide range of personal and social situations and that this pattern leads to significant distress or impairment in social, occupational settings. This pattern can be traced back to adolescence or early childhood and is not a result of medications, substance abuse, head trauma, or some general medical condition.

The types and characteristics of the various personality disorders include: *paranoid*—a pervasive distrust and suspiciousness of others; *schizoid*—a pervasive pattern of detachment from relationships, including limited expression of emotions; *schizotypal*—social and interpersonal deficits, eccentric behaviors that inhibit the development of close relationships; *antisocial*—extreme disregard and violation of the rights of others; *borderline*—instability in interpersonal relationships and self-image, and extreme impulsivity; *histrionic*—excessive emotionality and attention seeking; *narcissistic*—grandiosity, need for praise, lack of empathy; *avoidant*—social inhibition, feelings of inadequacy, hypersensitive to criticism; *dependent*—need to be cared for, fear of abandonment, submissive and clinging behavior; *obsessive-compulsive*—preoccupation with orderliness, perfectionism, mental and interpersonal control, inflexible and inefficient behaviors (pp. 275–276).

Personality disorders appear to be the most resistant to change. Their pervasive nature allows for the comingling of symptoms, which creates problems in identifying dominant disorders. Antisocial personality disorder (ASPD), common among violent offenders, includes a history of antisocial behavior beginning no later than age 15 for males, and for females anytime during the teen years. Antisocial behaviors may include one or more of the following: incorrigibility, theft, fighting during childhood, deceitfulness, excessive alcohol/drug use, reckless regard for the safety of self or others, impulsivity, and aggressive behavior during adolescence. As adults antisocial persons have particular difficulty in developing and sustaining relationships. They tend to demonstrate poor work habits and lack of responsibility; view the world in negative, hostile terms; and frequently show lack of insight into their problems and future plans.

Serial killers have often been portrayed as antisocial personality types manifesting aggressive, hostile behavior and a tendency to avoid developing close relationships. However, some serial murderers appear to be well-adjusted persons leading rather normal lives; their closest friends and family members have been surprised and shocked by their confessions of multiple homicides. The point is: Offenders do not always come from the same mold. Each killer has evolved through different life events and has responded to those experiences differently. Although it may be argued that serial killers possess "fatal flaws," it remains indefensible to say that such flaws are overtly manifested. In short, some offenders may never reveal enough of themselves in daily life to allow the identification of particular personality disorders. In hindsight we are always able to identify fatal personality flaws once we know what the offender has done. Accurate prediction of homicidal behavior, particularly serial killing, continues to evade researchers and clinicians alike. Understanding the psychopathology of these Jekyll-and-Hyde-like personalities appears increasingly complex as we explore the minds of serial murderers.

What we are seeing in the psychopathology of serial killers is that all serial killers exhibit antisocial qualities, but not all in the same manner. One way in which to conceptualize the personalities of serial killers is that they all share some common characteristics but also differ significantly. Serial killers share antisocial qualities but much of what they reveal about themselves appears to be linked to intelligence and skill levels.

CONSTRUCTING THE PSYCHOPATH

The term *psychopath* was introduced by J. L. A. Koch in his 1891 monograph *Die Psychopathischen Minderwertigkeiten* in his description of "psychopathic inferiorities." In 1939 Henderson described psychopaths in his book *Psychopathic States* as those afflicted with an illness:

> The term psychopathic state is the name we apply to those individuals who conform to a certain intellectual standard, sometimes high, sometimes approaching the realm of defect but yet not amounting to it, who throughout their lives, or from a comparatively early age, have exhibited disorders of conduct of an antisocial or asocial nature, usually of a recurrent or episodic type, who, in many instances, have proved difficult to influence by methods of social, penal, and medical care and treatment and for whom we have no adequate provision of a preventive or curative nature. The inadequacy or deviation or failure to adjust to ordinary social life is not a mere willfulness or badness which can be threatened or thrashed out of the individual so involved, but constitutes a true illness for which we have no specific explanation (1939, p. 19).

Cleckley (1976) in *The Mask of Sanity* outlined 16 characteristics of psychopaths:

1. Intelligent
2. Rational
3. Calm
4. Unreliable
5. Insincere
6. Without shame or remorse
7. Having poor judgment
8. Without capacity for love
9. Unemotional
10. Poor insight
11. Indifferent to the trust or kindness of others
12. Overreactive to alcohol
13. Suicidal

14. Impersonal sex life
15. Lacking long-term goals
16. Inadequately motivated antisocial behavior

Thompson (1953) in *The Psychopathic Delinquent and Criminal* viewed such persons as those who seek momentary gratification, lack discretion, and fail to profit from experience, which leads to repeated failures.

The term *psychopath* operates as a label to describe a potpourri of individuals determined by societal and medical standards to possess antisocial qualities or characteristics. Often used interchangeably with the label of *sociopath,* the psychopath often has turned out to be exactly what we want him or her to be. Working in a sex-offender unit, the present author quickly learned that most of these offenders were also regarded by the professional staff as psychopaths. In another section of the hospital were housed the habitual criminals, often also called "psychopaths or sociopaths." Even on the unit designated for persons on civil commitment, "psychopaths" were in abundance (author's files).

Psychopaths are generally viewed as aggressive, insensitive, charismatic, irresponsible, intelligent, dangerous, hedonistic, narcissistic, and antisocial. These are persons who can masterfully explain another person's problems and what must be done to overcome them, but who appear to have little or no insight into their own lives or how to correct their own problems. Those psychopaths who can articulate solutions for their own personal problems usually fail to follow them through. Psychopaths are perceived as exceptional manipulators, capable of feigning emotions in order to carry out their personal agendas. Without remorse for the plight of their victims, they are adept at rationalization, projection, and other psychological defense mechanisms. The veneer of stability, friendliness, and normality belies a deeply disturbed personality. Outwardly there appears to be nothing abnormal about their personalities, even their behavior. They are careful to maintain social distance and share intimacy only with those whom they can psychologically control. They are noted for their inability to maintain long-term commitments to people or programs.

Differentiating the Sociopath, Psychopath, and Primary Psychopath

The author proposes a rather simplistic but helpful framework in which to examine sociopaths, psychopaths, and primary psychopaths. The author recognizes the tremendous contributions Dr. Robert Hare has made in his examination of psychopathy and the distinctions made among these terms. To further illustrate some of these distinctions, let us first consider these three typologies in terms of intelligence and social skill levels. The *sociopath* is antisocial. This individual possesses the demeanor of one familiar with the insides of jails and correctional facilities, and also has a history of criminal behavior. In addition, this person has acquired certain attributes that facilitate criminal activity: callousness, anger, indifference, and revenge fantasies. Of average to below average intelligence the sociopath is commonly found throughout our state prison systems. The *psychopath* usually does not have the lengthy history of criminal behavior. That is not to say that this person is never arrested but is more careful in avoiding arrest. The psychopath possesses all the attributes as described by Dr. Hare in the PCL-R. This individual tends to have average to above average intelligence, and is less obvious to the investigator and therapist because psychopaths are less prone to show their antisocial attitudes. Psychopaths differentiate themselves from sociopaths in that psychopaths tend to display a higher level of skill in their criminal trade. Thus, they tend not to be arrested as often as sociopaths. Better adapted to their own deeply seated issues than sociopaths, the psychopath is less obvious as a predator. The psychopath often does not physically harm a victim. Remember, the core of psychopathy is power and control over the victim through whatever means necessary to maintain or improve his or her status. The *primary psychopath* also is antisocial but the untrained eye will never see the true nature of the offender. The victim may even defend his or her predator believing wholeheartedly in the innocence of this person. Never underestimate the power of denial. Primary psychopaths are social chameleons, who can blend into any environment. They are above average intelligence to highly intelligent and have developed skill levels far superior to other criminal types. They become consummate predators. They can lie so well that their words carry complete credibility. The primary psychopath personifies the PCL-R and can outmaneuver law enforcement for lengthy time periods. Sometimes the distinctions can become blurred. The salient factor for the investigator is the level of control exhibited by a person. Emotionally healthy people do not need to control others because they are already in control of themselves.

Measuring Criminal Psychopathy

Currently, the best methodology in measuring criminal psychopathy is Hare's (1991) *Psychopathy Checklist* (PCL-R). Based on Cleckly's observations of psychopathy, this instrument is used for the assessment of male offenders incarcerated in prisons or psychiatric institutions.

Revised Psychopathy Checklist

Factor 1: Measures a selfish, callous, and remorseless use of others and contains most of the personality characteristics considered central to the traditional clinical conception of the disorder. These traits are inferred, as opposed to explicit.

- Glibness/superficial charm
- Grandiose sense of self-worth/narcissism
- Pathological lying
- Conning, manipulative behavior
- Lack of remorse or guilt
- Shallow affect

- Callousness/lack of empathy
- Failure to accept responsibility for actions

Factor 2: Measures social deviance, as manifested in a chronically unstable and antisocial lifestyle. These traits are more explicit than those in the Factor 1 group.

- Need for stimulation/proneness to boredom
- Parasitic lifestyle
- Poor behavioral controls
- Early behavioral problems
- Lack of realistic, long-term goals
- Impulsivity
- Irresponsibility
- Juvenile delinquency
- Revocation of conditional release

Other factors:

- Promiscuous sexual behavior
- Many short-term marital relationships
- Criminal versatility

These factors appear to vary with the age, social class, cognitive abilities, alcohol and drug abuse or dependence, violent behavior, and recidivism of the psychopath.

The perception of and research on psychopaths indicate that most psychopaths are not violent but that they are more dangerous than most other people. Although many psychopaths are not physically violent, they appear to be more prone to violent behavior than other people. Perhaps another way of viewing psychopaths is that they are all dangerous because that is their nature. Every psychopath wants control to some degree over his or her surroundings. It is this quest for control that makes them psychologically, if not physically, dangerous. They are dangerous in that they constantly seek control over others. If the notion is correct that psychopaths seek to control their environment, then what happens when they are unable to maintain that control? Meloy (1993), in his impressive text *Violent Attachments,* states:

> The nature of the psychopath's violent behavior is also consistent with his callous, remorseless, and unempathic attitude toward his victims. I theorize that the psychopath was psychobiologically predisposed to predatory violence, a mode of aggression which is planned, purposeful, and emotionless (pp. 72–73).

Hare and Jutai (1959) note that psychopaths do not "peak" in their careers as do other criminals but instead are able to maintain a consistency in their criminal behavior. Psychopaths are commonly found in institutions and constitute approximately 20–30% of prison populations.

A common trait of psychopaths is their constant need to be in control of their social and physical environment. When this control is challenged, the psychopath can be moved to violent behavior. One example from the present author's experience is David, an intelligent man who was charming and engaging, and who possessed tremendous skills for deceiving others. Transient, he moved from one locale to another, seeking out those whom he could use. He had married several times, often before the divorce from his previous spouse had been finalized. He carefully and systematically siphoned off, diverted, and used the financial resources of each new spouse. He embezzled money from his stepchildren by forging their names on government bonds. Constantly he borrowed money from others with no plans for repayment. Fastidious in his dress, versed in etiquette, and articulate in speech, he impressed everyone who had never been victimized by him as a responsible, gentle, and kind person. David also had a passion for organization. He constantly reviewed everything about his life, his daily plans, and his goals. He always knew where he had been and what he did on any given day, week, month, or year. Indeed, he spent so much time planning and creating checklists he never really accomplished anything. When confronted, he deftly sidestepped the issues, carefully staying out of the focus. He rarely allowed himself to be in situations in which he might not have control. On occasion he would engage in an athletic contest, such as basketball. A personality transformation inevitably occurred if his team was losing or if he did not give a stellar performance. Seething with anger and frustration, he would resort to vulgar language, extreme physical aggressiveness, and shouting at other players. The moment he was confronted about his behavior he switched back to his former, kind self, until he returned to the game. He was a true Jekyll and Hyde. Although he had never been in prison, it was only because of his manipulative abilities that he remained free (author's files).

The problem with the label *psychopath* is that researchers and clinicians alike have yet to arrive at a consensus as to the proper definition of the term. Constructing a framework for the sociopathic personality type is still in the early stages. The etiology of personality disorders has given rise to a plethora of literature describing various forms of dysfunctional personalities.

For the serial killer, the term *psychopath* seems to "fit." Heretofore, killers could, by societal standards, be labeled through generally accepted standards of stereotyping. Gradually, however, the public was introduced by the media to the "nicest-guy-in-the-world" killers, and the public discovered that psychopaths had no apparent overt characteristics to enable stereotyping. The catch-all label of *psychopath* serves adequately to describe serial killers mainly because there appears to be a variety of types of serial offenders. This "variety," however, may be more of style than substance. The underlying pathology of serial killers typically is frustration, anger, hostility, feelings of inadequacy, and low self-esteem. These feelings may be manifested in many ways, but the source or underlying pathology appears as a common denominator. Meloy (1993, pp. 78–80) notes that psychopaths live a "presocialized emotional world" in which feelings are experienced only in relation to self and never to others. Psychopaths are more narcissistic and self-absorbed than nonpsychopaths and express themselves through self-aggrandizement and omnipotent control of others. This control is possible to achieve, as psychopaths are significantly detached individuals possessing little capacity to form emotional bonds with others.

The continuum of psychopathic personalities includes representatives of many groups, including adolescents, sexual deviants, intellectual types, hard-core criminals, recluses, and extroverts, to name but a few. Many people may at one time or another play "mind games" with others in order to gain the upper hand in a relationship. This does not make one a psychopath. Psychopaths become adept at this psychological game playing and ultimately become proficient at controlling their environment. It is very much a learning and adaptation process. Profile 3.3 examines the developing mindset of a psychopathic offender arrested for stalking. Much of the information was obtained from hundreds of diary entries found in the offender's computer upon his arrest.

Psychopaths are easily misidentified because so often their behavior is inconsistent. Although they may show contempt, anger, and hatred toward certain types or groups of people, they may be particularly accepting of other groups or types. Feelings are compartmentalized and victims rationalized into objects by the psychopath who seeks outlets for his hostilities. In 1985 in Wisconsin, dozens of women received telephone calls from an individual described as an "emotional rapist." His goal was to psychologically gain control over his victims' emotions by persuasively convincing them that they were dying of cancer or a rare blood disease. The only cure for their acute disease, he insisted, was to inflict extreme embarrassment on themselves. Some were ordered to walk down city streets with their breasts exposed, and two others pierced their nipples and walked mutilated among the public. His ability to manipulate his victims amazed everyone, especially those who obediently followed his commands (*Newsweek,* pg. 3a, 1985). The purpose of his ruse was to inflict as much pain, degradation, and humiliation on his victims as possible.

Sex offenders use sex as a vehicle to gain control over their victims by inflicting pain and suffering. It is believed that the sexual involvement of many serial killers is a result of childhood experiences. According to Gebhard (1965), "It appears that fewer sexual psychopaths than other offenders were able to make good adjustments with their parents and their peers throughout their childhood" (p. 856). De Young (1982) notes that "the sadist sees the child victim as a representation of everything he hates about himself as well as the dreaded memories of his own childhood" (p. 125). Karpman (1954) notes similar characteristics of masochists: "Aggressive sexual crime symbolizes the inferiority feelings of the masochist and expresses his hostility toward the objects of his lust; these tendencies are integrated in the personality of the sexual psychopath as a result of long-standing emotional conflicts and stresses" (p. 72). The offender, through violent acts, attempts to gain the control he or she has sought since his or her childhood experiences. As Stoller (1975) observes, "Many childhood defeats and frustrations feed into the dynamics of risk, revenge, and triumph" (p. 128).

The *sexual psychopath* is often referred to in serial-murder cases as a "lust killer" or one who practices erotophonophilia. The notion of lust suggests

PROFILE 3.3 Mr. Carter, a Psychopath Exposed

Carter's behavior and writings indicate a man who is a prisoner of his own obsessive ambivalence. The journal clearly and repeatedly documents Carter's fears, anger, and frustrations with himself and others. He presents himself as a person controlled by his obsessions and compulsions. Although he attempts to portray himself to others as a successful and productive individual, his journal tells a very different story. Carter, reflecting upon his unhappy state writes:

> My inheritance has afforded me the luxury of not having to do anything with myself. Because of this, I have had a hard time joining society. My self-esteem has suffered as a result. I latch on to a girl and want to be consumed by the relationship. I smother them, and this causes them to tend to reject me. I lose myself too quickly and easily in the girl. I "set myself up" to be alone. It's almost like I set myself up for hard times.

By his own account he places blame on his family, especially his parents, as the source of much of his inner conflicts. Carter chronicles in his journal his deep resentments toward his parents for the many perceived and actual pains they caused him:

Things Mom and Dad did:

1. Dad held me under the water in pool when I was 5—made me afraid of the water. Later I conquered it windsurfing.
2. Left me at boarding school
3. Mom went crazy and killed herself
4. Dad used to beat me for no reason
5. Broke bass guitar
6. Kicked me for selling colt pistol
7. Gave vacuform for straight "A" 2nd grade (instead of love)
8. Mom called me a sociopath
9. Dad built my tree house
10. Knocking my head with the ring
11. Knocking my head against the wall
12. Pulled me out of the house by my hair with Pat watching
13. Cut me off ($) when I left GA Tech
14. Left us at grandparents for three months, repeatedly
15. Forced me to stay in library every day during spring break
16. Threw out all my toys when house we grew up in was cleaned out
17. Didn't want to see me when I moved to GA Tech to be close to him
18. Wrote will such that his wife got to dispense with everything

The death of his parents and his unhappy childhood set the stage for his need to project his own self-loathing and insecurities onto others while at the same time appearing to be a congenial, understanding, and tolerant person. For example, Carter accepted invitations to visit his sisters and stayed in their homes while at the same time he vividly described his negative personal feelings about them in his journal. Regarding Stacy he writes:

> Well—Stacy is really a spoiled child. I am really done with her this time. I don't give a shit if she does kill herself. At least then we would be done hearing her whine about how she is all bummed out about whatever the excuse of the week is. Think of the money I am going to save by not traveling to her house ever again. Frankly, I hope I live long enough to see her die. She will get hers. It is just a matter of time. She is such a bitch. Such a self-important, self-righteous bitch. Remember: I am better than they are. They have more security now, but it ain't over YET. When Al has a heart attack and dies, I won't be around to do anything for them. FUCK THEM!!

Of particular importance in these excerpts are the several references made by Carter regarding his death wishes for his sister Nancy, his desire to see Nancy "get hers," and his matter-of-fact indifference to the possibility that his other sister Stacy might take her own life. His systemic anger that frames his thoughts about his family and his desire to see them suffer for treating him poorly is a recurring theme in his journal. Carter demonstrates these same attitudes toward his friends and ultimately his victims. The following statements from Carter's journal highlight his pent up anger toward others who have intentionally or inadvertently angered him. Please note the forms of punishment Carter has selected for each person.

1. Pat C. had affair with dad, ended up with all his property. Make it look like an accident.
2. Carol L. . . Trash her car. "Father" Tom. Meddling mother fucker. . . He will get what he deserves! I will see to it!
3. Nancy C. . . (Crusader Yacht Sales)—deserves something special: vandalize boats w/crusader signs on them!!!
4. Lisa (M sister) child/husband
5. Michael D. Wind surfing vacations—kill.
6. Steve H., lawyer—kill.
7. Norbert C.—find, kill.
8. Eric Z.—find, kill.
9. Don't get mad get even. Revenge is best served cold.
   Light bulb filament in gas tank—powered by car elec. system—when car is started: BOOM.
10. Scott W.—Fuck with car.

His inability to adequately resolve his personal inner conflicts is a core issue to his conviction for stalking activity. Unable to bring resolution regarding his conflicts with his deceased parents, Carter focuses his fantasies, frustrations, insecurities, and anger into developing relationships where he can be in control. These relationships are specific in that he is attracted to women who are assertive, goal-oriented, and self-confident: everything that he, according to his own account, is lacking. An example of his need to control is noted in his journal regarding his destructive relationship with his former girlfriend, Jane C.

> The things I did to her: Never let her have any time with friends. Never let her have any time alone. Couldn't talk to any guy without interrogation following. Physical violence. Being cruel when I knew that she couldn't get away or I wouldn't let her get away. Destroying things she gave me. Destroying her things. Threatening with violence. Saying mean things. Can't control myself.

Mary, another victim, would often attempt to break off the relationship. In his journal Carter expresses his rage toward her by threatening to kill her.

> She was not happy with this, and used her old threat of saying "goodbye then." I really don't think she has any idea what she is dealing with. I will kill her if she fucks with me this time.

Her friends stopped calling because they were uncomfortable speaking to or being around Carter. Often, following one of his jealous tirades Carter showed displays of affection and kindness in an effort to convince her that life would be better now, that all the ugliness was behind them. This tactic inevitably was followed by more acts of rage. Eventually his anger intensified and he punched her on the arm and threw her against a

(continued)

PROFILE 3.3 Continued

window. She moved out and tried to hide. In retaliation, Carter cut up her clothing and other personal property and erased her computer hard drive that contained important data she used for her business. On occasion he was so angry that he again wiped out her computer hard drive and filled her coffeemaker with detergent. His aggression toward his victim was manifested in other ways including killing her cat by crushing its head with a flashlight. Carter refers to the killing:

> Did kill the cat. After it bit me, it deserved as much. (Bashed its head with her roommate's flashlight.)

During the attack Carter was bitten severely on one of his fingers. After killing the animal, Carter returned to the residence and explained to Mary that, as he was leaving her residence, he tried to pet the cat when it suddenly turned and attacked him. Sympathetic, Mary bandaged his wound and then she and Carter spent an hour looking for her cat, which she believed, had run away. It was not until weeks later that Carter informed her by telephone of the actual demise of her cat.

He would then call and harass her followed by expressions of contriteness and apologies. His behavior follows the same pattern seen in domestic violence cases: the escalation of rage, the blowup, and finally the placating apologies, which become the hallmark of an abuser before the next cycle of acting out.

These incidents were punctuated over time with a series of telephone threats, several of them suggesting either physical or psychological harm to Mary:

1. "And I'll tell you something else cold-blooded bitch. I know where you are and the fun has just begun."
2. "Hmm, remember the nightmares you used to have? Aaah, they're nothing compared to what reality could be."
3. "You've wasted my time. The bill will come due. Rest assured the bill will come due."

one who possesses a particular urge, not only to kill, but to ravage the victim. Even among lust killers, methods of killing vary widely, as do the types of mutilations that may occur before or after the victim has died. In one case an offender described his feelings about killing, focusing on the urge to mutilate and destroy his victims before he could find temporary relief:

*Uncensored Exotics**

Vainly I crouch at the fireside,
For the flames on the hearth cannot warm me.
Vainly I put on coats
Against the cold of the star winds,
Blowing from Outer Gulfs in the darkness beyond Time.
Thick walls and roofs, you are useless

*From J. Paul de River, *The Sexual Criminal,* 1949, pp. 210–211. Courtesy of Charles C. Thomas, Publisher, Springfield, Illinois. Reprinted by permission.

4. Kissing sounds, music. "Nowhere to run, nowhere to hide."
5. "By the way you bitch, I enjoyed killing your little cat. Purr, purr, purr, till I crush your skull."
6. "I went out tonight and I found the dog. It was an annoying dog and I fed it Drano mixed in with hamburger and I watched it die. And I thought about various things."

All of these behaviors are clear manifestations of Carter's desire to control and/or harm his victims. In the beginning, his relationships appear to be positive. In the case of Mary, both parties seemed quite enamoured with each other. Over time, Mary began to see and hear behavior that she found disturbing. As the relationship deteriorated and she tried to break off with him, Carter began to employ a variety of maladaptive behaviors in order to maintain control of the relationship. Moving from harassing phone calls to threatening phone calls, from minor vandalism to serious property destruction, from knocking a victim down to showing up at her home with a gun, from killing animals to dousing the victim's planter box and front porch with gasoline—each scenario denotes escalation toward increasingly violent behavior. The etiology of violent attachments is grounded in an internal drive for control. Carter can maintain the pretense of respectability and detachment from others but internally he is drawn to women with whom he can develop an obsessive love/hate relationship. At an individual level dysfunctional relationships created by Carter culminate in the forced termination of the relationship. Carter then retreats for a period of time to rethink his relationships. He reemerges to seek another relationship, only to have it also destroyed. The pathological cycle appears endless, as do his levels of frustration and aggression. Carter may appear rehabilitated while under the scrutiny of the courts, but the prognosis is not good for future, unsuspecting victims. At the time of this writing Carter is serving 3½ years in federal prison for stalking (author's files).

Against the breath of the star winds.
Red logs, why do you crackle,
Since you are mocked by the star winds?
And my bones are chilled within me
And my blood is become as water.
And now from the void behind me
Comes the piping of the piper,
That senseless, complaining piping,
That tuneless, high, thin piping.
Swiftly I turn to assail him
But he keeps ever behind me,
So that I catch but a glimpse of him,
Piping behind the shadows.
Faceless, with malformed hands
Holding a flute of silver,
Blowing his senseless music.

Piping his high, thin piping.
During an age does his playing
Beat to my brain through my eardrums,
Covered by helpless fingers.
Then, with a shout, I surrender,
And leap to do the bidding.
From the wall I snatch my weapons
And rush from the house to the forest.
Where the road winds down the mountain,
Panting I lie in ambush,
Waiting for some poor traveler
Who shall bring me my release.
When he comes with laggard footsteps,
Sudden and fierce is my onslaught.
Like a beast I overcome him
And utterly destroy him.
And I cut out his heart and eat it,
And I guzzle his blood like nectar,
And I cut off his head and scalp him,
And hang his scalp at my belt.
Homeward I walk through the snowdrifts,
And my heart is warm within me,
And my blood and bones are new again,
And the star winds cease to chill me,
And the piping of the piper
Will be heard no more for a season.

Such an urge to kill is fueled by well-developed fantasies that allow the offender to vicariously gain control of others. Fantasy for the lust killer is much more than an escape, it becomes the focal behavior. Even though the killer is able to maintain contact with reality, the world of fantasy becomes as addictive as an escape into drugs. Ressler and his colleagues (1988) argue that psychological motives for homicide do not find their roots in traumatization or stimulation; rather, offenders murder as a result of their thinking (p. 34). Thought processes, however, are influenced by life experiences that ultimately can affect the types of fantasies developed by individuals. Thus, negative experiences give rise to negative thoughts and fantasies, and positive experiences lay the foundation for positive thoughts and constructive fantasies. It is unlikely to find individuals who fantasize about helping others and then go out and kill other human beings. People who feel good about themselves do not kill others. The better a person's self-concept, the higher an individual's self-esteem, the less need he or she has to control and dominate others. One may wonder why so many people subscribe to magazines or prefer entertainment established and operated on the premise of violence. Perhaps those who have carefully controlled lives allow others to stand proxy for them in acting out their fantasies of hostility and aggression. The boxer smashing his opponent's face, splattering blood; the matador who is gored by the horns of an enraged bull; the hockey player who slashes his opponent with his stick—each brings the fans to their feet, eager for more.

But most people do not kill, they just enjoy watching others do it on television and at the movies, or reading about it in books. Murderers take their fantasies further. Perhaps some of us have fantasies that resemble those of the murderer, yet we maintain control. Edmund Kemper spoke of the rage inside him that would not subside. He also discussed his fantasy of performing his next murder. By the time Kemper shoved a gun in the face of his first college coed, he had already mentally rehearsed the scenario "hundreds of times." Once he pulled out the gun, he knew there was no turning back (Home Box Office, 1984). How often and how close do the fantasies of nonoffenders take them to the brink of killing?

Ressler and his colleagues (1988), in their study of 36 sexual murderers, explain fantasy as a process rather than merely an experience. Fantasies may begin at a very early age and appear to escalate over time. They report several cases in which offenders were involved in early construction of aggressive fantasies, including "sexualized rituals" or the repetition of sexual acts. They challenge the notion that murderers involved sexually with their victims make the decision to kill as adults: "The power of life and death and the realization that one decides whether to control, injure, or kill is a very early experience for these men" (p. 38). Given that many serial killers report histories of traumatization, including sexual abuse, it might be useful for researchers to note exactly when these offenders remember wanting to kill. However, one must always recognize the degree to which this type of offender can "color" his or her responses. Reliable information might indeed be hard to come by.

INTERVIEWING SERIAL MURDERERS

Many readers have asked me, the present author, about my experiences interviewing serial killers. It is difficult for most people to comprehend what it is like to sit across from someone who has killed 15 to 20 people. In questioning such an individual, I apply the same principles that I teach my university students: requisite objectivity; a dispassionate search for new perspectives; and, most important, a recognition that the questions I ask will be of greater import than any answers I may obtain. I am cognizant that these offenders lie. Indeed, this is part of their profile. Most of them could not do otherwise, given their careers of killing. Their ability to reconstruct the past in nearly obsessive detail is fascinating. I am not there to judge the offender, nor can you, if you are seeking greater understanding of serial behavior. The offender has already been convicted and sent to prison. I am there to learn and gather information just as any social scientist does in an honest pursuit of understanding.

I am not caught up in the allure of the offender or the sensational nature of the murders. These offenders are not Hannibal Lecters, but distinctively violent offenders who have something to teach us, albeit dark and disturbing, about

PROFILE 3.4 Juan Corona

Juan was a 29-year-old Mexican living illegally in California. He was captured in 1994 after a robbery and kidnapping incident in northern California. Depicted by the prosecution as a very dangerous man deserving harsh punishment, Corona was given two life sentences. Angrily he remarked that if they (the prosecution) thought what he had done was bad, they were going to be very impressed with what he had done during earlier crimes. Corona then confessed to killing six white, middle-aged males, all homosexuals. He would go out by himself into the gay districts of Los Angeles pretending to offer sex to unsuspecting victims. Once victims were undressed, Corona used a cord to strangle them slowly, so they would suffer as much as possible.

Upon his arrest he insisted the victims themselves were to blame, that they were asking for it. He also forced victims to reveal their automated-teller-machine personal identification numbers. After murdering them, he stole their jewelry and money. He also committed thefts atypical of serial killers: He stole a VCR and cable box but, instead of unscrewing the cables, Corona cut them with a knife, suggesting he was in a hurry and afraid of being caught. He stole several vehicles and gave one of them to a friend. One usually does not equate serial murder with such repetitive and ill-concealed property crime.

This case, however, is much more about rage than money. Juan appears soft-spoken, reflective, and very controlled. As your author sat at a small table across from the defendant in a supermaximum-security prison, Corona was clearly agitated. He said he really did not know why he killed his victims, but believed the "devil made me do it." He reiterated that he deserved to die for his crimes. Unlike most serial killers I have interviewed, Corona was deeply depressed. He spoke quietly and dispassionately, belying the rage that drove him to kill. He would not make eye contact with me but kept his head bowed, speaking in short, often monosyllabic words. For a moment I began to doubt his dangerousness. He was small in stature, but a handsome, almost timid man wanting to be left alone. His demeanor deceptively concealed his capacity for murder.

Juan was having a difficult time looking at me. I decided to move around to his side of the table in order to be closer to him. Just as I moved my hands along the table top Corona made brief but revealing eye contact with me. I was about to invade his space and he sensed it. The eyes were those of a man in horrible pain, a man living in hell. These were not the eyes one would ever wish to encounter alone. Nor were these eyes going to allow me into his space. Corona was doing all that he could to keep himself under control. Moving to his side of the table would have the same effect as entering a cage with a wild animal. Although I was not afraid, I sensed the danger zone I had nearly entered. I remained where I was, focusing more intently on this man.

I probed him for over an hour. Juan has one brother, whom he loves. His father deserted his family when he

the nature of violence. In 1995 I had the opportunity to interview a serial murderer in Los Angeles. Profile 3.4 is a summary of my observations regarding the offender. Names have been changed for reasons of confidentiality, because the defendant was being processed through the criminal justice system.

was a young boy. He expressed no animosity toward his father, yet clearly remembered the day his father left. I learned of Juan's deep hatred for his mother and grandmother. As a child he was frequently beaten and humiliated by his grandmother. She told young Juan that he should never have been born. His beatings became brutal. A beating with a lead pipe left him with serious head injuries. He pointed out the multiple indentations and scars on his head. The beatings appear to have left Juan with some possible brain damage. As an adolescent he was a heavy glue sniffer, which may have also impaired his cognition. I asked him what he would do if either his grandmother or mother were here, at this very moment. He responded: "I would hang them with a rope." The "rope" he was referring to was most likely the one he had used to strangle his victims. If he had been so abused by these two women, why was he not killing women? Corona's explanation was simple: "I came out of a woman." He also stated that he held women in high esteem.

Juan claims no sexual interest in men. He could not explain why he left all of his victims bound and nude in motel rooms. He says he just wanted their money and that he was not sexually involved with any of them. The autopsy reports, however, indicate Corona did engage in homosexual activity with his victims. Juan also expresses no sexual interest in women or men, although his brother remembers him sometimes being with females.

Juan expresses no remorse for his crimes and wants to be executed as soon as possible. He believes God wants him punished for his sins. He wants no media attention and wishes to spare his brother any trouble or pain. Juan is a man of average intelligence who prefers to be alone. He has no friends and his sense of alienation is profound. Other inmates keep their distance from him. Even though he is smaller than some at the prison, inmates are uncomfortable around him. He does not exude machismo; he radiates anger and hate. A man of very low self-esteem and clinically depressed, Juan claims to have attempted suicide.

Juan is a very dangerous man. He is a very real threat to others, especially males. Although he expresses no anger toward his father, he seems to harbor very real feelings of rejection and abandonment. His father was not there to protect him from his mother and grandmother, which may have exacerbated his negative feelings toward men. Juan also denies being attracted to males or having any sexual connection to men, but given his sexual involvment with his victims, he probably has latent homosexual feelings that have caused him considerable dissonance and ambivalence. He awaits execution.

You have been exposed to several biological and psychological explanations for violent behavior, in particular, serial murder. Which explanations, in your opinion, best help to explain Juan Corona's behavior? What other possible motivations do you think he may have had for killing, and for killing only gay men?

Another approach to the question of multiple homicide focuses on sociological explanations. Chapter 4 explores the various structural and social-process theories that seek to elucidate the dynamics of serial killing.

4

Social Construction of Serial Murder

Those involved in criminological research often find themselves drawing on various sociological theories. Two theories that are often quoted are social structure theory and social process theory.

SOCIAL STRUCTURE THEORY

Social structure theories focus on individuals' socioeconomic standing, suggesting that poor people commit more crimes because they are stifled in their quest for financial or social success. Specifically, offenders, as a result of their racial, ethnic, or subcultural standing, are blocked in various ways from achieving the "American dream" through legitimate means. Consequently, they seek success through deviant methods. Structural theories offer cogent explanations for many types of crimes except for serial murder. Generally, serial killers do not belong to a racial or ethnic minority and do not appear to be particularly motivated, although there are a few exceptions, by social or financial gain. Certainly, serial offenders exist who rob their victims, but even then the financial reward is peripheral to the attraction of killing another human being. The few exceptions to this often are found among female serial killers, who constitute a small portion of the total number of serial murderers (see Chapter 7). Occasionally, as in the case of Belle Gunness of Indiana, who advertised in newspapers for suitors, then promptly killed them once she gained access to their money, women will kill their husbands, fiancés, or lovers in order to improve or maintain their lifestyle. Over a 14-year period one offender is believed to have murdered seven of her eight children for insurance purposes. Each time she needed money another child would suddenly pass away. Even in these cases, however, we cannot be sure that money was actually the primary motive.

One structural theory that may at some point provide greater insight into serial murder is the perspective of urbanism. Murder rates tend to be highest in densely populated cities such as Gary, Indiana; Detroit; Miami; Birmingham, Alabama; New York City; and Washington, D.C. Urban homicide rates tend to be associated with social disorder, alienation, drugs, fear, disassociation, poverty, and broken homes (Messner & Tardiff, 1986). High-density populations increase the probability of victimization because of impersonalization and frequent encounters with strangers (Sampson, 1987).

Serial killers have been located in and around most major U.S. cities, although they also appear in some of the most isolated areas in America. Where the offenders commit their crimes, of course, depends on what type of serial killers they are and what kinds of victims they are after. High-density populations are attractive to those wishing to "melt" into their environment. Several of the most "effective" serial killers have operated in some of the more populated areas of the country. Whether serial murderers are attracted to such locales or they already live in the area is not exactly clear. We do know that California, followed by Florida, New York, Texas, Illinois, Georgia, and Ohio report the highest frequencies of serial killing in the United States. However, Rossmo (1995) correctly notes that those states with the highest *per capita rates* of serial murder, or states with more than twice the overall rate for the United States are Alaska, Idaho, Wyoming, Utah, North and South Dakota, Kansas, Delaware, Vermont, and Rhode Island. For the serial offender who is specifically looking for women or children, the larger cities obviously offer an ample supply of unsuspecting victims. Ted Bundy was particularly at ease when working the crowds of people in shopping malls. Christopher Wilder specifically went to shopping malls to lure his victims by posing as a photographer. Yet, for some of these offenders, it is not the crowds they seek but the potential victims who walk, work, or play alone. Jeffrey Dahmer frequented gay bars, looking for attractive young males whom he could cull out of the crowd and lure to his apartment. Although areas with dense populations would seem likely places for serial offenders to find victims, further research is warranted on the connection between population density and occurrence of serial murders.

SOCIAL CLASS THEORY*

Leyton (1986), in his pivotal work *Hunting Humans: The Rise of the Modern Multiple Murderer,* examines the status aspirations of serial murderers. He noted that a serial killer is "most often on the margins of the upper-working or lower

*The author strongly encourages those interested in the issue of social class and serial murder to read Lynn Gunn's (2000) study.

middle classes who comes to feel excluded from the class he (sic) so devoutly wishes to join. In an extended campaign of vengeance, he murders people unknown to him, but who represent to him (in their behavior, appearance and their location) the class that has rejected him" (p. 23). Leyton points out the killer's perceived social status of the victims becomes a catalyst for murder. Ritzer (1992, p. 336) notes that some feminists are of the opinion that "the theme of violence as overt physical cruelty lies at the heart of radical feminism's linking of patriarchy to violence: rape, sexual abuse . . . enforced prostitution . . . sadism in pornography are all linked to the historic and cross-cultural practices of witch burning, the stoning to death of adulteresses . . . and the savage practices of clitorectomy." Once patriarchy was established Ritzer states that other power resources including economic, legal, emotional, and ideological were used to support it.

Caputi (1989) examines power and serial murder and suggests that females are usually selected as victims by male serial killers because of female powerlessness. She argues that we glorify serial killers in American society and that as hierarchy dictates such murders carry sexually political importance. These are murders rooted in a system of male dominance in a manner similar to the way the lynching of blacks was based on white supremacy. Caputi states that serial murder is the "ultimate expression of sexuality that defines sex as a form of dominant power; it, like rape, is a form of terror that constructs and maintains male supremacy" (1990, p. 2). Egger (1984) observed that the majority of victims are women who share common characteristics and are considered to be without power and prestige—women in lower economic groups including prostitutes, runaways, homeless, minorities, the poor, and the elderly. Gunn (2000) in her exceptional examination of social class and serial murder found a connection between violence and social class. She noted that homicide patterns tend to be prevalent among the lower classes. Serial killers in her study came primarily from the working and/or underclass and chose victims at the same social standing or lower. She concluded that serial killers chose male victims based on their lower social class and female victims based on gender. Gunn supports other researchers who contend a distinctive linkage between serial murder and social class.

SOCIAL PROCESS THEORY

Social process theories contend that criminal behavior is a function of a socialization process. This includes a host of sociopsychological interactions by the offender with institutions and social organizations. Offenders may turn to crime as a result of peer group pressure, family problems, poor school performance, legal entanglements, and other situations that gradually steer them to criminal behavior. Process theories recognize that anyone, regardless of race or socioeconomic status, has the potential for criminal behavior. Central to the social process theory, as to some aspects of psychoanalytic theory, is the effect of the family on youths who engage in delinquent or violent behavior. Considering the dramatic rise in divorce rates from 35 per 1,000 married in 1960, to 131 per 1,000 married today, and the growing number of single parents, extensive research continues in the area of family dynamics ("U.S.," 1988).

Theories of aggression vary extensively, but for understanding the etiology of serial murder, Albert Bandura's book *Aggression* (1973) provides valuable insights. According to social learning theory, a component of social process theory, one might explain the aggressive behavior of the serial murderer by examining the offender's past (see Chapter 3). Special attention by researchers should be given to childhood experiences for evidence of victimization or the witnessing of violent behavior. In earlier studies, Bandura and Walters (1963) noted that particularly aggressive boys were also hostile and antagonistic and that they experienced feelings of rejection from their fathers.

Brown (1984), in an application of social learning theory, found that emotional neglect and abuse were correlated with all forms of reported delinquency. However, he also noted a lack of correlation between physical abuse and any form of delinquency. This may suggest to those who study the psychodynamics of the serial killer that evidence of the social learning of aggression may be subtle. Children who witness family violence are (according to ratings by their mothers) likely to demonstrate diminished social competence and behavioral problems (Wolfe et al., 1985). This "exposure to violence may have an indirect, yet significant, effect on children" (p. 663). The social learning of violence, therefore, need not be the result of one's having been a victim but simply a result of viewing violence. Wolfe and his colleagues add: "It is suspected by some researchers and clinicians that girls from violent families may not express signs of maladjustment in childhood, yet they may suffer higher rates of mental health and family problems in adulthood than many girls from nonviolent homes" (p. 663). Again, this suggests that the evidence of learned social aggression may not manifest itself in some cases for several years. The direct and indirect influence of family violence on future adjustment difficulties of boys was examined by Jaffe and his colleagues (1986), who found similar patterns of adjustment problems for those who had been abused by parents and those who had witnessed violence between their parents. Both of these groups differed from a control group in that they exhibited more aggressive behaviors toward others.

Ruth Inglis, in her book *Sins of Fathers* (1978), notes a strong relationship between abused children and subsequent violent behavior. In comparing abusive and nonabusive families, Webster-Stratton (1985) found that, in addition to low family income, "family history of parent abuse as a child was highly correlated with more negative and controlling interactions with children, which was correlated with the abusive family. This finding seems to support the social learning model that parents learn abusive parenting techniques from their own parents and then carry them out with their children, thus continuing the 'coercive cycle' across generations" (p. 67).

In another study done by Dean and associates (1986), maltreated and nonmaltreated children were asked to tell stories about kind or unkind behavior initiated by a child toward a child, by an adult toward a child, or by a child toward an adult and then asked to explain what the recipient would do next. In contrast to their nonmaltreated counterparts, maltreated children between the ages of six and eight years told more stories in which children reciprocated the kind acts of adults and fewer stories in which adults or peers reciprocated the kind acts of children. A second finding was that maltreated children of all ages justified their parents' unkind acts on the basis of their own bad behavior (pp. 617–626). This finding is echoed in many of the statements and accounts of serial killers.

Alice Miller in *For Your Own Good* (1984), an examination of child rearing and the roots of violence, provides a subjective qualitative study of child abuse in which she explores the private hells of children who later become offenders. She discusses "soul murder" or the extraordinary beatings and sexual abuses perpetrated upon young children by parents and relatives. She argues that "the earlier this soul murder [takes] place, the more difficult it will be for the affected person to grasp and the less it can be validated by memories and words. If he wants to communicate, his only recourse is acting out" (p. 231). Put another way, children may forget or repress what you say or do to them, but children never forget how you make them feel. It is these feelings that fuel the flames of anger and violence. Having interviewed several serial killers, your author finds considerable validation for this perspective. Other theoretical frameworks also warrant examination.

NEUTRALIZATION THEORY

Sykes and Matza (1957) and Matza (1964) view the process of delinquent youths becoming criminals as a matter of neutralizing their personal values and attitudes as they drift between conventional behavior and illegitimate behavior. Matza points out that people are not criminals all the time. Often criminals participate in the normal functions of everyday life. Occasionally they drift toward illegal behavior just as they sometimes drift toward conventional behavior. In order for them to rationalize their drift toward illegal behavior they must use learned techniques of neutralization. These techniques include denial of responsibility, denial of injury, denial of the victim, condemnation of the condemners, and the appeal to higher loyalties—in other words "it was not my fault," "no harm was done," "they had it coming," "society is to blame," and "I did it for them, not me."

Denying the victim is a technique commonly used to shift blame and accompanying guilt. It also serves to lessen the value of the life destroyed. Bandura (1974) describes methods by which offenders can make inhuman behavior legitimate:

> Attribution of blame to the victim is still another exonerative expedient. Victims are faulted for bringing maltreatment on themselves, or extraordi-

> nary circumstances are invoked as justification for questionable conduct. One need not engage in self-reproof for committing acts prescribed by circumstances. A further means of weakening self-punishment is to dehumanize the victim. Inflicting harm upon people who are regarded as subhuman or debased is less likely to arouse self-reproof than if they are looked upon as human beings with sensitivities (pp. 861–862).

Current research into the behavior of serial killers suggests they frequently dehumanize their victims before taking their lives. It appears to expedite the murder when, psychologically, instead of attacking another human being, they attack something without name, feelings, or identity. Henry Lucas, who confessed and recanted confessions to dozens of murders, once stated that when he had found a victim he would never ask her name and if she gave it he would forget it immediately because he did not want to know his victims' names or anything about them. Charny (1980), in explaining the process of dehumanization of others, notes that the process is actually much more subtle and commonplace than we would expect:

> Dehumanization is a process of ridding the other of the benefit of his humanity. The process extends along a continuum, leading to the ultimate step of removing the other person's opportunity to live. The "little" everyday dehumanizations we practice on one another are stations on a way toward the ultimate act whereby one person takes away another's very life. Thus, it is not simply the insult that we inflict upon another that is at stake in everyday dehumanizations. The fact is that we are learning to practice a devastating process, rehearsing it, achieving gratification from it, and perhaps preparing ourselves to participate one day in the removal of other people's actual lives (p. 100).

One might argue that serial murderers drift between conventional and nonconventional behavior. Several serial killers have been known to be gainfully employed, married with families, active in civic organizations, and educated, and they were considered part of mainstream society.

Complete denial of injury to victims by offenders is a common ploy used by many serial killers. Others not only deny any involvement but readily name another person as the guilty party. One serial killer was found guilty in 1983 of murdering several women and presently awaits execution on San Quentin's death row. His female accomplice received two lengthy prison sentences. In December 1988 the male offender, in a letter to the present author, reaffirmed his complete innocence with regard to any of the killings.

> The sum total would prove beyond doubt to you that [she] was following a script for murder, and that she was and at times is . . . wife of Theodore Robert Bundy. . . . It is utterly easy to show that [she] selected her own internalized victim/motivation and externalized it into the script of a book about a man she idolized.

> She lived one of the most bizarre lives from that point forward of any serial killer to date. She became a practicing lesbian. She engaged in degradation-sex, and S/M. She leapt the gender line with such frequency in her life, even marrying a flagrant homosexual, that her roles in sex and S/M became so blurred she would often be involved in utterly contradictory encounters with gender-blended persons, groups or persons, and in such a role-blended way with her sadomasochism she wanted to torture her deceased victims as she wished she dared be so tortured.
>
> You won't find a cesspool as vile as this case. But god damn it, I can prove I am a mere "substitute" for her partner . . . whom she murdered. She could not testify against a dead man, so the next best deal shown to her was to testify and accuse against some living person. I was a man who stayed in her apartments, renting a room and bathroom, and on three occasions, dumb enough to let her talk me into sex with her. She had a man, proximate to vehicles, weapons, and herself. It was all the police wanted. In the aftermath of the terror of the Hillside Strangler case in Los Angeles, the authority-attitude was, solve this damned case fast.
>
> Within the first 18 days, August 11, 1980, to August 29th, 1980, they committed themselves trustingly to her stories.
>
> That sealed it.
>
> The Ted Bundy legacy is still going on. If you don't have the sense and energy to see that everything I've said, and tons more, proves truly that [she] is the strangest of them all, then live on in the mediocrity of assuming those who are on death row MUST be guilty . . . (author's files, November 30, 1988).

John Wayne Gacy, killer of 33 young males in Chicago, denied any involvement in the murders and suggested that someone else must have placed those 27 bodies in the crawlspace of his home while he was at work.

Other serial killers have admitted murdering women, especially prostitutes, but insist there have been no real victims because they were, in the offenders' eyes, scum of the earth. Thomas N. Cream argued that he had aided society and ended the suffering of scores of prostitutes. In 1995, an offender who murdered five homosexuals in Los Angeles stated to the present author that his victims "deserved what they got" and that "they were asking for it because they kept trying to pick me up." Another offender, Robert Carr, explained that those who died by his hands "grew" a great deal during their brief stay with the killer. Others killed because they believed it was God's will or because of allegiance to their partners or to assist the survival of society.

The problem with neutralization theory as an explanation for serial murder is its verifiability. One would have to be able to demonstrate that an offender first neutralized his moral beliefs before drifting into violent behavior. As it appears now, serial murderers who rationalize their behavior are believed to construct explanations ex post facto, or after the homicides have occurred.

Given the current understanding of serial-murder behavior, empirical evidence of neutralization will not likely appear in the foreseeable future.

SOCIAL CONTROL THEORY

Classical control theorists would argue that people do not commit crimes such as murder because of their fear of punishment. Punishment, they believe, can serve as a deterrent to committing crimes. However, for homicides in general, capital punishment or long prison terms usually do not deter people, because many homicides are "crimes of passion" in which the offender kills his or her victim as a result of an altercation. Briar and Piliavin (1965) have pointed out that fear of punishment alone is not sufficient for everyone to refrain from criminal behavior. They believe that a sense of commitment to society, family, and education serves as a deterrent to crime. Reckless (1967) has argued that youth can become isolated or insulated from criminal influences through what he terms "containments," including a positive self-image; ego strength; high frustration tolerance; goal orientation; a sense of belongingness; consistent moral front; reinforcement of norms, goals, and values; effective supervision; discipline; and a meaningful social role.

Hirschi (1969) expanded social control theory and introduced four elements of the social bond, which apply to all social classes. These four elements—attachment, commitment, involvement, and belief—are bonds that individuals strengthen or weaken in relationship to the society in which they live. He noted that attachment to peers, schools, various social institutions, and especially family, is critical if the individual is to develop a sense of conscious concern for others and a general acceptance of the social norms. Hirschi also believed that having a commitment to personal property, conventional goals, reputation, education, and so on, will make people less likely to commit crimes and risk losing what they have worked to establish. Similarly, involvement in conventional endeavors allows little time for criminal behavior. Finally, if one shares a set of common beliefs with others, there exists a greater likelihood of conformity to societal expectations.

Hirschi found that youths who appeared to be closely attached to their parents were less likely to commit crimes. In comparison, most serial killers do not appear to have close relationships with their families. The majority appear to have experienced gradual or traumatic breaks with one or both parents while in their youth. The lack of commitment to conventional values is noted in the histories of other serial murderers who became heavily involved in drugs, alcohol, and other "marginal" behaviors. In addition, serial killers usually do not have meaningful, close relationships with peers but remain distant and isolated.

The application of Hirschi's social control theory may eventually provide additional insight into serial killers. These offenders do not appear to have the requisite ties to family, peers, and community that Hirschi found among those who tended not to engage in criminal behavior. The theory, however, was developed for measuring delinquent youths, not adults. Although serial offenders report weakened social ties, we have yet to examine youths who later become serial offenders in order to determine whether they had experienced weakened social bonds before their acts of homicide. Certainly there are case histories of offenders that reveal weakened social bonds, but such reports are usually developed after the homicides. In short, we find what we want to find: Instead of a weak social bond causing one to become violent, becoming violent to the point of killing may cause the offender to weaken his or her social bonds.

LABELING THEORY

Erving Goffman (1961), in his classical treatise on institutions, noted the stigma attached to persons who have spent time in an institution such as a prison or a psychiatric facility. This stigma is the result of having attracted the attention of society through abnormal or unacceptable behavior. Labeling theorists Lemert (1951) and Schur (1972) viewed negative labels such as "former mental patient," "ex-convict," "delinquent," "stupid," and "slut" as inflicting psychological damage on those to whom the labels are attached.

Labeling theory views abnormal behavior as a process by which a person graduates from primary deviance to secondary deviance (Lemert, 1951). According to labeling theorists the original deviant act, of which the origins vary significantly, is called *primary deviance.* In turn, by being labeled a deviant, the offender is carried along in a societal process of negative social sanctions that inevitably engender hostility and resentment in the offender. Then the offender reacts negatively to the label by acting against society and so concludes the process by affirming the negative label or deviant status.

The labeling process takes a certain amount of time for the offender to absorb the labels and for those labels, in turn, to affect the offender's self-concept. The negative feelings created by the labeling multiply into feelings of inadequacy, low self-esteem, and anger. Clifford Olson, killer of eleven children in British Columbia, Canada, during the early 1980s, explained to me that society played a major role in his homicidal behavior. The courts had kept him in prison for nearly 30 years and then allowed him to go free. He was already an habitual criminal and a perceived threat to society. As Olson ruefully noted, "They never should have let me go." He claimed that the effects of prison made him much more dangerous. Combined with alcohol, he said, they triggered his murderous rampages (author's files).

The types of labels, their visibility, and the manner in which they are applied, including their intensity, duration, and frequency—as well as the individual's ability to cope with the process of labeling—may all help to determine an offender's commitment to a criminal career. The more an individual succumbs to the labels of failure and imperfection, as well as to remarks critical of his or her behavior, the more he or she discounts positive feedback.

The labeling process is expedited by the selective application of those labels. For example, Becker (1963) has described people who create rules as moral entrepreneurs: "Social groups create deviance by making rules whose infractions constitute deviance and by applying those rules to particular people and labeling them as outsiders. From this point of view, deviance is not a quality of the act a person commits, but rather a consequence of the application by others of rules and sanctions to an 'offender.' The deviant is one to whom the label has successfully been applied; deviant behavior is behavior that people so label" (p. 9).

Labels, by the nature of their construction, are inconsistently applied. The poor, racial minorities, and the socially disadvantaged are more likely to be labeled. The fact that most serial killers are white and many appear to maintain at least middle-class socioeconomic standing does not disprove labeling theory. It is plausible that some serial offenders have been affected by negative labels created to differentiate between the rich and the poor, white and nonwhite, the powerful and the powerless. In essence, labeling can create psychological disparities between individuals regardless of their race or socioeconomic standing. Wayne Williams, who is believed to have been involved in the murders of 22 to 28 young black men and boys in the Atlanta, Georgia, area, was described as one who hated his own race and preferred white people and who killed blacks because they reminded him of his own standing.

It is unlikely, however, that all serial killers destroy human life because of their socioeconomic status or race or because the law is applied to favor the powerful people in society. Individuals who have experienced a traumatic event or process of events involving extreme criticism, or those who are forced to feel the pain of failure when their egos allow only perfection, may eventually respond negatively. Inevitably their feelings of low self-esteem and worthlessness become their internalized "master status," constantly reminding them of their weaknesses. Psychologically, the stress and anxiety of labeling may be viewed as *cognitive dissonance,* which feeds a need to right the wrongs and restore balance. Labeling theory, then, is not concerned with the origins of serial killers' behavior but with the formation of the killers' perceived status as the result of experiencing traumatic events during their formative years.

THE MACDONALD TRIAD

The childhoods of serial killers are varied and complex. Some are much more sociopathic than other children because they are more aggressive and more manipulative, express less remorse, and experience fewer feelings of guilt. Yet similar characteristics can be observed in children who never grow up to become violent offenders. In truth, each child processes experiences differently. Children also react differently to stress. It is this author's contention that stress is the generic predisposer to many maladaptive behaviors in childhood. Because children do not possess the same coping skills to deal with life's stressors, some children are at greater risk of developing inappropriate behaviors. Psychopathology during childhood can be manifested in a variety of behaviors, some of which are more noticeable or detectable than others. Serial killers have been linked to childhood maladaptive behaviors such as torturing animals; enuresis, or chronic bed-wetting; and fire-setting. Any of these three behaviors is not a good predictor of later adult violent behavior. Even a youth displaying all three behaviors does not guarantee a life of violence during adulthood. However, such behaviors appear more often among the serial-killer population than among nonoffenders.

Psychological profiles of those who commit homicide reveal portraits of frustration and intrapersonal conflict stemming from childhood. Justice, Justice, and Kraft (1974) note that, although the MacDonald Triad may indicate a troubled child, it is not certain that that child will grow up to commit violence. Hellman and Blackman (1966) suggest,

> The triad is proposed as a pathognomic sign, as an alert to both the parents and the community that the child is seriously troubled; that if this readiness to project and elicit fear or pain, to be violent and destructive, is not alleviated nor remedies found for it, this pattern of hostile behavior may well lead to adult aggressive antisocial behavior (p. 1434).

These authors also suggest that a relationship exists between parental loss or rejection and the development of mental illness or personality disorders. "This loss or rejection of a parent causes not only primary separation anxiety but also aggression, the function of which is to achieve reunion. The aggressive outbursts of adults who murder are associated with a history of maternal or paternal deprivation" (p. 1431). The child who suffers consistently under these circumstances develops defense mechanisms including withdrawal and denial of stress. If, however, the child chooses to revolt, he begins to act out his feelings of rejection and resentment, exacting aggression and violence on society.

Kathleen Heide (1995), in her study on why children kill parents, noted that emotional neglect is damaging to a child's healthy development. "Parents who do not give their children clear messages that they are loved, whether by words or appropriate displays of affection, such as being held, cuddled, hugged, kissed, having hands shaken, and being patted on the back, are not meeting their sons' and daughters' emotional needs" (p. 30). Cummings and Davies (1994) write that child neglect when begun early "disrupts virtually all aspects of development, including attachment, cognition, play, and social and emotional skills." Children who continue to suffer this deprivation act out in vengeance and sometimes kill the parent responsible. By the age of 14, Ed Kemper had suffered much cruelty and rejection by his caustic mother. She berated and belittled him for not living up to her social expectations. Being sent away to live with his grandparents (whom he killed at age 15) was further evidence of her contempt for him. Studies support the findings that children as young as one or two years of age may be hurt by the rejection or criticism of others (Leibman, 1989). Leibman also suggests that:

> Resentment brought about as a result of such rejection is frequently repressed by those who later commit murder. Repression often becomes a pattern of behavior leaving little need for release of anger. Upon reaching adulthood, the individual who thus far has adequately repressed rage since childhood may find himself in situations where he is unable to suppress hostile feelings (p. 41).

It was not until Kemper's killing career had claimed several lives that he found he could no longer repress the hatred he felt for his mother and killed her savagely.

The Triad also reveals that the psychopathology of violent adult offenders often stems from the prevalence of such etiologic factors as paternal neglect, abuse, and rejection suffered in childhood. In a homicide study of four men who killed with extreme violence, authors Rosen, Satten, Mayman, and Karl Menninger (1960) found that they all had extensive histories of losing control over aggressive impulses. Each case involved a history of extreme parental violence and emotional deprivation during childhood.

From a young age, children raised in dysfunctional and abusive homes develop coping skills to deal with the inherent stress. Heide (1995) writes,

> Persons in dysfunctional families characteristically do not *feel* because they learned from a young age that not feeling is necessary for psychic survival. Family members generally learn it is too painful to feel the hurt or to experience the fear that comes from feelings of rage, abandonment, moments of terror, and memories of horror (p. 48).

Some parents cannot distinguish between punishment and discipline. Anyone can punish a child and many parents do it out of frustration. Discipline requires time, patience, and love and may include some punishment. To punish children without discipline usually involves a parent who is frustrated and has turned to anger. Most Americans believe that spanking, for example, is an appropriate way to raise children despite compelling evidence to the contrary. Although some children do not connect the spanking with rejection, some most certainly do. If parents would not spank when they are angry, they would seldom spank at all. As one 11-year-old insightfully penned in his journal after being spanked by his father for not cleaning his room, "Yesterday Dad spanked me again. Why is it that Dad's pain is always my pain too?" Parenting by instinct does not work well.

The pathology and psychological disturbance that can develop in children who have suffered the trauma of severely poor parenting is indicated by behaviors outlined in the Triad and the DSM-IV. Conduct disorders can develop in preschool years but are not fully apparent until later childhood. These individuals often display low impulse control and failure to observe social norms through rebelliousness against authority. Emotionally truncated, they lack empathy and aggress arbitrarily with little apparent provocation. The psychopathology of animal cruelty, enuresis, and fire-setting can surface in some children concomitantly. Unfortunately all too often parents and authorities are quick to punish without recognizing these behaviors as "red flags" that the child is suffering and needs help.

Animal Cruelty

> . . . the custom of children tormenting and killing beasts, will, by degrees, harden their minds even towards men, and they who delight in the suffering and destruction of inferior creatures, will not be apt to be very compassionate, or benign to those of their own kind (Locke, 1705).

Even though some serial killers have displayed delight in harming animals, more appear to have enjoyed the vivisection and exploration of dead animals. The morbid curiosity of cutting into dead animals may facilitate the development of deviant sexual fantasies. To understand the role that animal cruelty plays in later homicidal aggression we must first examine the etiology of animal abuse.

In America, a pet can be the object of affection or the target of displaced scorn. Many violent offenders report incidents of childhood cruelty toward animals. According to the Humane Society, animal cruelty "encompasses a range of behaviors harmful to animals, from neglect to malicious killing. Intentional cruelty, or abuse, is knowingly depriving an animal of food, water, shelter, socialization, or veterinary care or maliciously torturing, maiming, mutilating, or killing an animal." Felthous and Kellert (1985), in their study of 102 men serving time in federal penitentiaries, found that cruelty to animals during childhood occurred much more often among aggressive criminals than among nonaggressive criminals or noncriminals. In their study, they identified nine motivations for the childhood maltreatment of animals:

1. To control the animal
2. To retaliate against the animal
3. To satisfy a prejudice against a specific species or breed
4. To express aggression through an animal
5. To enhance one's own aggressiveness
6. To shock people for amusement
7. To retaliate against another person
8. Displacement of hostility from a person to an animal
9. Nonspecific sadism

Of pathognomic importance, Margaret Mead (1964) suggests that, "The torturing or killing of 'good animals' by the child may be a precursor to more violent acts as an adult." Elana Gill (1994), a family therapist, notes how children who are physically or sexually abused seem to mimic their mistreatment on their companion animals. Gill says that children learn the lessons of abuse: that people who love them hurt them, and that power and dominance are preferable to the victim's plight of helplessness. In some cases Gill observed that animal cruelty may signify a child's preoccupation with death and that they may be rehearsing their own suicide. In one case, of a severely abused child named Miriam, Gill writes,

> I learned this from Miriam, a six-year-old who had been abused sexually. When I asked her to make a picture of herself, she drew a bleeding dog and herself in heaven. Miriam's drawing revealed the depth of her despair. Her mother later informed me that Miriam had recently begun slapping and choking her dog and had injured him with scissors.

According to Patterson et al. (1989), there are two approaches to understanding risk factors that signal development of aggression and antisocial behavior in children: *coercive family interaction patterns* and *children's attributional biases.* The first factor is found in modeling theory where children emulate the parents' behaviors. Patterson found that "ineffective parenting styles, relying heavily on punitive or aversive control, present children with models of coercion such that family members become enmeshed in a cycle where parent and child use aversive techniques to terminate each others' behavior" (1989, pp. 329–335). The implications of this approach suggest that a cycle of violence develops where children subjected to harsh and abusive treatment will view their abuse as normal and emulate this behavior in their interpersonal relationships. The second approach according to Price and Dodge (1989) suggests that boys who show atypical aggression have deficits in *intention-cue detection.* These boys display attributional bias where they interpret ambiguous or neutral peer actions (e.g., being accidentally bumped in a lunch line) as being hostile and aggressive. This bias leads them to act aggressively, often causing strong peer retaliation. The parallel to animal abuse is apparent. The fact that a peer's intention cues can be ambiguous to a rejected child suggests that intention cues by animals, both companion and noncompanion, may also be misinterpreted. In one case a young boy brutalized, sexually assaulted, and eventually killed a stray dog. The boy stated that, when he heard the dog barking at him, he interpreted the dog's demeanor as personally directed aggression, something he was not going to allow.

Animal abuse has been included in the DSM-IV diagnoses of conduct disorder since 1987. According to Lockwood and Ascione (1998), as of July 1997, 18 states now have felony-level provisions within their animal cruelty codes. Margaret Mead (1964) notes, "One of the most dangerous things that can happen to a child is to kill or torture an animal and not be held responsible" (pp. 11–22). Repeated acts of violence toward animals are a harbinger of adult violence. Lockwood and Hodge (1986), in *The Tangled Web of Animal Abuse: The Links between Cruelty to Animals and Human Violence,* note the importance of preventing animal cruelty by disciplining all such acts, even minor ones. Without proper intervention, children may graduate to more serious abuses including violence against people.

Enuresis

The trauma some children experience as the result of physical, sexual, or emotional abuse can trigger frequent bed-wetting. Like those who practice animal torture or experimentation, chronic bed wetters appear to cease the maladaptive behavior as they approach adulthood. Defined as unintentional bed-wetting during sleep, persistent after the age of five, enuresis evokes emotional and social distress for the child sufferer. It is embarrassing as well as frustrating for the child and parents find it annoying because it means persistent interrupted sleep. For approximately 80% of children who suffer enuresis, the causes have biological roots and heredity is a major contributing factor. According to Houts et al. (1994) enuresis is, most often, caused by a failure of muscular responses that inhibit urination or by a hormonal imbalance that permits too much urine to accumulate during the night. A prescription of antidepressant drugs, which reduce the amount of urine produced, usually eliminate the problem. In some cases, children simply outgrow the problem. However, for about 20% of children with enuresis it is an indicator, a red flag, of something more serious.

Enuresis, in some cases, is considered to be an overt manifestation of internal turmoil usually caused by disturbance in the home. In one study conducted by Hellman and Blackman (1966), it was found that enuresis was tied to aggression and fantasies of destruction. Of the 84 prisoners who served as subjects, 31 were charged with aggressive crimes against the person and 53 were charged with misdemeanors and minor felonies. Thirty-six were found to have enuresis. Of the 36, 33 had enuresis past the age of eight years and in 70% this trait persisted into their teens.

Though relatively insignificant by itself and not as visible as other traits in the Triad, it is no less important a red flag in identifying maladaptive development in a child. However, unlike animal cruelty and fire-setting, enuresis is not listed as a diagnostic criterion for conduct disorder in the DSM-IV. Enuresis is an unconscious, involuntary, and nonviolent act and therefore linking it to violent crime is more problematic than animal cruelty or fire-setting.

Fire-Setting

> He who lights a fire during the day will wet his bed that night (German and Mexican-Spanish proverb).

The term *fire-setting* is generally used to describe the actions of juveniles, whereas *arson* describes adult behavior. Frequently the distinction is not clearly understood and the terms are used interchangeably. Some children display an abnormal fascination with or interest in fire. They engage in excessive fire watching, fire play, or compulsive collecting of fire paraphernalia. They are also more prone to trigger false fire alarms (Fineman, 1995, p. 32). California has experienced a significantly large number of fires set by juveniles. Nationally, juveniles set about 50–60% of all arson fires. Males are responsible for over 90% of all of these fires. Fresno, California, reporting the highest per capita rates of arson fires in the United States in 1994 and 1995, had over 70% of their fires set by juveniles.

Fire-setting is best understood as part of a process, not merely an act. Recent research of 1,200 juvenile fire-setters in Fresno found a disturbing pattern of psychopathology within the families of fire-setters. Family dysfunctioning included low marital satisfaction, little or no display of affection, ineffectual role modeling, and excessive physical force in disciplining children (Hickey, 1996). Children frequently report deep feelings of maternal or paternal rejection or neglect. The absence of a father is thought to contribute to aggressiveness and fire-setting in boys. Felthouse (1980) notes that deprivation by the father due to such dysfunctions as alcoholism frequently results in rejection of the boy. Other factors including divorce and separation from the father due to incarceration contributed to boys' fire-setting behavior.

Juvenile fire-setters commonly report anxiety, depression, and resentment when feelings of abandonment surface about their relationship with parents or significant others. In turn, the perceived rejection affects self-esteem, and fosters feelings of anger, hatred, and revenge fantasies. Similar to profiles in psychopathy, fire-setters have less capacity for internalization, are less able to tolerate anxiety, and are less empathetic and able to form attachments to others. They are often diagnosed as having a conduct disorder and display antisocial personality characteristics. Incapable of feeling adequate remorse or guilt, juvenile fire-setters are more prone to be in conflict with authority figures. The most common psychological and behavioral problems observed in the Fresno group of juvenile fire-setters were:

1. Learning problems
2. Poor school behavior
3. Poor concentration
4. Lying
5. Excessive anger
6. Fighting with siblings
7. Disobedient
8. Influenced by peers
9. Attention seeking
10. Impulsive
11. Impatient
12. Preoccupied with fire
13. Very unhappy in dysfunctioning family
14. Pronounced need for security and affection

These 14 characteristics parallel many of those noted in Fineman's profile (1995) of fire-setters. These children display distinct personality pathology, and fireplay is but one of many maladaptive behaviors. Among the types of fire-setters identified by Fineman that fit the profile of certain types of serial killers were those who *cry for help.* The offenders consciously or subconsciously bring attention to themselves as a result of interpersonal dysfunctioning. Offenders are those with a hero fantasy, who "discover" a fire and may even help extinguish the flames. Sometimes a firefighter will be caught setting fires in order to draw attention to himself and be recognized for his heroics. Similarly,

PROFILE 4.1 Portrait of a Serial Arsonist and Pyromaniac

Ricki A. has spent several years in prison for serial arson. The tall, thin, Hispanic male, 29, who is gay, has set hundreds of fires. He was instrumental in making Fresno the arson capital of California until his arrest and incarceration. The fire and the men who fight the flames sexually motivate him. He likes to visit fire stations, meet the firemen, and learn all he can about the fire equipment and the fire district. Ricki has memorized the boundaries of each fire district in Fresno. He would often set two fires in a district to cause more excitement. He watched the fire and in his fantasies directed the firefighters in their work. Ricki has collected a box full of souvenirs from his 23 major fires and buried them. He often drives by the area and thinks about digging up the box of trophies. He has a long history of other crimes including prostitution at 15, theft of a police car, fraud, sexual assault, burglary, impersonation of a police officer, and assault. Ricki set fires over an 11-year period. His first intentional fire-setting was at age 12, beginning with trash fires and escalating to burning down businesses at night. He never killed anyone, although several persons needed to be evacuated from an apartment complex when a fire he set spread out of control.

He is a friendly, talkative person who masks tremendous anger. His father abandoned the family when he was very young. At age five a neighbor sexually molested him and the molestations continued for several years. The man threatened Ricki into compliance by threatening to harm the dog that lived with the man. The man also inserted a barrel of a gun into Ricki's rectum and pulled the trigger. Ricki found that even negative attention was still attention. He harbors anger toward his mother for not protecting him from the neighbor and for not meeting his childhood emotional needs. At age 14 he was raped by a 24-year-old male he met while making crank phone calls. Once diagnosed as a paranoid schizophrenic, Ricki is now on parole and takes medication. He sees his parole officer and has a one-hour visit with a psychiatrist once a month. He has great difficulty in finding work because most employers will not risk having an arsonist in the building. Ironically, Ricki never sets fires to places he is affiliated with such as school, home, and work. However, the prognosis for Ricki is not good. He harbors pathological attitudes and behaviors and still maintains his interest in fire. He still collects fire memorabilia and admits to having urges to start another fire, especially when he becomes stressed. He frequently calls the author just to talk when he becomes anxious and starts fantasizing about starting fires. Indeed, there are no acceptable excuses for Ricki's criminal behavior but there are reasons. Although highly dangerous today, he was once a true victim.

some of the most prolific serial killers on record have entered the profession of care providers to gain themselves easy access to extremely vulnerable victims. A second typology, the *delinquent or antisocial* fire-setter, generally displays little empathy or remorse for his crimes or victims. Much of his psychopathology has roots within his family dynamics. (See Profile 4.1.)

In the Fresno study, in which about half of the offending children are age eight or younger, parental absenteeism is high. Parents consistently indicate being "present" about 80% of the time, even though the child's perception is considerably less. The main point is that *perception* is the key factor. It does not really matter what the parents say they are doing as much as it matters what the child perceives parents are doing or not doing. Young children perceive their surroundings differently than adults. In addition, fire-setters are more frequently spanked or isolated from others on a weekly or sometimes daily basis over periods of time. These children report "bad" experiences in homes often facing financial problems, family restructuring, or relocation.

But fire-setting appears to be a transitory method of pathological self-expression. Fineman points out that adult fire-setters usually have a history of setting fires as children but that most child fire-setters do not set fires as adults. Does this mean that children who are chronic fire-setters resolve their personal conflicts or mature out of the maladaptive behaviors? In all probability, many children do resolve the conflicts or mature out of the behavior. For other children, adolescence provides a transitory period during which time the youth begins to find more personal, more deviant methods to express himself or herself.

The presence of the Triad indicates a pattern of creating hurt because of hurt: The victim becomes the victimizer. Other behaviors also indicate pathology in children, including temper tantrums, excessive fighting, and truancy. Some experts feel the Triad is not a sufficient diagnostic tool. Justice, Justice, and Kraft (1974) suggest that these other symptoms may be more predictive of the violence-prone individual. When correlated with the Triad they become even more useful as childhood predictors of violence. However, the predictive value of all three traits found in the Triad, persistent in childhood, is found in many studies of violent adults. As Hellman and Blackman (1966) illustrate:

> Albert was a 15-year-old male charged with murder and assault with intent to rob with malice. He was the second of three children. Enuresis occurred until age 8 and persisted as occasional bed-wetting into adolescence. As a child he frequently made small fires in ashtrays, wastebaskets, and played with matches. At the age of 12 he obtained a rifle and enjoyed shooting birds, dogs, cats, and other animals. Since the age of 8 or 9 he liked to stick pins and needles in his sisters' dolls.
>
> The boy's father was a chronic offender who had served time in prison, was twice dishonorably discharged from the Army, and had committed acts of oral sodomy on both of his daughters. The patient repeatedly gave instances where his mother had shown marked favoritism towards his two sisters. She often told him he would grow up to be a thief, a bum, and a sexual pervert like his father.

ETIOLOGY OF SERIAL KILLING

So far we have briefly examined a number of psychological and social theories of deviant behavior. But how can we then explain the phenomenon of serial murder in a manner that will include all varieties of serial murderers and satisfy the psychologist, the psychiatrist, the criminologist, the geneticist, the sociologist, the biologist, the phenomenologist, and other scientists and researchers who investigate homicidal behavior? Because research into serial murder is in its infancy, the haste to draw quick conclusions about its etiology is not only speculative but also dangerous.

Some data and literature, however, allow researchers some leeway in formulating tentative models to explain the construction of serial murder. We do know that alcohol and drugs are often cited as contributing factors to serial murder; some offenders even suggest it as a primary causal factor. Ted Bundy's declaration that pornography led him to his career in killing caused considerable debate regarding the degree of influence such material has on people who become murderers. Many people believe that pornography and/or alcohol cause people to kill. Yet millions of people in the United States frequently consume alcohol and indulge in pornography and never physically harm anyone.

The current belief in pornography and alcohol as causal factors in serial murder belies a much more complex set of variables. If our society were to ban pornography, should one expect the incidence of serial murder to decrease? If we restrict or ban the use of alcohol, would that affect serial murderers' behavior? Such a Band-Aid approach to a cure for serial killing ignores a host of more obscure factors. Also, by joining the bandwagon of "porno makes murderers," we continue to avoid issues of responsibility that point in some way to nonoffending citizens.

As long as we continue to seek quick answers without first constructing a framework for the discussion of serial murderers' behavior, we will continue to treat the symptoms of the illness rather than the illness itself. For example, we continue saying that anyone who kills, especially serial killers, must be insane. No one would argue that what these offenders *do* is insane by society's standards, but the vast majority of serial killers not only are judged sane by legal standards but are indistinguishable from nonoffenders as they move within our communities. However, there exists a degree of security for us in believing that such crimes occur as a result of insanity or violent pornography. Such cause-and-effect thinking creates a dichotomy of "them" and "us." "Normal" people are not considered to be at high risk for insanity, nor do they generally indulge in violent pornography. Therefore, criminal behavior is completely out of our control, and in no way must we bear any responsibility for such actions.

Ultimately, the common belief that pornography, drugs, alcohol, or insanity directly causes serial homicides is not only simplistic but fallacious. Certainly such factors *can* contribute to serial murder, but only as appendages to an etiological process.

TRAUMA-CONTROL MODEL OF THE SERIAL KILLER

We are beginning to learn that serial offenders are influenced by a multitude of factors that inevitably lead them to kill. It is unlikely that any one factor is directly responsible for homicidal behavior. People are no more likely to be

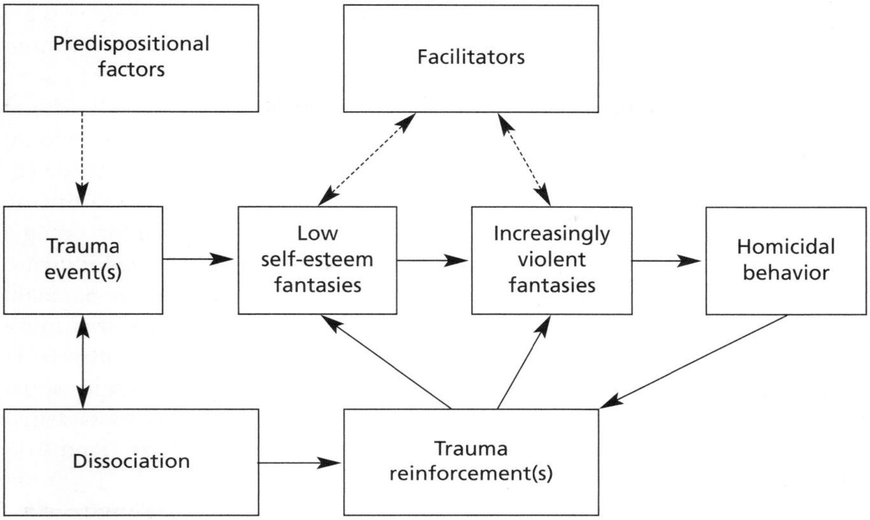

FIGURE 4.1 Trauma-Control Model for Serial Murder (Predispositional factors and facilitators may or may not influence the serial killing process.)

born to kill than offenders are to acquire homicidal inclination from watching violence on television. However, this general truth does not preclude the existence of a predisposition for violent behavior or the fact that we may be influenced by what we see.

In addition, no one factor has been useful thus far in predicting who may be prone to serial murder. Social scientists have long engaged in creating models for predicting criminal behavior. Unfortunately, in serial-murder research, everyone wants to be the first to predict causation. Whether the explanation is excessive television viewing, head traumas, biogenics, childhood victimization, or a host of other "causes," it has been offered too quickly, without the support of sufficient and valid data.

Among serial killers there may exist one or more predispositional factors that influence their behavior. As mentioned in Chapter 3, some violent offenders have been known to possess an extra Y chromosome, but some men who possess an extra chromosome never become violent offenders. Similarly, there are many who drink heavily and indulge in pornography—even violent pornography—and never become serial killers. Thus, even for those influenced by predispositional factors, whether they be biological, sociological, psychological, or a combination thereof, an event or series of events, or traumas, seem to be required that gradually influence a person to kill. Figure 4.1 shows a proposed trauma-control model for understanding the process by which individuals become involved in serial murder.

In discussing the trauma-control model, the destabilizing event(s) that occur in the lives of serial offenders will be referred to as *traumatizations.* These include unstable home life, death of parents, divorce, corporal punishments, sexual abuse, and other negative events that occur during the formative years of the offender's life. Literally millions of U.S. citizens experience one or more of these traumatizations in their lives and never become offenders of any sort. Also, it is possible that individuals who have some predilection for criminal behavior and who experience some form of traumatization do not become violent offenders. However, Lange and DeWitt (1990), in their worldwide research of 165 "motiveless" murderers from 1600 to the present, state that many serial killers have had some form of head injury or organic brain pathology. They point out that neurological malfunctioning as a result of head injuries, epilepsy, or deep temporal-lobe spiking can generate interictal or postictal seizures that may lead to compulsive autonomic behavior. Thus, serial murderers act out during periods when they are experiencing uncontrollable brainwave activity. Although head trauma may well be correlated with serial murder, the present author suggests that the trauma is most likely exacerbated by social and environmental issues. Many people with similar head trauma do not become violent or antisocial.

Childhood trauma for serial murderers may serve as a triggering mechanism resulting in an individual's inability to cope with the stress of certain events, whether they are physical, psychological, or a combination of traumatizations. For serial murderers the most common effect of childhood traumatization manifested is rejection, including rejection by relatives and parent(s). It must be emphasized that an unstable, abusive home has been reported as one of the major forms of rejection. The child or teen feels a deep sense of anxiety, mistrust, and confusion when psychologically or physically abused by an adult. Eth and Pynoos (1985) note some of the effects of traumatization on children who have witnessed murder, rape, or suicidal behavior. These effects include images of violence involving mutilations; destabilization of impulse control; and revenge fantasies. However, instability in the home environment may not be sufficient to trigger homicidal behavior. Other factors may be involved that in combination create a synergistic response, or enhanced reaction.

The combined effect of various traumatizations is greater than any single trauma. In other words, the combined effects should be viewed exponentially rather than arithmetically. As Nettler (1982) observes, "In synergistic situations, a particular effect may be 'more than caused.' It is not merely a metaphor to speak of 'causal overkill' " (p. 77). Other possible contributing forms of rejection include failure, ostracism in school, and exclusion from a group. Most individuals appear to cope constructively with rejection or at least to deal with the stress of rejection from a "self-centered" perspective. In other words, the individual deals with his or her feelings without the involvement of others, resorting to physical exercise, hobbies, travel, and so on. Others may become self-destructive through, for example, excessive eating, anorexia nervosa, bulimia, and other types of eating disorders. In more severe cases, rejection may prompt individuals to take their own lives rather than live with such uncomfortable feelings. Rejection as a stressor may contribute to a number of psychosomatic illnesses. For some people, confronting rejection may necessitate seeking out others who are able to provide emotional support to restore their psychological equilibrium.

Some individuals deal with rejection within a more destructive framework—perhaps by beating the family dog, breaking objects, or assaulting a spouse, a friend, or a relative. Each person deals with rejection differently depending on its perceived degree, frequency, and intensity. Similarly, children cope with various childhood traumatizations in numerous ways. In the case of children who later become serial killers, many have experienced some form of childhood trauma that was not or could not be effectively countered by therapeutic strategies. In some cases there appeared to be series of traumatizations that psychologically affected these offenders. Cleary and Luxenburg (1993) in their study of 62 serial killers found common characteristics of abuse and dysfunctional families. At this juncture in our research we can only speculate as to the number or strength of predispositions or predilections offenders may have had toward violent behavior. However, we do know that most of them have a history of childhood traumatizations. Hazelwood and Warren (1989) reported in their study of 41 serial rapists that 76% had been sexually abused as children. Considering that some serial killers in this study were rapists before they graduated to murder, we must not ignore the implication that sexual victimization during childhood may readily manifest itself in a negative manner during adulthood.

Traumatization experienced by the offender as a child may nurture within him or her feelings of low self-esteem. A common characteristic of most, if not all, serial offenders is feelings of inadequacy, self-doubt, and worthlessness. They do not cope constructively with the early trauma(s) and subsequently perceive themselves and their surroundings in a distorted perspective. It is during this time of childhood development that a process of dissociation may occur. In an effort to regain the psychological equilibrium taken from them by people in authority, serial offenders appear to construct masks, facades, or a veneer of self-confidence and self-control. The label of psychopath, given to most serial killers, may actually describe a process of maintaining control of oneself, of others, and of one's surroundings. Indeed, a psychopath must become adept at perfecting rationalization and developing unconscious pretense, or the illusion that he or she is in perfect control of himself. The truth is just the opposite—the psychopath, internally, is a social and moral cripple. He must devote his life to maintaining and living his image. For the psychopath, it becomes both his best defense and best offense against conflicts he cannot resolve.

The offender may suppress traumatic event(s) to the point where he or she cannot consciously recall the experience(s). This can be referred to as splitting off, or blocking out, the experience. Tanay (1976), in describing this state of dissociation, noted that the murderer appears to carry out the act in an altered state of consciousness. Such an ego-dystonic homicide, whereby the individual is faced with a psychologically unresolvable conflict, results in part of the psychic structure splitting off from the rest of the personality. Danto (1982) noted that dissociative reactions are types of anxiety states in which the mind is "overwhelmed or flooded by anxiety" (p. 6). For some children, certain traumatizations can generate extremely high anxieties. To defend oneself against a psychologically painful experience a person may block it from recall or, instead, not consciously suppress the fact the trauma occurred but suppress the hurt, fear, anger, and other feelings caused by the event(s). However, the pain of a traumatic event will eventually surface in some way. For the offender, a cycle of trauma and quest for regaining control can be generated at a very early age. Vetter (1990) suggests that serial killers resemble those with *Mephisto Syndrome,* who exhibit a combination of dissociation and psychopathy.

Facilitators

At some point in the trauma-control process the offender may begin to immerse him- or herself in facilitators. Facilitators may include alcohol and other drugs, pornography, and books on the occult. Alcohol appears to decrease inhibitions and to inhibit moral conscience and propriety, whereas pornography fuels growing fantasies of violence. During the Reagan administration, the Meese Commission found that violent pornography was linked to violent sexual behavior. However, the connection made between pornography and violence can be misleading, because saying the two are "linked" can be interpreted in several ways. In any case, that certain serial murderers have insisted that pornography was a major factor in their killing young women and children should not be ignored. In February 1989, Richard Daniel Starrett was arrested and charged in the murder of a 15-year-old girl in South Carolina. He was also believed to have participated in the abduction and sexual assault and murders of several other young women and girls. Starrett claimed that pornography had influenced his violent behavior. As police searched a rented miniwarehouse, they seized 935 books and magazines belonging to Starrett that displayed nudity and sexual violence. Also found were 116 posters depicting bondage, violence, or sex, 18 calendars depicting sex or violence, and books on sex crimes, as well as dozens of hardcore videos.

Murray Straus and Larry Baron (1983) found that states with the highest readership of pornographic magazines, such as *Playboy* and *Hustler,* also had the highest rape rates. Dr. Victor Cline (1990), of the University of Utah, outlined a four-factor syndrome that appears similar to the process experienced by serial killers who are reported to have used pornography extensively. The offender first experiences "addiction" similar to the physiological/psychological addiction to drugs, which then generates stress in his or her everyday activities. The person then enters a stage of "escalation," in which the appetite for more deviant, bizarre, and explicit sexual material is fostered. Third, the person gradually becomes "desensitized" to that which was once revolting and taboo-breaking. Finally the person begins to "act out" the things that he or she has seen. Wasserman (2000), in her study of adolescent sexual offenders found that their motivation stemmed from sexual ignorance and sexual repression during puberty. Some youth, due to poor parenting skills, were forced to seek sexual information from pornographic sources that distorted reality and confused them. Puberty is a critical time for male youths when some learn to masturbate to pornography.

We must remember, however, that many serial murderers do not use pornography. Given the current state of limited research on serial homicide, it is dangerously premature to suggest facilitators as *causal* factors. What we can say is that a tendency to use pornography, alcohol, and texts on the occult has been noted frequently in serial offenders. But, we must recognize that pornography is produced in many different forms, both qualitatively and quantitatively. There exists not only difficulty in defining the parameters of pornography but also in discerning the effects it may or may not have on any particular person. In a recent study conducted by the Federal Bureau of Investigation, it was found that 36% of serial rapists collected pornography (Hazelwood & Warren, 1989). Does this mean they all read *Playboy, Penthouse,* and *Hustler,* or perhaps the many publications that include hardcore acts of sadomasochism, bestiality, and other forms of sexual degradation? Can we give the same weight to all forms of pornography, including acts of violent sexual conduct?

Also, can we exclude the possibility that pornography, like alcohol, may affect those people who harbor a predisposition for such stimulation more than others? In addition, pornography may actually serve as a retardant to serial offenders. If we are to believe, regardless of the presence or absence of pornography, that serial killers will commit acts of murder, then it is possible that some people may find sufficient gratification in and catharsis through various forms of pornography to avoid violence. As a release valve, the pornography lessens the demand for victims. We might argue that some serial offenders might have been motivated to kill earlier if pornography had not been available through which they could exercise their fantasies of control.

Proper scientific verification of these and other implications of pornography are needed in the construction of serial-murder etiology. We must be cautious in suggesting that there exists anything more than a tendency for pornography to affect those offenders involved in serial killing, regardless of how any of us may feel about pornography. If an argument is to be made that pornography (hardcore) is a primary causal agent for serial murder, then how are we to explain the behavior of serial killers who lived before the media explosion of the twentieth century? Serial murderers have existed for several hundreds of years, if not longer. Before technology permitted society to produce violent and sexually graphic material, serial killers were at work in America.

However, one could also argue that the emergence of large numbers of serial killers beginning in the 1960s was a direct result of the recent media explosion. Alcohol and pornography are not mandatory elements in the construction of a serial killer, but they tend to provide vehicles the offender uses to express the growing rages from within. In most instances these facilitators tend to be present to some degree in the profile of a serial killer. It is my contention, however, that without alcohol or pornography the offender in all likelihood would kill anyway. The circumstances of the acts may be altered, but the murders would inevitably occur. The offender still must gain control of inner feelings, anxieties, anger, rage, and pain. Using alcohol, pornography, or other such types of graphic literature may be useful in expediting the offender's urge to kill. (See Profile 4.2.)

PROFILE 4.2 Jeffrey Dahmer, 1978–1991

On July 22, 1991, Jeffrey Dahmer, age 31, was arrested in Milwaukee, Wisconsin, and entered the annals of America's most notorious serial killers.

With all the broken pieces sometimes it is impossible to see exactly which piece broke first. Jeffrey Dahmer was raised in a family in which his father was oblivious to the inner struggles of his son. At age eight Jeffrey is believed to have been sexually abused by a neighbor boy. His father recalls that Jeffrey was a loner and a poor student. He was unaware of his adolescent son's use of alcohol, his more than scientific interest in dissecting road kills, and his penchant for young men. Only three weeks after his senior high school prom, at age 18, Jeffrey would kill and dismember his first victim, a 17-year-old male—a deed kept secret from everyone. After several years of apparent family turmoil, Jeffrey's parents divorced. His mother took the youngest son to live with her while Jeffrey remained with his father. Jeffrey joined the military but was discharged for abuse of alcohol. He began working a night shift at the Ambrosia Chocolate Company in Milwaukee. In 1986 he received a year's probation for exposing himself to young boys. He struggled with his sexual orientation and felt that being gay was wrong. His inner struggles found him frequently contemplating suicide, but he was also developing aberrant sexual fantasies. His capacity for killing was being enhanced by these increasingly deviant sexual fantasies. He struggled against the urge to harm other human beings but was torn by sexual fantasies and driven by his need to control his life by controlling others. After the first homicide, at age 18, Dahmer is believed by some to have visited graveyards in hopes of retrieving a corpse rather than kill another person. Unsuccessful, Jeffrey Dahmer finally yielded to his growing fantasies. Succumbing to their ever-tightening grip, Jeffrey continued to fail in his attempts to succeed in his education or employment.

To most of his victims he seemed like a very average person wanting to be sociable. A resident of Milwaukee's West Side, Dahmer lived alone in an apartment. He frequented bars, some of them gay, looking for contacts. Initially he used his grandmother's basement to have sex with drugged men and act out some of his deviant fantasies. He often rented cheap rooms at bathhouses, where he gave alcohol laced with drugs such as Halcion (a sleeping pill) to his victims. He had gotten the routine down very well. Potential victims, many of them African American or Asian, were then brought to his apartment. Others he brought directly to his apartment, had sex with them, and then offered them tainted alcohol. Dahmer then handcuffed his victims, who were unaware that the alcohol had been laced with drugs, and led them into the bedroom. This was his killing room, where he kept and disposed of his victims. Most of his victims he strangled to death. One 14-year-old boy, a Native American, was sexually assaulted, drugged, strangled, dismembered, and his corpse pulverized with a sledgehammer. While some of his victims lay unconscious, Dahmer would drill holes into their skulls in an attempt to make zombies out of them. In this state he either hoped or fantasized they would become his sex slaves and never leave him. Dahmer also cannibalized several of his victims. The goal of all this carnage was, in fact, pitiful. Dahmer had a fantasy: By consuming his victims, they would become part of him and make him more powerful. He fantasized having his two favorite victims, fully skeletonized, standing on either side of him. He, Dahmer, would be sitting in a large black chair like the one used by the antagonist in the movie *Star Wars.* Directly behind him on a shelf and between the two skeletons would rest the shrunken skulls of several of his victims. This scene was a powerful one for Dahmer. In his mind he would achieve the ultimate. Surrounded by his victims who now had become part of him, Dahmer fantasized a sense of power and control unlike any he had ever felt before.

The last victim he attempted to lure into the killing chamber managed to escape and alert two police officers on patrol. (Over the years four other potential victims had also escaped and told their stories to police and friends, but still Dahmer had remained free.) Responding to the man's complaint that Dahmer had tried to handcuff him and that his bedroom contained photographs of dead men, the police went to the apartment. Dahmer greeted them at the door and appeared very cooperative. Stepping into the apartment, the officers noticed a severe stench, like that of rotting carcasses. One of the officers asked for the key to the handcuffs still attached to the arm of the man. Dahmer insisted on retrieving it himself from the bedroom. Concerned for their own safety, one of the officers moved past him and entered the bedroom.

What he found would soon become international headlines. A blue barrel containing human body parts stood in one corner and two skulls lay unconcealed in a box. Restraining Dahmer, the officers looked around the apartment and counted at least eleven skulls (seven of them carefully boiled and cleaned) and a collection of bones, decomposed hands, and genitals. Three of the cleaned skulls had been spray painted black and silver. These were to be part of the shrine fantasized by Dahmer. A complete skeleton suspended from a shower spigot and three skulls with holes drilled into them were found throughout the apartment. Dahmer had attempted to lobotomize some of his victims by pouring muriatic acid through the drilled holes and into their brain tissue. Chemicals, including muriatic acid, ethyl alcohol, chloroform, and formaldehyde, were also discovered, along with several Polaroid photographs of recently dismembered young men. A complete human head sat in the refrigerator. The next day, Dahmer confessed to murdering and dismembering 15 to 17 young men and boys. He blamed no one or anything for his crimes, including his parents, society, or pornography.

Jeffrey Dahmer was sentenced to 15 consecutive life sentences (957 years) and incarcerated at the Columbia Correctional Facility in Portage, Wisconsin. There he was the recipient of much fan mail and letters from curiosity seekers. Several writers, some from as far away as South Africa and Europe, sent him money. In contrast, the families of the victims obtained judgments against Dahmer totalling more than 80 million dollars. Dahmer admitted that he should never be allowed freedom again because he still felt the compulsion to kill. Nor did he wish to remain in prison. On November 28, 1994, Dahmer was beaten to death by Christopher J. Scarver, another inmate serving time for murder. His remains were cremated, although efforts were made by his mother to have her son's brain donated to science.

How do we explain Jeffrey's criminal behavior? Like other serial

(continued)

PROFILE 4.2 Continued

killers, there is no single causal factor. Jeffrey's biological father, Lionel Dahmer, outlines several possibilities that in combination may have triggered his son's urge to kill. Mr. Dahmer (1994) points out that Jeffrey's mother, Joyce, frequently used medications such as phenobarbital and morphine during her pregnancy with Jeffrey to deal with both psychological and physiological problems. Could these medications have affected Jeffrey's fetal development, or did Jeffrey inherit mental illness from his mother or antisocial personality traits from his father? From a neuropsychological perspective, was there some genetic predisposition to violence inherited by Jeffrey? Mr. Dahmer does mention his own obsession with fire and a fascination with bombs and making explosives. Another possible factor was the constant family discord that seemed to alienate Jeffrey and led to divorce and further family disruption. Eventually, Jeffrey turned to alcohol to assuage his pain of abandonment, his feelings of low self-esteem, and his perceived pattern of failure in life. How do you explain Jeffrey's diminished conscience, lack of empathy, and cold-blooded attitude as he hunted, selected, and killed each victim?

Fantasy

The most critical factor common to serial killers is violent fantasy. Prentky and colleagues (1986), who studied repetitive sexual homicides, found that daydreams of causing bodily harm through sadism and other methods of sexual violence were common among offenders. The researchers concluded that the offender attempts to replicate his fantasies. Because the offender can never be actually in total control of his or her victim's responses, the outcome of the fantasy will never measure up to his or her expectations. In any case, each new murder provides new fantasies that can fuel future homicides. Ressler and his colleagues (1988) concluded that "sexual murder is based on fantasy" (p. 33). Fantasy becomes a critical component in the psychological development of a serial killer. Although fantasies are generally associated with sexual homicides, they are likely to be found in the minds of most, if not all, serial killers.

The following case, of a young man arrested for attempted rape and murder, illustrates how consuming and powerful fantasies can become: Visiting a young woman in whom he was interested, Carl suddenly attacked and tried to rape her. During the course of the attack the girl's mother returned home. Enraged, Carl killed the mother and fled the home. Carl was adjudicated to be insane at the time of the attack and was confined to a mental institution until he could be considered safe to return to the community. After seven years and extensive therapy in a sex offender program, Carl was permitted to begin a community reintegration program. Working as an electrician's helper, Carl worked during the day and stayed at the hospital at night. He was also allowed certain weekend privileges, provided he followed the specific rules of his therapy program.

One of Carl's problems had been his propensity for fantasy. When he was younger, he loved to set fires so he could view the flashing lights of the police and fire trucks. Over time he had graduated into some extremely violent fantasies that were believed by psychiatrists to have contributed to his homicidal behavior. During his years in the sex offender program Carl appeared to learn how to control his fantasies. On weekends he attended dances, movies, and other recreational activities. He was not permitted, however, to attend movies that contained any explicit sexual violence for fear he could still become caught up in his own fantasies of violence. One evening he violated his weekend pass by attending the movie *Dressed To Kill,* featuring Angie Dickinson. Later, he would report how he had attempted to "pick up a girl" during the movie but was rejected. Even before the violence in the movie had ended, Carl was also ready to kill. Going to his car engulfed in raging fantasies of violence, Carl located his electrician's knife and waited in the shadows while four unsuspecting female college students exited from the theater. His fantasy was to enter their car and cut each girl's throat. Walking quickly to the rear door of the vehicle, Carl reached for the handle. Just as he was about to open the door, the driver, unaware of his presence, stepped on the accelerator and drove off.

Frustrated and in the grips of his violent fantasies, Carl later explained how he had then gone to the local park, hunting for a lone female jogger. He had decided to cut her into pieces. Waiting in some bushes for several minutes, Carl saw a woman jogging toward him. It was 11:30 P.M., and the park was deserted. Fortunately for his intended victim, a male jogger emerged from another direction at about the same time. Thwarted in his bid to kill and in fear of detection, Carl returned to his car. After driving around for a while and unable to locate any more suitable victims, Carl calmed down and returned to the hospital, where he explained to hospital staff his evening's experiences. It was decided that Carl was still in need of closer supervision, and his passes were revoked (author's files).

Most people's fantasies generally are perceived as harmless and often therapeutic. Fantasies can involve a continuum of benign to aggressive thoughts that usually generate little or no action on the part of the fantasizer. For serial offenders, however, fantasies appear to involve violence, often sexual in nature, whereby the victim is controlled totally by the offender. The purpose of the fantasy is not the immediate destruction of another human being but total control over that person. The element of control is so intense in the serial killer that in some cases the actual death of the victim is anticlimactic to the fantasized total control over the victim. In a case mentioned in an earlier chapter, an offender who is believed to have killed 14 young women used to place his revolver on the forehead of his victim and order her to perform fellatio. Those victims who cried and begged for mercy would invariably receive a bullet in their heads during the sexual assault. Those victims who cooperated with the killer but remained calm and did not show fear were spared. During an interview with one of the victims who survived the assault, this author was told how she had been ordered to kneel on the floor. In this instance the offender had placed tape over his victim's mouth. After he had taped her mouth, the killer proceeded to rub his penis against her face and insisted she look him in the eyes while he performed his sexual assault. The victim later recalled how she managed to remain calm and did exactly as he ordered her to do even though her attacker held a gun to her head. After a few moments the killer realized his victim was not responding the way he expected (and according to his fantasies), and so he abruptly fled the store (author's files).

The control fantasy becomes the highlight of the attack. The sexual assault is one vehicle by which the offender can attempt to gain total control of a victim. Sexual torture becomes a tool to degrade, humiliate, and subjugate the victim. It is a method to take away from the victim all that is perceived to be personal, private, or sacred. The offender physically and mentally dominates his or her victims to a point where he or she has fantasized achieving ultimate control over another human being. Once that sense of control has been reached, the victim loses his or her purpose to the offender and is then killed. One serial killer noted in a personal interview that he had developed a ritual for torturing his victims and that he seldom varied from those methods.

It is during the sexual assault, torture, and degradation that fantasies of the original childhood trauma may manifest themselves in acts of violence. In some cases, 10 or 20 years may have lapsed since the traumatic event(s) occurred; in others, only a short period of time may have passed. During the time elapsed between the traumatic events(s) and the homicides, the offender may have completely disassociated from the traumatic experience (which had split off from his consciousness) and may have protected him- or herself further by assuming a life of control and confidence. Psychologically the offender has been experiencing less and less self-control but desperately seeks to retain control of his inner self. Often the victims selected by the killers stand as proxies for the traumatic event(s) experienced by the offenders. In one instance an offender had received electroshock treatments as corrective therapy for his involvement in a gang rape while he was a teenager. In 1984, 22 years after his electroshocks, the offender tortured some of his victims by wiring their toes to electrical outlets and then turning the power on and off. In yet another case, an offender had been sexually abused, beaten, bound with heavy cords, and left in terrifyingly dark closets. Several years later he began torturing boys by beating them, tying them with heavy cords, and holding them captive in dark places. His attempts to replicate his childhood traumas were nearly successful except that the sense of control he sought remained elusive. Each victim experienced more extensive tortures and depravities than the previous victim until he died, at which time the killer butchered the corpse. His last victim was slowly dismembered and disemboweled while still alive (author's files).

Fantasies may be fueled by pornography and facilitated by alcohol. The anger that has continued to grow over the years is allowed to be expressed in images of violence and death. Once the total domination and destruction of the victim has occurred, the killer momentarily regains the sense of equilibrium lost years before. One offender described this moment as the "restoration stage," which allows the killer to "feel good" again. He explained that for many serial killers, the frequency of victimization is a direct function of the degree of completion of the restoration. In other words, if the offender is stymied or frustrated in some way in the act of ritualistically killing a victim, he or she may be prompted to quickly seek out another. Once the killer is able to complete the ritual of killing and feels that sense of control restored, he or she may not need to kill again for some time.

But fantasies can never be completely fulfilled or the anger removed or the missing self-esteem restored. For some, the experience of killing may generate new fantasies of violence. Exactly what does occur in the killer's mind between murders? It is possible for some offenders to become so consumed by their attempts at fantasy fulfillment that killing becomes a frequent experience. Yet there are many serial killers who wait long periods of time, months or even years, before they seek out their next victim. According to one offender, he felt good about himself and more in control of his life directly following a murder. Eventually he would experience another failure in his life, such as criticism of job performance or rejection by a girlfriend. He believed that such events should not have bothered him, but they seemed to act as catalysts for depression and low self-esteem. The sense of failure or rejection never failed to put him into a spiral of self-pity, anger, loss of confidence, and increased fantasies. Sometimes it would be months, but inevitably he would go hunting for young women to torture and kill (author's files). Frequently, serial offenders escalate their hunt for prey as they seek to fulfill deviant sexual fantasies of control. By the end of Jeffrey Dahmer's killing career he was hunting another victim even before completely disposing of his most recent victim's corpse (see Profile 4.2).

As a postscript to this case, the present author asks the reader to consider the perspective of the offender's family—a view seldom recognized or appreciated. This author came to know personally some of Jeffrey Dahmer's family. Since the murders, the author spent time with both Jeffrey's brother, David, and his mother, Joyce. If Jeffrey was angry or unhappy with his mother, these emotions were well concealed after his arrest. Both his mother, now deceased, and his brother were two of the kindest people a person could ever hope to meet. They have suffered immensely and struggle to understand how and why Jeff, a brother and son, could act so violently. Their lives, too, have been changed forever.

STALKING

The role of stalking in serial murder merits exploration, because it can help to explain both cognitive and behavioral aspects of victim selection and subsequent murder. The act of *stalking* did not become a crime until 1990, when the state of California passed antistalking statutes to protect individuals or groups from harassment, intimidation, or violence. Since then, every state has implemented some form of antistalking legislation. Stalking generally requires three elements: a pattern of harassment over a period of time, implied or explicit threats, and intent to harm, intimidate, or create great emotional stress. We usually consider stalking in reference to celebrities such as tennis star Monica Seles, who in 1993 was stalked and stabbed during a tennis match. We are more likely to see stalking in cases of domestic problems in which the offender relentlessly pursues a former spouse, lover, or friend.

The Threat Management Unit of the Los Angeles Police Department has classified stalkers into four categories: *simple obsessional,* in which the offender knows his victim and stalks as a result of perceived mistreatment or separation; *love obsessional,* which involves stranger-to-stranger stalking in which the offender harasses the victim to draw attention to himself; *erotomania,* which typically involves a celebrity, who the offender believes is in love with her (most offenders are female); and the rare *false-victimization syndrome,* in which the offender falsely accuses another person, real or imaginary, of stalking him or her in order to assume the role of the victim. Most of these forms of stalking seldom end in actual violence to the victim. Oddie (2000) provides insight into the prediction of violence in stalking cases and notes that prediction is a most difficult process.

Hickey, Margulies, and Oddie (1999), in their study of 210 victims of stalking, revised the manner in which we view the process of stalking, the offenders, and the victims. Hickey identifies two general categories of offender-initiated stalking: *domestic* and *stranger,* each with its own types of stalkers. A third category involves victim-initiated stalking or *factitious* reporting. An important clarification is that Hickey views some stalking as noncriminal. The fact that someone may be demonstrating stalking behaviors does not prove intent to do harm. Indeed, in American society and given the many ways that humans can interact with one another, attempting to repeatedly make contact with someone does not always imply criminal intent. Consider a person wanting an autograph, a person wanting to meet another person and feels awkward in initiating contact, people sending e-mails; all of these commonplace events may or may not be construed as stalking depending upon the contextual cutting point of the relationship, the duration, intensity, and frequency of the contact, past behavior of the initiator, and the level of dangerousness created by the initiator. Much of everyday social discourse may involve low levels of noncriminal stalking, or *nuisance stalking.* The author is aware that nuisance stalking can and often does quickly develop into various forms of criminal stalking. The following classification system is designed to assist potential victims of stalking in identifying, understanding, and dealing with offenders. Critical to this discussion is the linkage of serial murderers to stalking behaviors. All serial murderers utilize various forms of stalking in order to lure their victims. Each category of stalking has different types of stalkers:

1. Domestic	**2. Stranger**	**3. Factitious**
Power/Anger	Power/Anger	False Victimization
Obsessional	Obsessional	Hero Fantasy
Nuisance	Nuisance	
	Sexual Predator	
	Erotomania	

Domestic Stalking

This form of stalking commonly involves persons who are related to the victim, friends, or acquaintances and usually can be associated with one of three types of stalkers. The *domestic-power/anger* stalker harbors feelings of hatred, revenge, and domination over their victim. Sometimes offenders are so consumed by their anger that they are inappropriately designated as being obsessed. These offenders may exhibit antisocial characteristics, low self-esteem, lack of self-confidence, insecurity, and fear, but they are not obsessed in a clinical sense. Their inability to manage their personal or public life creates a state of perpetual frustration and anxiety. In turn, their frustrations and emotions lead them into increasingly violent acts. This is the most common type of domestic stalker and the most likely to do physical harm to the victim. The victims are usually women caught up in dysfunctional relationships who leave their husbands, lovers, boyfriends, or even acquaintances because they fear for their own personal safety and/or the safety of their children. Enraged, the offender often begins a campaign of relentless pursuit by harassing, threatening, and assaulting and, in some cases, killing the victim.

The *domestic-obsessional* stalker usually has motivations less obvious than the power/anger stalkers. Their victims are former friends or lovers, coworkers, acquaintances, and relatives. Often plagued by psychological disorders including schizophrenia, paranoia, and personality disorders, the offender becomes fixated upon their victim and relentlessly pursues them. What separates the obsessional from other types of stalkers is their often irrational and illogical behavior caused by psychological dysfunctioning. These offenders sometimes are persons who are gainfully employed and may appear to most others as quite normal. For the victim however, contact with the obsessional offender becomes a series of frequent telephone calls, house calls, letters, gifts, followings, and harassments. Caught in obsessions the offender will often make claims that the victim wants to be with the offender and that they are meant to be together.

In other instances the offender believes the victim to be an enemy who is plotting to do harm and must be stopped. The obsessional attachment is based in delusional beliefs that the victim is an enemy to the offender and community in which he/she resides. The offender believes that no one else is truly capable of stopping this threat and feels they are on a mission to save everyone.

The *domestic-nuisance* stalker is an offender who uses various forms of harassment as his or her primary tool. The victims are coworkers, acquaintances, relatives, and former friends. The offender does not attempt to harm or threaten the victim. In many cases the offender is trying to establish a friendly relationship with the victim but through unconventional means. The offender is either misguided and lacking in adequate social skills or derives pleasure through fantasy and the behavioral process of harassment. They may think that the victim actually finds the harassment a bit thrilling and looks forward to hearing from the offender. Such harassment may even begin in a joking manner and escalate into stalking.

Stranger Stalking

This category of stalking involves an offender who has no known prior relationship to the victim and includes five types of stalkers:

Stranger-power/anger stalkers are primarily men who look for random victims to control, intimidate, and harm. The Internet is quickly becoming a popular tool for such offenders. These men exhibit antisocial characteristics and, as a result of their own lack of self-confidence and self-esteem, they hunt for proxy victims upon which to vent their anger. In times of economic hardship such men turn to others upon which to place blame. Neo-Nazis, skinheads, right-wing extremists, men marginalized by society, and sexists all want to vent their rage and frustrations. The Internet is proving to be an excellent tool for harassing others and spreading their messages of hate toward minorities and women. Much of what appears in e-mail as threats tends to be cathartic and goes no further in stalking escalation. However, these offenders are not passive and are known for their boldness in striking out at random victims. The Internet is another way for them to band together for those wanting to affiliate. Other power/anger stalkers prefer anonymity and will send repeated messages of hate to public officials, minorities, and women. In most cases the messages tend to be cathartic and end quickly. Those who pursue sending threatening e-mails should be considered extremely dangerous.

Stranger-obsessional stalkers are individuals who suffer from a variety of psychological disorders including paranoid schizophrenia, and bipolar and dissociative disorders. They generally should be considered dangerous because of their level of unpredictability. The object of their attachment is a stranger. Obsessionals attach because they have come to learn or believe something about another person or organization that may be completely false but that acts as a catalyst for the attachment. The Internet is attractive to obsessionals because it allows them unlimited access to their victims. Often, obsessionals will use additional means to reach their victims.

Stranger-nuisance stalkers tend to be loners looking for opportunities to connect with others in some medium. They range from teens to middle-aged men who frequently use the Internet to meet and harass victims. They enjoy the sense of freedom they have in hacking into victim's e-mails, tampering with Web pages and sending obscene messages. They are offenders who derive satisfaction from honing their computer skills and demonstrating their prowess. The stalking usually is short in duration and low in intensity.

Stranger-sexual predator stalkers are some of the most dangerous offenders known to our criminal justice system. They include rapists, pedophiles, child molesters, and paraphiliacs. They are dangerous because the outcome is frequently the actual sexual assault of a victim or psychological sexual violence of a victim. The Internet is a perfect medium for sexual predators to solicit potential victims and do it with relative impunity. Offenders frequently have criminal histories, display various psychopathic characteristics, act alone, and become very adept at using tools such as the Internet to find victims.

Stranger-erotomaniac is a stalker who attaches himself or herself to another person because this stalker believes that person wants and is in love with him or her. The victims are usually persons of public prominence. The offenders are often irrational and obsessive in their stalking behaviors. Women are more likely to become involved in such stalking cases. In cases where the offenders are schizophrenic, psychotic, or suffering from a delusional state, there have been several instances when the stalking turned physically violent. In such cases the offenders are more likely to be males than females.

Factitious Stalking

In some cases those reporting being stalked actually have fabricated the story in order to receive attention. This deception may be manifested by the person reporting the crime as someone who is following her and always watching her every move. She may report being attacked, assaulted physically, or even tell investigators that she will soon be murdered. Although extensive efforts are made by law enforcement to substantiate the victim's claims, no acceptable evidence materializes. The LAPD refer to such cases as *false victimization*. The payoff for the "victim" is repeated visits by police and other officials that provide her with the desired attention. Often these are women who have experienced severe trauma or have long-term issues involving feelings of abandonment, neglect, and rejection by significant others through death, divorce, and familial dysfunction. This form of Munchausen's Syndrome may also be transferred to a child, known as Munchausen Syndrome by Proxy, where the illness, or in this case, stalking, involves the child. The mother or guardian makes every effort to protect her child. This entails repeated calls to the police. Other factitious reporters exhibit a hero fantasy and want to be recognized for their efforts in tracking down their ever-elusive stalker. Again, these factitious reporters will be extremely vigilante in assisting investigators.

Site and Nonsite Stalking

The level of personal and physical dangers to a victim can usually be measured by whether the offender is participating in *nonsite* or *site stalking*. Nonsite stalking refers to offenders who do not make personal, direct contact with the victim but instead engage in one or more of the following behaviors:

1. Telephone calls
2. E-mails
3. Fax messages
4. Letters
5. Gifts
6. Voice mail
7. Other forms of recorded messages

These offenders, although often creating tremendous psychological stress for their victims, do not pose a physical danger. For the offender, nonsite stalking can be cathartic and provide a sense of control and power over their victim without actually having physical contact. Indeed, some types of nonsite stalkers would not feel comfortable nor in control were they to come face to face with their victims. Offenders who are married or have careers and reputations they do not want placed in jeopardy will employ nonsite tactics to harass, intimidate, and control their victims. In cases of domestic, nonsite stalking offenders are careful to avoid any acknowledgement of their stalking behaviors to their victims who may also be their coworkers, acquaintances, or relatives.

Other nonsite stalkers will escalate their activities into site stalking where the offender makes direct contact with the victim. Site stalking is preferred by some stalkers over nonsite stalking because they feel a greater sense of control and the direct contact fulfills physical and sexual fantasies. Site stalkers engage in one or more of the following behaviors:

1. Following
2. Workplace visits
3. Home visits
4. Signatures
5. Vandalism
6. Sending or leaving "gifts"
7. Displaying weapons

Some stalkers will only use nonsite stalking, whereas others will exclusively use site stalking and some will engage in both site and nonsite stalking. A critical factor for law enforcement and victims is understanding that site stalking opens a Pandora's box of both physical and psychologically dangerous behaviors.

Cyberstalking

Cyberstalking is best viewed as a *method* of stalking employed by either domestic or stranger stalkers. Typically, we find that most cyberstalking appears to be committed by strangers given the vast number of sexual predator, celebrity, and nuisance stalkers currently using the Internet. The stalking landscape will continue to fluctuate as more individuals from all socioeconomic statuses, ethnic/racial backgrounds, political persuasions, and religious belief systems embrace the ether world. For example, the fastest growing group of persons now gaining access to the Internet is that earning a wage of under $25,000 per year.

The greatest focus surrounding those who cyberstalk and their victims involves sexual predators. Most commonly noted are pedophiles and child molesters. Differentiating between pedophiles and child molesters is not an easy task because they are not mutually exclusive in their fantasies and behaviors. Pedophiles prefer the company of children both socially and emotionally. Although many pedophiles work in adult settings, they always prefer the company of children. They usually are not married and live alone or with a relative. Their fantasies involve being emotionally attached and, if possible, physically involved with a child. They appear on a continuum from reclusive and self-gratified (where the pedophile does not actually seek out children but instead uses movies, props, photographs, etc., to fulfill fantasies and sexual desires) to the aggressive pedophile who seeks out children for sexual purposes, including murder. The child molester also prefers children but is more likely to be married and have a family. The key distinguishing factor is sexual contact with children. Once the pedophile begins to approach children, he is no longer in a benign status engaged in only sexual fantasies involving children. Pedophiles and child molesters can be found affiliated with NAMBLA (North American Man-Boy Love Association), Free Spirits, the Renee Guyon Society, Pedophile Liberation Front and other organizations of similar ilk.

The Internet has become a labyrinth in which such predators lurk. Internet chat rooms, especially those designed for younger persons, have become virtual playgrounds for sexual predators. Pedophiles who may have kept their fantasies to themselves now have a forum to discuss their thoughts with other pedophiles as well as daily opportunities to visit chat rooms and begin relationships with unsuspecting victims. In California, a 60-year-old opthamologist contacted a 13-year-old girl and after a few e-mail exchanges began sending her sexually explicit photographs. Eventually the doctor asked to meet the girl and she agreed. The girl turned out to be a police officer working Internet sex crime cases. The doctor felt that law enforcement was overreacting because there was no proof of intent to harm the child. In his words "I only sent her a couple of photos and asked to meet her."

The Internet now provides the predator with a plethora of tools and options to use in the process of stalking children. Photographs, drawings, e-mail, online chats, chat rooms, videos, and music are some of the devices now available via the Internet that allow predators to connect with children. Potential rapists can use the same tools in hunting victims. From a criminal's perspective, barrooms have been places of gathering for men seeking women to rape. The advent of the Internet now provides a forum for would-be rapists to stalk women. Unfortunately people find themselves more willing to talk openly about personal topics on the Internet than if they were face-to-face with a stranger. The computer provides a false sense of anonymity and security that leads potential victims into sharing too much information.

In one case the predator used his computer to lure victims to his home for sexual activities or promises of employment. Thus far the bodies of eight of these women have been located after the predator raped, tortured, and murdered them.

Stalking Fantasy

Stalkers have been psychologically categorized as having antisocial, borderline, or narcissistic personalities but also have been diagnosed with impulse-control, intermittent explosive, and substance abuse disorders. Some of the most noted celebrity stalkers, such as Ralph Nau, known as the Hollywood stalker who sent thousands of letters to over 40 celebrities, or Michael Perry, who escaped from a mental institution and managed to murder five people, including his parents, while stalking Olivia Newton-John, were found to be psychotic or paranoid schizophrenics.

For most sex offenders such as rapists, pedophiles, voyeurs, and exhibitionists, *stalking fantasies* are critical in the process of offending. Consider the voyeur who goes about looking for opportunities to watch people undressing or engaging in sexual activities. Voyeurs derive a sense of personal control when they secretly watch unsuspecting victims. Thinking and completing the act of voyeurism provides the offender with reinforced fantasies that will once again need to be satisfied. Like many acts of sex offending, voyeurism causes the offender's fantasies to escalate and increases the risk of victim contact.

This author once consulted on a case in California in which a woman had separated from her husband as a result of his continuous lying, manipulation, and intimidation. He then began stalking her. On one occasion she arrived home from work to find a pair of her underwear lying on the driveway. Another time she looked out of her classroom where she taught school and noticed her nightgown hanging on the school fence. She had changed the locks on her home, but he was still gaining entrance. Fearing for her safety, she filed for a restraining order. A few days later the estranged husband violated the order and was arrested as he was driving his car. Police found two boxes of photographs chronologically organized.

During the two years the couple had been married the husband had taken many photographs of his wife. In the beginning the pictures were snapshots of her face, walking alone, or lying down. Eventually he had insisted she pose in attire, such as leather and chains, which made her uncomfortable and nervous, but she complied in order to humor him.

Her husband had special plans for those pictures. He had purchased some horror magazines depicting various monsters. Cutting out pictures of his wife, he taped them onto scenes of monsters lurking in dark corners of rooms or parking lots while she stood innocent-looking in the scene. He had taken other photographs of her and penned in red cut marks on her neck and drops of blood on her dress. Other scenes depicted monsters killing her while she lay bound in chains and leather. Police were concerned that he was about to kill her. Although that was certainly possible, the present author suggested that the offender was probably stalking other women (by voyeurism) in his neighborhood. His wife was a successful woman who had self-confidence and high self-esteem. He did not feel in control around her and felt she could see through his facade. Consequently, he was probably searching for victims he could control, at least in his own fantasies.

Indeed, serial killers also engage in psychological stalking prior to physically stalking their victims. This form of psychological foreplay is an essential component for many serial murderers. Ed Kemper recounted how he would visualize female victims sitting beside him in his car while he pulled out a gun. Stalking fantasies prepare an offender for opportunities to physically stalk selected victims. In other cases, stalking is accomplished in fantasy only. Eventually, when the "right" victim appears, the offender is prepared to move quickly in isolating her. Indeed, the more focused the fantasies, the greater the danger to potential victims.

SIGNATURES

Cases of serial killing share commonalties and characteristics. Anger, low self-esteem, fantasy, facilitation, and objectification of victims all are common denominators in understanding the general etiological roots of serial murder. Some cases, however, have distinctive behaviors that make the crime and the offender(s) unique. These are referred to as the *signature,* or personal marking of the offender. For example, most cases of serial murder are described in terms of patterns of murder customized to fit the special needs and fantasies of each killer. This pattern is not part of the modus operandi and sets the case apart from other murder cases. Signatures are actions of the offender usually unnecessary to completing the murders. Frequently the signatures are extensions of paraphilic fantasies. Sometimes postmortem mutilation becomes the signature of a particular killer. Others collect souvenirs such as body parts, pieces of clothing, or newspaper clippings. One offender liked to remove the eyeballs from his victims. Another cannibalized the sexual organs of his young victims, whereas still another skinned his victims and made lampshades, eating utensils, and clothing. Signatures also help the offender actualize his fantasies. (See Profile 4.3.)

CYCLICAL NATURE OF SERIAL KILLING

The trauma-control model of violent behavior describes, in effect, the cyclical experience of serial offenders. Fantasies, possibly fueled by pornography or alcohol, reinforced by "routine" traumatizations of day-to-day living, keep the serial killer caught up in a self-perpetuating cycle of fantasies, stalking, and violence. Contrary to some claims, serial killers do not all wish to be caught, although some do, and even allow themselves to be apprehended. One may argue that serial killers allow themselves to be caught because their need for recognition overwhelms their desire to remain hidden. Others may briefly experience a moment of clarity in considering their deeds and decide to end the killing. Although this has happened, such offender behavior appears to be rare. Ed Kemper, after murdering several women in California, drove to Colorado, called the police, and told them he was the killer they were searching for. Kemper was accommodating enough to wait by the pay phone until the police arrived and arrested him. Some serial killers can go on for many years and never allow their fantasies to become so consuming that they lose control of their surroundings and their abilities to remain obscure. For the killer, the cycle becomes a never-ending pursuit of control over one's own life through the total domination and destruction of others' lives.

PROFILE 4.3 Cary Stayner, the Yosemite Signature Killer, 1999

Cary Stayner could have easily been a model gracing the pages of GQ magazine. Tall, dark, and striking, he rated high on "attractiveness" in an opinion poll solicited by the author. Due to his artistic giftedness, Cary was voted "most creative" by his graduating class and was expected to become a famous cartoonist. Later the author would have the opportunity to examine several drawings done by Mr. Stayner around 1995. These drawings depicted scenes of death and destruction, with heads of victims on the ground. The backdrop was Yosemite National Park.

Those who know him describe him as amiable, easy going, and quiet. He is described as a naturalist, with a penchant for nudity, frequenting secluded lake areas to sunbathe unencumbered. His acquaintances were shocked at his confessions of multiple murder, and even more so, the macabre means by which he killed.

First born of five children, Cary was eldest brother to Steven Stayner, who in 1972 was kidnapped and held prisoner by a child molester for almost eight years. He escaped, bringing with him a 5-year-old child who had also been abducted. Making national headlines, Steven became the hero, his notoriety pushing his sibling into obscurity. Disgusted by the book written about his brother and the made-for-TV movie, Cary's resentment grew.

At Merced High School, Cary was considered a good student and was thought well of. But his home-life was deteriorating with the separation of his parents. He moved in with his uncle, Jesse Stayner, until 1990 when tragedy struck and an intruder shot Jesse to death. Cary was never considered a suspect and was believed to have been at work. His employers considered him a diligent worker and a proven employee, always showing up on time and never the object of customer complaints.

Between 1996 and 1997, Cary moved to El Portal in Yosemite National Park where he worked as a handyman at several hotels. Those who knew him described him as likeable, a loner who never dated and was not inclined to close friendships. Though he occasionally smoked marijuana, he was not disposed to drinking, even when generous tourists at the hotel offered to indulge everyone with a "round." But such benign behavior only masked the brooding predator within. Rarely does evil not masquerade. For many years, Cary Stayner had fantasized about killing women.

In the spring of 1999, Eureka, California, resident Carol Sund, 42, her daughter Julie Sund, 16, and an

Argentine friend, Silvina Pelosso, 16, were visitors to Yosemite National Park in California. On February 14, they checked in at Cedar Lodge where Stayner worked and lived. They were last seen alive February 15.

One month later, Carol and Silvina's charred bodies were found in the trunk of their burned out rental car. On March 25, Julie's decomposed body was found several miles away. Her throat was cut so severely she was almost decapitated. Stayner was not considered a suspect.

Almost five months later, after she was reported missing by her friends, Yosemite naturalist Joie Armstrong's body was found in a creek near her home. She was decapitated. A similar vehicle to Stayner's had been seen in the vicinity of Armstrong's home. Three hours after the body was found, Stayner told authorities he had nothing to do with her death. When he didn't show up for work the next day, authorities began searching for him and found him at a nudist colony in Wilton. He has confessed to all four slayings. The FBI had originally arrested other suspects and kept reassuring the public they had the right people in custody, only to suddenly retract those statements when Stayner gave them specific incriminating information that was privy only to law enforcement. Stayner has since pled guilty to the Joie Armstrong murder. He is currently awaiting trial for the other murders, which could take years to conclude. The death penalty is being sought.

One of the most important clues linking these murders is the manner in which the victims died. Decapitation or nearly severing a person's head is not just about murder but is also about sexual fantasy and gratification. The offender becomes sexually gratified by the fantasy of cutting into a victim's throat. The sense of sexual power overwhelms the offender. Stayner had been fantasizing and drawing his fantasies of decapitation for several years. The method of killing became his sexual signature that could link him to other similar murders.

In one of his public statements he said, "I would like to say how deeply sorry I am for all the pain and sorrow I've brought upon so many people. Not only the Sunds, Pellossos (sic), Carringtons and the Armstrongs, but my fellow employees at Cedar Lodge, the community of El Portal, the people of Argentina, and all those across the nation who felt the sorrow of my victims' families. I am truly sorry." He also wants a movie to be made and requested an interview with NBC's Jane Pauley.

5

The Male Serial Murderer

Male serial killers in the United States appear with amazing regularity. They are found in local bars, working blue-collar jobs, or may be hitchhikers and transients. They are also men working in hospitals, independent business owners and most recently, predators "surfing the net" hunting for just the right person. Victims of serial killers continue to be found throughout the United States. Some are found in boarding houses, homes for the elderly, hospitals, and private homes. Other victims will be found in wooded areas, ravines, and other isolated areas—victims of male serial killers. Usually these victims die much more violently than other homicide victims. In 1999, Gerald Parker, known as the "Bedroom Basher" was convicted of murdering five women and a full-term fetus in their homes. DNA evidence finally caught up with Parker. The personalized violence inflicted on helpless victims has no boundaries or limitations to which offenders subscribe. For example, during 1990, a supposed male serial killer in San Diego, California, murdered at least five young women. One of the victims, a 20-year-old San Diego university student, was stabbed more than 50 times. That same year five students were stabbed to death in Gainesville, Florida, with a surgical instrument. One of the women was decapitated. Male serial killers wage their own personal wars against humanity, indifferent to the lives of others in their constant quest for control. Charles Starkweather, after his killing spree, casually observed "shooting people was, I guess, a kind of a thrill. It brought out something" (Reinhardt, 1960, p. 78). Edmund Kemper, reminiscing about the start of his killing career remarked "I just wondered how it would be to shoot grandma."

Male serial killers represent the darkest, most sinister side of human existence, yet we are fascinated to read about them, to watch them portrayed in movies and learn of their obscenities. Drukteinis (1992) reminds us that serial murder is "at the extremes of conduct" defined in human interaction. These killers are especially dangerous because we understand so little about their actual motivations, their lives, and their personalities. Pollock (1995), in reviewing clinical and theoretical motivations for serial murder, concluded that most offenders exhibit malignant narcissism, an extreme form of narcissistic personality disorder manifesting as "pathologically grandiose, lacking in conscience and behavioral regulation with characteristic demonstrations of joyful cruelty and sadism." These summary descriptors of serial killers assist researchers in restructuring definitions of serial murder. From Cormier's (Cormier et al., 1972) coining the term multicide to Keeny and Heide's (1994, 1995) concise and logical redefining of serial murder as "premeditated murder of three or more victims committed over time, in separate incidents, in a civilian context, with the murder activity being chosen by the offender," our understanding of this phenomenon has significantly accelerated. Our search for "commonality" helps us to create descriptive parameters and taxonomies, yet the horror generated by these offenders distorts their profiles, actual body counts, and inevitably our perception of them. In March 2000, Tommy Lynn Sells confessed to killing 13 people in seven different states. He killed men, women, children, and babies by using guns, knives, a bat, a shovel, an ice pick, and his bare hands. That same year Darrell Rich, a California serial killer, was executed for the brutal murders of four female victims. Most of his victims were teenage girls he sexually assaulted, then shot, beat to death, or crushed their skulls. His last victim, 11-year-old Annette Selix was thrown off a train bridge. Contrast that form of rage serial killing to a person who quietly lived with the knowledge that 25 decomposing bodies lay under the floorboards of his house. Masters (1986) chronicled the life of Dennis Nilsen, a British serial killer and necrophile, and described how involved the murderer became with his victims after death. They were a source of company for him. In one instance, Nilsen stored the body of a young male under his floor and frequently would retrieve him for an evening's entertainment. This included propping the boy in a chair next to Nilsen, who carried on conversations, bathing him, watching television "together," and performing sexual acts on the decomposing child.

Other serial killers have sex with their victims just before or immediately after death. Some are known for their habits of collecting trophies or souvenirs. For example, when the police arrived, Gary Heidnik was found to have several pounds of human flesh stored in his freezer while other body parts were simmering in a stew pot. Others have collected lingerie, shoes, hats, and other wearing apparel. Some serial killers do not have any apparent sexual involvement with the victims, but their method of killing is so bizarre one can only speculate about their actual motivations.

EMERGENCE OF MALE SERIAL MURDERERS

Intrigue and horror have generated several peculiar and chilling monikers for male killers since the mid-1800s. The following names are a sampling of monikers given to male offenders who acted alone.

Monikers Given to Male Serial Killers in the United States

1846–1871	Edward H. Rulloff	The Educated Murderer
1874–1909	James P. Miller	"Deacon" Jim
1879	Stephen Lee Richards	Nebraska Fiend
1890–1905	Johann Otto Hoch	Bluebeard
1892–1896	Harry Howard Holmes	The Torture Doctor
1895	William H. T. Durrant	Demon of the Belfry
1910–1920	James P. Watson	Bluebeard
1910–1934	Albert Fish	The Cannibal The Moon Maniac
1911–1919	Joseph Mumfre	New Orleans Axeman
1921–1931	Harry Powers (a.k.a. Herman Drenth)	American Bluebeard
1926–1927	Earle L. Nelson	The Gorilla Murderer
1933–1935	Major Raymond Lisemba	Rattlesnake Lisemba
1942–1947	Jake Bird	Tacoma Axe Killer
1945–1946	William George Heirens	The Lipstick Murderer
1949	Harvey Louis Carignan	The Want-Ad Killer
1957–1960	Melvin David Rees	Sex Beast
1958–1983	Richard F. Biegenwald	The Thrill Killer
1962–1964	Albert Henry DeSalvo	The Measuring Man The Green Man The Boston Strangler
1964–1965	Charles H. Schmid	Pied Piper of Tucson
1964–1973	Edmund Emil Kemper	Coed Killer
1965	Posteal Laskey	Cincinnati Strangler
1967–1969	John N. Collins	Coed Murderer
1970	Richard Macek	The Mad Biter
1970–1987	Donald Harvey	Angel of Death
1972–1978	John Wayne Gacy	Killer Clown

1974–1975	Vaughn Greenwood	Skid Row Slasher
1974–1978	Theodore Robert Bundy	Ted
1974–1994	Ricardo Caputo	The Lady Killer
1976–1977	David R. Berkowitz	Son of Sam .44-Caliber Killer
1977–1978	Carlton Gary	Stocking Strangler
1977–1980	Richard Cottingham	The Ripper Jekyll/Hyde
1978	Richard T. Chase	Vampire Killer
1978–1979	Gerald Parker	Bedroom Basher
1978–1996	Theodore Kaczynski	The Unabomber
1979–1980	William Bonin	Freeway Killer
1980s	Roger Kibbe	I-15 Killer
1980s	Paul M. Stephanie	Weepy Voiced Killer
1980s	Craig Price	Slasher of Warwick
1980s	Randy Kraft	Score Card Killer
1980–1981	David Carpenter	Trailside Killer
1980–1982	Randall Woodfield	The I-5 Killer
1981	Masrion A. Pruett	Mad Dog Killer
1981–1982	Coral Eugene Watts	Sunday Morning Slasher
1984	Cleo Green	Red Demon
1984–2000	John Edward Robinson	Slavemaster
1985	Richard Ramirez	Night Stalker
1987	Richard Angelo	Angel of Death
1989–1990	Danny Rolling	Campus Killer Gainesville Ripper
1990–1995	Keith Jesperson	Happy Face Killer
1990–1991	Cleophus Prince	Clairmont Killer
1992	David L. Wood	Desert Killer
1992	Thomas Huskey	Zoo Man
1993–1995	Glenn Rogers	Cross Country Killer
1994–1995	Roy Enrique Conde	Tamiami Strangler
1994–1996	Anthony Balaam	Trenton Strangler
1997–1999	Angel Maturino Resendez	Railroad Killer

It is these bizarre killings that have contributed to the often distorted caricaturizations of serial offenders during the past 100 years. Many of the males since 1800 in the present study earned some type of moniker. Unlike the monikers for female serial killers, most names for males were designed to

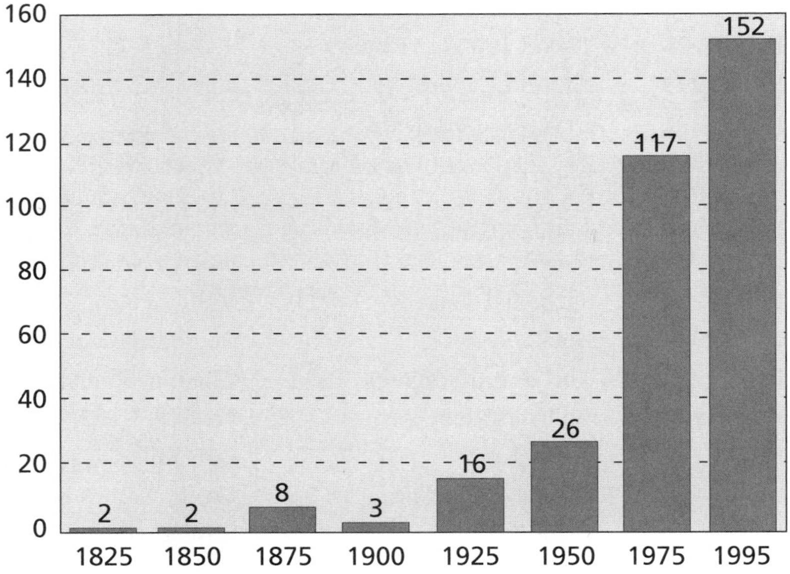

FIGURE 5.1 Frequency of Male Serial Killers in the United States, 1800–1995

N = 326 offenders

create an aura of mystery and fascination. Some male serial killers, because of extended killing careers or notoriety, earned more than one name.

Male serial killers have murdered men, women, children, the elderly, prostitutes, hitchhikers, transients, and patients. Each case brings with it unique situations, methods, weapons, and motivations. Following World War II, an increase in serial murders began that sharply accelerated during the late sixties and seventies. This rather dramatic "emergence" began to attract national attention in the mid- to late-1970s. During the 1980s serial murder became an increasing concern for law enforcement professionals and an important research area for social scientists. By the mid-1990s several law enforcement agencies had begun addressing multiple homicide during inservice training and seminars as well as colleges and universities offering special-topics courses in serial crime and multicide. Of the 337 male offenders in this study,* approximately 94% began their killings since the year 1900 (Figure 5.1). Between 1900 and 1924, 5% of offenders appeared; 8% between 1925 and 1949; 35% between 1950 and 1974; and 45% between 1975 and 1995. More offenders were identified in the 20-year time frame between 1975 and 1995 than during any previous 25-year span. Between 1995 and 2000 serial killers

*Coincidentally, the total number of male serial killers and the total number of cases of serial murder in this study are the same: 337.

have made regular appearances. Although the incidence of serial-killing cases is not as high as cases of mass murders (one every five to six days including both public and domestic cases) in the United States, serial murders have become part of our culturally violent landscape. They provide script for our slasher movies, sound bites for our newscasts, and fodder for crime novels. Table 5.1 lists a sample of films since 1995 with serial-murder themes.

The causes have yet to be determined for the sharp rise in serial homicides. In brief, some of these causes include (1) a belief in the emergence of a new breed of predatory criminal, (2) previous underreporting of such homicides, (3) self-fulfilling prophecy—you find what you expect to find by focusing specifically on serial killing, (4) inconsistency in defining the phenomenon, (5) the media's proliferation of "splatter" and "snuff" movies, (6) pornography depicting violence and other sado-erotic material, (7) a belief that changes in the economy are connected to surges of violent behavior, and (8) a feminist belief that serial killing is an extreme form of male domination of women based on patriarchy. Whatever the reasons for the apparent surge, we still must sort through and evaluate each case.

MYTHS OF SERIAL MURDER

The result of such an array of cases of serial murder as well as media focus has given rise to several general myths surrounding the phenomenon. With every myth, just as in every stereotype, there is a measure of truth. The following are long-held myths surrounding serial killers.

Myth	Fact
1. They are nearly all white.	One in five serial killers are black.
2. They are all male.	Nearly 17% are female.
3. They are insane.	Insanity is a legal term. Very few offenders (2–4%) are legally insane.
4. They are all lust killers.	Many are, but several cases do not involve sexual assaults, torture, or sexual mutilations.
5. They kill dozens of victims.	A few have high body counts but most kill under 10 victims.
6. They kill alone.	About one in four have one or more partners in murder.
7. Victims are beaten, stabbed, strangled, or tortured to death.	Some victims are poisoned or shot.
8. They are all very intelligent.	Most are of average intelligence.
9. They have high mobility in the United States.	Most offenders remain in a local area.
10. They are driven to kill because they were sexually abused as children.	Many kill as a result of rejection and abandonment in childhood.

Table 5.1 Sample of Films in the United States between 1995 and 2001 with Serial Murder Themes

1. The Glimmer Man	1996
2. The Mask of Sanity	1997
3. American Strays	1996
4. Crimetime	1996
5. Freeway	1996
6. Nightwatch	1998
7. Ratchet	1996
8. La Sindrome di Stendhal	1996
9. Turbulence	1997
10. Labyrinth of Dreams	1997
11. 8 Heads in a Duffel Bag	1997
12. Wana	1997
13. American Perfekt	1997
14. Kiss the Girls	1997
15. The Ugly	1997
16. Switchback	1997
17. Self Storage	1997
18. The Ripper	1997
19. Al Limite	1997
20. Fallen	1998
21. The Limbic Region	1996
22. Bloodmoon	1997
23. Bride of Chucky	1998
24. Closer and Closer	1996
25. Sailor Moon	1996
26. Inspector Morse	1997
27. Evil Obsession	1997
28. Angel Dust	1996
29. Cyberstalker	1996
30. Dr. Ice	1996
31. Revenge Quest	1996
32. Tails You Live, Heads You're Dead	1996
33. Deadly Sister	1996
34. Curdled	1996
35. Bloody Friday	1996

36.	Jack Frost	1996
37.	Humanoids From the Deep	1997
38.	Profile for Murder	1997
39.	Scream	1996
40.	Scream 2	1997
41.	Scream 3	2000
42.	Superstar	2000
43.	Wedding Murders	2000
44.	Serial Killing 4 Dummys	1999
45.	Hypnotic Murders	1998
46.	Postmortem	1998
47.	Sweetheart Murder	1998
48.	Serial Lover	1998
49.	Papertrail	1997
50.	Seaside Murder	1997
51.	Rough Draft	1997
52.	Showgirls	1996
53.	Moonlight Murder	1996
54.	Countdown	1996
55.	Serial Bomber	1996
56.	Paradise Lost	1996
57.	Serial Numbers	1996
58.	American Psycho	2000
59.	Clay Pigeons	1998
60.	Eye of The Beholder	2000
61.	The Bone Collector	1999
62.	I Know What You Did Last Summer	1997
63.	I Still Know What You Did Last Summer	1998
64.	Kiss The Girls and Make Them Die	1997
65.	The Minus Man	1999
66.	Summer of Sam	1999
67.	The Watcher	2000
68.	The Cell	2000
69.	Along Came a Spider	2001

Table 5.2 Distribution of Cases Involving Male Offenders across the United States, 1800–1995

State	Number of Cases in Which One or More Victims Were Killed	State	Number of Cases in Which One or More Victims Were Killed
California	57	Alaska	1–4
		Arizona	
		Arkansas	
Florida	19–27	Colorado	
Illinois		Delaware	
New York		Hawaii	
Texas		Idaho	
		Iowa	
		Kansas	
Alabama	5–9	Kentucky	
Connecticut		Louisiana	
Georgia		Maine	
Indiana		Maryland	
Massachusetts		Minnesota	
Michigan		Mississippi	
Nevada		Missouri	
New Jersey		Montana	
North Carolina		Nebraska	
Ohio		New Hampshire	
Oklahoma		New Mexico	
Oregon		North Dakota	
Pennsylvania		Rhode Island	
Washington		South Carolina	
Wisconsin		South Dakota	
		Tennessee	
		Utah	
		Vermont	
		Virginia	
		West Virginia	
		Wyoming	

The proliferation of serial-murder cases has been experienced in varying degrees by most states. It is unlikely that any states have not dealt with at least one or two cases in the past two decades. As far as the male offenders in the present study are concerned, every state reported having at least one case of serial murder since 1800 (Table 5.2). In all probability, cases have occurred in some states but have not been officially recorded because of lack of evidence or, as Egger (1990) observed, linkage blindness, which prevents related cases of serial murder from being connected to each other.

California by far surpasses any other state in identified cases. This high number may be explained in part by the pattern of high mobility of people relocating to or exiting the state. Also, many serial killings occur in densely populated areas. Note that the second category of states includes some highly populated areas. As mentioned earlier, serial murders can occur anywhere, but anonymity is more likely among crowds of strangers, and the probability is greater for more randomized killings in large cities than in small ones. Even these explanations, however, do not fully explain the wide disparity between California and other states. Of course, these are absolute figures and not related to population densities. Rossmo (1995) identified areas of the United States by comparing rates of serial-murder cases. Some states that are significantly less populated have higher rates of serial murder cases per 100,000 population.

In the present study, males were involved in over 90% (303 cases) of all serial-murder cases. In examining the age of offenders at the start of their killing careers, male offenders tended to be in their late twenties, with the average age at approximately 27.5 years. Where race or ethnicity could be determined, 73% of male offenders were white, 22% African American, 3% Hispanic, 1% Asian, and 1% other racial or ethnic groups ($N = 226$).

Most of the cases involving black male offenders have been documented in recent years. Chicago produced at least three black serial killers in 2000. Given the growing concentration of blacks in several major U.S. cities, coupled with the plight and blight of urbanization that has especially affected black people, we should not be surprised to see the "emergence" of the black serial killer. Some of the outward motivations for killing may appear different for blacks, including poverty and various forms of discrimination, but the final product will be the same. In truth, when blacks are killing blacks especially when the victims are black prostitutes, national press coverage is usually very limited in comparison to white offenders killing white victims. The author contends that African American serial killers are actually disproportionately overrepresented when comparing race and ethnicity of serial killers.

Serial murder in this study generally remained intra-racial, but cases such as the Stocking Strangler (see Profile 5.1) in Columbus, Georgia, and the black serial killer in Jackson, Mississippi, who murdered whites, suggest that racial boundaries are not sacred. Rarely, however, do blacks and whites team up as accomplices in serial killing.

MOBILITY AND VICTIMIZATION

Over half (55%) of all male offenders have been categorized as local serial killers—those who stay within the general area of a city or county but do not carry on their killing patterns in more than one state (Table 5.3). Approximately one-third of all male offenders killed victims in more than one state,

PROFILE 5.1 Carlton Gary, 1977–1978

Between September 16, 1977, and April 20, 1978, seven elderly white females were strangled to death in their homes in Columbus, Georgia. Two attempted murders of elderly women also occurred during this period of time. Eventually Carlton Gary, 34, "The Stocking Strangler," was arrested and charged with three of the homicides. Initially, Gary admitted he had been involved in all seven cases, but later he insisted that he was only present and did not participate in the murders. He was simply there to burglarize the residences, claimed Gary, but his history of crime seemed to suggest otherwise. His police record revealed a history of crimes involving robbing fast-food restaurants and steak houses in South Carolina, Georgia, and Florida. In 1970 he had been charged with the robbery, rape, and murder of an elderly woman in New York. He plea-bargained his way out by testifying against his partner.

Gary is described as a charmer, a ladies' man, very intelligent, and a "chronic talker." It was not until 1984 that police received a tip about a stolen gun that eventually linked Gary to the homicides. After his arrest he seemed to enjoy the notoriety he had gained so quickly. Eventually he attempted escape and when that failed he tried to kill himself. As the trial date drew closer, Gary attempted to feign mental illness but was unable to convince anyone.

Raised in a home without a father and then sent to his grandmother's house when his mother left, Gary had little home life. He dropped out of school in 1966, married, and was soon arrested for auto burglary. He and his wife moved to New York and started raising two children while Gary worked as a janitor and played drums in a band. By 1970 Gary had deserted his wife and children. His former wife described Gary as "gentle, kind, and dangerous." Gary traveled around under several aliases until he became involved in the murder of 74-year-old Nellie Farmer in New York.

Gary escaped from prison in New York one month before the stranglings began in Georgia, where he had moved to hide out. In 1979, after the killings in Georgia had ceased, he was arrested for a series of robberies in South Carolina and sent to prison for 21 years. Gary again escaped from prison in 1984, when he walked away from Goodman Correctional Institute in South Carolina, and headed to Florida to see his wife. Shortly afterward, Gary was arrested as the "Strangler."

Gary was found guilty of three of the Stocking Strangler cases, although a definite pattern had been established in the other cases and some palm prints had been found. He was convicted of murder, rape, and burglary in all three cases and sentenced to death for the crimes.

Carlton Gary's Victims

DATE	NAME	AGE	MARITAL STATUS	METHOD	SEXUAL ASSAULT
9/16/77	Mary F. Jackson	59	Widow	Strangled	Possible
9/25/77	Jean Dimenstein	71	Single	Strangled	Yes
10/21/77	Florence Scheible*	89	Widow	Strangled	Yes
10/25/77	Martha Thurmond*	69	Widow	Strangled	Yes
12/28/77	Kathleen Woodruff*	74	Widow	Strangled	No
2/12/78	Mildred D. Borom	78	Widow	Strangled	Possible
4/20/78	Janet T. Cofer	61	Widow	Strangled	Possible

*Gary officially charged with the murder.

Table 5.3 Victims of Male Offenders in the United States, 1800–1995, by Mobility Classification

Mobility Classification of Killers	1800–1995 Percentage of Victims (*N* = 2,613–3,807)	1800–1995 Percentage of Offenders (*N* = 337)	1975–1995 Percentage of Victims (*N* = 986–1,450)	1975–1995 Percentage of Offenders (*N* = 158)
Total	100	100	100	100
Traveling	36–37	35	26–35	27
Local	45–48	55	53–59	63
Place-specific	16–19	10	12–15	10

and 10% used their own homes or places of employment as killing sites. These data refute the stereotype that serial killers are men who primarily travel across the country in search of victims. Based on cases examined here, most offenders (65%) never killed outside the state in which they began their killing careers. However, we often associate serial murder with offenders who travel (see Profile 5.2).

By narrowing the time frame to the most recent years, when traveling would be expected to be at its highest rate, the percentage of offenders moving from state to state actually decreased. The number of male killers identified as place-specific, however, remained constant. In contrast, the number of offenders killing locally increased markedly from 1975 to 1995. Again, this increase may be in part due to rapid urbanization and a lessening need to travel in order to maintain anonymity. Finding, killing, and disposing of victims in and around cities may appeal to offenders in their quest to avoid detection.

Overall, the greatest percentage of victims were killed by local offenders. In recent years, nearly two-thirds of all victims were murdered by local killers. A significant decrease was noted in the number of victims of traveling offenders, challenging the popular myth that this group inflicts the greatest number of victims. A slight decline was also discovered in victims involving place-specific offenders. Proportionately, the mobility type of offenders responsible for the greatest percentage of victims are those who remain local. Male offenders who roamed the streets of U.S. cities and towns and remained relatively close to their killing sites appear to have been the most common type of serial murderer in recent years as well (see Profile 5.3).

Data on offenders were also examined relative to mobility and the average number of victims killed by each offender (Table 5.4). Overall, male offenders identified as place-specific were reported to have killed on the average more victims each than the other mobility types did. This finding suggests that killing at home or work offered perhaps a greater degree of "invisibility." Another explanation for the higher body counts of place-specific male serial killers may involve the type of victims targeted by these killers.

PROFILE 5.2 Traveling Serial Killers

A. John E. Armstrong, 26, a Navy veteran of seven years, confessed in 2000 of murdering 11 victims, all prostitutes he found in Seattle, Hawaii, Hong Kong, Singapore, Bangkok, and Virginia. An amiable and professional petty officer, Armstrong had a dark side that harbored a deep hatred for whores. He would pay for sex then afterward yell "I hate whores" and strangle them. His last three victims were in the Detroit area. He was arrested once DNA evidence conclusively linked him to some of the earlier murders.

B. Wayne A. Ford, 36, a long-haul truck driver, turned himself into California police in November of 1998 claiming to have killed four female prostitutes or hitchhikers dating back to 1997. The victims had been killed in different counties in California. To prove that he was serious Ford produced a bag from his jacket pocket containing a woman's breast. Ford said that he was angry with his ex-wife who denied him visitation with their son. Ford started killing and dismembering the women as his frustrations and anger toward his exwife increased. The victims were strangled and beaten to death. One corpse he kept in a refrigerator but would not explain his motivations for doing so.

C. Angel M. Resendez, 39, also known as Rafael Resendez-Ramirez, "The Railroad Killer," is believed to have killed between 8 and 13 victims in five states. All the killings occurred in homes near the railroad tracks. Resendez entered the United States illegally several times since 1976. He killed both men and women and then hopped freight trains to other areas of the state or country. Married with a young child, no one suspected this mild-mannered man to be someone who used over 30 aliases and raped, shot, and beat victims to death. Angel claims to have killed many, many more victims and investigators are looking for connections between Angel and nearly 200 young women abducted and killed in northern Mexico.

Local offenders each killed fewer numbers of victims in relation to other mobility groups. In recent years, as illustrated in Table 5.4, the victim-offender averages dropped slightly for both traveling and local mobility types. Place-specific offenders decreased more noticeably but still maintain the highest average number of victims per offender. This could simply mean that reporting of body counts in recent years has become more accurate. For example, in several historical accounts H. H. Holmes was reported to have killed at least 200 women in Chicago in his "Murder Castle" during the late 1800s. However, a report citing police investigations indicated a body count of 27 victims. Clearly, cases with large body counts should always be critically examined. Often high victim counts are more the result of sensationalism than of what actually occurred. Certainly high victim counts are possible but they should always be questioned.

In summarizing the connection between mobility and victimization, it appears that place-specific offenders in recent years killed the greatest number of

PROFILE 5.3 Robert Joe Long, 1984

During an eight-month period in 1984, at least ten young women ranging in age from 18 to 28 were abducted in the Tampa Bay, Florida, area. Each victim was bound, sexually assaulted, and then murdered. The victims, most of whom were prostitutes, were strangled, although one had her throat cut and another died from gunshot. The perpetrator, Robert Long, 31, generally drove his car around an area frequented by prostitutes and then lured his victims into his vehicle. Long, who was on probation for assault, was divorced and unemployed. He experienced sadistic pleasure from fashioning a collar and leash from rope and using them on his victims. Shortly before his capture, Long abducted Lisa McVey from a doughnut shop in Tampa. He took her to an apartment and subjected her to 26 hours of sexual assault and then released her. The information she provided allowed police from three jurisdictions to "zero in" on Robert Joe Long. The impressive forensic work, involving the comparison of his clothing fibers, carpet fibers, semen, tire treads, ligature marks, and rope knots, influenced Long to make a full confession. Fiber evidence alone linked most of Long's victims to his vehicle. Long pled guilty in a plea-bargain arrangement to eight of the homicides and the abduction and rape of Lisa McVey. He received 26 life sentences, 7 requiring no parole for 25 years. Long then received two separate death sentences for the murders of Virginia Johnson and Michelle Simms. He now sits on death row in Florida (Terry and Malone, 1987).

Robert Long's Victims

DATE VICTIM MISSING	DATE VICTIM FOUND	NAME	AGE	OCCUPATION	METHOD	MUTILATION
5/10/84	5/13/84	Long thi Nguyen	20	Exotic dancer	Strangled	Bludgeoned
5/25/84	5/27/84	Michelle Simms	22	Prostitute	Cut throat	Head bludgeoned
6/8/84	6/24/84	Elizabeth Loundeback	22	Factory worker	Unknown	Unknown
10/1/84	10/7/84	Chanel Williams	18	Prostitute	Gunshot to head	Neck puncture
10/13/84	10/14/84	Karen Dinsfriend	28	Prostitute	Strangled	Head bludgeoned
9/31/84	10/31/84	Kimberly Hopps	20s	Prostitute	Unknown	Unknown
10/15/84	10/16/84	Virginia Johnson	18	Waitress/ prostitute	Strangled	Unknown
11/9/84	11/12/84	Kim Swann	21	Student/ nude dancer	Strangled	No
9/7/84	11/16/84	Vicky Elliot	21	Waitress	Strangled	Unknown
3/28/84	11/22/84	Artis Wick	18	Unknown	Unknown	Unknown

Table 5.4 Average Number of Victims by Mobility Classification of Male Offenders, 1800–1995

Mobility	1800–1995 Average Number of Victims per Offender ($N = 337$)	1975–1995 Average Number of Victims per Offender ($N = 158$)
Traveling	8–12	6–12
Local	7–9	6–8
Place-specific	12–20	9–11

victims each. This helps refute the media stereotype of serial killers in recent years—a male who is extremely mobile. Although place-specific offenders were responsible for many victims, on the average most serial killers in recent years have been local offenders. Local killers were much more common than traveling killers but did not appear to have each killed as many victims per offender. Also, the data in this study indicate that local offenders as a group are responsible for the greatest total number of victims.

Place-specific cases often receive limited press coverage unless they involve high body counts and the victims died violently. For example, most Americans know who Ted Bundy was but have never heard of Donald Harvey (Profile 5.4). This can be partially explained by the types of victims selected. Harvey quietly poisoned and suffocated male hospital patients, whereas Bundy brutally tortured and sexually mutilated young females.

VICTIMS

As mentioned earlier, findings from this study support the belief that serial murder involves primarily stranger-to-stranger violence. Overall, 90% of all male offenders since 1975 killed at least one stranger (Table 5.5). The killing of family and acquaintances by male serial killers all but disappeared in recent years. Although male offenders killed a large variety of strangers, they appeared to have their preferences. Table 5.6 provides a list of strangers, acquaintances, and family victims sought out by the offenders in this study.

Young females, especially if they were alone, ranked the highest in general preference of offenders. Of this category, prostitutes appeared to be the most readily accessible victims who could also be easily disposed of. However, many women who never engaged in prostitution were also victimized. Hitchhikers, students walking alone, women living alone or seeking employment, and women engaged in certain professions and jobs (such as nurses, models, and waitresses) sometimes or frequently increased their risk factor by associating with total strangers. Females who had lifestyles or employment that tended to bring them into contact with strangers appeared to increase their chances of being victimized. (Prostitutes and hitchhikers were at the highest level of risk.) In some cases

PROFILE 5.4 Donald Harvey, 1970–1987

Donald Harvey, "The Angel of Death," started killing when he turned 18 and began working as a nurse's aide at Mary Mount Hospital in Laurel County, Kentucky. He first killed an aunt, then committed what he referred to as "accidental homicides," followed by 10 more patient deaths—a total of 13 dead in 10 months. Some were suffocated, others had their oxygen supply shut off, and one victim died when Harvey shoved a wire coat hanger up his catheter tube, tearing his bladder.

Harvey then joined the Air Force, where he attempted suicide on two occasions. Unable to cope, he was discharged after only nine months of service, but he continued to receive psychiatric care. In 1975 he joined the nursing staff at the Veterans Administration Hospital in Cincinnati, Ohio. During a two-year period he is believed to have murdered another 17 patients. His remaining eight years at the hospital were spent working as an autopsy assistant in the morgue. Being exposed to death and corpses seemed to satisfy Harvey, and apparently he killed no one during this time. In 1985 he was asked to resign when a gun, books on the occult, syringes, and slides of human tissue were discovered in his hospital locker.

He then joined the staff at Drake Hospital, also in Cincinnati, without anyone ever checking his references. Most of the patients at Drake were the elderly and the terminally ill. Using cyanide, arsenic, and sometimes injections of cleaning fluids, Harvey was able to kill at least 21 victims in a two-year period. When he had no poison for their food or IVs, Harvey suffocated his victims. Harvey later referred to his actions as mercy killings. He had become the angel of death and held the power over who would live and who must die. He finally confessed when investigators discovered large amounts of cyanide in the stomach of a victim. This final victim brought Harvey's total number of homicides to between 54 and 58. Almost all his victims were male; among his possessions police discovered a list of victims yet to be killed by Harvey. One of his female coworkers had hepatitis serum poured into her coffee by Harvey but miraculously survived her ordeal. Harvey also slowly poisoned his roommate only to nurse him back to health.

During his confession, Harvey explained that during a 13-year period, starting when he was five years old, he had been subjected to sexual molestation by an uncle and a male neighbor. He did not believe that this frequent molestation had anything to do with the fact that almost all his victims were helpless males, older than himself; nor did he feel it had anything to do with the fact he was a homosexual. He claimed to be a compassionate, caring person, which seemed to be validated by his fellow workers. They found Harvey to be dedicated, polite, and a good colleague. The courts found Harvey to be sane under law and competent to stand trial.

Harvey gave his confession only after being allowed to plea-bargain and thereby escape the death penalty. Dozens of bodies were exhumed, and the victims were found to have died as Harvey described. Never showing remorse or guilt, Harvey received three consecutive life sentences and will not be eligible for parole until he has served at least 60 years. He was also fined $270,000 and received a life sentence for the murders in Kentucky. After several years in prison Harvey has changed his mind about what influenced him to kill. He now states that the sexual abuse he experienced as a child was indeed a major contributing factor fueling his urges to kill.

Table 5.5 Percentage of Male Offenders Murdering Family, Acquaintances, and Strangers in the United States, 1800–1995

Relationship	1800–1995 Percentage of Offenders (N = 316)	1975–1995 Percentage of Offenders (N = 150)
Strangers	70	73
Strangers/acquaintances	13	16
Acquaintances	8	7
Strangers/family	3	1
Family	3	1
Acquaintances/family	3	1
All	1	1

Table 5.6 Rank Order of Types of Victims Selected by Male Serial Killers

A. Strangers

1. Young females alone
   - Prostitutes
   - Hitchhikers
   - Students
   - Women at home selected randomly
   - Women seeking employment
   - Nurses, models, waitresses
2. Children alone
   - Boys
   - Girls
3. Travelers
   - People in cars
   - Campers
4. Young males alone
   - Hitchhikers
   - Skid-row derelicts
   - Laborers
   - Military
5. Employers/business
   - Gas stations
   - Fast-food outlets
6. Elderly alone
   - Female
   - Male
7. Patients
   - Elderly
   - Infants
   - Others
8. Police
9. Racial targets
   - Blacks
   - Whites

B. Acquaintances

- Young women
- People in community
- People in own group/coworkers/employers
- Neighbors
- Children
- Visitors, transients
- Schoolmates
- Patients
- Roommates

C. Family

- Wives
- In-laws
- Children
- Mothers, brothers, grandparents

the community was aware that a serial killer was operating in the area. Yet some women would continue to take risks because, as Edmund Kemper, serial killer "extraordinaire," pointed out, "They [the victims] judged me not to be the one" (Profile 5.5). This does not mean that female victims should bear culpability but that in most cases women are much more vulnerable to men than men are to women by nature of physical strength and perceived motivation to kill.

Male serial killers also frequently targeted children as victims (category A2 in Table 5.6). Primarily, the majority of victims were the powerless being exploited by the more powerful. (As one researcher pointed out, you don't ever hear of these offenders going after bodybuilders.) The rest of the categories also include victims who were easily isolated and taken by surprise.

The next-largest group of target victims, after strangers, was acquaintances. Again, young women were the most frequent victims identified. Finally, in the category of family victims, wives were most likely to be killed, followed by in-laws and children. Although people are more likely to be spanked, whipped, beaten, and killed in their own homes by family members than anywhere else or by anyone else (Gelles & Cornell, 1990), serial murderers seldom are the perpetrators. Despite the fact that much of what they have become is rooted in family dysfunction and trauma, serial killers usually do not kill family members, except for mothers. According to an in-depth study by Underwood (2000), siblicide, or the killing of a sibling by another sibling, very often is initiated by alcohol and culminates in a shooting death. Serial killers are much more likely to direct their aggression outside the family. Although we often hear of serial killers who hated their mothers, mothers are rarely victims. A myth has been created and perpetrated about serial offenders killing their mothers because such cases tend to be frequently dramatized (Lucas and Kemper, for example). There exists a much greater likelihood that offenders wanting to kill their mothers inevitably find themselves killing someone else. These proxy killers continue to kill their mother's image repeatedly by seeking out unsuspecting females.

Patterns in victimization should also be examined for additional insight into the mind of the murderer. Approximately 40% of male offenders targeted females only, whereas one-fifth killed males exclusively (Table 5.7, p. 149). Only 37% of offenders killed both males and females.

As expected, males were more likely to kill females than males. Four-fifths of offenders killed at least one female victim. Surprisingly, however, nearly 60% of male offenders killed at least one male victim. Often the primary targets were females, but frequently males were killed, which suggests that a person's gender often did not preclude victimization. Over 40% of all offenders killed only adults, whereas only small percentages of offenders specifically targeted children, teens, or the elderly.

Approximately one in five offenders killed at least one child, 45% killed at least one teenager, and eight out of ten offenders killed at least one adult. In addition, one in six offenders murdered at least one or more elderly persons. If we account for only the past few years, the elderly were increasingly being selected by male serial killers.

PROFILE 5.5 Edmund Emil Kemper III, 1964–1973

"I just wondered how it would feel to shoot grandma," Kemper, a boy of only 15 years of age, explained to police. His confession was calm and very matter-of-fact. He walked up behind his grandmother and shot her in the back of the head, shot her two more times in the back, and repeatedly stabbed her. Then he waited for grandpa to come home and shot him to death on the porch.

Born in 1948, Ed was raised by a domineering mother who frequently berated him in public. His parents were divorced when he was nine. When he was eight, his mother had forced him to sleep in the cellar of the house for nearly eight months, his only exit through a trap door that usually had the kitchen table on it. Ed would later claim a deep love-hate relationship with his mother, which for him was a constant source of frustration. His mother married several times while Kemper was young, preventing him from ever drawing close to male role models.

As a child Ed sometimes acted out his own death through mock executions. His younger sister would act as the executioner, and Ed would role-play a person in the death throes in the gas chamber. He later admitted to fantasizing about killing his family, especially his older sister, who he believed received more love and attention. His sister remembered receiving a doll for Christmas only to find it a few days later with the head and hands cut off. Kemper's fantasies became more violent, and he killed the family cat by burying it alive and then decapitating it. He placed the head on a spindle and prayed over it. One day his sister teased him about the fact that he liked his school teacher and wanted to kiss her—to which he replied, "If I kissed her I'd have to kill her first." Years later this statement proved to be extremely insightful.

At 13, Ed ran away to see his father but was then quickly sent to live with his grandparents. Ed's mother warned her exhusband that sending Ed to his grandparents could be very dangerous. A year and a half later Ed killed them. Kemper turned himself in and was subsequently placed in the Atascadero State Psychiatric hospital. During his incarceration he behaved as a model patient and impressed one psychiatrist so much that he allowed Kemper to administer psychological tests to other patients. Kemper learned the requisite psychological jargon and therapeutic skills to convince a parole board, against the advice of psychiatrists, to release him after only six years. Kemper returned to live with his mother and soon became embroiled in their usual fighting. However, Ed was now fully grown—280 pounds and 6 feet 8 inches tall. His IQ had been measured at 136, but he could only manage holding a job as a flagman for a construction company. At this point, his outward interests appeared normal for a young man, yet inwardly his violent rages and fantasies continued to grow.

In 1970–1971, Kemper began picking up young female hitchhikers, psychologically preparing himself for his mission. At the age of 23, Ed started killing again, a task that would entail nearly a year and eight more victims. He shot, stabbed, and strangled them. All were strangers to him, and all were hitchhikers. He cannibalized at least two of his victims, slicing off parts of their legs and cooking the flesh in a macaroni casserole. He decapitated all of his victims and dissected most of them, saving body parts for sexual pleasure, sometimes storing heads in the refrigerator. Ed collected "keepsakes," including teeth, skin, and hair from the victims. After killing a victim, he often engaged in sex with the corpse, even after it had been decapitated.

On one occasion Kemper visited at length with psychiatrists, who stated at the conclusion of the interview that Ed was now safe and would not harm another person. They agreed at the meeting to have Kemper's juvenile record sealed to allow him to lead a normal life. Only Ed knew that, at that very moment, the head of one of his victims was in the trunk of his car in the parking lot. Kemper recalls an incident in which he was returning to his apartment with the head of a college coed he had just murdered. As he mounted the staircase carrying the bowling bag with the head, he encountered a young couple descending the stairs apparently going on a date. Ironically, he mused that they were going on a date and so was he, but those realities were so very far apart. Kemper finally decided to kill his mother; early one morning on Easter weekend, he entered her bedroom carrying a hammer and a large hunting knife (which he called "General"). After smashing her in the head, he slashed her throat, cut out the larynx, and placed it in the garbage disposal. Severing her head, he had sex with the corpse.

Ed would later explain that he was killing his mother all along, and once she was dead he could stop the murder spree. Perhaps as a final insult to his mother, he invited her best friend over for Sunday dinner. When she arrived, Kemper also strangled her and severed her head. Leaving a note for the police, Ed drove east to Colorado, where he had thoughts of climbing up a hill near the highway and shooting travelers as they drove by. Instead he called the police and, after being told to call back several times, convinced them he was the "Coed Killer," so named by the news media. Hours later, while Kemper was still waiting at the pay phone, police arrived and placed him under arrest.

In his confession Kemper stated five different reasons for his crimes. His themes centered on sexual urges, wanting to possess his victims, trophy hunting, a hatred for his mother, and revenge against an unjust society (Leyton, 1985, p. 70).

Elliot Leyton insightfully integrated Kemper's often bizarre reasoning into one single theory for his murderous behavior:

> As he slipped into the social niche of celebrated multiple murderer, he cured society's indifference to him and did so while exacting his fearful revenge and indulging all his repressed sexuality. . . . He had come to terms with that "total frustration," which all our multiple murderers remedy in their crusades. . . . This should not be any surprise, for he has confronted all the major issues in his life and resolved them. Kemper has, in his own terms, rewritten his personal history and, in the lunacy of destruction, created himself (1986a, p. 72).

Edmund Kemper was sentenced to life imprisonment. He was denied parole at his first hearing in 1980 and at this writing remains incarcerated in a California prison.

(continued)

Profile 5.5 Continued

Edmund Kemper's Victims

DATE OF MURDER	NAME	AGE	RELATIONSHIP	METHOD	SEXUAL ASSAULT	CORPSE MUTILATION
8/24/64	Maude Kemper	66	Grandmother	Shooting/ stabbing	No	No
8/24/64	Ed Kemper I	72	Grandfather	Shooting	No	No
5/7/72	Mary A. Pesce	18	Stranger	Stabbing	Body parts	Decapitated, dissected
5/7/72	Anita Luchessa	18	Stranger	Stabbing	Body parts	Decapitated, dissected
9/14/72	Aiko Koo	15	Stranger	Suffocation/ strangulation	Necrophilia	Decapitated, dissected, severed hands
1/8/73	Cindy Schall	19	Stranger	Shooting	Necrophilia	Decapitated, dissected
2/5/73	Rosalind Thorpe	23	Stranger	Shooting	Possible	Decapitated
2/5/73	Alice Liu	21	Stranger	Shooting	Necrophilia	Decapitated, severed hands
4/20/73	Clarnell Kemper	40s	Mother	Hammer/ cut throat	Necrophilia	Decapitated, dissected
4/20/73	Sara Hallet	40s	Mother's friend	Strangled	No	Decapitated

Table 5.7 Percentage of Male Serial Killers Murdering People in Specific Victim Age and Gender Categories, $N = 329$

Age Only		Gender Only	
Children	4	Females	40
Teens	6	Males	22
Adults	43	Both	37
Elderly	3		
At least one		**At least one**	
Child	21	Female	78
Teen	45	Male	58
Adult	82		
Elderly	16		
Combinations		**Variations**	
Adults and children	6	One or more female adults	67
Adults and teens	28	One or more adult males	48
Teens and children	3	Both adult males and females	30
All age groups	7	One or more female teenagers	34
		One or more male teenagers	16
		Both male and female teens	5
		One or more female children	13
		One or more male children	13
		Both male and female children	4

Table 5.8 Degree of Victim Facilitation in Being Murdered by Male Offenders, 1800–1995

Facilitation	1800–1995 Percentage of Offenders ($N = 303$)	1975–1995 Percentage of Offenders ($N = 145$)
Low	66	56
High	13	18
Both	21	26

Female adults were victimized by over two-thirds of these offenders, whereas only about half reported killing at least one adult male victim. Less than one-third of offenders was found to have killed at least both male and female adults. Often offenders killed both adults and teens, but they rarely killed both adults and children. In short, adult victims appeared to be the most frequent targets sought out by male serial killers. Children were frequently victimized, but not as often as adults. The elderly appeared to be picked as victims more frequently in recent years, possibly as a result of their rapidly increasing numbers, as well as their accessibility to offenders.

Table 5.8 gives the percentages of victim facilitation. Overall, most victims did not place themselves in particularly vulnerable positions at the time

PROFILE 5.6 Albert Henry DeSalvo, 1962–1964

Perhaps he could have been stopped, but the signs were ignored or missed, and Albert DeSalvo—also known as "The Measuring Man," "The Green Man," and "The Boston Strangler"—murdered 13 innocent women. Born in Chelsea, Massachusetts, in 1931, DeSalvo was forced to live in extremely impoverished conditions. Often hungry and cold, he was subjected to cruel beatings at the hands of his alcoholic father. He was also forced to watch while his father abused and beat his mother. On one occasion he watched as his father broke each of his mother's fingers one after the other. On another occasion his father sold him and his sister into slavery to a farmer for several months. In 1944 Mrs. DeSalvo divorced her husband, taking her six children with her.

His love for his mother and his hatred for his father seemed to bring out the worst in Albert. He remembered later how much he enjoyed shooting cats with his bow and arrow, especially when the arrows protruded through their bellies. His father had trained him well in stealing from stores, and Albert became proficient at the task. He gradually developed a liking for breaking and entering homes, which he began to do frequently.

By the time he was 12, Albert had been arrested twice, once for larceny and once for breaking and entering. He was incarcerated at Lyman School for delinquent boys, where he learned a great deal more about burglary. After his release he began to apply himself full time to breaking and entering homes. Albert constantly seemed to try to bridge the gap between himself and those who had money and possessions. He was no more able to attain middle-class respectability than he was able to satisfy his apparently enormous sex drive. He became sexually active with both girls and homosexuals in the neighborhood and gained a reputation for his remarkable sexual capacity. At 17 he joined the military and served with the occupation forces in Germany. Before returning, he won the U.S. Army middleweight boxing championship and married his wife, Irmgard. In 1955, at age 23, Albert was charged with his first sex offense, involving the molestation of a 9-year-old girl. The charges were dropped when the parents refused to proceed with the case. In 1956, he was honorably discharged from the military.

In 1958 Albert's first child was born and he briefly ceased his breaking-and-entering activities. However, his wife refused to submit to his excessive sexual demands, and his financial status seemed to be worsening. In a short time Albert received two separate suspended sentences for breaking and entering. Before long, he earned the nickname "The Measuring Man" by conning his way into scores of apartments by explaining that he represented a modeling agency and was in

they were targeted, but this appears to have changed slightly in recent years. Since 1975 nearly one in five offenders attacked and killed victims who had facilitated their own deaths by placing themselves at risk. One-fourth of all offenders in recent years targeted victims in both high and low categories.

In cases of serial murder, seldom do we perceive of victims as having precipitated their own deaths through acts of provocation. Most victims were unaware of the immediate danger when first they met their killers, especially in cases where males targeted females. In addition, not all offenders concerned themselves with the easiest target. In one case, the offender felt the

search of talent. Producing a measuring tape, he would take occupants' personal measurements, touching them inappropriately whenever possible. He later would claim that most of his victims were quite willing to have their measurements taken, that few complained and a few even removed their clothing. He never attacked or harmed any of them but promised they would soon be hearing from his agency.

Eventually Albert was arrested once again for breaking and entering and was sentenced to two years' imprisonment. He earned his release in 11 months. According to police, at that time DeSalvo was still known only as a breaking-and-entering criminal. He returned home, only again to be rejected by his wife until such time that he could prove he had mended his ways. Overwhelmed with frustration, Albert began changing from the harmless "Measuring Man" to an aggressive, violent personality. He began tying up some of his victims and raping them. He always wore green pants during these forays and was soon dubbed "The Green Man." Police estimate he attacked several women. Feelings of rejection, sexual frustration, and inferiority to others became intolerable by June of 1962, when he attempted his first murder of a woman in her apartment. Apparently, during the attack he saw himself in a mirror by the bed and it jolted his sensibilities, so he stopped. A week later he began killing in earnest.

Most of DeSalvo's victims were strangled and sexually assaulted. Over 60% were older women, although most of his last few victims were young women. He seemed to enjoy desecrating the corpse and then ransacking the apartment.

Although DeSalvo was unsure of his motives for killing, he was even less sure why he suddenly stopped in January 1964. Perhaps he felt he had given the supreme insult to society through the explicit humiliation of his last victims. DeSalvo continued to enter the homes of unsuspecting women as "The Green Man," tying them up and raping them, but he no longer killed his victims. Eventually, after a description had been given to the police by one of his victims, Albert was arrested as "The Green Man" and was linked to sexual assaults in Massachusetts, Connecticut, New Hampshire, and Rhode Island. He was sent to Bridgewater, a mental institution, for evaluation, but not until the spring of 1965 did he confess to being "The Boston Strangler."

DeSalvo's confession, however, was given under special circumstances that protected him from prosecution for the murders. He never came to trial for the murders but instead was sent to prison for his many sexual assaults committed as "The Green Man." In 1967, he entered Walpole State Prison to serve a life sentence. Six years later Albert DeSalvo was stabbed to death by a fellow inmate.

(continued)

urge to kill and tried to abduct a woman who was sitting in her car at a street intersection waiting for the light to change. Another just moved around neighborhoods, knocking on doors, until he found somebody at home.

The element of surprise is particularly operative in serial murder. Consequently, offenders take time to stalk a victim without giving warning signals. Thus, a "selective" hitchhiker—one who is careful about getting in with "just anybody"—probably incurs the same risks as anyone else who hitchhikes. One investigator described serial killers as "charming" people; however, once they get you into their "comfort zone" it's too late to back out (see Profile 5.6).

PROFILE 5.6 Continued

Albert DeSalvo's Victims

DATE OF MURDER	NAME	AGE	METHOD	SEXUAL ASSAULT	CORPSE DESECRATION	RESIDENCE SEARCHED
6/14/62	Anna Slesers	55	Blow to head/ strangulation	No	Bow under chin	No
6/28/62	Mary Mullen	85	Strangulation	No	No	No
6/30/62	Helen Blake	65	Strangulation	Yes	Bite marks; legs apart; bow under chin	Yes
6/30/62	Nina Nichols	68	Strangulation	Yes	Bottle in vagina; legs apart; bow under chin	Yes
8/19/62	Ida Irga	75	Strangulation	Yes	Legs apart and propped up on chairs; bite marks; twisted pillowcase around neck	Yes
8/20/62	Jane Sullivan	67	Strangulation	Yes	Body left in kneeling position, face down in bathtub; exposed	Yes
12/5/62	Sophie Clark	20	Strangulation	Yes	Legs apart; gag in mouth; bow under chin	Yes
12/30/62	Patricia Bissette	23	Strangulation	Yes	Bow under chin	Yes
3/9/63	Mary Brown	69	Fractured skull/ stabbing/strangulation	Yes	Table fork embedded in breast	Yes
5/6/63	Beverly Samans	23	Multiple stab wounds to throat and breast	Yes	Gagged; legs apart tied to bed posts; bow under chin	?
9/8/63	Evelyn Corbin	58	Strangulation	Yes	Underpants stuffed in mouth; bow tied on ankle	Yes
11/23/63	Joann Graff	23	Strangulation	Yes	Bite marks on breast; bow under chin	Yes
1/4/64	Mary Sullivan	19	Strangulation	Yes	Legs apart; broom handle in vagina; bow under chin; Happy New Year card	?

Table 5.9 Selected Occupations of Male Offenders before or during Their Career of Murder

Skilled	Semiskilled	Unskilled
Aircraft company	Woodsman	Laborer
Shoemaker	Truck driver	Hotel porter
Car upholsterer	Warehouse employee	Gas attendant
Electrician/carpenter	Bartender	Garbage collector
TV repairman	Boiler operator	Kitchen worker
Plumber	Farmer	**Criminal**
Electronics technician	Nurse's aide	Thief
Building contractor	House painter	Con-artist
Computer operator	Barber	Pimp
Mechanic	Factory worker	Burglar
Nurse	Construction worker	Robber
	Motel clerk	
	Store clerk	

Government/professional	Other
Security, auxiliary police officer	Transient/drifter/vagrant
Military personnel	Cult follower
Minister	Student
Business owner: hotel, plantation, ranch, bakery	Former mental patient
Lecturer	
Physician	
Clerk	
Salesman	
Musician	
Social worker	
Postal worker	
Accountant	
Photographer	

OFFENDERS' BACKGROUNDS AND OCCUPATIONS

The male serial killers in this study came from a wide variety of backgrounds and occupations. Educational attainment was often only high school or less, some vocational training, or a year or two in college. Very few offenders held college degrees. Offenders generally held blue-collar jobs, but a few managed to secure professional work as teachers, doctors, musicians, and ministers.

Table 5.9 provides an overview of various types of employment held by male offenders before or during their killing careers. Some offenders held responsible positions that provided regular employment. Some used their employment to facilitate victim selection: For example, a building contractor lured boys in search of work; a nurse's aide killed patients; a bartender killed his female employees; a farmer killed his laborers; a hotel clerk killed tenants; a physician killed his patients; a few salesmen killed their customers. Other offenders did not connect their employment in any way to their victims, and still other offenders were transients, unemployed, or recently out of jail or prison.

Contrary to popular opinion, male serial killers in this present study, as in the previous one, were not usually highly educated nor did they commonly hold professional or even skilled careers. Occasionally an offender did appear to be extremely intelligent or had a prestigious occupation, but this type of offender tended to be the exception, not the rule. Because of the sensational nature of the serial-murder phenomenon, it is not surprising that we tend to seize on unsubstantiated evidence, especially if such information tends to create further distortion of offender profiles. Indeed, offenders' ability to kill reportedly without detection appears to be more a function of cunning and deceit than intellectual abilities or academic attainments. Commonly, offenders have been profiled as the "law student," the "lecturer," or the "businessman" when in reality they have had very little exposure to those roles. This appears to happen most often in the more sensationalized cases. For example, Ted Bundy was portrayed as a law student, but he had never completed any coursework. "Law student" was merely a status symbol that Bundy used to infiltrate more easily the communities in which he roamed. In short, we have perpetuated a myth about male serial killers that is based on only a few sensational cases. Blue-collar work and unskilled labor have been found to be much more common among male offenders than higher-level employment.

Two of the most important factors in the construction of the stereotypic serial killer are found in the methods and motives of offenders. Table 5.10 provides a breakdown of methods used by offenders to kill their victims, based on police and autopsy reports, which specify the exact cause of death as well as other contributing factors, including nonlethal injuries. In serial killing we are often faced with a process of murder rather than a brief act. Consequently, offenders were frequently found to have used a variety of nonlethal, potentially lethal, and lethal attacks on the victim. In contrast to typical homicides, domestic or otherwise, male serial offenders do not commonly use guns as their sole means of killing. In this study, firearms were used in approximately 40% of the cases, but not as the main mode of death.

The victims in this study may have actually died from strangulation, a bullet to the head, or a stab to the heart, but these often were the final acts committed after the victim had been successfully tortured, mutilated, and/or beaten by the offender. Conversely, a few offenders, such as necrophiles, would kill their victims as quickly as possible before they began their sexual assaults, mutilations, and trophy collecting. Other offenders engaged in physical assaults before, during, and after the death of the victim. In one case the offender tortured his victims for several days before finally killing them. The fact that such acts of torture, beatings, and mutilations often preceded the act of murder indicates they should be viewed as part of the methodology of serial killing. One offender stated in an interview with me that "the response of the

Table 5.10 Methods and Motives of Male Serial Murderers in the United States, 1800–1995

Methods (*N* = 337)		Motives (*N* = 337)	
Some firearms*	41%	Sex sometimes*	46%
Some strangulation/suffocation	37	Control sometimes	29
Some stabbed	34	Money sometimes	19
Some bludgeoning	26	Enjoyment sometimes	16
Firearms only	19	Sex only	9
Stabbed only	13	Racism	7
Strangulation/suffocation only	11	Money only	7
Bludgeoning only	9	Mental problems	6
Some poison	6	Cult-inspired sometimes	5
Poison only	5	Hatred	4
Some drowning	3	Urge sometimes	3
Other	2	Attention	2
Combination of the preceding methods	42	Enjoyment only	2
		Combination of the preceding motives	50

*"Some" or "sometimes" denotes that offenders killed one or more victims by a specific method or for a specific reason.

PROFILE 5.7 Robert Hansen, 1973–1983

Robert Hansen, 44, admitted having a "severe inferiority complex with girls." To compensate, he began raping women and inevitably started torturing and murdering them. Hansen, considered to be Alaska's worst mass murderer in history, confessed to killing 17 prostitutes, nude dancers, and other women whom he resented. Hansen described to police how he—while working as a baker in Anchorage—abducted young women over a ten-year period. Hansen later worked as a respected businessman and was nationally known for his big-game hunting. He explained how he had abducted more than 50 women and taken them in his plane to his mountain retreat. If they gave him free sex, he would spare their lives, but any demand for money sealed their doom. Hansen would often strip his victim naked and then give her a head start to escape from him in the wilderness. He explained how much he enjoyed hunting victims down with his .223-caliber Ruger mini-14 rifle, a weapon used by hunters. He usually kept his victims tied up in his cabin for several days of sadistic rape and torture before sending them naked into the woods to be hunted.

victim was everything." This meant that without torture, killing a victim was merely going through the motions (see Profile 5.7).

Another commonly held myth about male serial killers is that their primary motivations for murder are sexually rooted. Consequently, the typical

Table 5.11 Percentage of Male Offenders Reporting a History of Violent, Criminal, or Abnormal Behavior

History	Percentage of Offenders (N = 198)
Prior incarceration in prison or mental institution	67
Property crimes	45
Sex-related crimes	37
Crimes against children	18
Illegal drugs	17
Fire-setting or animal abuse	14
Homicide	13
Assault	6
Combination of preceding behaviors	68

stereotype of the offender is the "lust killer," who is driven to kill for sexual gratification. Most serial killings we hear and read about involve lust murders. Thus, it becomes that much easier to view sex as the primary motivating force behind the serial offender. Some serial killers, however, never become sexually involved in any way with their victims. Some experts may argue, however, that "enjoyment" is related to sexuality.

Sexual motivations were found to be the most common explanations of serial murder, but only 9% of offenders gave it as the sole reason for killing. Similarly, offenders frequently stated that they enjoyed killing but rarely killed for enjoyment only. Money was a factor for approximately one in five of the offenders, yet infrequently did they kill for money only. Even those who killed in order to engage in perverted sexual acts seldom committed the murders to carry out perverted acts only. As discussed in Chapter 4, sex may serve much more as a vehicle to degrade and destroy. Ultimately, by depriving a victim of things she or he holds sacred, such as dignity and self-respect, the offender achieves his most important goal, which is to have complete control over the victim. In short, many of the offenders' stated "motivations" may actually have been methods by which they achieved ultimate power and control over other human beings. One offender pointed out how good it made him feel to completely control another person's life. To have that control over life and death, he noted, gave him a special thrill.

Another area of research pertaining to the male offender is his prior history of violent, criminal, or abnormal behavior. We tend not to think of male serial killers as having criminal records but rather as embarking on a unique form of criminal activity.

After careful examination of the lives of 198 male serial killers, the present author compiled data indicating that two-thirds of them had had prior incarceration(s) in prison(s) or mental institutions (Table 5.11). Over one-third were found to have histories of sex-related crimes, whereas nearly half (45%) had been convicted of thefts, burglaries, and robberies. Thirteen percent re-

PROFILE 5.8 Paul John Knowles, 1974

Paul Knowles had a history of criminal behavior long before he started his killing spree. As a teenager and an adult, Knowles had spent time in jails for petty theft, car theft, and burglary. By the time he was released from prison, the 28-year-old Florida resident suffered from loneliness, rejection, and failure. Sandy Fawkes, a woman he met (but chose not to kill), described Knowles as a man who could be thoughtful and even protective. He also appeared to be confused as to his sexuality. Some of the rapes he confessed to were never completed because of his sexual inadequacies. One of his male victims appears to have been associated with homosexual behavior. Knowles met him in a gay bar and was invited to spend the night at his home but killed him following an argument. Knowles decided to make his mark on society and began a four-month killing rampage that would cover seven states and include at least 18 victims. He later claimed to have killed at least 35 people; the admissions were never confirmed.

Knowles's killings were generally random; he often murdered someone to conceal detection or to rob him or her. Some of his victims he simply killed for enjoyment. He murdered children, teenagers, adults, and elderly persons. Most of his victims died by strangulation, although at least five were shot to death. Most of them were female, but he raped or attempted to rape only a few. He managed to elude law enforcement through cunning and sheer luck as he drove thousands of miles, killing along the way.

Finally he abducted a police officer and another male traveler, handcuffed them to a tree, and shot both in the head, killing them instantly. After running a road block, he smashed his car into a tree and fled into the woods. He surrendered moments later when confronted by a local resident pointing a shotgun at him. After his arrest Knowles reveled in the notoriety and gave several interviews. He made a point of telling the press he was the "only successful member of his family." The next day Knowles was shot and killed as he attempted to escape from the police.

(continued)

ported prior homicide records, whereas 17% of male offenders were discovered to have had illegal drug involvement and 14% had been charged with animal abuse or fire-setting. Over two-thirds were found to have a history of a combination of criminal activities. In short, most of the offenders examined were found to have some form of criminal history. Instead of being faced with a new breed of offender, we may have failed in our criminal justice system to adequately deal with the "old" criminal before his career of serial killing began (see Profile 5.8).

Another important area of background research is the killer's childhood history. In 62 cases of male offenders, various degrees and types of traumatization occurred while they were young (Table 5.12). This does not preclude the possibility that other offenders also may have had similar experiences. Trauma was defined as rejection, including being abandoned by parent(s), being neglected by parent(s), and being rejected by significant others. Rejection was

PROFILE 5.8 Continued

Paul Knowles's Victims

DATE OF MURDER	NAME	AGE RANGE	GENDER	STATE	METHOD	SEXUAL ASSAULT	AREA OF KILLING OR WHERE BODY FOUND	ITEMS STOLEN
7/74	Alice Curtis	Elderly	F	Fla.	Suffocation	No	Home	Money/car
7/74	Mylette Anderson	Child	F	Fla.	Strangled	—	Swamp	—
7/74	Lillian Anderson	Child	F	Fla.	Strangled	—	Swamp	—
7/74	Marjorie Howe	Adult	F	Fla.	Strangled	—	Home	TV
8/74	Hitchhiker	Teen	F	Fla.	Strangled	Rape	Woods	—
8/74	Kathie Pierce	Adult	F	Fla.	Strangled	No	Home	—
9/74	William Bates	Adult	M	Ohio	Strangled	Possible	Woods	Car
9/74	Emmett Johnson	Elderly	M	Nev.	Shooting	No	Camper	Credit cards/car
9/74	Lois Johnson	Elderly	F	Nev.	Shooting	No	Camper	Credit cards/car
9/74	Unidentified	Adult	F	Nev.	Strangled	Rape	Car	—
9/74	Ann Dawson	Adult	F	Ala.	—	—	—	—
10/74	Dawn Wine	Teen	F	Conn.	Strangled	Rape	Home	Records/tape recorder
10/74	Karen Wine	Adult	F	Conn.	Strangled	Rape	Home	—
10/74	Doris Hovey	Adult	F	Va.	Shooting	No	Home	—
11/74	Carswell Carr	Adult	M	Ga.	Stabbing	No	Home	—
11/74	Miss Carr	Teen	F	Ga.	Strangled	Attempt	Home	—
11/74	Officer Campbell	Adult	M	Ga.	Shooting	No	Woods	Car
11/74	James Meyer	Adult	M	Ga.	Shooting	No	Woods	Car

Table 5.12 Percentage of Male Offenders Who Experienced Forms of Traumatization as Children

Traumatization	Percentage of Offenders (*N* = 62)
Rejection	48
Unstable home	37
Physical abuse	35
Mental/Emotional abuse	34
Divorce	19
Alcoholic parent	18
Adopted	13
Sexual abuse	13
Parents deceased	11
Illegitimate	10
Poverty	8
Prostitute mother	6

by far the most common theme surrounding the lives of these killers as children, which very likely originated from the experience of a dysfunctional family, sexual abuse, alcoholism, and so on. The feelings of rejection and anger appear to be the residual of the traumatization. However, most people have experienced rejection to a lesser or greater degree than serial killers have, yet they do not become violent killers. Many people have lost their parents; experienced divorce, poverty, and unstable homes in which parents drink heavily; used drugs; or been involved in prostitution or sexual abuse. However, most people who have had such experiences do not turn to homicide. Serial killers may be different in that they were not prepared or able to cope with the stresses the trauma created (see Chapter 4). Such an explanation will require more extensive research but may eventually provide us with greater insight into causation. For the present, it appears that early childhood trauma can and will influence future behavior to the extent that some individuals will become violent offenders.

DISPOSITION OF SERIAL KILLERS

There has been considerable concern about the disposition of serial offenders. Given that some states* do not have capital punishment and that several serial killers were removed from death row when capital punishment was struck down by the U.S. Supreme Court in 1972, many offenders are spending the rest of their lives in prison instead of waiting to be executed (Table 5.13).

*Thirty-eight states currently impose the death penalty.

Table 5.13 Disposition of Male Serial Killers after Apprehension

Disposition	Percentage of Offenders (N = 337)
Prison Sentences	45
Death penalty sentence	28
Pending in courts	5
Suicide	3
Killed before trial	3
Confined to mental institution	3
Escaped	1
Now free	1

Of the 337 male offenders examined for sentencing, 35% have been executed or await execution on death row as of this writing. A few committed suicide or were killed before a trial could be held. In total, 40% of all offenders are now dead or currently await execution. At least half of all male offenders spent or will spend the rest of their lives in prison or confined to psychiatric institutions. The chances of parole or early release for any of these offenders is at present extremely small, if not nonexistent.

MEN WHO KILL WOMEN: THE SOLO KILLER

Given the variations among the types of serial killing, the cases can also be subdivided into a number of taxonomies, subgroups, or categories. These subgroups may also provide valuable information about the methods, motives, victim selection, or mobility patterns of particular serial killers. Examination of different subgroups may, in the final analysis, provide insight into the mind and behavior of serial killers, as well as generate new areas of research. This section focuses on male serial offenders who primarily killed young women. This subgroup was selected for a number of reasons: (1) the public tends to associate the phenomenon of serial murder with young women as victims; (2) young women are the most likely targets of serial killers; (3) these murderers generally receive more extended media coverage than some other groups of serial killers; and (4) these offenders display habits and traits that tend in some ways to set them apart from other serial offenders.

These are the types of killers we so often hear or read about in the media. These are the rapists who enjoy killing and often indulging in acts of sadism and perversion. These are the men who have engaged in necrophilia, cannibalism, and the drinking of victims' blood. Some like to bite their victims; others enjoy trophy collecting—shoes, underwear, and body parts, such as hair clippings, feet, heads, fingers, breasts, and sexual organs. Offenders in this subgroup have earned monikers like "Bluebeard," "The Torture Doctor,"

"Demon of the Belfry," "Sex Beast," "The Thrill Killer," and "The Coed Killer," which are designed to evoke our disgust, horror, and fascination.

Compared with serial killers who pursued victims other than young women, these offenders tended to kill more victims. Perhaps males who target young women are more devious, more obsessed, and more intelligent than other males who kill solo. Or young women may simply be the easiest targets and more accessible. In this subgroup, most of the offenders killed young women. The majority of these women-killers were classified as local offenders. Other killers who are more mobile also have made a significant impact in the American landscape. These are the offenders who have been known to travel thousands of miles in a month eluding police, in search of easy victims. However, like other types of information regarding serial murder, this has been subject to exaggeration. For example, Henry Lee Lucas, a self-confessed serial killer in Texas, said he had killed in nearly every state and claimed he sometimes drove his car 100,000 miles in a month. This means he would have averaged 3,225 miles per day, in a 31-day month, if he drove nonstop, maintaining a speed of 134 mph for the entire month. Obviously, such statements are ludicrous, but it is exactly this type of misinformation that helps to create stereotypes. Some serial killers do travel throughout the United States and Canada, and a few even travel overseas. They commit crimes in several different law enforcement jurisdictions, which they often use to their own advantage. In such situations, poor interagency communications, as well as limited cooperation among agencies, can keep a strong police response from ever developing. As you will see in Chapter 11, efforts are being made to deal with the particular problems created by the traveling serial killer.

The remaining serial killers in this subgroup maintained their territoriality by staying place-specific. Few of these types were strictly stay-at-home killers; some waited for victims to come to their homes, but they also roamed locally in search of prey. Jerry Brudos, about whom Ann Rule wrote *The Lust Killer* (1983), would return to his home with his captured victims; however, he also victimized women who made the fatal mistake of knocking on his door.

LUST KILLERS

Our discussion of sexual homicides in Chapter 1 briefly introduced the concept of homicides motivated, at least at some level, by lust. Malmquist (1996) states that sexual homicide is a broad term that includes different types of sexual killing including rape killings, sexual lust killings, and killings after a sexual act in order to destroy evidence. Sexual serial killers tend to be either killing after a rape or are involved in lust murders. These sexual killers are more inclined to seek out strangers for victims than other solo male offenders. Generally the women were prostitutes, hitchhikers, or students. For example:

> In late 2000, Robert L. Yates plead guilty to the murders of 13 mostly prostitutes in the Spokane/Tacoma WA area. The female victims were

> raped, shot in the head and buried. He killed his first prostitute in 1988. However, in 1975 and only 23, Yates was working as a correctional officer. While target shooting he came upon two college graduates who were on a picnic. On a whim he killed them both. Yates continued to fantasize more and more about raping and killing women and now will spend the rest of his life in prison (author's files).

Sometimes nurses, models, or waitresses were targeted. Although a few offenders randomly selected women who were at home alone, most victims succumbed to the ruses and con games played by offenders in both public and private areas. One offender, who now resides at the Florida State Prison in Starke, Florida, was able to talk his way into anyone's trust. Charismatic, irresponsible, unfaithful to his wife and family, he always blamed others for his problems. He felt completely invincible as he stalked his prey. After talking an attractive 38-year-old real estate agent into showing him some very expensive property, he led her into a wooded area in the backyard, where he beat and stabbed her to death.

Compared with other male offenders who acted alone, this subgroup similarly often targeted women who placed themselves at risk, including those who hitchhiked, worked as prostitutes, or walked alone at night. The majority of these offenders, however, sought out women who generally did not perceive themselves to be at risk. Swimming at a crowded beach, shopping in a mall, and walking home are not activities one generally considers to be risky, yet there are potential dangers in practically all public and many private activities. For serial killers like Ted Bundy (Profile 5.9), the challenge is to exploit situations in which the risk of danger appears so remote that the victim never feels a need to be on guard.

It is especially this subgroup of killers that reinforces the belief that sex is the primary driving motive behind the murders. Because of these offenders' sexual abuse of their victims, the public believes that serial killers are motivated by particularly bizarre and perverted sexual urges. Certainly they experience a degree of sexual arousal and gratification in what they do, but this does not mean that sexual gratification is the primary motive for killing. When we begin to evaluate sexual acts as vehicles to gain control, maintain power, and degrade and inflict pain on the victim, we inevitably are making headway toward understanding the mind of the serial killer. Most offenders in this subgroup can be described as "lust killers" because sexual acts and associations are both overtly and subtly interwoven into their assaults. The DSM-IV terms lust killing as *Erotophonophilia* or *Dacnolagnomania,* which is sexually sadistic murder involving sexual arousal and gratification as part of the killing. The need for control was never more manifest than in this particular group of male offenders. Postmortem acts of mutilation and desecration were common, as were repeated and prolonged acts of sexual sadism and torture. Necrophilia also was very common. The fear of rejection appeared to be so powerful that some offenders would have sex with the victim only after she had died. In the perception of the offender, a corpse permits him to be intimate without risk of rejection. As discussed briefly in Chapter 1, paraphilia are very common to serial killers. However, many paraphilia are not illegal nor do they lead to criminal behavior. For the male serial killer, the paraphilia they engage in usually have escalated from softer forms to those that are considered not only criminal but violent as well. They range from unusual to incredibly bizarre and disgusting. The author contends that as paraphilia develop, men who develop them often engage in several over a period of time. Most men who engage in paraphilia exhibit four to five different forms. For those with violent tendencies, *soft* paraphilia can quickly lead to experimentation with hardcore paraphilia that often involves the harming of others in sexual ways.

Paraphilia are considered by the DSM-IV to be: sexual impulse disorders characterized by intensely arousing, recurrent sexual fantasies, urges and behaviors (of at least 6-months duration) that are considered deviant with respect to cultural norms and that produce clinically significant distress or impairment in social, occupational, or other important areas of psychosocial functioning. Many paraphilia involve various forms of *fetishes,* which are defined by the DSM-IV as: occurring over a period of at least 6 months, recurrent intense sexually arousing fantasies, sexual urges, or behaviors involving the use of nonliving objects.

The Internet is replete with paraphilia, many of which have little documentation or import. Of most concern is that readers view the sexual assaults as a process of sexual fantasy development culminating in lust murder. The author has selected a few forms of violent paraphilia referred to as *attack paraphilia* (sexual violence involving others, including children) for readers to consider in context with *preparatory paraphilia,* or paraphilia that have been found as part of the lust killers sexual fantasies and activities. This does not mean that having a preparatory paraphilia makes one a serial killer. The preparatory paraphilia listed here are those believed to be common to this group of serial killers. The process of sexual fantasy development may include stealing items from victims. Burglary, although generally considered to be a property crime, also is sometimes a property crime for sexual purposes. Stealing underwear, toiletries, hair clippings, photographs, and other personal items provides the offender with souvenirs for him to fantasize over. One offender noted how he would climax each time he entered a victim's home through a window. The thought of being alone with people sleeping in the house had become deeply eroticized. Another offender likes to break into homes and watch victims sleep. He eventually will touch the victim and will only leave when she begins to scream. He "began" his sexual acting out as a voyeur. This *paraphilic process,* detailed in Chapter 4, is also examined by Purcell and Arrigo (2000). They note that the process consists of mutually interactive elements: paraphilic stimuli and fantasy; orgasmic conditioning

PROFILE 5.9 Theodore Robert Bundy, 1973–1978

In the end, society gave Ted what he so eagerly sought throughout his life: infamy, notoriety, and the attention of millions of people. Even though the lives of 30 to 40 young women, including several teenagers and a 12-year-old girl, were sacrificed, the final price Ted would pay was never a real issue for him. Like some other serial killers, Ted Bundy found his fortune in the recognition and celebrity status he acquired through his involvement with the judicial system of the United States.

Ted was born out of wedlock in Burlington, Vermont, in 1946, to Louise Cowell. During the next few years, Ted and his mother lived with Louise's parents. Some relatives believed it was during this period of time that Ted was deeply traumatized by his violent grandfather.

At age 4, Ted and his mother Louise relocated to Tacoma, Washington. In a short time his mother married an army cook, Johnnie Bundy. Ted was forced to live a meager lifestyle and grew up deeply resenting not having money or respectable social-class affiliations. He nurtured feelings of inadequacy, of being unable to compete with others who possessed upper-middle-class standing. Michaud and Aynesworth (1983), who later interviewed Bundy, discovered: "Even the Little Teddy was deeply class conscious." As Leyton (1986b) explained in his profile of Bundy, "The status anxiety seemed particularly intense in his relationships with women" (p. 98). He dated infrequently while in high school and, as Leyton points out, "he ultimately captured and killed sorority girls, or their idealized models, for it was an obvious way in which his class-scarred soul could conceive of the possession" (p. 99).

His quest for identity served as a catalyst for constantly presenting himself, especially in physical disguises, to be somebody else. One person he truly did not want to be was Ted Bundy, the Nobody. Yet Ted seemed to lack the ability to comprehend the dynamics of social life, of being able to fit in, and admitted to his interviewers: "I didn't know what made people want to be friends. I didn't know what made people attractive to one another. I didn't know what underlay social interactions" (Michaud & Aynesworth, 1983, p. 68). Consequently Ted created a series of social fronts and disguises to help him blend into the "right groups." In truth, Bundy became the "mirror image" of himself. He lived to portray an image that he so desperately wanted to be but could never attain.

His decision to begin killing, however, was spurred only in part by his social-class paranoia. Ted later explained, using the third person, that he was eventually overcome by an internal force or an "entity" that constituted a "purely destructive power." In essence, Ted began to delve deeper into a world of sexual fantasy that became increasingly violent in nature. He consumed quantities of pornographic material depicting sexually violent acts. Bundy explained pornography "as a vicarious way of experiencing what his peers were experiencing in reality. Then he got sucked into the more sinister doctrines that are implicit in pornography—the use, abuse, the possession of women as objects" (Winn & Merrill, 1980, pp. 116–117).

He fed his sexual fantasies through voyeurism. For years he peeped through windows to watch women undress. Combined with his increasing appetite for alcohol, Ted was gradually preparing himself to begin his killing career. During this time he established what appeared to be an impressive record. He had been in the Boy Scouts, worked as an assistant programs director at the Seattle Crime Commission and wrote, ironically enough, a booklet for women on rape prevention. He was even accepted to the University of Utah Law School but attended only a few classes. This was all part of the image, the illusion he maintained in order to move freely about in fulfilling his growing deviant sexual fantasies.

His efforts to "fit in" vanished as he dealt with the sting of rejection. Each setback was perceived as devastating, regardless of its true magnitude. Like some other serial killers, Bundy began to act out his fantasies by first stalking his women and then attacking them. As Leyton observed, "He decided to commit himself to another career . . . having failed at social mobility" (p. 106). Like Ed Kemper, Bundy had already picked out some dumping sites for his victims. It is unlikely we will ever know exactly how many victims Bundy accrued, but there exists sufficient evidence to link him to at least 30 homicides, though many people believed he killed nearly 40.

The victims were all young, attractive females who appeared to come from middle- or upper-middle-class families, and many were students. He killed victims in at least five different states between 1973 and 1978, usually leaving the bodies in secluded wooded areas.

Several bodies were not found until all that remained were a few bones scattered by animals. Some victims were never recovered. Robert Keppel, a former detective who investigated eight Bundy killings in the Seattle area, believes he may have murdered over 100 victims. Ted was usually able to lure the intended victim to his car by asking them for assistance. He was always polite and friendly and sometimes wore his arm in a sling to appear as a harmless, well-bred young man simply in need of help. At other times he was known to lurk in dark shadows and attack women who were alone. An early victim was abducted from her basement apartment where she was sleeping.

Ted usually attacked his victims with a blunt instrument, such as a tire iron or a wooden club, and rendered them unconscious. Some of them died quickly from having their skulls crushed, whereas others would linger for hours or days until Ted strangled them. Once Ted had maneuvered his victim into a position that allowed him to be in control, the woman's fate was inevitable. Only one victim managed to escape death after he had placed her under his control. He raped most, if not all, of his victims; several were subjected to sodomy and sexual mutilations. Some of the victims had vaginal lacerations caused by foreign objects. In the Chi Omega sorority house killings in Tallahassee, Florida, Bundy left teeth marks on the breast and buttocks of at least one victim. In some instances Bundy would keep the body for days and is believed by some investigators to have shampooed the hair of and applied makeup to more than one victim.

Ted also liked to match wits with law enforcement personnel, and on two occasions was able to escape from a jail and a courthouse in Colorado. Ted was able to avoid apprehension because of his degree of mobility. Moving from state to state, he drew in dozens of police agencies, all wanting to capture him.

In the end, Ted's own psychopathology appeared to have caused his downfall. Before his last kill, Bundy drank heavily and resorted to frequent thefts of wallets and sprees of shoplifting. In his last few days of freedom he was overcome with desperation, paranoia, and the inability to make and act on decisions that would allow him to remain free. His frequent and excessive use of stolen credit cards and his impulsive purchases of clothing, especially socks, were not the actions of the "old" Ted who had been in control. Fueled by his paranoia, fetishes, and constant intake of alcohol, perhaps he foresaw or even wished his inevitable capture. Bundy's final victim, Kimberly Leach, whom he randomly selected from a grammar school, was only 12 years of age. A few days later after murdering her, Ted was pulled over by a suspicious patrol officer, and eventually police discovered that he had been placed on the FBI's Ten Most Wanted list.

Bundy was convicted of three murders and sentenced to die in Florida's electric chair. Reveling in the notoriety, he defended himself in court and used his trial to bask in the light of national TV and newspaper coverage. He finally

(continued)

gained the prominence and self-validation he so desperately sought. In an interview with Dr. Ron Holmes of the University of Louisville, Bundy discussed the classic characteristics of serial killers but could not recognize those traits in his own personality (author's files). He continued to the very end to employ legal maneuverings to avoid the electric chair. His trial and appeals cost approximately $9,000,000. Bundy's court record was one of the longest in Florida's history, more than 28,000 pages, or about the size of the Encyclopedia Britannica. For Ted that was also a way to satisfy his desire for revenge on a society he believed had maligned him. For Ted there was no guilt, and as he declared on one occasion, "I don't feel guilty for anything . . . I feel sorry for people who feel guilt" (Winn & Merrill, 1980, p. 313). As his interviewers, Michaud and Aynesworth, came to realize, Ted did not act under some irresponsible uncontrollable urge; rather he consciously used his free will, his agency, to create the killer within himself. Bundy's fame attracted many young female followers who continued to send him letters of love and support. During his incarceration in Florida, Ted married and even managed to father a child. He had absolutely no remorse for his crimes. As Ted so aptly observed, "I'm the coldest mother-fucker you'll ever put your eyes on. I don't give a shit about those other people" (author's files).

But in the end Ted decided to confess his crimes, possibly to buy additional time for himself. The consummate psychopath lived out his image until the very end when he allowed some well-intentioned minister to interview him. The meeting was vintage Bundy. The minister wanted Bundy to explore the role of pornography in his life and its influence on him in committing the murders. Like a master craftsman, Bundy controlled and molded the interview. In the end Bundy gave the minister what he wanted without ever scratching the veneer of his own image. Finally, his confessions, his efforts to show he was insane, that he did not receive a fair trial, that he could take authorities to more burial sites, all faltered.

As Bundy's execution hour drew near, the nation watched with increasing interest. Talk shows, newscasters, and newspaper editors all began exploring the life of Ted Bundy and the phenomenon of serial murder in general. Some individuals and groups eagerly awaited his last moments. T-shirts with slogans such as "Fry-Day" and bumper stickers that read "I'll buckle up when Bundy buckles up" were common in Florida and other states where the killer had murdered young women. Radio stations played a song parody, "On Top of Old Sparky," and an Indianapolis station fried bacon on the air and held a "Bundy countdown" one hour before his execution. Dances and cookouts called "Bundy-Ques" were held in several locations. The execution in many respects took on the atmosphere of a circus. Even those strongly opposed to capital punishment were few in number at the Florida State Prison in Starke as dozens of people anxious to see him die cheered, set off firecrackers, and chanted "Burn, Bundy, Burn" as the appointed hour approached. Indeed, it was a disgusting end to a disgusting life. On January 24, 1989, at 7:00 A.M., Theodore Robert Bundy died in the electric chair. His last words before a black hood was placed over his head were "Give my love to my family and friends."

The following statements by Bundy attempt to add a rational note to his murderous career.

- "Sitting there in a cell, I could convince myself that I was not guilty of anything."
- [Regarding confession:] "Walking right up to the edge is a thrill, but I can't do it. I haven't allowed myself to choke."
- "They [society] will condemn Ted Bundy while walking past a magazine rack that contains the very things [pornography] that send kids down the road to being Ted Bundys."

Ted Bundy's Victims

DATE OF MURDER OR DISAPPEARANCE	NAME	AGE	OCCUPATION	LOCATION	METHOD
1/31/74	Lynda Ann Healy	21	Student	Wash.	Clubbing
3/12/74	Donna Gail Manson	19	Student	Wash.	?
4/17/74	Susan Rancourt	18	Student	Wash.	Clubbing
5/6/74	Roberta K. Parks	22	Student	Oreg.	Bludgeoning
6/1/74	Brenda C. Ball	22	Unemployed	Wash.	Clubbing/strangulation
6/11/74	Georgeann Hawkins	18	Student	Wash.	?
7/14/74	Janice Ott	23	Probation officer	Wash.	Bludgeoning
7/14/74	Denise M. Naslund	19	Secretary/student	Wash.	Bludgeoning
8/2/74	Carol Valenzuela	20	—	Wash.	Strangulation/clubbing
8/2/74	Unidentified victim	17–23	—	Wash.	?
10/2/74	Nancy Wilcox	16	Student	Utah	?
10/18/74	Melissa Smith	17	Student	Utah	Strangulation/fractured skull
10/31/74	Laurie Amie	17	Student	Utah	Strangulation/fractured skull
11/8/74	Debbie Kent	17	Student	Utah	?
1/12/75	Caryn Campbell	23	Nurse	Colo.	Fractured skull
3/15/75	Julie Cunningham	26	Ski instructor	Colo.	Fractured skull
4/6/75	Denise Oliverson	25	—	Colo.	—
1/15/78	Lisa Levy	20	Student	Fla.	Fractured skull
1/15/78	Margaret Bowman	21	Student	Fla.	Clubbing/strangulation
2/9/78	Kimberly Leach	12	Student	Fla.	Strangulation/slashed throat

Bundy also confessed to, or is believed by investigators to, have also murdered:
1973 Rita Lorraine Jolly, 17, Clackamas County, Oregon; 1973 Vicki Lynn Hollar, 24, Eugene, Oregon; 1973 Katherine Merry Devine, 14, Seattle, Washington; 1974 Brenda Joy Baker, 14, Seattle, Washington; 1975 Nancy Baird, 21, Farmington, Utah; 1974–1975 Sandra Weaver, 17, Utah; 1974–1975 Sue Curtis, 17, Utah; 1974–1975 Debbie Smith, 17, Utah; 1975 Melanie Suzanne Cooley, 18, Nederland, Colorado; 1975 Shelly K. Robertson, 24, Denver, Colorado.

process; and facilitators (drugs, alcohol, pornography). The probability of the offender harming a victim is extremely high given the progressive nature of his sexual fantasies.

Attack Paraphilia

- **Amokoscisia—**arousal or sexual frenzy with desire to slash or mutilate women
- **Anophelorastia—**arousal from defiling or ravaging a partner
- **Anthropophagolagnia—**rape with cannibalism
- **Biastophilia—**those preferring to violently rape their victims; also called raptophilia
- **Dippoldism—**sexual arousal from abusing children
- **Pedophilia—**sex with minors
- **Pyromania—**arousal from deliberate and purposeful fire-setting
- **Sadism—**empowerment and arousal derived from injuring others

Preparatory Paraphilia

- **Agonophilia—**person who is aroused by partner pretending to struggle
- **Altocalciphilia—**high heel fetish
- **Alvinolagnia—**stomach fetish
- **Anililagnia—**arousal from older female sex partner
- **Autonecrophilia—**imaging oneself as a corpse or becoming sexually aroused by simulated corpses
- **Bondage—**physical or mental restriction of partner
- **Coprolalia—**arousal from using obscene language or writing
- **Dacryphilia—**person who is aroused by seeing their partner cry
- **Erotomania—**people who develop an unreasonable love of a stranger or person not interested in them
- **Exhibitionism—**exposing body to inappropriate and nonconsenting people for arousal
- **Frottage—**rubbing body against partner or object for arousal
- **Gerontophilia—**attraction to a partner whose age is that of a different generation
- **Hebephilia—**men aroused by teenage boys
- **Hyphephilia—**arousal from touching skin, hair, leather, fur, or fabric
- **Kleptolagnia—**arousal from stealing
- **Mastofact—**breast fetish
- **Mixoscopia—**orgasm dependent on watching others having sex
- **Necrophilia—**sex with corpses

PROFILE 5.10 John Edward Robinson, the "Slavemaster," 1984–2000

The 56-year-old predator with a criminal history dating back to the 1960s met several of his young, female victims in sadomasochistic Internet chat rooms. His Internet moniker was "slavemaster." He pretended to own two international businesses to impress potential victims. At least five women were lured to his Kansas home with promises of work or kinky sex. After torturing and beating them to death, Robinson sealed each victim in a steel drum and placed some of them in a storage locker over the Missouri state line. Robinson was caught after two other intended victims managed to escape during their S&M encounters. They realized just in time that the rough sex was only going to get worse. The other victims all died from blunt head trauma. He was also charged with stealing over $ 900 of sex toys from one of his victims. Robinson depicted himself as a businessman and philanthropist who lived with his wife in a mobile home park that she managed. One associate of the Slavemaster claimed that Robinson was involved in a sex cult in which rape, bondage, and torture were practiced. Robinson enjoyed the sexual degradation of women and the Internet became a useful tool in procuring his victims.

- **Retifism—**shoe fetish
- **Scatophilia—**arousal by making phone calls, using vulgar language, or trying to elicit a reaction from the other party
- **Somnophilia—**fondling strangers in their sleep
- **Voyeurism—**arousal by watching others without their consent

Deviant sexual acts usually are part of the killing process, not the actual reasons for killing. News accounts of these lust killers portray them as sex fiends when in reality sex is another tool he uses to appease sexual fantasies and express total domination over his victim. The primary motive is control; such offenders must control others in order to feel that they themselves are in control of their own lives. The vehicle to achieve control is through sexual acts. Other male killers may use different methods, such as guns, to achieve a similar sense of control. In our study, offenders in this subgroup frequently carried out acts of rape and were also likely to express enjoyment or pleasure about the murders. Offenders often cited personal reasons for the murders such as an "urge to kill." Efforts to gain control are also influenced by technology. Some serial killers are now using the Internet to lure victims to their deaths (see Profile 5.10).

Another important characteristic of these lust killers was the "perversion factor." This subgroup was often prone to carry out bizarre sexual acts. These acts most commonly included necrophilia and trophy collection. Jerry Brudos (Profile 5.11) severed the breasts of some of his victims and made epoxy molds.

PROFILE 5.11 Jerry Brudos, 1968–1969

At an early age, Jerry Brudos developed a particular interest in women's shoes, especially black, spike-heeled shoes. As he matured, his shoe fetish increasingly provided sexual arousal. At 17 he used a knife to assault a girl and force her to disrobe while he took pictures of her. For his crime he was incarcerated in a mental hospital for nine months. His therapy uncovered his sexual fantasy for revenge against women, fantasies that included placing kidnapped girls into freezers so he could later arrange their stiff bodies in sexually explicit poses. He was evaluated as possessing a personality disorder but was not considered to be psychotic.

Jerry completed high school, served in the military, and then became an electronics technician. His sexual fixations carried into marriage; he insisted his wife, Ralphene, stay nude while in the house. He would take pictures of her naked, and, according to his wife, he occasionally dressed in her panties and bra. He continued to collect women's undergarments and shoes. Prior to his first murder, he had already assaulted four women and raped one of them. At age 28, Jerry was ready to start killing. His first victim came to his home quite by accident, looking for another address. On January 26, 1968, Linda Slawson, 19, working in book sales, knocked on Jerry Brudos's door. He took her to his garage, where he smashed her skull with a two-by-four. Before disposing of the body in a nearby river, he severed her left foot and placed it in his freezer. He often would amuse himself by dressing the foot in a spiked-heel shoe.

His fantasy for greater sexual pleasure led him, on November 26, 1968, to strangle Jan Whitney, 23, with a postal strap. After killing Ms. Whitney, he had sexual intercourse with the corpse, then cut off the right breast and made an epoxy mold of the organ. Before dumping her body in the river, he took pictures of the corpse. Unable to satisfy his sexual fantasies and still in the grasp of violent urges, he found his third victim, Karen Sprinker, 19, on March 27, 1969. After sexually assaulting Karen, he strangled her in his garage, amputated both breasts, again took pictures, and tossed her body into the river. Four weeks later, on April 23, 1969, he abducted his last victim, Linda Salee, 22, from a shopping mall. He sexually assaulted Linda, and, after strangling her in his garage, he shocked her torso with electric charges and watched her body jerk with spasms. Investigators also found needle marks on her body.

All of Brudos's victims were young, white, female strangers, whom he methodically killed in his garage under the special mirrors he had installed to help feed his fantasies. He later confessed that he enjoyed the killing, especially how his victims looked once they were dead. Brudos was sent to Oregon State Prison for the murders.

Twenty years later, Brudos is now granted a parole hearing every other year under Oregon's old parole system. He has adjusted to prison life and has turned his energies to his personal computer and printer, which make life in a cell much more meaningful. It is unlikely he will ever be paroled, but Brudos has not given up hope.

Brudos, like others, also photographed his victims in various poses, dressed and disrobed. The photos served as trophies and a stimulus to act out again. Other lust killers engage in cannibalism including Albert Fish, Richard Chase, Ed Kemper, Jeffrey Dahmer, Ottis Toole, Ed Gein, and Robin Gecht.

There also tends to be a high correlation between men who cannibalize and Satan worship. Gary Heidnik in Philadelphia kept sex slaves and when two died he dismembered them and cooked them for meals.

The lust killers had a frequent history of sex-related crimes and time in prison or mental institutions. Again, offenders in the subgroup were likely to have had more than one previous social or psychological problem. This may suggest that lust killers are influenced to commit violence as a result of such problems. Another explanation, and probably more accurate at this point in the development of serial-murder research, is simply that lust killers receive more attention from both law enforcement and researchers. Consequently, we are probably going to find more information on the sensational cases, especially if research is based primarily on the more gruesome statistics and facts and pays less attention to other details.

Regardless of the subgrouping of male serial killers who act alone, a recurrent problem noted in most of them is feelings of low self-esteem and worthlessness. These feelings, according to offenders, appear to stem from periods of rejection or denial by loved ones, especially parents, or by society in general.

MEN WHO KILL MEN: THE SOLO KILLER

Serial killers select a variety of victims contingent on their own perceived needs and abilities. Given the apparent reality that male solo offenders prefer to attack women, what types of men would elect to kill males? During the settlement and expansion of U.S. territories, men killing men was a common phenomenon, especially during the taming of the "Wild West." Gunslingers and other outlaws were a constant threat to those wishing to establish order and preserve the peace. By definition, gunslingers who roamed the country in America's early days met some of the criteria of what a serial killer was and is supposed to be. However, given the fact that carrying guns was established as the rule of law for many years, it is not surprising that men frequently killed men. Most people carried weapons, especially guns, for protection. Others carried guns in order to commit property crimes, and some killed during the completion of such crimes. The term "cold-blooded killer" was commonly affixed to outlaws such as the members of the Dalton gang, Jesse James, and other robbers because they often killed men who tried to interfere with their pursuit of criminal activity. But these men are not the types of offenders generally thought of as serial killers, even though they killed over time. Generally, they are excluded from the definition of serial killers because their primary objective was to rob, not kill. However, the question could be asked: How do we know the exact intent of their criminal activity? Some outlaws who robbed may have also looked forward to killing innocent bystanders. The same question could be asked about organized-crime figures, military personnel, or even police officers.

As with other subgroups of serial killers, efforts were made in our study to identify offenders of earlier eras using the contemporary definition of serial murder. Even by omitting most outlaws, certain offenders who fit the intended definition

PROFILE 5.12 Randy Kraft, the Southern California Strangler, 1972–1983

The California Supreme Court upheld Randy Kraft's death sentence in 2000 for the murders of several young men, many of them military personnel or hitchhikers. He is believed to have tortured and killed at least 16 victims in southern California, Oregon, and Michigan and is linked to as many as 45. Considered highly intelligent and a graduate of Claremont Men's College, Kraft was stopped one day in 1983 for suspicion of drunk driving. The patrol officer found a dead marine in the passenger seat along with pictures of other victims and a death list with addresses of victims. Kraft became known by the media as the "Scorecard Killer" because he kept a detailed record of all his murders. Kraft developed his own "signatures" when he killed yet was not concerned about changing "signatures" when it suited him. Victims frequently had a cigarette lighter burn on their left nipple, had their left testicle removed while still alive, and objects such as tree branches rectally inserted. When the torture was complete, victims were strangled slowly with their own belts. Most victims had been given Valium along with alcohol before they were bound and raped. Torture was a critical part of the slow killing process. One victim had his eyelids cut off so that he might witness all the horror being inflicted upon him. Once victims were dead, they were often pushed out of a speeding vehicle. J.J. Maloney, once a reporter for the Orange County Register and assigned to investigate the numerous freeway killings in southern California noted that many of the murders could have been averted had prosecutors done their job. In 1975 Kraft had been arrested in connection with one of the murders but prosecutors declined to pursue the case. Maloney also points out the confusion created when investigating serial-murder cases that have similar characteristics. Kraft was erroneously dubbed the "Freeway Killer" when in fact the title belonged to William Bonin, who murdered 21 men between 1979 and 1980. He was executed in San Quentin in 1996. Kraft maintains his innocence and has, like so many serial killers, attracted numerous "groupies" to champion his cause.

of serial killers were identified. These men were identified as serialists because their primary objective was clearly to kill others. It was not until the twentieth century that information about the sexual involvement of serial offenders who killed men began to surface. This may have been more a function of limited recordkeeping than a puritan spirit. Eventually, as recordkeeping became more complete and crimes of sexual nature were more openly discussed, in the cases of men killing men an array of perversities began to be documented.

In our study, serial killers who murdered men came from a wide spectrum of educational levels and social classes, including transients and local politicians, farmers, and racists. The most common thread among this particular subgroup, which also sets them apart, appears to be that offenders were involved homosexually with their victims or killed as a result of homosexual liaisons. Bonin, Dahmer, Gacy, Baumeister, and Kraft are examples; see Profiles 5.12 and 5.13. Lust killers use sex as a vehicle to destroy their victims; often men who kill men

PROFILE 5.13 John Wayne Gacy, 1972–1978

Few other serial killers have attracted as much attention as John Wayne Gacy, "The Killer Clown," one of the most prolific murderers of all time. Born on March 17, 1942, he appeared to have experienced a rather normal childhood, but there were a few dark sides. His father, Gacy Sr., was an alcoholic and frequently mistreated the family by beating his wife, abusing John, and terrorizing his daughters. John could never seem to gain the approval of his father regardless of the efforts he made. As a child, John was accidentally struck in the head by a swing. For five years he experienced blackouts until a blood clot was diagnosed and dissolved by medications. He dropped out of high school in his senior year and left home for a short time, working in a mortuary in Las Vegas. But Gacy had been strongly influenced by his mother since childhood, and, succumbing to that influence, he returned home to live. After finally graduating from a business college, he began selling shoes. His friends found him to be a braggart, because he frequently talked about his time in the military. However, Gacy had never served time in the military.

In 1964, Gacy, now 22, married and went to work for his father-in-law as a worker for, then manager of, a chain of Kentucky Fried Chicken establishments. Gacy joined the local Jaycees and became chaplain of the Waterloo, Iowa, chapter and chairman of the group's first citywide prayer breakfast. In 1967 he was named outstanding vice president and honored as the best Jaycee club chaplain in the state of Iowa. In the spring of 1968, Gacy started his downward spiral, a trip that would take ten years before ending. A grand jury indicted Gacy for handcuffing an employee and trying to sodomize him and also for paying a youth to perform fellatio on him. He had also hired someone to beat up the youth after the youth testified against him. He pled guilty to one charge and was incarcerated at the Psychiatric Hospital, State University of Iowa. After being diagnosed as a bisexual with a personality that was "thrill-seeking or exploratory," Gacy was sent to prison. Because he was a model prisoner and an active community member, Gacy was paroled after serving only 18 months.

Gacy's first wife, who had had two children by John, divorced Gacy during his trial. Upon his release from prison, Gacy went back to Chicago to live with his mother again. For a while he worked as a cook and then told his mother he had decided to buy his own home. In 1971 he was arrested for picking up a teenager and attempting to force the youth to engage in sex. The case was dismissed when the youth failed to appear on the court date. Gacy was now living in Des Plaines, near Chicago, and had begun his own construction business. He married again, to Carol Hoff, who remembered how John started bringing home pictures of naked men. After four years the marriage ended because of a lack of sexual relations between the couple and because John would often stay out very late at night in his car. John's wife had also learned not to ask questions about personal items she found while cleaning. Gacy had become enraged when she asked him about her discovery of some wallets belonging to young men.

Gacy had begun to add onto his home, and part of the construction included building a large crawl space under the addition. He frequently had some of his young employees help in digging a trench in the crawl space. During this time Gacy was actively involved in the community. In 1970 he claimed to be a Democratic precinct captain and even had his picture taken with First Lady Rosalynn Carter shortly before his arrest in 1978. He became a local celebrity, dressing up as Pogo the Clown and performing at children's parties and at hospitals. He frequently held summer parties at his home, inviting local dignitaries and

(continued)

PROFILE 5.13 Continued

neighbors. Sometimes people would comment about the peculiar smell, but John simply explained that in the crawl space there was a lot of dampness that created the odor.

Only Gacy knew that the crawl space held his personal collection of bodies of young males whom he had sexually tortured to death. Some of his victims were young males who had worked for Gacy; others were male prostitutes he had picked up late at night at "Bughouse Square," a well-known locale in Chicago frequented at night by homosexuals and male prostitutes. Gacy would lure the victim to his home, promising money or employment. When they arrived, he would talk his victim into participating in his "handcuff trick." Once he had the youth in handcuffs, he would chloroform the victim and then sodomize him. Next followed the "rope trick," usually when the victim was conscious. Gacy would tie a rope around the victim's neck and, after fashioning two knots, would insert a stick and proceed to twist it slowly like a tourniquet. The terrifying deaths sometimes were accompanied by Gacy reading passages from the Bible.

John managed to bury 29 victims in the crawl space and cement driveway. Four other victims, for want of space, were discarded in the Des Plaines River. The police were led to Gacy after one of his intended victims escaped and reported him. Investigators eventually demolished Gacy's house and dug up most of his yard in search of bodies. Gacy confessed at least five times, only to recant his statements later. He claimed other people must have put the bodies there. "Where the hell could I have found time? I was working 16 hours a day, and the rest of my time was devoted to the community, charity affairs, and helping you people." During the determination of Gacy's sanity, he was described as a veritable Jekyll-and-Hyde. His defense attorney, Mr. Amirante, cited passages from Robert Louis Stevenson's *The Strange Case of Dr. Jekyll and Mr. Hyde,* quoting Dr. Jekyll: "If I am the chief of sinners, I am the chief of sufferers, also. Both sides of me were in dead earnest." The prosecution, however, described Gacy as having an "antisocial personality," as "a psychopath, a person who commits crimes without remorse."

In 1980, John Wayne Gacy was found guilty of all counts of murder and sentenced to die in the electric chair at Menard Correctional Center in Chicago. Three years after his trial, Gacy stated he was opposed to capital punishment on religious grounds: "Let he who is free of sin cast the first stone." He believed a lengthy appeals process could save him from execution. While in prison Gacy claimed to be a quiet and kind person. He blamed some of the parents for the deaths of their own children because their sons were prostitutes. He said he was incapable of violence and allegedly received letters every day from "kind people," most of them women. "Ninety percent of the writers are women, and I have 41 people on my visiting list. I'm allowed three visits a month," explained Gacy. Although the prosecution portrayed Gacy as a skillful, competent torturer and killer who enjoyed the "God-like power" of life and death, Gacy said it was a lie: "How could I live on top of those bodies?" (Simons, 1983). Yet in a 1986 interview with author Tim Cahill, he remarked that if he could spend 15 minutes in a room with the parents of the people he killed, "they would understand."

Gacy spent much of his prison time painting pictures and having them sold to the public. He loved the attention. This present author received several letters from Gacy hopefully seeking assistance in his efforts to avoid the executioner. On May 10, 1994, John Wayne Gacy was put to death by lethal injection. Shortly after his death, several of his paintings were purchased at an auction for $20,000. The buyer, wanting to send a clear message to the public, burned Gacy's artwork.

PROFILE 5.14 Herb Baumeister, 1980–1996

On July 3, 1996, with police closing in, Herb Baumeister committed suicide while eluding police in a provincial park in Canada. He typified the Jekyll-and-Hyde personality cycles common to many serial killers. He was a very successful businessman who had built a chain of thrift stores in Indianapolis. He was known for being an entrepreneur and generous in his gifts to charities. Married and father to three children, he was respected by his family, peers, and community. The man appeared so normal, calm, and secure: exactly what every sexual psychopath practices, the art of pretense. Baumeister was very discreet when and how he lured young, gay men to his estate for sex, torture, and murder. His wife was unaware of his penchant for autoerotic asphyxia or his desire for gay men. For 20 years she believed that her husband was everything good and was shocked to learn that he was actually one of Indiana's most prolific serial killers of gay men. In all, he probably killed 20 or more victims in Indiana and Ohio. Police linked him to 16 murders. Several of his victim's bones were found buried on the Baumeister estate. His 13-year-old son accidentally came upon the remains of one of the victims that opened the door for investigators to search the property.

use sex in a similar fashion. Some of the offenders in this subgroup committed their crimes while traveling; others searched for victims locally or used their own homes or places of employment for the killing sites. For the most part, these offenders were single, lower-middle-class or middle-class, and had histories of deeply troubled lives. Other offenders are highly intelligent, educated, and successful in careers (see Profile 5.14).

MEN WHO KILL CHILDREN

Several of the male serial killers we researched had killed at least one child, and some had killed children only. The effects on families and communities of those who were victimized were devastating. Most offenders in this subgroup were in some manner involved sexually with their child victims, either before or after death occurred. Like other offenders, these men demonstrated a need to control their victims and have power over them. Some carried on their killings for many years. Given the amount of publicity and attention crimes against children generate, especially those shrouded in ritualistic abuse, we naturally can expect the media to focus on such cases.

In these particular child murders, there appeared to be a high degree of emotionalism among some offenders, including hatred expressed through acts of sadism. Some offenders looked forward to killing more children, whereas other offenders expressed deep regret for their crimes. Like other serial killings, the murders in this subgroup tended to be intraracial. Wayne Williams of Atlanta was the most publicized case of a black offender killing black children (Profile 5.15). Offenders usually presented themselves as nice,

PROFILE 5.15 Wayne B. Williams, 1980–1981

For 22 months the residents of Atlanta lived in growing fear and outrage as a serial killer methodically hunted their children. The body count reached 30 victims before the killer was apprehended. They ranged in age from 7 to 28, and most were young males. Some were shot or strangled; others were stabbed, bludgeoned, or suffocated. All the victims were black. The deaths of so many black young people gave rise to a variety of theories and accusations, including belief in a plot by white supremacists to systematically kill all black children. Others began to think the children were being killed by Satan worshipers, blood cultists, or even copycat murderers. The Ku Klux Klan came under close scrutiny, but no link could be made between their members and any of the murders. Atlanta became like a city under siege and inevitably attracted the attention of the entire country, including the resources of the federal government.

It appeared the murders would never stop until one night, as police staked out a bridge over the Chattahoochee River, they heard a car on the bridge come to a stop, followed by a distinct splash caused by something being dropped into the river. They pulled Wayne B. Williams, 23, over for questioning and finally arrested him as a suspect in the child murder cases. Williams was found to be a bright, young, black man who lived with his retired parents and involved himself in photography. A media and police "groupie," Williams would often listen on his shortwave radio and respond to ambulance, fire, and police emergency calls. He would then sell his exclusive pictures to the local newspapers. At age 18, he was arrested for impersonating a police officer. He spent one year at Georgia State University but dropped out when he felt his "rising star" was moving too slowly.

Wayne's freelance work as a cameraman was never steady, and he began to focus his energies on music. As a self-employed talent scout, he eventually lured his victims into his control. He was known to distribute leaflets offering "private and free" interviews to blacks between the ages of 11 and 21 who sought a career in music. At his trial, Williams was depicted as a man who hated his own race and wanted to eliminate future generations. He was described as a homosexual or a bisexual who paid young boys to have sex with him. A boy, 15, claimed he had been molested by Williams, and several witnesses testified they had seen him with some of the victims.

Williams denied everything, and the prosecution had only elaborate forensics on which to base their case against him. The forensic evidence suggested a distinct link between Williams and at least ten of the homicides and indicated a pattern surrounding the murders. The judge ruled the evidence admissible, and Williams was found guilty of murdering two of his older victims, Nathaniel Cater, 27, and Ray Payne, 21. Because of the nature of the circumstantial evidence, the judge sentenced Williams to two consecutive life sentences. He was eventually named as being responsible for 24 of the Atlanta slayings, although some believe the child killings have not ended with Williams's arrest.

normal, trustworthy people, thus gaining the trust of their child victims. The more normal they appeared, the more caution they exercised, and the more premeditation they engaged in, the greater their homicidal longevity appeared to be.

MEN WHO KILL THE ELDERLY

This subgroup includes cases of male offenders who primarily murdered elderly persons. The most publicized case was that of The Boston Strangler. People tend to think of Albert DeSalvo as a man who raped and strangled young women; however, he attacked mostly older women: 8 of his 13 victims (62%) were 55 years of age or older. As mentioned earlier, rape is not necessarily motivated by sexual desire. The reality of these killings suggests that raping women has much more to do with power, control, and desecration than it does sexual desire. A 30-year-old man raping and sodomizing an 86-year-old woman is not only disgusting, vicious, and perverted but also forces us to reconsider our perceptions of exactly what motivates rapists.

Many of the cases in this subgroup involve men who killed older women. In these cases, most of the women had been sexually assaulted. The patterns in the killing of these elderly victims were just as distinct as the patterns in the murders of young women. The sexual assaults and tortures rivaled those inflicted on younger victims. The theme of control was pervasive throughout these cases of elderly serial killings.

The victims generally lived alone or were institutionalized. Either way, offenders could obtain relatively easy access to their intended victims. In addition, most older victims were completely powerless against these offenders. As America "grays," more elderly people become potential victims. Although young women are still the most frequent victims, cases of elderly serial murder appear to have increased from 1975 to 1995. Future policies of the health care industry will undoubtedly focus on the aged. As of 1995, work has been done to provide better security for the elderly at the hospital or in the nursing home. Elderly people who are alone and unprotected unknowingly provide accessible targets for serial offenders (see Profile 5.16).

MEN WHO KILL FAMILIES

Most serial killers are portrayed as offenders who seek out individual victims. Occasionally some killers elect to abduct two victims at the same time. However, few offenders attempt such abductions because dealing with more than one victim tends to weaken their control. Serial killers, especially the lust killers, often wanted "private" time alone with the victim. Team killers tend to be the exception (Chapter 6).

PROFILE 5.16 Calvin Jackson, 1973–1974

Calvin Jackson, 26, worked as a porter at the Park Plaza Hotel, a run-down building in New York City. Many elderly and those on fixed incomes lived there, trying to make ends meet. They did not realize that their porter was an ex-convict who had a long history of robberies and burglaries. He also was a regular drug user and had been involved in several assaults. On one occasion Jackson had plea-bargained a robbery charge, and, instead of getting a 15-year sentence, he served 30 days. For years he moved from one dilapidated hotel to another. On his arrival at the Plaza, he decided to start burglarizing apartments there, except this time he would kill the occupant. He ransacked each victim's apartment and stole radios and television sets along with other items of small value. He attacked and killed at least nine women, most of them older. He usually strangled or suffocated his victims, although at least one was stabbed to death. All the victims were sexually assaulted, some after death, and, except for his final victim, they all lived in the Plaza Hotel.

Jackson was finally captured after he was seen carrying a TV set down a fire escape at 3:00 A.M. He confessed to all the pattern killings and was judged sane by the courts. His defense argued that Jackson would often make something to eat after he had killed his victim and sit and watch her, sometimes for an hour, to make sure she was really dead. The defense believed that only an insane person could do that. The courts did not agree and convicted Jackson on nine counts of homicide. He was given 18 concurrent life sentences, making him eligible for parole in the year 2030.

A few offenders have killed several victims at once, including entire families. However, such occurrences appear to be rare in serial killing; also, these types of murders by male offenders occurred mostly before 1940. Some of these cases involved "Bluebeards," or men who killed one spouse after another (Profile 5.17). Most of these cases did not include sexual attacks, and often money appeared to be a primary motivating factor in the killings. Guns and poisons were more likely to be used, with less emphasis on torture and strangling.

MEN WHO KILL MEN AND WOMEN

The final subgroup in this chapter includes offenders who kill both men and women. Some of the cases could be referred to as "spree serial killings" because they occurred within a relatively short time frame. Anger, revenge, greed, madness, sadism, and delusions of heroism were often associated with these killers' homicidal actions. This subgroup includes some well-publicized cases, including "Son of Sam" (Profile 5.18), Charles Starkweather, and the "Night Stalker" case in California. In several of these cases, guns were used as the sole means of killing the victims. Some of the killers were extremely violent in their attacks, whereas others quietly poisoned or

PROFILE 5.17 James P. Watson, 1910–1920

Like many con artists, James P. Watson, "Bluebeard," went by several aliases. When asked by police for his real identity, he simply replied, "I don't know." His last official residence was in California, but Watson operated from Mexico to Canada. A very bright individual but not without his own peculiar sexual quirks, Watson was married to at least 18 women and possibly as many as 26, several of them at the same time. He frequently placed ads in newspapers luring women into marriage.

> Personal: Would like to meet lady of refinement and some social standing who desires to meet middle-aged gentleman of culture. Object matrimony. Gentleman has nice bank account, as well as a considerable roll of government bonds.
>
> H. L. Gorden
> Hotel Tacoma
> (Pearson, 1936, p. 132)

There were always several women who eagerly responded and happily accepted the fact that he worked for the secret service and would need to be on the road frequently. He was very careful to marry women of wealth, which he quickly maneuvered into his control. He began to act out his fantasies of killing women, because he believed they were the root of all evil. He murdered at least 7 and possibly as many as 15; the exact count was never established. Some of them he drowned; others he beat to death with a hammer. They died in Washington state, Idaho, California, and probably other states. His fantasies led him in at least one murder to sexually mutilate his victim. He would later confess to investigators:

> All I felt after killing seemed largely, in each instance, some kind of relief, yet unexplainable. The sensation experienced was a sensation of ease as if I had been relieved. Instead of remorse, I had passive satisfaction or passive pleasure. I had no sexual sensation at the time but maybe for a day or two afterwards feeling more that way than normal. The greater sexual desire shortly after was from a memory of the killing. Sometimes I have looked at the body in a way of satisfaction, a kind of pleasure. Yet there was no reason why I should do that because I had seen the same person in married relations (Ellis & Gullo, 1971, p. 20).

Watson agreed to lead them to the body of one of his victims in return for a guarantee he would receive a life sentence and not death row. The courts agreed, and he went to San Quentin, where he eventually died.

suffocated their victims. In contrast to the lust killers, most offenders in this subgroup were not involved in sexual attacks or particularly perverted acts. This type of serial killer tended to resemble the profile of the mass murderer, who kills all his victims in a few minutes or hours. Although some of the offenders had developed a distinct pattern in their murders, several cases involved a high degree of randomness in victim selection. Except for the "Night Stalker" case, which was allegedly connected to some form of self-styled satanism, most of the cases were less ritualistic and more impulsive and spontaneous.

PROFILE 5.18 David Richard Berkowitz, 1976–1977

For 13 months David Berkowitz, "The Son of Sam," or "The .44-Caliber Killer," was able to hold the attention of millions of people in New York City and across the country. During that time he shot 13 young men and women on eight different occasions. Six of his victims died, and seven others were severely injured after he fired on young women or couples parked in their cars at night. Investigators finally tracked him down through a parking ticket placed on his car while he was in the area looking for someone to kill. They expected to find "The .44-Caliber Killer" to be a monster but instead found a well-mannered, 24-year-old postal worker who lived alone. His apartment was filthy, littered with liquor bottles and the walls scratched with graffiti. On one area of the wall he had scrawled: "In this hole lives the wicked king."

To those few who knew him, he lived a rather uneventful life. Born out of wedlock, he had been placed for adoption. He was an exceptional student who frequently was taunted by his classmates for being Jewish. He served three years in the U.S. Army, worked as a security guard, and once worked as an auxiliary New York police officer. His main character trait seemed to be that he was introverted and liked to roam the streets alone at night. On July 29, 1976, two young women, Donna Lauria, a medical technician, and Jody Valenti sat talking in their car when David walked out of the shadows and fired five shots through the windshield. Donna died quickly; Jody was wounded in the thigh. In October, he fired on a young couple through their rear windshield, wounding the young man. In November David walked up to two women sitting in their car in Queens and, as he asked for directions, pulled out his .44-caliber gun and fired at both women, paralyzing one of them. On January 30, 1977, a young couple were saying goodnight to each other when the windshield shattered with gunfire. Christine Freund died a few hours later of her injuries. On March 8, 1977, an Armenian student, Virginia Voserichian, was approaching her mother's house when David met her on the sidewalk and shot her directly in the face, killing her instantly. On April 17, 1977, in the same area as some of the other attacks, David shot to death Alexander Epaw and Valentina Swiani as they sat in their automobile. A note was found at the scene that read in part: "I love to hunt. Prowling the streets looking for fair game—tasty meat. The women of Queens are prettiest of all." The .44-Caliber Killer had identified himself as "Son of Sam" in letters he had sent to a New York columnist, James Breslin. By now the city was beginning to panic, but David still easily found victims. In June he shot out the windshield of another car but only wounded the two occupants.

In July David decided to relocate his killing to the Brooklyn area in order to throw off the police. At 1:30 A.M. he fired four shots through the windshield of a car, striking a young couple. Stacy Moskowitz died a few hours later, and her friend Robert Violante was blinded for life. It was here that David's car was ticketed and shortly thereafter linked to the killings. David was arrested exclaiming, "You finally got me!" But he had planted several clues during the long year's ordeal. David had sent threatening notes to his Yonkers neighbors. Sam Carr had made reports to police that David was out to get him because his dog barked too much. Carr's dog had been shot by David with his .44-caliber gun on April 27, shortly after David sent him the letters. David's capture proved to be providential for several young New Yorkers. He told police that he was planning a raid on a Hampton discotheque that night and that authorities "would be counting bodies all summer." Police found a submachine gun and a note to authorities lying on the seat of his car (Leyton, 1986a, Chapter 5).

At first Berkowitz claimed he committed the killings because demonically possessed dogs commanded him to do so. Years later, he would recant those claims publicly by saying that it was the need to justify those shootings in his own mind that caused him to fabricate the demon story. He said he simply wanted to pay back his neighbor, Sam Carr, for all the noise his dog made, so he created the story that Sam was telling him to kill by using the dogs as a medium. In a letter he sent to David Abrahamsen, a psychiatrist who determined Berkowitz to be competent for trial, he conceded:

> I will always fantasize those evil things which are part of my life. I will always remain a mental pervert by thinking sexual things, etc. However, almost everyone else is like me, for we commit numerous perverted sexual acts in our minds day after day. I will always think of violence, for only a monk, perhaps, could ever succeed in eliminating these desires and thoughts. But what I hope to do is mature to such a point in which I will develop a deeper respect for human life and an increased respect and appreciation for humanity (Abrahamsen, 1985, p. 23).

David Berkowitz received six 25-to-life consecutive sentences for the murders to which he confessed, with a recommendation that he never be paroled. He is now serving his time at Sullivan Correctional Facility in Fallsburg, New York. New York passed a "Son of Sam" statute prohibiting criminals from profiting financially from their crimes, which has been challenged in the courts in recent years. He converted to Christianity in 1987 after reading a bible given to him by an inmate. In 1998 in a collaborative effort with evangelical pastors, Berkowitz helped produce two Christian videos "Son of Sam/Son of Hope" and "The Choice is Yours With David Berkowitz" in efforts to persuade others to repent.

6

Team Killers

On February 23, 1996, William George Bonin, age 49, known as the "Freeway Killer," was executed by lethal injection in the state of California. Between 1978 and 1980, Bonin is believed to have sodomized, beaten, and murdered at least 21 young men and boys. He was convicted in 14 cases of murder in the Los Angeles and Orange County areas. As a neglected and sexually abused child, Bonin matured into a young man with a keen interest in young boys. He spent five years incarcerated in a psychiatric hospital and then in prison for sexually assaulting five boys. He finished his sentence and within 16 months he was caught for raping yet another boy. From then on he left no witnesses. Most of his victims were in their teens and each had died a gruesome death by strangulation or stabbing. One victim was fed chlorohydrate acid and then had an ice pick jammed into his right ear and into his brain. Bonin knew no boundaries. He also enjoyed having accomplices who assisted him in his constant search for victims. This chapter focuses on serial killers who prefer to hunt in packs.

The primary catalyst for serial-murder victimization stems from a perceived need to acquire power and control over others. Of course, human nature, practically by definition, includes a drive for power of some type, in some degree. For some people, however, the road to power is strewn with human sacrifices. Power can be all-consuming and justifies every means and method to obtain it.

In the drive for domination, the intensity, the frequency, and the subsequent interpretation of murder are more fulfilling for some killers than for others. The lust for power is the chameleon of vices and as such can be perceived and experienced in many different ways. For some multiple killers, murder must be simultaneously a participation and a spectator endeavor; power can be experienced by observing a fellow conspirator destroy human life, possibly as much as by performing the killing. The pathology of the relationship operates symbiotically. In other words, the offenders contribute to each other's personal inventory of power.

In the mid-1960s, Walter Kelbach and Myron Lance went on a killing spree for several days. In some of the murders, the killers would toss a coin to see which one would get to stab the victim to death. Alone, they may never have killed. What they could never become alone, they could aspire to collectively. Inhibitions and fears were dissipated by the interaction of the two men. History is replete with examples of the destructive forces of group behavior. In groups of people who kill, there are often a few who play subservient roles. They provide an immediate audience "privileged" to experience or witness the destructive power of the main actors. Serial-killing groups are frequently masterminded by one person—for example, Angelo Buono, in the "Hillside Stranglings" in California; Douglas Clark in the "Sunset Strip" killings in Hollywood; Charles Manson and his "Family"; and Gary Heidnik, "The Fiend of Franklinville" in Philadelphia.

Like other subgroups of serial offenders, team killers, or those who kill with one or more accomplices have been documented for many generations. They have generally been considered anomalies that occur infrequently; thus little attention has been given to the nature of team killing.

IDENTIFYING TEAM KILLERS

Forty-seven cases, comprising 110 offenders, represented the base for the analysis for this subgroup of serial killers in our study. Female offenders participated in 17 of the 47 cases of team serial killing. Seventy-four percent of team killers were white, 25% African American, and 1% Asian. The majority of cases involved only two offenders, whereas the remaining cases had three or more offenders in each group. The largest group was identified as having five offenders. Several of the cases or offenders involved were labeled by the media, by the community, or by themselves with creative monikers, such as the Zebra Killers, the Lonely Hearts Killers, and the .22-Caliber Killers.

Several of these cases attracted public attention and have inspired books and movies, including *The Hillside Strangler* and *Helter Skelter,* both of which were popular at the bookstore and the box office.

As indicated in Figure 6.1, the emergence of team killers has mirrored the rise of solo offenders. Although predicting criminal behavior has never been the forte of researchers, assuming that such cases will continue to appear as they have during the seventies, eighties, and nineties, we will likely see a continued rise in such cases. First, law enforcement is becoming educated about serial killings and is more likely now to recognize patterns of serial murders.

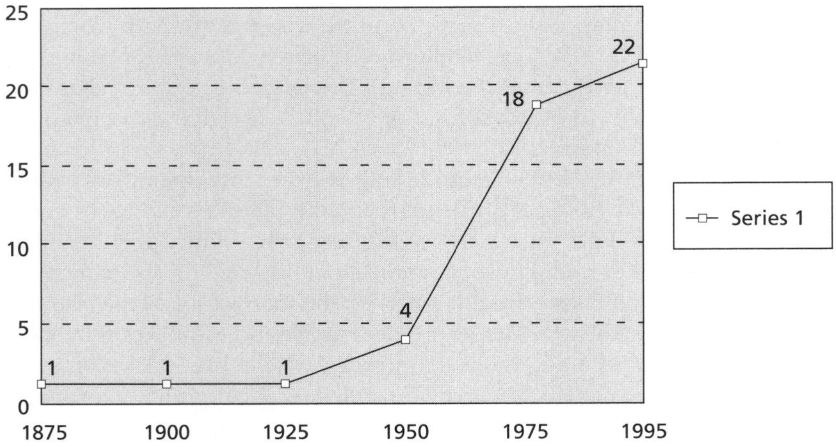

FIGURE 6.1 Frequency of Team Serial Killers in the United States, 1875–1995

N = 47 cases

Table 6.1 Relationship Groupings of Team Offenders, 1850–1995

A. Relatives	B. Nonrelatives
1. Husband/wife	7. Male-dominated teams
2. Father/son	8. Heterosexual lovers
3. Brothers	9. Gay lovers
4. Mother/son	10. Lesbian lovers
5. Father/mother/daughter/son	11. Female-dominated teams
6. Cousins	

Second, law enforcement now has much improved forensic technology and expertise with which to investigate serial crime. Third, fluctuations in the stability of the U.S. economy have a profound effect on the psychological well-being of some individuals. Fourth, desensitization of portions of our communities toward the value of human life is continuing as a result of violence portrayed in the movies, on TV, and in the media. Fifth, the elderly are a fast-growing group of particularly accessible, potential victims.

Only time will prove the accuracy of the gloomy predictions of an increase in serial murders. In the meantime, understanding some of the characteristics of team killing may assist in unraveling its etiology. As briefly discussed earlier, relationships between or among team killers can reveal a great deal about the offenders and the motivations for murder. Table 6.1 indicates that team offenders form dyads, triads, and even larger groupings; sometimes they are both legally or blood related; sometimes they are strangers and acquaintances (see Profile 6.1).

PROFILE 6.1 Kenneth Bianchi and Angelo Buono, 1977–1978

October 18, 1977, the nude, strangled body of Yolanda Washington was discovered in Los Angeles. She had been a part-time waitress and prostitute who worked the streets of Hollywood. On October 31st, the body of 15-year-old Judith L. Miller, a runaway, was found along a roadside, strangled and sexually abused. The child had been severely tortured. There would be at least eight more victims of Bianchi and Buono, "The Hillside Stranglers." Except for Yolanda Washington, who was killed in a car, all the victims were taken to Buono's house, where they were bound, gagged, raped, sodomized with instruments, beaten, and finally strangled to death. The corpses were dumped along the highways and hillsides of Los Angeles and Glendale, except for Cindy Hudspeth, who was found in the trunk of her car in a ravine.

Buono, age 44, and Bianchi, 26, were cousins who decided to kill someone just to see what it would feel like. Each killing, sexual attack, and torture session became easier for them, a game that they looked forward to with excitement. Lauren Wagner was burned with an electrical cord placed on her body. Kristina Weckler was injected with a cleaning solution so they could watch her convulse and then was gassed by having a bag placed over her head with a hose attached to a stove. The killers abducted not only prostitutes but schoolgirls, like 12-year-old Dolores Cepeda and 14-year-old Sonja Johnson. In a span of five months, at least ten homicides had been linked to the Hillside Stranglers.

Bianchi relocated to Bellingham, Washington, and the murders ceased in Los Angeles. A year later, the bodies of Karen Mandic and Diane Wilder, college roommates, were found raped and strangled, and Bianchi, a prime suspect, was arrested. The similarities in the killings and other circumstantial evidence linked Bianchi to the Hillside killings. Bianchi first tried to convince authorities he suffered from multiple personalities and was not responsible for his actions. When that failed, he agreed to plea-bargain and testify against Buono in order to avoid the death penalty. Although they both had developed a taste for killing, Buono and Bianchi were quite different in personality. Bianchi was a bright, smooth-talking ladies' man, a con artist, who had nearly mastered the art of lying. Buono, much less articulate, remained silent throughout his trial. He had been married three times and fathered at least seven children. With only a ninth-grade education, Buono had begun his own upholstery business and also pimped for prostitutes. He enjoyed sex with pain and had abused many women sexually. Bianchi, who was married at the time of some of the murders, had concealed his actions from his wife and newborn son, Sean.

It was California's longest criminal trial at the time and was very costly. Several witnesses spoke on behalf of the killers, especially Buono, but there were always those who knew of his dark side as well. In 1984, Buono received life in prison without parole, and Bianchi is required to spend 26 years and eight months in prison before his first parole hearing can be scheduled. Judge George, who had remained impartial throughout the long trial, commented to the two sadistic killers, "I'm sure, Mr. Buono and Mr. Bianchi, that you will only get your thrills by reliving over and over the tortures and murders of your victims, being incapable, as I believe you to be, of ever feeling any remorse."

In 1986, in a brief ceremony at Folsom Prison, Angelo Buono, then 52 years old, married Christine Kizuka, 35, a supervisor at the Los Angeles office of the State Employment Development Department. His conviction in nine murders apparently did not diminish his attractiveness to at least one woman (Levin & Fox, 1985, Ch. 11).

PROFILE 6.2 Martha Beck and Ray Fernandez

Martha was born in 1920 into poverty. Raped at 13 by her brother she continued to gain weight, appeared emotionally unstable, suffered from low self-esteem and self-worth. She would eventually marry and divorce three times. Authorities removed her two young children when she was declared an unfit mother. One of the children was illegitimate. When Martha pressed for marriage, the father elected suicide rather than marrying her. Martha completed high school and worked as a nurse until she was fired in 1947 from a city maternity hospital. She began sending letters to the "Lonely Hearts Club" only to meet her future murder accomplice. Ray Fernandez was born in Spain in 1914. Considered a shy, introverted man Ray was happily married until he received a head injury at age 31. His demeanor changed as did his personality and he began to believe that he possessed psychic powers that enabled him to get women to fall in love with him. For the next few years he was described as a "sleazy gigolo with a toupee and a gold tooth" who managed to swindle dozens of women out of their financial assets. He was caught in 1949.

Beck proposed that she and Fernandez become partners to continue the confidence games. She would pose as his sister. Although Fernandez found her unattractive, they became sexual partners as well, engaging in extremely "degenerate" practices. Martha eventually became jealous of the relationships Ray developed with their victims and began putting barbiturates into their food. Ray would then kill the unsuspecting victim. In one case Ray killed a woman and Martha assisted by drowning the woman's two-year-old child in the bathtub. She initiated the killing and appeared to enjoy watching the small child struggle for life as she held it in a death grip. Another she killed by striking the victim repeatedly on the head. The duo were linked to approximately 20 murders when they were apprehended, convicted, and executed on March 8, 1951 (Seagrave, 1992).

In our study, the relationships were widely distributed, including several sibling and parent-child combinations. Nonrelated team killers were subdivided into four groups, some of which included offenders who were intimately involved. Other groups had either males or females who provided leadership to the group.

Females as Masterminds in Serial-Murder Relationships

In the nonrelative category, males almost exclusively assumed leadership. Cases were extremely rare in which nonrelated females masterminded multiple homicides. The Martha Beck and Raymond Fernandez case is one such example (Profile 6.2).

This also tended to be true for cases of male/female lovers. In short, although women frequently became involved in serial murder as a part of team killing, they generally were not the decision makers or main enforcers. Pearson (1995) suggests that such perceptions, in part, explain why the FBI Behavioral Science Unit, which develops psychological profiles of male serial

PROFILE 6.3 Tene Bimbo Gypsy Clan, 1984–1994

Five elderly men, all in their eighties and nineties died in San Francisco between 1984 and 1994. Their bodies were exhumed and each was found to have died from overdoses of the drug digitalis, a heart drug. Each man had been involved in May-December romances and each of their sweethearts were females associated with Tene Bimbo, a gypsy clan. Prosecutors believe that the women seduced the elderly men, swindled them, and then killed them with digitalis, a drug from the foxglove plant that is lethal in high doses and mimics natural death. The Clan gained notoriety in Peter Maas's 1974 book *King of the Gypsies* and a film by the same name. In each case younger women in their twenties and thirties from the Clan sought out wealthy elderly men. In some cases the women actually married the men in order to gain access to their money. In one case investigators found that immediately following the death of one victim, $70,000 was drained from his estate and funneled to an Atlantic City casino (Cole, AP).

killers had, by 1995, only one category "compliant victim" for female perpetrators. A FBI study of seven women offenders involved with male offenders who were their husbands or lovers described the relationship as "straightforward male coercion." The Bureau concluded that females took part in the killings as a result of compliance, fear, or stupidity. Such findings are based upon bias and lack of objectivity. Women do become the leaders in some murder cases, albeit rare. There are other types of male-female team serial killers that do not fit traditional concepts of serial murder yet they are serial killers by definition. Consider the case of the Tene Bimbo Gypsy clan (see Profile 6.3).

Indeed, female "Rippers" have yet to make their mark in the United States. Such perceptions do not, however, refute the fact that women can be as deadly as men, as witnessed in the case of Aileen Wuornos (see Chapter 7). Pearson (1995) argues that females who commit murder have the "best of both worlds" because the female offender is empowered during the killing and is able to fulfill her own fantasies, sexual or otherwise. Following the murder(s) the female offender can revert to a submissive, compliant role. Several of the females in this text who are part of the subgroup of male-female team killers tend to be, with a few exceptions, followers, not leaders. However, some of these followers quickly learned how to kill, became "equal partners in the killing," and participated directly in some of the bloodiest murder cases ever chronicled (see Profile 6.4).

Males as Masterminds in Serial Murder Relationships

Without exception, every group of offenders had one person who psychologically maintained control of the other members of the team. Some of these leaders were Charles Manson types who exerted an almost mystical control over their followers; others used forms of coercion, intimidation,

PROFILE 6.4 Alton Coleman and Debra D. Brown, 1984

A man with an explosive temper and ready to fight, Alton Coleman had committed a long list of violent crimes and sex offenses by the age of 28. He was living with Debra Brown, whom he frequently beat and threatened. Alton was raised in the black slums of the Midwest, the son of a prostitute who died when Alton was a teenager. Having no father and being rejected by his mother while still an infant, Alton went to live with his grandmother. She apparently provided a good home for Alton, who nevertheless was characterized as an unhappy, bitter child, who was called "Pissy" by schoolmates because he wet his pants so often. As he grew older, he became more aggressive. He gambled frequently and began to hustle women, whom he usually abused through beatings and sexual assaults. He spent at least three years in prison, where he was known for his aggressive homosexual behavior. His brutality with women and his fascination for bondage, violent sex, and young women ended his first marriage after only six months. He is believed to have raped several women and young girls before his murder spree.

His first victim was 9-year-old Vernita Wheat, whom Coleman had abducted from an acquaintance. She was raped, strangled, and stuffed into a small closet. While police investigated her disappearance, Alton and Debra left the area. Three weeks later they attacked two girls, ages 7 and 9. The younger, little Tamika, was kicked in the face and chest and strangled until she died. Alton then beat and raped the second child and left her unconscious. For the next several weeks, the couple traveled back and forth through five different states, including Ohio, Indiana, Illinois, and Michigan, where they murdered, raped, and robbed several more people, both black and white, young and elderly, male and female. A mother, Virginia Temple, and her 10-year-old daughter were beaten, raped, and strangled and left in a basement crawl space. Coleman possessed a real talent for gaining the trust of strangers and

and persuasive techniques. In team murders, not all the participants shared equally in the "thrill" of the kill. As one offender pointed out, real serial killers are people who make it their life's work. Certainly not all team offenders in this subgroup shared exactly the same motivations or abilities for killing. Given time, however, several became molded to the task.

Truman Capote, in his acclaimed *In Cold Blood* (1965), described the relationship between two killers, Dick Hickock and Perry Smith. In the aftermath of the vicious murders of the entire Clutter family, Perry begins to question the normality of people who could do such a thing. Dick's response reaffirms in his own mind his superiority over Perry: " 'Deal me out, baby,' Dick said. 'I'm a normal.' And Dick meant what he said. He thought himself as balanced, as sane as anyone—maybe a bit smarter than the average fellow, that's all. But Perry—there was, in Dick's opinion, 'something wrong' with Little Perry to say the least" (p. 108).

Such relationships tend to be built on deception, bravado, and intimidation. Often in the aftermath of apprehension by police and eventual incarcer-

eluding the police, who placed him on the FBI's Most Wanted list. One psychiatrist, who was familiar with Coleman, described him a "pansexual," a person who enjoys sex with anyone—man, woman, or child. His sexual enjoyment was surpassed only by his ability for sadism and viciousness.

Debra Brown was described as a high school dropout, from a family of 11, who was easily influenced and dominated. On meeting Coleman, she almost immediately broke off her engagement to another man. Her ability to kill seemed to come easily. In one instance Coleman and Brown attacked a husband and wife, who lived in suburban Cincinnati, using an array of devices, including a four-foot wooden candle stick, a crowbar, vise-grip pliers, and a knife. The wife, Marlene Waters, died after being bludgeoned to death. Other victims were shot to death.

After eight weeks, the two killers were captured without a struggle while watching an outdoor basketball game in Evanston, Illinois. Bond for Coleman was set at $25 million, full cash, and $20 million cash bond was set for Brown. They are believed to be guilty of at least eight murders in addition to a variety of abductions, beatings, robberies, thefts, and sexual assaults. Brown remained loyal to her lover; moments before his first sentencing they signed legal documents creating a common-law marriage. Perhaps in efforts to save Coleman from the death penalty, Brown stated in court regarding one of the victims, "I killed the bitch and I don't give a damn. I had fun out of it." When the courts finished with Coleman, he had received four separate death sentences and more than a hundred years in prison. Debra Brown, after receiving her second death sentence, life in prison, and dozens of additional years in prison, apologized for her part in the killing and wrote "I'm a more kind and understandable and lovable person than people think I am." They are currently awaiting execution (Linedecker, 1987, Ch. 2).

ation, the leaders of some groups tend to go through a process of self-abdication and place culpability for the murders on the followers. In one case the group leader, denying absolutely any involvement in a series of horrific mutilation murders, contended that his exgirlfriend had conceived and executed the murder plans. From his perspective, he was always just a bystander. The case involving Douglas Clark and Carol Bundy (Profile 6.5) also illustrates this point.

Parents and children as well as husbands and wives have also been serial killers. Imagine the dynamics of a family whose mom, dad, son, and daughter systematically killed 14 victims! In one case, the wife had never been involved in any form of violent criminal behavior. By the end, she helped in luring victims to an automobile that she then drove while her husband raped, beat, and strangled them in the back seat.

At what point does a person acquiesce and agree to assist in murdering victims? What enables someone to convince others that murdering people is the direction to follow? It appears unlikely that some male and female

PROFILE 6.5 Douglas D. Clark and Carol A. Bundy, 1980

Clark, son of a retired U.S. Navy admiral, liked to call himself "The King of the One-Night Stands." He enjoyed exploiting women emotionally, sexually, and financially. Since childhood, his sexual fantasies had been fueled by the wearing of women's underclothing. He acted out perverted sexual fantasies with women who would care for his bizarre needs, regardless of their sometimes dowdy appearance. He met Carol Bundy, a nurse, while working as a boiler room engineer at a Burbank, California, soap factory. Carol had recently been jilted and was quickly attracted to the smooth-talking Clark. She felt that he might be the solution to her problems because she was lonely, had poor eyesight, was diabetic, and in need of comfort. Clark immediately moved in with Carol, but, much to her dismay, he insisted on regularly cruising Sunset Boulevard in Hollywood, California, in search of young prostitutes. He told Carol of his fantasies to have sexual intercourse with the corpses of recently murdered girls. Carol, believing she really loved Clark, became a compliant assistant in his efforts to actualize his fantasies.

Carol began photographing Clark while willing teenage girls he had brought home performed oral sex on him. She even watched while he had sex with an 11-year-old girl who had been rollerskating in a nearby park. Clark next targeted two female hitchhikers, whom he shot to death and then had sex with: Gina Marano, 15, and Cynthia Chandler, 16, had run away from home to enjoy the excitement of living on Sunset Strip. To display his work, Clark later took Carol to the site where he had disposed of the bodies. Female corpses began appearing with regularity. The body of a female was found behind a restaurant in Burbank. The same morning, a man discovered a headless woman lying in an alley. Three days later, the severed head appeared in a box at the entrance to another neighbor's driveway. The head had been cleaned, frozen, and made up with lipstick and other cosmetics. Both of these victims, Karen Jones and Exxie Wilson, had been young prostitutes. Clark, now dubbed the "Sunset Slayer" by the press, had developed a pattern of abducting and shooting young hookers and runaways in order to engage in necrophilia.

Carol later confessed how Clark kept the heads of some of the victims in the refrigerator. On at least one occasion, she applied cosmetics to a victim's head that Clark then used sexually while in the shower. He claimed that he hated prostitutes and loved to watch them die. He frequently hired prostitutes for oral sex and, as he reached a climax, shot them in the head. Panties became another trophy Clark would save after he had sex with the corpse. He even carried a "killing bag" in his car that contained a knife, rubber gloves, and plastic sacks. One victim abducted from a shopping mall managed to pull

offenders ever would have indulged in such crimes had they not been exposed to group dynamics and the power of persuasion and manipulation. Some of those who led groups of team offenders experienced a sense of power and gratification not only through the deaths of victims but also through getting others to do their bidding. Robin Gecht in Chicago sur-

free from her two captors but only after she had been stabbed 27 times (Linedecker, 1987, Ch. 12).

Although Carol was a willing participant in the murders, it was Clark who initiated the hunts for victims along the Strip. Clark allegedly told her on one occasion that if Carol ever told, he would kill her two young children. Later Carol would inadvertently disclose information about the killings to her former boyfriend. When he decided to tell the police, she lured him to a secluded spot where they had sex together. She then stabbed him to death, slashed open his buttocks, and decapitated him. The head was never found.

Eventually Carol decided she wanted no more of the killing and told her story to her coworkers. She became the star witness for the prosecution but still claimed to love Clark. While in jail awaiting trial, Clark began to exchange letters with a woman who was in custody for attempted murder. She had tried to establish a fake alibi for yet another serial killer, Kenneth Bianchi, one of the "Hillside Stranglers." They appeared to derive great pleasure in writing letters that made reference to necrophilia, murder, blood, torture, and mutilation. In 1983, Clark was found guilty of six counts of first-degree murder and sentenced to die in San Quentin's gas chamber. Carol, who admitted killing at least one prostitute and her former boyfriend, was given consecutive sentences of 25 years to life and 27 years to life and currently resides in Central California's Women's Prison in Chowchilla (Linedecker, 1987, Ch. 12).

Clark, on death row in San Quentin, California, at the time of this writing, vehemently denies any involvement in any murders. He claims that his accomplice, Carol A. Bundy, was the real mastermind and the person who carried out all the killings. Her actual partner, claims Clark, was John Murray, her former boyfriend, whom she murdered. After Murray was killed, Clark was left to "take the rap" because he had stayed in one of her rented apartments. Clark claims that Carol Bundy fantasized herself to be the wife of the now-deceased serial killer Ted Bundy and that she was merely mimicking his pattern of murders. Since Clark's arrival on death row, he has married a woman who champions his quest for freedom while he continues his appeals process. He expresses great bitterness toward law enforcement and the criminal justice system, which he feels has used him as a scapegoat to cover up their own failure to prosecute the real offender.

The author, on a prison visit, spoke with Carol Bundy, now frail and ill with diabetes. I asked her if she ever communicated with Clark. She responded "Oh no, he is not allowed to send me mail anymore." As I was leaving her cell, she reflected on Clark and said "You know Dr. Hickey, Douglas Clark is a very disturbed man." Unfortunately, I did not have a mirror to give her.

rounded himself with loyal followers who obediently killed with and for him. Charles Manson needed only to provide direction for his eager band of devotees. Dean Corll, involved in killing dozens of young males, used his charisma to entice delinquent youths into his gang of procurers. This does not negate in any way the culpability of team offenders. Indeed, many of them were quite anxious to become involved, but they became killers because of another's influence. For some of these followers, killing first became acceptable and then desirable. Others continued to kill solely as a result of their relationship with whoever held the reins of leadership. The next sections explore social data surrounding team offenders that may be helpful in further understanding group killers.

OCCUPATIONS OF TEAM SERIAL KILLERS

For the most part, team offenders who held jobs were employed in blue-collar work that required limited training. The occupations listed below reflect some types of employment held by team offenders. In contrast to the myth that serial killers often are financially successful, economically stable individuals, offenders in this subgroup were not from the professional occupations. Similarly, with only a few exceptions, most of these offenders did not receive college educations, and only a few received postsecondary education, such as vocational training. In brief, they were generally ill prepared to achieve occupationally successful careers.

Occupations of Team Offenders before or during Their Career of Murder

Skilled

Aircraft company employee
- Shoemaker
- Car upholster
- Electrician
- Carpenter
- Nurse

Semiskilled
- Woodsman
- Truck driver
- Warehouse employee
- Bartender
- Boiler operator
- Farmer

Unskilled
- Laborer
- Waitress
- Gas station attendant

Government

Security/auxiliary police
- Military personnel
- Minister

Criminal
- Thief
- Scam artist
- Pimp
- Burglar
- Robber

Other
- Transient
- Cultist

TEAM KILLING AND MOBILITY

Team serial offenders (110 offenders) were responsible for 408–564 murders or 15–16% of all deaths in this entire study. Twenty-eight percent of all offenders ($N = 399$) were identified as team killers. This means, in general, that group offenders did not kill on the average as many victims as other serial offender subgroups. Team offenders on the average were responsible for four to five killings per offender (Table 6.2).

In general, it seems that solo serial killers caused greater destruction than team killers did. Certainly there were exceptions: Bianchi-Buono, Corll-Henley-Brooks, the Benders, and Lake-Ng all killed more than the average number of victims. But several teams managed to kill "only" three, four, or five victims. By dividing the number of cases into the number of victims, team killers averaged nine to twelve victims per case, whereas solo killers averaged slightly more. In brief, having more than one offender involved in serial killing did not increase the number of victims per case. Solo offenders were a little more likely, on the average, to kill more victims. This discrepancy might result in part from the greater number of offenders involved in team killing, which may increase the possibility of discovery by law enforcement. When two or more offenders are involved in a case, the chances of somebody talking or leaving evidence at or near the crime scene increase.

Offender mobility data indicated that team killers were most likely to remain in local proximity to their killing sites and least likely to be classified as place-specific offenders. The greatest number of victims were killed by these local team offenders, in some contrast to those with greater mobility (see Profile 6.6, Henry Lee Lucas and Otis Elwood Toole).

Place-specific offenders had the fewest number of cases and were responsible for the smallest percentage of team victims, yet they averaged the highest number of victims per case. By contrast, local team killers represented double the number of place-specific cases but averaged significantly fewer victims per

Table 6.2 Victims of Team Killers in the United States by Mobility Classification, 1850–1995

Mobility Classification of Killers	Percentage of Victims (408–564)	Percentage of Cases (N = 42)	Percentage of Offenders (N = 110)	Average Number of Victims per Case	Average Number of Victims per Offender
Total	100	100	100	9–12	4–5
Traveling	33–34	37	31	8–10	4–6
Local	44–48	48	48	8–12	3–5
Place-specific	20–23	15	12	13–15	7–8

PROFILE 6.6 Henry Lee Lucas and Otis Elwood Toole, 1976–1982

"Joe Don . . . I've done some bad things" was something of an understatement from Henry Lee Lucas to a jailer when he was incarcerated for illegal possession of a .22-caliber weapon. Within a few days Lucas had confessed to killing about 100 victims in several states. Within a few months the figure rose from 100 to 600 victims. He claimed to have killed in most of the 50 states and to have had at least a dozen victims in Canada.

Born in Blacksburg, Virginia, in 1936, to a woman who worked as a prostitute and suffered from alcoholism, Henry seemed to be doomed from the beginning of his life. Lucas experienced rejection from both within and outside his family. His IQ was considered to be slightly below normal. He dropped out of school in the fifth grade after his brother accidentally gouged out his right eye with a knife. By the time he was 13 he had already served time in Maryland for auto theft. At age 14 he killed a girl, also 14, in order to conceal a sex crime. He continued to accumulate a history of criminal behavior of burglaries and thefts. At age 23 he murdered his 74-year-old mother by stabbing her. He was sent to prison in Michigan and was paroled in 1970, only to return quickly for another four years for attempted abduction. He was released in 1975, and a year later he teamed up with Otis Toole, a tall, rough-looking character who served at times as Lucas's homosexual lover. Toole also had been involved in various criminal activities. He would later confess to allegedly having killed several homosexuals and to have started several fires simply because he found them exciting. Apparently Toole enjoyed killing his victims, then mutilating the corpses.

The pair traveled through many states picking up hitchhikers to kill along the way. Most of the victims were female, although Lucas did confess to killing a few males, such as a police officer in Huntington, West Virginia. Many of the victims were sexually abused, and necrophilia and even cannibalism may have been involved. During an eight-year period, Lucas had another traveling companion and sexual partner, 13-year-old Freida "Becky" Lorraine Powell. Toole was her uncle and had managed to gain custody of the orphan girl from a state institution. While in Texas, the slightly retarded girl became involved in an argument with Lucas about leaving the state. Lucas later confessed how Becky reached over and slapped him, to which he immediately responded by stabbing her to death. According to Lucas, he then raped her, dismembered the body, stuffed the pieces into pillow cases, and left the

case. This may suggest that place-specific offenders, although few in number, were much more difficult to detect. Such offenders could carry on seemingly routine lives while they methodically killed and disposed of victims in their own homes or places of employment. In some cases of local team killing, offenders were less difficult to detect because bodies of victims were discovered quickly.

remains in a field. Ironically, this young girl was the only person for whom Lucas claims to have had affection.

Lucas claimed to have killed his victims in every imaginable fashion. He never wanted to know their names, and if a victim did give his or her name, Lucas would put it out of his mind. He claimed to have killed very young children and people 80 years of age. Lucas's first confession after he was jailed in 1983 solved the unexplained disappearance of 80-year-old Katherine Rich, who had been living in north Texas not far from Lucas. He chopped her into pieces and tried to incinerate the remains in his stove. Investigators would later find pieces of human bones in the trash of Lucas's home. Most of the Lucas/Toole victims were female hitchhikers who willingly got into their car. Lucas perceived that women who hitchhiked rides were like prostitutes, and he harbored a real hatred for them. As a child, Lucas remembers having to watch his prostitute mother have sex with men and how poorly he was treated by her.

Other victims were killed during robberies or while Toole was sexually attacking a male victim. When asked if he (Lucas) had any morals at all, he responded that he never stole from the victims; he never took their money or their jewelry. After Lucas started his confessions, he decided to help locate the bodies of the victims. He claimed that God helped him get over his hate, and it was time to change his life and start again. But did Lucas/Toole actually kill as many as 600 victims? One investigator was quoted as saying "This is a man who will confess to anything you want." He is believed to have confessed to many of the murders because of the publicity he received (Peyton, 1984).

Lucas was convicted of ten homicides, but in early 1985 he began to recant most of his confessions, claiming that law enforcement officers pressured him into confessing or tried to bribe him with special perks. He now claims that police are simply trying to clear cases and use him as a scapegoat. In early 1988, shortly after interviewing Lucas, one investigator stated that Lucas probably killed between 40 and 50 victims. He killed mainly because he enjoyed the experience; most of his killings were probably done in Florida, Texas, and Louisiana, although authorities in other states believe he was involved in additional homicides. Lucas's death sentence was commuted to life in prison by then Texas Gov. George W. Bush, while Toole died of cirrhosis of the liver in a Florida prison.

Team offenders in this subgroup appeared in several states, the majority surfacing in California. Table 6.3 indicates that distribution of team killings and the number of offenders by state. Except for California the number of cases was relatively even and did not appear to be concentrated in any particular area of the country. However, along with California, a few states, including Illinois, Texas, and Pennsylvania reported noticeably higher numbers of offenders per case than all other states.

Table 6.3 Distribution of Cases and Team Killers by State, 1850–1995

State	Number of Cases	Number of Offenders	State	Number of Cases	Number of Offenders
California	16	43	Montana	2	4
Florida	6	8	Virginia	2	4
Illinois	5	19	Utah	2	4
Texas	5	13	Tennessee	1	2
Ohio	4	4	Oklahoma	1	2
Washington	3	6	Nevada	1	2
Pennsylvania	3	12	New Jersey	1	2
Arizona	3	5	Iowa	1	2
Indiana	3	6	Minnesota	1	2
Michigan	2	4	South Carolina	1	2
Nebraska	2	4	Vermont	1	2
Oregon	2	4	Georgia	1	2
New York	2	7	Massachusetts	1	2
Kansas	2	4	Louisiana	1	2
Colorado	2	4			

RITUALISM, CULTS, AND CHILD VICTIMS

In recent years, considerable attention has been given to ritualistic crimes, including child abuse and murder. Conspiracies organized by groups of adults have been credited with using daycare centers as fronts for exploiting children. These allegations have included a litany of abuse and sexual exploitation. Finkelhor, in his book *Nursery Crimes* (1988), concluded that, although abuse does occur in daycare centers, he did not find any abnormally high rates of abuse. Instead, he pointed out that such abuse was much more likely to happen in the home, caused by parents and relatives. What this may suggest is that abuse is indeed a social concern but that it has not become as institutionalized as some people believe. Instead, abuse continues to be primarily a function of private, rather than collective, interests. However, only a few cases involving groups or organizations are needed to influence public perception, because of the tremendous publicity, scandal, and arrests.

For example, in 1989, 16 Catholic priests, former priests, and other men in the Roman Catholic community in the Province of Newfoundland, Canada, were charged with or convicted of sexual offenses against young boys. Because of priests' high community visibility, what started as a focus on one suspect quickly became a witch hunt for anyone affiliated with the Catholic priesthood. In 1984, in the McMartin preschool case in Manhattan Beach, California, seven people were accused of the ritualistic torture of children. After the longest trial ever in United States history, charges against most of the defendants were dropped because of insufficient evidence, and the key suspects were acquitted. Similar cases have surfaced in Bakersfield, California; Jordan, Minnesota; and Annawaakee in Douglasville, Georgia.

On April 11, 1989, a mass grave was unearthed near Matamoros, Mexico, just south of the Texas border. The grave contained 15 corpses, many of which appeared to have been ritualistically sacrificed. Cauldrons with animal remains mixed in a broth of human blood and boiled body parts were found not far from a bloodstained altar. Suspects arrested said the victims were "killed for protection." This group of drug smugglers was practicing a form of black magic in which sacrifices to the devil, both human and animal, were believed to provide protection from bullets and criminal prosecution (Fox & Levin, 1989, pp. 49–51). Kahaner, in his book *Cults That Kill* (1988), noted that satanism and murder are increasing and that an epidemic of youth violence is sweeping the country. The Robin Gecht case supports this claim (see Profile 6.7).

Such cases continue to surface and ignite public outrage, especially those that center on families and children. Marron, in his book *Ritual Abuse* (1988), described the complexity of a case in which parents allegedly performed ritualistic tortures on their own children. By the time the courts, investigators, and social service agencies had all been involved, affixing blame and determining culpability had become extremely difficult.

In attempting to sort out the connection, if any, between satanism, cult activities, and serial murderers, investigators should recognize that many murders in general are carried out by nonstrangers. Also, acts of satanism or cult worship are much more likely to be self-styled than part of any organized effort. In one case, Robert Berdella, a serial killer involved in the murders of several young men, was accused of Satan worship. Indignant, Berdella requested an interview with the press and, although he admitted to the murders, he categorically denied any association with cultists, Satan worship, or occult activities (author's files). In only a few cases of team offenders who targeted children were there any hints of satanism, rituals, or other cultlike activities.

The connection of satanic worship and child sacrifices never fails to generate near hysteria in a community. The reality, however, is that people are much more likely to be killed in a domestic argument, by an intoxicated driver, in an accident, or by disease than by Satan worshipers. The cases of those few who do fall prey to such bizarre practices generate such publicity that people believe the problem has suddenly become epidemic. To add to the confusion, some serial killers may give the appearance of killing children for cult-related purposes.

Such self-styled "satanism," in which each offender adapts rituals to his or her own purposes, appears to be more common than organized satanic sacrifices. In a 1994 survey of 11,000 psychiatric and police workers across the United States, the National Center on Child Abuse and Neglect found more than 12,000 accusations of group cult sexual abuse using satanic ritual. Except for a few cases of solitary offenders adapting cult rituals, not one report could be substantiated. It is exactly these forms of disinformation that generate and

PROFILE 6.7 Robin Gecht, Edward Spreitzer, and Andrew and Thomas Kokoraleis, 1981–1982

Robin Gecht, 28, could be described as charismatic in his ability to draw others to him, especially those who were easily led. Raised on the north side of Chicago, he went to live with his grandparents after he allegedly molested his sister. He eventually became a carpenter-electrician in order to provide for himself, but his strongest skills were his abilities to manipulate and use others. Gecht also had a developing interest in satanism, cults, and secret rituals. On one occasion he remarked to a friend that through his study of ancient torture practices, he discovered that some female victims were mutilated and their breasts removed to be used later as tobacco pouches. But Robin seemed to be a harmless individual, and no one suspected him, at least not those who knew him, to be involved with the wave of female abductions in the city.

Meanwhile Robin sought out those who might help him realize his sexual fantasies. He had already hired Ed Spreitzer to work for him and eventually met the Kokoraleis brothers, who joined his group. They were all young men: Andrew Kokoraleis, 19; Thomas Kokoraleis, 22; and Ed Spreitzer, 21. One investigator described the three as "classic followers" and "generic nobodies." Using a van belonging to Gecht, they roamed the city, usually at night, hunting for female victims. Police confirmed eight murders carried out by the group, although some of the killers claimed between 10 and 12 victims, and others went as high as 17. The victims were raped, beaten, stabbed, or strangled to death and often sexually mutilated. Following Gecht's arrest for slashing an 18-year-old prostitute, police began to probe deeper into the assailants' backgrounds. They undoubtedly became more suspicious when they discovered that Gecht had worked for John Gacy, the killer of 33 males. Gecht had commented to a friend that Gacy's only mistake had been to bury the bodies under his house. In one place where Gecht had recently lived, police found crosses painted in red and black on the walls of the attic.

perpetuate beliefs that satanic groups are preying upon children ("Study Belies Reports," *New York Times,* 1994). Recently, a few persons have claimed to have been ritualistically victimized or watched as members of satanic groups sacrifice children. Known as repressed memory syndrome, many adult patients under the care of psychotherapists have reported being victimized by cult groups or being part of a group that has victimized children or other adults. Very few of these cases have actually been verified.

VICTIM SELECTION

Team killers did not appear to be gender-specific and equally selected both males and females as targets, especially those who were adults. About half of all team cases and offenders killed both males and females. Strangers were the most common type of victim selection as well as a preference for adults over

Thomas Kokoraleis admitted that the room had contained an altar on which cult members dissected both animal and human parts as sacrifices.

As the probe continued, police found a common trait among the victims whose bodies had not completely decomposed. In each of the cases the victim's breasts had been mutilated and cut off with a knife or piano wire. At least one of the killers admitted that they had been told by their leader Gecht to "bring a breast back to the house." Apparently the trio wanted to do Gecht's bidding in order to please him. Once a victim had been found and killed, her breasts would be placed on the altar. Gecht would then read Bible passages while the group engaged in cannibalism.

After five years, the four were convicted of various offenses. Gecht, whom prosecutors described as being similar to Charles Manson, has yet to be convicted of any murders even though the others testified against him. Instead he received a 120-year sentence for the attack on the 18-year-old prostitute, on the evidence of one eyewitness. His lengthy sentence includes time for attempted murder, rape, deviant sexual assault, armed violence, aggravated kidnapping, and aggravated battery. Police continue at this writing to collect more evidence against him. Ed Spreitzer pleaded guilty to six murders and received a death sentence. Some of the victims included Lorraine Borowski, 21, a secretary; Rose Beck Davis, a housewife; Sandra Delaware; Linda Sutton, 28; Shui Mak, 30; and Rafail Tirads, 28, a male who was shot from a car. Andrew Kokoraleis also received a death sentence for his part in the murders. Thomas Kokoraleis had his murder conviction reversed on technical grounds, and after a second trial and a plea bargain he received a 70-year sentence. It is unlikely that the remains of all their victims will ever be recovered, because many of them were buried in forested areas (Baumann, 1987).

children. In one case offenders would cruise in their van along city streets looking for opportunities to drive up beside an intended victim and pull her in through the side door. The victim was then gagged, tied, and tortured to death. Overall, in 73% of the cases, at least one female was murdered.

As indicated in Table 6.4, very few cases or offenders that specifically targeted children or teenagers were identified. Nearly one-fifth of all cases included one or more male or female children. Females were also the most common targets among teenage victims. Overall, team offenders targeted female teens twice as often as male teens. In addition, when team offenders killed victims from more than one age category, adults and teenagers were the most likely targets. Conversely, team offenders, in all cases, were least likely to select both teenagers and children as victims.

The majority of cases involved stranger-to-stranger violence (Tables 6.5 and 6.6). Two-thirds of all female team offenders and three-fourths of male team offenders targeted strangers. Again, this reinforces the belief that strangers

Table 6.4 Percentage of Team Offenders Murdering Specific Victim Age and Gender Categories, 1850–1995

	Percentage of Cases (*N* = 47)	Percentage of Offenders (*N* = 110)
Gender		
1. Females only	27	23
Males only	27	29
Both	46	48
	100	100
2. At least one female	73	70
At least one male	73	75
Age Grouping		
Adults only	42	45
Teens only	8	9
Children only	2	2
Gender and Age Grouping		
1. Adults:		
One or more females	67	63
One or more males	60	64
Both males and females	40	40
2. Teens:		
One or more females	38	38
One or more males	19	24
Both males and females	6	12
3. Children:		
One or more females	17	14
One or more males	17	15
Both males and females	10	7
4. Age combinations:		
Adults and teens	23	25
Adults and children	6	4
Teens and children	2	3
All ages	15	14

are preferred as victims by serial killers. Very few cases involved the killing of a family member or an acquaintance.

Stranger-to-stranger homicide facilitation was influenced by several circumstances, including time of attack or abduction, accessibility to victims, age and race of victims, and location of potential victims and offenders. Although research has yet to explore some of these factors, it would appear that not all strangers were equally at risk. Individual lifestyle appeared to be a critical factor in determining the types of strangers who fell prey to team offenders or any other serial killers. Risk-takers such as prostitutes and hitchhikers appeared to be at greater risk than those who avoided such lifestyles.

Table 6.5 Percentage of Team Offenders Murdering Family, Acquaintances, and Strangers in the United States, 1850–1995

Relationship	Percentage of Cases (*N* = 46)	Percentage of Female Offenders (*N* = 19)	Percentage of Male Offenders (*N* = 89)	Percentage of Total Number of Offenders (*N* = 108)
Strangers	74	68	80	78
Strangers/acquaintances	11	5	7	6
Strangers/family	4	11	2	4
Acquaintances	—	11	4	6
Acquaintances/family	2	—	1	1
Family	4	5	3	4
All	4	—	2	2

Table 6.6 Order of Types of Victims Selected by Team Killers

A. Strangers

1. Females: young females walking alone
   Hitchhikers
   Prostitutes
   College students
   Handicapped
   Respondents to newspaper ads
2. Travelers/campers
3. People at random in homes
4. People at random on street
5. Young boys
6. Employees/business people
7. Children at play
8. Police officers

B. Acquaintances

9. Neighbor children
10. Females: people on street
    Waitresses
11. Males: group members
    Visitors
    People in authority

C. Family

12. Children
13. Wives/brothers/mothers

Table 6.7 Degree of Victim Facilitation in Being Murdered by Team Offenders, 1850–1995

Facilitation	Percentage of Cases (*N* = 47)	Percentage of Offenders (*N* = 107)
Low	57	64
High	11	10
Both	33	26

Table 6.7 compares cases and offenders with the degree of facilitation provided by the victims. Did the victim walk alone at night? Did he or she hitchhike or pick up partners in bars? Perhaps the person was too trusting of strangers instead of exercising caution. In any case, recent team offender cases appeared to involve more frequency of facilitation by victims than in earlier years. For example, overall since 1800, 57% of these cases were reported to have one or more victims rating low in facilitation. Since 1975, however, that number has dropped considerably. This in turn raises questions of whether victims are actually taking more risks, taking greater risks, or whether offenders are merely exploiting a pool of risk-takers they had earlier ignored. What has changed considerably from the first study is that several more offenders who target victims with both low and high facilitation ratings have been identified.

METHODS AND MOTIVES

Guns were commonly used by team offenders during the commission of their crimes (Table 6.8). However, guns only were used in approximately one out of four cases as the sole method of killing. As in other serial murders, the purpose was usually not to dispose of victims quickly but to keep them alive so they could be subjected to tortures and mutilations. Consequently, more than half of team offenders used two or more methods to kill their victims. Mutilations, including stabbings, dissections, and other forms of cutting, were particularly common. Several offenders expressed enjoyment in being able to perform acts of sadism. The case of Dean Corll and followers graphically illustrates this point (see Profile 6.8).

Team killers were more likely than other offenders to kill for cult-related reasons. A few team offenders were involved in ritualistic torture of victims. Most of these offenders belonged to larger teams of killers and were not the planners and decision makers. As mentioned earlier, cult activities involved extensive torturing of victims and using human blood and body parts for altar offerings. Enjoyment of torture and killing was more frequently expressed by this group of team killers than by other serial offenders. This, in part, may be due to the bravado some of the group members may have felt was necessary for the public to hear and see once they were apprehended.

Table 6.8 Methods Used by Team Offenders to Kill Their Victims, 1850–1995

Methods	Percentage of Cases (*N* = 43)	Percentage of Offenders (*N* = 100)
Firearms	65	60
Strangulation	35	33
Stabbing	33	36
Bludgeoning	30	33
Firearms only	28	28
Suffocation	9	7
Poison	7	9
Drowning	5	4
Combinations of methods	56	55

Almost identical to other serial offenders, team killers most likely had motives of a sexual nature (Table 6.9). Rape, sodomy, fellatio, and so on, were recurrent forms of sexual acting out. As discussed earlier, such "motives" appear to fall under the category of methods; the sexual assaults appeared to be methods of gaining control over victims. Money was found to be commonly cited as a motive for murder, although it was much less likely noted as the sole reason for killing. Similar to all serial killers, team offenders could rarely be legally classified as insane. Regardless of how obscene some of the murders were, insanity could not be established.

OFFENDER HISTORY

Research data were sometimes limited regarding certain biographical information on team serial killers. In approximately half of team offender profiles, sufficient data existed to examine previous violent, criminal, or abnormal behaviors. Offenders having such histories were most likely to have been incarcerated in prison or a mental institution. Team offenders reported similar records of incarceration in comparison to their male solo counterparts (Table 6.10). They were also likely to have criminal records for theft, sex-related crimes, or histories of psychiatric problems. Considering that 26% of all serial killers report a history of various psychiatric problems, team killers are only slightly higher (30%). However, team offenders (25%) were less likely to have criminal records for sex-related crimes than solo killers (37%).

Team offenders were likely to come in contact with one another as a result of prior incarcerations and criminal records. There appeared to be somewhat more interest in financial gain among team serial killers than solo offenders in

PROFILE 6.8 Dean A. Corll, David O. Brooks, and Elmer Wayne Henley, 1970–1973

Born in Fort Wayne, Indiana, Dean Corll relocated to Houston, Texas, about the time his parents were divorced. A model student, he played trombone in the high school band and was never a disciplinary problem. He was often referred to as "good ole Dean." He became active in his family's candy business and eventually became vice president. For a two-year period he left the Corll Candy Company to care for his widowed grandmother. He later served time in the military and received an honorable hardship discharge to return and help his mother with the family business. Dean's generosity and kindness became well known among the local children and they came regularly for candy handouts. The candy company dissolved in 1968, and Dean entered an electricians' training program. He began to move frequently, and in 1969 met David Brooks, who became attracted to Dean's personality.

Brooks's parents had also divorced. He had a short history of theft before he was sent to live with his grandfather, then with his grandmother; finally he moved in with Corll. He always maintained to his friends that "nobody can figure me out." He continued to steal, shoplift, and burglarize while Corll helped him purchase a Corvette. The two became sexually involved, and Dean began giving money to Brooks for sexual favors. Elmer Wayne Henley, 17, also began associating with Corll. He too had come from a broken home and helped support the family after his father left. As his grades dropped, Wayne left school in the ninth grade. He had tried to enlist in the Navy at 16 but was rejected. Life worsened for Wayne, and he was arrested for breaking and entering and assault with a deadly weapon. He began drinking heavily and associating with Dean Corll, but unlike the bisexual Brooks, Wayne was not interested in any homosexual liaisons.

The two young men, however, were willing to procure young males for Corll to sexually abuse. They would later state in confessions that Corll agreed to pay them $200 for every boy they picked up. The two found male hitchhikers and brought them to Corll's apartment for glue-sniffing parties. When the boys passed

Table 6.9 Motives Reported by Team Offenders for Killing Their Victims, 1850–1995

Motives	Percentage of Cases (N = 47)	Percentage of Offenders (N = 97)
Sexual	49	43
Money	32	33
Control	32	28
Enjoyment	26	27
Cult expectations	13	19
Racism	9	20
Combination of motives	58	59

out, Corll would molest them. Eventually Corll wanted more and began torturing and killing the boys. He would tie or handcuff them to a seven-by-three-foot board and then sodomize, strangle, and shoot the boys. Their deaths often were gruesome; Corll would sometimes chew off the victim's penis or assault the youth with a 17-inch double-headed dildo. Most of the victims came from the Heights area in Houston, and some were neighbors. The victims ranged in age from 9 years to college age. Corll killed several of his victims in groups of two, and on at least two occasions he killed brothers. Henley seemed to enjoy the sadistic killing; on one occasion he fired a bullet up the nostril of one of the victims and then shot him again in the head. Brooks later testified that Henley "seemed to enjoy causing pain." The killing went on until Corll decided to kill Henley after they had disagreed. Henley managed to convince Corll not to kill him, and when Henley was freed, he grabbed a gun and shot Corll five times, killing him on the spot.

The story became public when Henley decided to call the police and tell the entire story. Police found 17 bodies of young white males under a boathouse near Pasadena, Texas. They had been placed in sheets of heavy plastic and covered with lime. Various smaller plastic containers held an assortment of body parts, primarily sex organs. Ten other bodies were exhumed at two additional sites under the guidance of Henley. Some observers believe police stopped searching for bodies once they had surpassed the existing number of homicide victims found in a single case at that time.

Elmer Wayne Henley eventually was found guilty of helping to murder six of the boys and sentenced to six sentences of 99 years each. A Texas appeals court in 1978 overturned his conviction as a result of pretrial publicity, but in a second trial, in June 1979, Henley was convicted and sentenced again. David Brooks was convicted of only one murder and sentenced to life in prison. Ironically, Dean A. Corll's coffin was covered in an American flag in keeping with the tradition that we honor those who have served their country honorably (Nash, 1981a).

Table 6.10 Percentage of Team Offenders Reporting a History of Violent, Criminal, or Abnormal Behavior, 1850–1995

History	Percentage of Cases (*N* = 47)	Percentage of Offenders (*N* = 53)
Theft	45	51
Prior incarceration in prison or mental institution	45	45
Psychiatric problems	28	30
Sex-related crimes	26	25
Drug/alcohol-related crimes	13	21
Crimes as a juvenile	13	11

PROFILE 6.9 Leonard Lake and Charles Ng, 1983–1985

On June 2, 1985, a man arrested in San Francisco was detained and charged with illegal possession of a weapon with a silencer. A few moments later the man swallowed a cyanide capsule and collapsed; he died four days later after being removed from life support systems. Fingerprints indicated his name was Leonard Lake, a 39-year-old Vietnam veteran who was described by neighbors as "quiet, strange, and somewhat arrogant."

He allegedly attended weekly Bible classes. It is also believed that he and an accomplice, Charles Ng, who fled to Canada, may have murdered 25 or more males and females in a specially constructed cinder-block bunker located near Sacramento in a mountain retreat that was used as a torture chamber. Some victims were lured to the house by a promise of work, whereas others answered classified ads. Apparently, some of the earliest victims were relatives, friends, and neighbors because they were easiest to lure to the bunker. The goal was to seek out sexually attractive females who would then be used as sex slaves, subjected to sexual torture, and often killed. Males were targets simply because they were companions of the women or because they had credit cards, cash, or desirable identification. It has been speculated that some of the men may have actually worked at the retreat prior to their deaths.

Some reports indicate that Lake was involved in clandestine cult meetings where human sacrifices were discussed. Some photographs show Lake wearing robes worn by modern-day witches and posing with a goat made up to look like a live unicorn. Police also discovered that Lake had skipped bail in 1982 after he was arrested on charges of possession of explosives and illegal automatic weapons. Shortly after this arrest, Lake's wife divorced him. Two years earlier Lake had been arrested for grand theft for stealing building materials from a low-income housing project. Later he was arrested after police found an arsenal of bomb material, machine guns, silencers, and other weapons at a ranch where he worked as caretaker.

Ng, a 24-year-old who also had many encounters with the law, had been involved in several incidents of stealing and shoplifting as a youth. Following a hit-and-run accident, Ng joined the Marines, where he was arrested for stealing a variety of weapons, including grenade launchers, machine guns, and handguns. Ng es-

considering past crimes. Indeed, some team killers grouped themselves together in almost businesslike ventures that culminated in murder. Such is the case of Leonard Lake and Charles Ng (see Profile 6.9).

Another important area of biographical data concerned the degree to which team offenders had experienced traumatization while in their youth (Table 6.11). In comparing male team killers to male solo killers, changes from the original study were found. For example, in the original study, team killers were twice as likely to come from unstable homes as solo killers. With a much larger data set of solo killers it was found that little difference existed between the two groups. This included alcoholic parents, prostitution by mother, incarceration of parent(s) (see Profile 6.10), periodic separation from parents due to troubles at home, and psychiatric problems involving the parents. We do

caped from marine detention, and after seeing an ad placed by Lake in a magazine for mercenary soldiers, he joined forces with Lake in a spree of killing.

When investigators went to the secluded ranch where the bunker was located, they found a sign posted on a vehicle that read, "If you love something, set it free. If it doesn't come back, hunt it down and kill it." Entries found in one of Lake's diaries indicated that some of the men brought to the ranch may have been used as game animals to be hunted down and executed. Wrote Lake, "Death is in my pocket and fantasy my goal" and "the perfect woman is totally controlled; a woman who does exactly what she is told and nothing else. There is no sexual problem with a submissive woman. There are no frustrations, only pleasure and contentment."

The diaries revealed graphic illustrations of sexual abuse, torture, murder, kidnapping, and cremation. Lake believed he would be a survivor of the nuclear holocaust in his concrete bunker filled with sex slaves, weapons, and food. Police found several tapes and pictures of women being sexually abused and tortured. Some of the tapes showed Lake and Ng raping and sodomizing their victims. When the two had finished, they executed their victims by shooting or strangling them. It appears that victims then may have been cut up into pieces with power saws and tree trimmers found at the site and placed in metal drums for incineration. The remaining bones were then pulverized and buried. Police found 45 pounds of bone fragments, including many teeth. Some victims, including some campers, were buried around the ranch area. Lake had made a map of "buried treasure," which police thought meant grave sites. The exact number of the victims of Lake and Ng will never be known. Ng, while incarcerated in a Canadian prison, fought extradition to the United States but after several years was returned to stand trial in California. After nearly 14 years Ng was brought to trial, convicted, and sentenced to death. His conviction is currently on appeal. Lake was cremated but his brain was preserved for scientific research into the causation of homicidal behavior.

The seven-month trial of Charles Ng was so traumatic and emotionally draining for the jurors, after being forced to repeatedly watch video recordings of the grisly murders, that several had to seek professional counseling.

Table 6.11 Percentage of Male Team Offenders Who Experienced Forms of Traumatization as Children, Compared with Male Solo Offenders

Traumatizations	Male Team Killers ($N = 21$)	Male Solo Killers ($N = 45$)
Unstable home	42	40
Rejection	33	58
Beatings	25	40
Divorce of parents	0	27
Illegitimate	25	7
Sexual abuse	17	11
Parents died/orphaned	8	13
Poverty	8	9

PROFILE 6.10 Gerald A. Gallego, Jr., and Charlene Gallego, 1978–1980

When Gerald Gallego, Jr., was born, his father, a 19-year-old convict, was doing time in San Quentin prison. Gerald Jr. was 9 years old when in 1955 his father was executed in Mississippi for having killed two correctional officers. His father, whom Gerald Jr. thought had died much earlier in a car accident, wrote a letter telling others, especially youth, to avoid breaking the law. But less than a year later Gerald Jr. began getting into trouble. At age 13, he was detained by the California Youth Authority for sexual involvement with a 6-year-old girl. From that point on his life gradually continued to self-destruct.

By the age of 32, Gerald Jr. had been married seven times, one wife having married him twice. He was known to have been married to more than one woman at the same time, and when he married Charlene he did not bother to divorce his previous wife. By this time, Gerald was developing a real penchant for violence and sadism. By the time of his final arrest, Gerald had compiled an amazing history of murder, deviant sexual conduct, a jail escape, an armed robbery, and several other crimes.

Unlike her husband, Charlene apparently grew up in a family that provided love and support and had the respect of neighbors and friends. Why she decided to attach herself to an exconvict who referred to her as "Ding-a-Ling," is unknown, but she quickly accepted his lifestyle, including his bizarre and perverted sexual fantasies.

Gerald decided it was time to seek out young female virgins that he could keep in a secluded hideaway where he would be able to use them as his personal sex slaves. His first two victims, 17-year-old Rhonda Scheffler and 16-year-old Kippi Vaught, were abducted September 11, 1978, from a Sacramento shopping mall. Their bodies were later found badly beaten, both having been shot in the head with a .25-caliber handgun. Autopsies indicated both girls had been sexually abused. On June 24, 1979, in Reno, Nevada, two more girls, 15-year-old Brenda Judd and 14-year-old Sandra Kaye Colley, were abducted from a crowded fairground. Their bodies were never recovered. On April 24, 1980, 17-year-old Stacy Ann Redican and Karen Chipman-Twiggs disappeared from a Sacramento shopping mall. In July,

continue to see a gap between the two groups when reporting on rejection. Solo offenders were much more prone to report feelings of rejection than team serial offenders. Other areas were also higher for the solos including remembering beatings as children (40%), being adopted (13%), and parents dying or the offender recalling his youth as an orphan (13%).

DISPOSITION OF OFFENDERS

Of this study's group of team killers, 23% have been executed or await execution on death row (Table 6.12). Six percent were either killed before a trial could be held or committed suicide. In total, 69% were incarcerated for life or

picnickers near Reno discovered the girls' bodies in shallow graves. They too had been beaten severely with a blunt metal object and sexually abused. On June 6, 1980, Linda Teresa Aguilar, age 21 and expecting her first child, was abducted while hitchhiking from Port Orford, Oregon, to Gold Beach. She too was later found in a shallow grave, tightly bound with her skull crushed in by blows from a metal object. The autopsy report indicated she had been buried while still alive. The next victim, 34-year-old Virginia Mochel, mother of two, was abducted while walking to her car from the bar and grill where she worked as a waitress. Three months later her body was discovered outside Sacramento. On November 1, 1980, Mary Beth Sowers and her fiancé, Craig Raymond Miller, were kidnapped from a parking lot. Gerald had no particular interest in Craig, and on arriving in a secluded area, shot him in the head three times. Later Gerald raped and sexually abused Mary Beth and also shot her in the head three times.

Police were finally able to apprehend Gerald and Charlene after a friend of the engaged couple witnessed the abduction and was able to memorize the license number of the car driven by Gerald. After a difficult manhunt that took authorities to several states, the Gallegos were captured. After their return to California, the couple pleaded innocent to charges of murder and kidnapping. Because Charlene was not legally married to Gerald, she eventually agreed to testify against him in exchange for a plea bargain. She explained how she would help lure the girls to the car where Gerald could overpower them. She admitted sitting in the front seat while Gerald would rape, beat, and sodomize his victims and force them to perform oral sex and sometimes kill them. Charlene also admitted holding a gun on two of the girls while Gerald raped them. She described in detail the ten gruesome murders in her husband's quest for the perfect sex slave. She admitted watching while Gerald used a hammer to beat his victims to death. The Gallegos were convicted of murder, and Gerald was sentenced by the state of Nevada to die by lethal injection. Charlene is now serving two concurrent 16-year-8-month sentences in Carson City, Nevada, for her part in the murders (Linedecker, 1987).

Table 6.12 Disposition of Male and Female Team Offenders after Apprehension

Disposition	Percentage of Offenders (N = 94)
Prison sentence	69
Death row	23
Killed before trial	4
Suicide	2
Confined to psychiatric institution	2
	100

sentenced to serve a specific number of years in prison. A few of these offenders are currently awaiting court dispositions. Occasionally an offender has been placed in a mental institution. Rarely has anyone convicted of such crimes escaped or been freed from prison. The problem, however, is not being able to keep these offenders incarcerated but rather freeing other convicted psychopathic felons every year who will go on to become some of America's most infamous serial murderers.

More than half of the serial killers in this study are destined to live out the rest of their lives in prison. What efforts, if any, are being made to study them or rehabilitate such offenders? What are the issues surrounding sentencing? Is capital punishment the best response to these offenders? Both physiological and psychological forensics must play a role in combatting serial crime.

7

The Female Serial Murderer

The orientation of criminological research focuses primarily on male criminality, especially in the area of violent crimes such as homicide. However, during the 1970s, when the United States experienced a growth in the women's liberation movement, some scholars hastily observed "a tremendous increase of serious crimes by women" (Deming, 1977). In her book, *Sisters in Crime,* Freda Adler predicted "a new breed of women criminals," who would be significantly involved in violent crimes (Adler, 1975, p. 7). Yet other research discounts such notions (Chapman, 1980; Schur, 1984; Steffensmeier & Cobb, 1981). Weisheit (1984b), in his review of women and crime perspectives, noted that "the factors leading to the current interest in female criminality—the perception that female crime was on the rise, the link between liberation and crime and the sexist nature of previous research on female criminality—have been challenged" (p. 197). In any case, the number of women who kill is still relatively low in comparison with the number of men who kill.

IDENTIFYING FEMALE SERIAL MURDERERS

Because of the constant focus on male criminality, women are seldom viewed by the public as killers. Certainly, our crime statistics support this view. Because those women who kill do so primarily in domestic conflicts, there is even less reason to suspect women to be multiple killers (Kirby, 1998; Hickey, 1986). Thibault and Rossier (1992) state:

> Although some women may kill in the home in self defense, female killers in the home also plan to kill and kill because they want to. We need to take a close look at the courts that are letting these women get away with murder. Has our sexist society, by defending these female murderers, made it open season for women to kill men, as long as the killing is in the home? (p. 126)

Consequently, those few females who are serial murderers may be even less likely to come under suspicion than their male counterparts or females who commit other types of murder. Of those women who commit multiple murders, rarely does one go on any kind of rampage like that of Richard Speck, who killed eight nurses in Chicago in 1966, or of James Huberty, who in 1984 during a ten-minute shooting spree killed 21 victims and wounded 19 others in a McDonald's Restaurant in San Ysidro, California. Female serial killers, especially when they act alone, are almost invisible to public view. Freiberger (1997) in her efforts to apply current serial murderer typologies to female serial killers concluded that such classifications were not adequate in understanding such offenders. These are the *quiet* killers. They are every bit as lethal as male serial murderers, but we are seldom aware one is in our midst because of the low visibility of their killing. Keeney and Heide (1994) conclude from their review of eleven studies of serial murder only two address the notion of females as serial killers. They note that such offenders are easily overlooked:

> For female serial murderers who have killed their patients, for example, health care facilities appear to have been extremely reluctant to bring charges against an employee with the resultant probability of trial and media attention. One case in this sample was indicative of this type of administrative bungle. Genene Jones, a Texas nurse, was continually employed in a hospital long after numerous complaints and charges that she was injuring the children in her ward. In addition, family and friends may be unwilling to confront female killers with their suspicion regarding murder. The husband of Mary Beth Tinning, the New York woman who murdered eight of her children, apparently did nothing to stop her behavior, suggest that she get therapy, or take steps to prevent further birth (p. 394).

Some controversy remains as to whether females who are multiple-homicide offenders fit the "true" definition of a serial killer. Consequently, when Aileen Wuornos was linked to killing seven men with a gun, the FBI quickly labeled her the nation's first female serial killer. Certainly she "fit" the profile of the male serial killer. She had many of the typical characteristics including past physical and sexual abuse, alcohol and drug abuse, abandonment by family, and possible organic brain damage from her extensive drug abuse. As a lesbian who had been brutalized by males, Wuornos harbored hatred for men. She was physically strong and could become very aggressive when provoked. She killed like a male, except for the fact that most of her victims were shot in the torso, which is more typical of female killers, than males who are more prone to shoot into the victim's head. Epstein (1995) notes that female serial killers are seldom portrayed to the public with accuracy:

> Actual murders by women who meet the definitional requirements of serial killing frequently involve the killing of children, the elderly, or the sick. This type of serial murder is not depicted in film. Rather, female serial killer characters are typically presented as avenging a gang rape, as reacting to a wrong, or as motivated by an evil supernatural force (p. 69).

Heckert and Ferraiolo (1996) conducted a study of college students in which they examined perceptions of female serial killers. Most respondents did not have a conceptualization of a female serial killer. The few who did have an image visualized the female serial murderer in a variety of ways. No dominant image emerged except that she would be in her thirties and have a slovenly appearance. Most respondents imagined that she was without any prior criminal record, was not a brutal killer, did not use torture techniques, and used a gun to dispatch her victims. They perceived her to have experienced extreme childhood/family trauma and to be distinctly mentally ill and of high intelligence. Not surprisingly then such perceptions ultimately distort an accurate depiction of female serial killers.

To say that a woman cannot be a "true" serial killer unless she acts like a male is myopic. Consider the case of Kristen Gilbert (see Profile 7.1). Given this information, does Gilbert fit any type of female serial killer profile? Could the prosecution simply be overreacting to a coincidence? What psychological factors exist to support or contest the prosecution's charges? What questions should be asked about this case in order to develop a more complete picture?

Women can be just as lethal as males but they use different methods to achieve their goals. The real issue is method. If Wuornos had used poison to kill men she never would have received her distinction as the first female serial killer. In brief, real killers use male methods to kill. This chapter challenges that assumption. Aileen Wuornos was not the first female serial killer, as the reader is about to discover, but rather an anomaly. Wuornos was an atypical female serial killer. We have almost no documentation of anyone similar to Wuornos, and there is nothing to suggest we will see more like her in the foreseeable future. In truth, every serial killer, male or female, has certain distinguishing features that identify them as serial killers and make them unique even though they fit the serial-killer mold. Female serial killers are some of the most fascinating criminals within American society. We have much to learn from them.

This chapter focuses on the cases of 62 females, approximately 16% of the total number of serial killers in this study. Some acted alone (68%), others with partners (32%), murdering altogether between 400 and 600 victims. Most of them are white (93%), and the remainder are African American (7%). Many of these killers, where identified, were predominantly unskilled, skilled,

PROFILE 7.1 Kristen Gilbert, 2000

Charged with the murders of four patients at a Veterans Affairs Medical Center in Setauket, New York, Nurse Kristen Gilbert, 33, may be yet another example of how women who kill serially target their victims. Her prosecutors say that she liked the thrill of medical emergencies and wanted to impress her boyfriend. She is believed to have injected her patients with large doses of adrenaline causing their hearts to beat rapidly and uncontrollably. The defense argues that the patients all suffered from serious illnesses, which ultimately caused their deaths. They insist that Gilbert's coworkers turned her in because they sided with Gilbert's husband when the couple divorced. The prosecution argues that she initiated medical emergencies so that she could respond and receive attention from her coworkers and boyfriend, who worked as a security guard at the hospital. They noted that each victim had a healthy heart upon entering the hospital intensive care unit where Gilbert worked and each died following a visit from the defendant. For so many patients with healthy hearts to suddenly die for no apparent reason so close together in the same unit was believed by the prosecution to be practically impossible. The prosecution compared it to the probability of lightning striking the same location many times. Gilbert is also accused of trying to kill three other patients. The prosecution also alleges that Gilbert falsified medical reports and confessed to the murders, saying, "I did it! I did it! You want to know? I killed all those guys by injection," to her boyfriend and exhusband.

or professional in occupation. Several of them were "black widows," nurses, and other types of care providers. (Black widows are women who kill their husbands, children, or other relatives.) Frequently they had remarried several times in order to kill again and again. Those who made up the nurse-and-care-provider group victimized people over whom they had control. Elderly men and women, and especially babies, became their targets. Of course, some female offenders were unemployed or were in jobs unrelated to their accessing victims.

We can speculate that the annual victim count produced by this group of females is very low. They appear to be atypical of female criminality. They tend to be viewed as anomalies, aberrations in female homicide patterns. They are ignored because there has not been an appropriate "pigeonhole" in which to place them and because of the belief that they represent a statistically small number of offenders. The public displays more amusement than concern about cases like that of Linda Sue Jones of Torrance, California. In September 1988, Mrs. Jones admitted having tried to kill two previous husbands in order to collect insurance. The day after she was sentenced to 20 years in prison, Jones married again in a ceremony performed by the same judge who sentenced her. It is less troublesome simply to label such people "insane" and somehow less important, at least statistically, than other female offenders. The Ted Bundys, the John Gacys, and the Jeffrey Dahmers are also atypical of males who commit homicide, but yet they have attracted international attention and a host of researchers. However, important comparisons can be made between women who are serial killers and other women who commit homicide.

EMERGENCE OF FEMALE SERIAL MURDERERS

Of the 62 female serial killers identified in this research, approximately 10% percent started their killing between 1826 and 1899, whereas the remaining 90% appeared since 1900. Several of the females had accomplices when they murdered and therefore are included in Chapter 6, which deals with team killers. This analysis focuses on the behavior, and when possible, the personal lives of these women, who ranged in age from 15 to 69 at the time they first began to kill. They are responsible for the deaths of 417–584 men, women, and children or 15–17% of all victims killed by offenders in this study. Figure 7.1 indicates the progressive increase in the number of female offenders since the year 1826 and the particularly sharp increase since 1950.

Approximately three-fourths of these females began their careers in killing since 1950. Like the statistics for male serial offenders, this number may be explained in part by improved police investigation and reporting procedures, population growth, and increased media attention. Although relatively few in number, female serial killers appear to be increasing in number and thus merit attention. Consider the number of victims believed to have been killed by

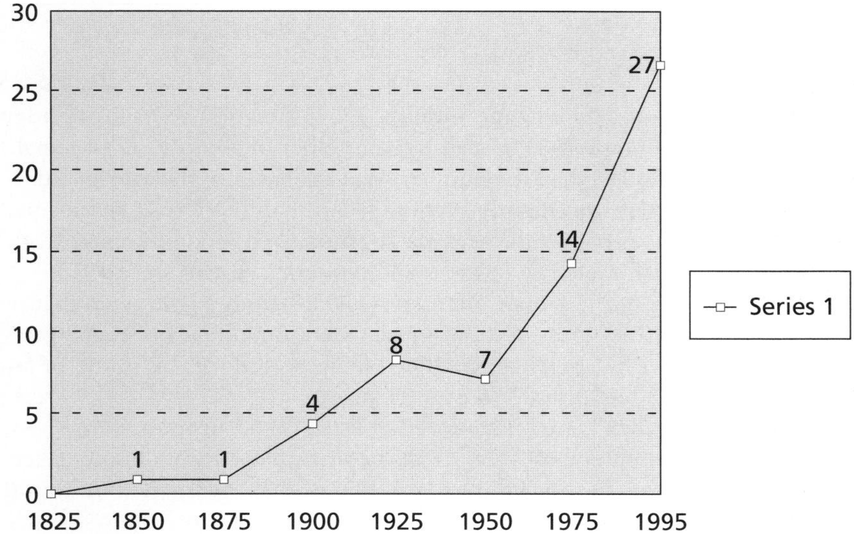

FIGURE 7.1 Frequency of Female Serial Murderers in the United States by Year, 1826–1995

N = 62 offenders

Table 7.1a Number of Cases of Serial Murder Committed by Females in the United States, 1826–1995

Years	Total Number of Cases	Number of Cases per Year	Number of Offenders	Percentage of Offenders	Percentage of Offenders per Year
1826–1995	59	.35	62	100	.20 (169 yrs)
1826–1969	31	.22	33	53	.23 (144 yrs)
1970–1995	28	1.08	29	47	1.10 (26 yrs)

Table 7.1b Victim/Female Serial Murderer Comparisons in the United States, 1826–1995

Year	Number of Cases	Number of Cases per Year	Number of Victims	Number of Victims per Case	Number of Victims per Year
Total	59	.35	417–584	7–15	3 (169 yrs)
1826–1849	1	.04	2–5	2–5	.1–.2 (24 yrs)
1850–1874	1	.04	11–30	11–30	1 (25 yrs)
1875–1899	4	.16	63–125	16–31	3–5 (25 yrs)
1900–1924	8	.38	45–46	6	2 (25 yrs)
1925–1949	7	.28	64–100	9–14	3–4 (25 yrs)
1950–1974	12	.48	59–64	5	2 (25 yrs)
1975–1995	26	1.24	173–214	7–9	7–8 (21 yrs)

these few offenders. The average number of victims per female offender ranged from 7 to 9 (Table 7.1). Because the number of actual cases of female serial killing (59) was less than the number of offenders (62), the average number of victims per case was slightly higher (7–10) than the 7 to 9 victims per offender. The number of victims per case has fluctuated modestly since 1900. There was also a noticeable rise in the total number of victims since 1975.

The average age of the female offender was 30, slightly higher than that of their male counterparts. Most of these females went on killing for several years before they were finally apprehended. The killing period for this group of females ranged from a few months to over 34 years.

Many of the women were unemployed or listed no occupation. Some were drifters or held jobs infrequently. Some of the unemployed were homemakers who found opportunities for killing. Very few of these women were found having a criminal history, or a criminal "career." Others hired out as housekeepers, worked as waitresses, or operated small businesses. Of those reporting, only 8% reported no particular employment status (Table 7.2). Most of these offenders were transient or living with relatives.

Table 7.2 Reported Occupation of Female Offenders in the United States, 1826–1995

Occupation	Percentage
Unemployed	8
Unskilled	10
Semiskilled	15
Skilled	5
Professional	10
Other	11
Unknown	41
	100

N = 62

Weisheit (1984a), in his research on incarcerated female homicide offenders, found that between 1981 and 1984 there were 77% of offenders who had been unemployed at the time of their offense. He reported that the median age during this time frame was 27 years, that 65% of the female offenders were black, and that 76% had children (p. 478). Although the percentage of female serial offenders having children is comparable to female homicide offenders in general, some interesting differences exist between the two groups. For example, the female serial offenders were older (median age of 30), and 95% were white. The contrasts diminish, however, when we examine the reasons for women committing homicide.

With regard to murders in general, Wolfgang (1967) noted a preponderance of killings among the lower socioeconomic classes, where interpersonal violence was more "acceptable":

> When homicide is committed by members of the middle and upper social classes, there appears to be a high likelihood of major psychopathology or of planned, more "rational" (or rationalized) behavior. The fact that they commit an act of willful murder, which is in diametric opposition to the set of values embraced by the dominant social class establishment of which they are part, often means that these persons are suffering severely from an emotional crisis of profound proportions. Or they have been able . . . to meditate and mediate with their own internalized value system until they can conceive of the murder act without the consequence of an overburdening guilt and thereby justify their performing the deed. This self-justificatory behavior undoubtedly requires the actor considerable time and much introspective wrestling in order to remain within, yet contradict his supportive value system. . . . Our thesis contains principally the notion that the man from a culture value system that denounces the use of interpersonal violence will be restrained from using violence because of his positive perspective that conforms to his value system, not because of a negation of it.

> The absence of that kind of value system is hardly likely to be a vacuous neutrality regarding violence. Instead, it is replaced by a value system that views violence as tolerable, expected, or required. As we approach that part of the cultural continuum where violence is a requisite response, we also enter a subculture where physically aggressive action quickly and readily can bleed into aggressive crime. The man from this culture area is more likely to use violence, similarly because of a positive perspective that requires conforming to his value system. Restraint from using violence may be a frustrating, ego-deflating, even guilt-ridden experience. Questions of the risks of being apprehended and the distant, abstract notion of the threat of punishment are almost irrelevant to he who acts with quick, yet socially ingrained aggressivity, neither reasoning nor time for it are at his disposal (pp. 6–7).

This notion of subcultural violence, Wolfgang noted, was based on a differentiation in value systems. He separated out middle- and upper-class people and explained homicide in those classes as a result of "major" psychopathology, of planned, rational behavior. This explanation may well fit the two-thirds of female serial offenders (author's data) who were classified within the various tiers of middle- and upper-class social hierarchies. Regardless of the social class, however, all but one of the offending women were white.

Weisheit (1984a) found that, between 1981 and 1983, 42% of the female homicide offenders in his study killed for money, up from 18% between 1940 and 1966 (p. 486). Overall, 74% of female serial killers were motivated at least partially by money, and 27% murdered only for money. Weisheit also reported that women were less likely now to kill in response to abuse than in the past. By contrast, female serial murderers are more likely to kill in response to abuse of various forms, although this motive appears to be less apparent than greed and the desire for money. Several of the cases in my study, especially those of recent years, report various forms of physiological and psychological abuse at the hands of husbands, lovers, friends, and other family members. In addition, women, regardless of social class, may be motivated to kill in response to a list of unfulfilled needs. Sometimes the needs are economic, and other times they are emotional. For some, the needs for economic and psychological well-being are virtually the same.

In earlier decades of American history, spouse abuse was not considered a justification or an explanation for female homicide. Today, however, emphasis is placed on understanding the nature of domestic violence and its relationship to murder. Women may be more likely now (than they were before the emergence of the women's movement) to explain homicidal behavior as a result of physical and/or mental abuse. The fact that women who commit homicides in general are increasingly reporting their motives as economic does not negate the possible link between societal discrimination against women and domestic violence. In short, women who kill more than once may manifest their behavior differently according to social class, but the stimulation for their behavior may stem from parallel class-related motivations. Whether the stimulation is psychopathology or a tolerance for violence, both may be the product of abuse the offenders have endured. Further discussion of motivations for killing will be discussed later in this chapter. Consider now the case of Aileen Wuornos, a woman who claims to have been victimized as a child and later achieved international attention as one of the most violent female serial killers of our era (see Profile 7.2).

PROFILE 7.2 Aileen Carol Wuornos, 1989–1990

On January 9, 1991, Aileen Wuornos, age 34, also known as Susan Lynn Blahovec, Lee Blahovec, Lori Kristine Grody, and Cammie Marsh Greene, was arrested near Daytona Beach, Florida, just outside the Last Resort Bar. This female drifter, who was living out of a suitcase and sleeping wherever possible, had been connected to the murders of seven men found along central Florida highways. Wuornos would eventually provide a three-hour videotape confessing to the murders and claim that the men were trying to hurt her and she was only acting in self-defense. Wuornos was erroneously dubbed by the FBI as the first true female serial killer.

Aileen was born in Oakland County, Michigan, in 1956 to a 16-year-old girl and a 19-year-old handyman. The marriage lasted only a few months. Her father was later imprisoned for kidnapping, rape, and other crimes and eventually committed suicide while in jail. Aileen, at 6 months of age, was abandoned by her mother. Her grandparents in Troy, Michigan, adopted her and raised her as their own child. Aileen at age 10 would learn from other children at school the truth about her real parents.

Aileen claims to have been raped at 13 and became pregnant. Her grandparents did not believe her and sent her to a home for unwed mothers. After giving the baby up for adoption, she was told to leave by her grandfather. Shortly after, her grandmother died. Aileen was only 15 when she began living on her own in an abandoned car. She earned money from prostitution and panhandling. Aileen dropped out of school in the ninth grade after much trouble with her teachers as a result of coming to school stoned on acid, pot, or mescaline.

Aileen became very adept at hustling men while hitchhiking but also remembers being raped and beaten between 10 and 12 times. Her life was an emotional roller coaster, and by the age of 22 Aileen claims at least six suicide attempts. At age 20 her grandfather committed suicide. She then married a man 70 years old but left him after only one month because of her claim of physical abuse. He explained that she beat him to get the car keys. In a suicide attempt at age 22, Aileen shot herself in the abdomen and was hospitalized for two weeks. At age 25, while under the influence of drugs and alcohol, Aileen robbed a convenience store. She was arrested, convicted, and did 14 months of a three-year sentence in prison for the robbery. While incarcerated Aileen was disciplined six times for disruptive behavior. One year after her release she entered a short-lived lesbian relationship with a woman she had met while job hunting. One day Aileen returned home to find her gone. A few months later Aileen was arrested for check forgery but failed

(continued)

PROFILE 7.2 Continued

Aileen Wuornos's Victims

DATE	NAME	AGE	OCCUPATION	METHOD
Dec. 1989	Richard Mallory	51	Store owner	Shooting
May 1990	David Spears	43	Equipment operator	Shooting
June 1990	Charles Carskaddon	40	Rodeo worker	Shooting
July 1990	Peter Siems	65	Missionary	Shooting
Aug. 1990	Troy Buress	50	Truck driver	Shooting
Sept. 1990	Dick Humphreys	56	Child abuse investigator	Shooting
Nov. 1990	Walter Antonio	60	Police reserve	Shooting

to appear for sentencing. She had moved on to Daytona, where she met Tyria Moore and moved in with her. Eventually, fearing for her own safety, Tyria returned home to her parents. By that time Aileen had begun her killing career.

Aileen claims to have killed only men who attacked her while she plied her trade of prostitution. Several of her victims were found nude or partially clad. They were all robbed and shot several times, most of them in the torso. Aileen might be viewed as fitting the profile of the typical serial killer because she sought out male strangers, killed them, and was very careful not to leave much evidence. Her victims were carefully selected, because she deliberately sought out men with more expensive cars. Like male serial killers, Aileen portrayed herself as dominant and aggressive. However, she also argues that she killed in self-defense, that she was handling many johns a day and only became violent when someone would become too physical or if she felt in danger of being raped, beaten, or killed. Prior to the trial, Aileen was adopted by Arlene and Robert Pralle and became Aileen Carol Wuornos Pralle, again adding to her list of names. She was convicted and sentenced to death in Florida's electric chair. For some she will always remain a battered woman trying to escape the trauma of abuse. For others, Aileen Wuornos is a sadistic woman who enjoyed watching men die.

VICTIM SELECTION

Regardless of gender, homicide usually involves an offender and a victim who are acquainted or related to each other. Weisheit (1984b) observed in studying victim-offender relationships in which the offender was female that "once again, the data fail to support the notion of a new breed of murderess" (p. 485). While this fact is true of homicides in general, such is not the case when females are involved in serial homicides. Instead, one-fourth of female serial killers reported having killed strangers only and nearly one-third had killed at

Table 7.3 Percentage of Female Offenders Killing Family Members, Acquaintances, and/or Strangers in the United States, 1826–1995

Relationship	Percentage
Family only	34
At least one family member	50
Acquaintances only	19
At least one acquaintance	35
Strangers only	24
At least one stranger	32

N = 62

Table 7.4 Distribution of Victims by Their Relationship to Female Offenders

Type of Victim	Number of Victims	Percentage of All Victims of Female Offenders
Family	104–132	22–25
Family and acquaintances	45–52	9–11
Acquaintances	47–88	11–15
Acquaintances and strangers	34–78	8–13
Strangers	125–141	24–30
Strangers and family	46–78	11–13
All	3	1

N = 417–584

least one stranger (Table 7.3). Overall, one-third of female offenders killed only family members, whereas half of all these offenders murdered at least one member of their family. Although overall, female serial offenders murdered more family members than strangers, since 1975 there has been an increase in killing strangers. Table 7.4 indicates the percentage of victims targeted by female offenders. Overall, victims were more likely to be strangers to their killers than an acquaintance or a family member.

Among the groupings of strangers, acquaintances, and family members, female offenders appeared to have preferences in the types of victims selected. Table 7.5 shows the rank order of victims; when the victims were classified as strangers, both young boys and girls were the most likely targets. However, in the case of female serial killers who acted alone, patients in hospitals, nursing homes, and other care facilities were the preferred victims. Either way, where strangers were concerned, offenders went after the weak and the helpless. When family members were victims, husbands overwhelmingly became the primary target. Indeed, some female serial killers have given new meaning to

Table 7.5 Rank Order of Types of Victims Selected by Female Serial Murderers

A. Strangers
Children: young boys and girls
Patients: hospitals/nursing homes
People in stores, businesses, and on streets
People in homes
Travelers
Others: e.g., older women, police officers, prostitutes

B. Family
Husbands
Children
In-laws
Mothers
Others: aunt, uncle, nephew, sister

C. Acquaintances
Friends/members of own group
Male suitors
Children
Older men and women
Others: landlord, neighbors, patients

the term serial monogamy. (For example, consider the case of Nancy Hazel Doss [1925–1954] described in Profile 7.3.)

In the case of child victims, some offenders took years to systematically kill each child. Of acquaintances, strangers, and family, acquaintances were least likely to be killed by offenders, but of those who were singled out, friends seemed to receive the most attention. Unsuspecting men wishing to marry the offenders did not fare much better.

Female offenders appear to have specific age groups of victims (Table 7.6). Nineteen percent killed children only, and one-third targeted adults only. Female offenders also killed from a variety of age groups, except for teenagers. Two-thirds murdered at least one adult, and 40% murdered at least one child. Nearly one-third of all female offenders killed at least one elderly person. Those offenders who selected their victims from more than one age group were most likely to have killed adults and children. Few offenders were prone to kill from all age groups.

Table 7.6 indicates that when the variables of age and gender are combined, female offenders were equally prone to kill female or male children. There was little difference between males and females when the victims were teenagers. Not surprisingly, female offenders were more likely to select at least one male adult victim but also were involved (53% of offenders) in killing

PROFILE 7.3 Nannie Doss— the "Giggling Grandma," 1925–1954

The media dubbed her the "Giggling Grandma" because Nannie laughed and smiled while admitting to police that she had killed four of her five husbands. In 1921, at age 15 and working in the Linen Thread factory, she met and married Charles Bragg. He would be the only husband to escape her murderous designs. In 1954, when Nannie was finally arrested, Bragg spoke with reporters and explained the very difficult eight years the two were together. Her constant infidelity finally forced Bragg to leave her, but most of their five children were not so fortunate. One died right after she was born. Two others died while they were still young, raising questions by some of the neighbors who felt something was not quite right.

Charles Bragg told another reporter, "Back at that time, I didn't know about poison. The undertakers told me at the time they were poisoned. Some of my folks warned me about Nannie, and when she got mad I wouldn't eat anything she fixed or drink anything around the house. She was high-tempered and mean." Bragg felt the reason she did not murder him was the fact that he had no insurance.

Her second husband, Robert F. Harrelson, married her in 1929, and 16 years later, when she was 39 years old, Nannie murdered him by putting liquid rat poison with arsenic into his corn whiskey. She told police he was an "awful drunkard" and decided to teach him a lesson. At the time, the coroner listed the cause of death as acute alcoholism. He was buried near his 2-year-old grandson, who, Nannie observed, "just might have gotten hold of some rat poison."

Two years later, Nannie married her third husband, Arlie J. Lanning, a factory worker, in northern California. Five years later she poisoned him because he "was running around with other women." One year later, Lanning's mother, Sarah E. Lanning, then 84 years of age, died while in Nannie's care. Nannie next married Richard C. Morton, Sr., whom she met through a lonely-hearts club. Four months after their wedding, she murdered him with arsenic because "he was fixing to run around with another woman." She collected on five insurance policies for a meager sum of $1,400.

Later, Nannie would smile and say she "didn't like to poison nobody, even if he wasn't no good." Yet the "feeling" that a husband was about to "pass on" seemed to provide her with morbid delight. She claimed to be a genuine romantic and was often seen perusing her favorite magazine, *True Romance.* Apprehended after poisoning her fifth husband, Samuel Doss, with her stewed prunes, Nannie finally confessed after questioning that she had killed several of her spouses. She insisted that she had killed for romance. "Yes, that's about it. I was searching for the perfect mate, the real romance of life," explained Mrs. Doss. Some thought Nannie had killed for financial gain, but the amounts collected on each victim were small, and Nannie was offended when asked if her motive was money.

The truth was that Nannie liked to kill. Whenever she got the "urge," she would select a victim. At the age of 30 she started a killing spree that lasted over 20 years. She murdered four husbands, her mother, two sisters, two children, one grandson, and one nephew. She denied killing her mother, claiming she loved her mother more than life. Very likely there were others who also sampled

(continued)

PROFILE 7.3 Continued

Nannie's stewed prunes. Each of her victims died agonizing deaths after being fed large amounts of liquid rat poison laced with arsenic. She was arrested in Tulsa, Oklahoma, October 6, 1954, where she was working as a babysitter and a housekeeper.

Nannie Doss was convicted and sentenced to life in prison, where she continued her obsessive reading of romance novels and wrote her memoirs for *Life* magazine. In 1965 she died of leukemia in prison at the age of 60.

Table 7.6 Percentage of Female Offenders Murdering Victims According to Specific Age and Gender Categories ($N = 62$)

Age Only		**Gender and Age Only**	
Children	19	Females	10
Teens	0	Males	18
Adults	32	Both	66
Elderly	13	Unknown	6
At Least One		**At Least One**	
Child	39	Female child	32
Teen	8	Male child	32
Adult	60	Both	26
Elderly	29		
		At Least One	
Combinations		Female teen	6
Teens and children	6	Male teen	2
Adults and children	19	Both	0
Adults and teens	8		
All age groups	3	**At Least One**	
		Female adult	53
		Male adult	61
		Both	44

adult females. Conclusions based on these data must be considered tenuous at best, considering the small numbers of victims. However, we do know that males are more likely to be victimized than females when the female serial offender concentrates on killing adult members of only one gender. In the case of children, it is unlikely that any real gender preferences exist considering the small difference between the numbers of male and female child victims.

Table 7.7 shows the mobility classification of female offenders. Traveling serial killers are almost exclusively males who move from city to city and

Table 7.7 Victims of Female Serial Murderers by Mobility Classification in the United States, 1821–1995

	Number of Victims	Percentage of Victims	Number of Cases	Number of Offenders	Percentage of Offenders	Average Number of Victims per Offender	Average Number of Victims per Case
Total	417–584	100	59	62	100	7–10	7–10
Traveling	99–134	23–24	14	14	23	7–10	7–10
Local	144–195	33–35	26	28	45	5–7	6–8
Place-specific	174–255	42	19	20	32	9–13	9–14

PROFILE 7.4 Terri Rachals, 1985–1986

In March 1986, registered nurse Terri Rachals was indicted on six counts of murder and twenty counts of aggravated assault stemming from alleged poisonings of patients at Phoebe Putney Hospital in Albany, Georgia. The grand jury accused 24-year-old Ms. Rachals of injecting eleven patients in the hospital's surgical intensive-care unit with potassium chloride, causing the deaths of six of them. (Potassium chloride is a colorless chemical used in small, diluted amounts in the treatment of nearly all surgery patients. It is used in large doses by states that perform executions by injection.) Her alleged victims ranged in age from 3 to 89 years, including both males and females. All died between October 17, 1985, and February 11, 1986. The twenty incidents of aggravated assault involved nine patients (many of them received more than one injection). Most of the patients injected by Ms. Rachals did not die because they were able to receive immediate attention.

Nine patients died of cardiac arrest in November 1985; the usual number was three to four deaths per month. The potassium levels in the bodies of several of the victims were found to be abnormally high. An investigation concluded that the only way the high potassium content in the IV line could be accounted for was through human intervention.

Nurse Rachals had worked at the hospital since 1981 and was described as an excellent, reliable surgical intensive-care nurse. There had never been any serious problems with Nurse Rachals at the hospital nor did she have any police record. Very active in her church, she sang in the choir and regularly attended Sunday School with her husband, Roger, who suffered from cerebral palsy, and was a printer at an Albany supply company. The couple resided with their 2-year-old son, Chad, in a middle-class suburban Albany neighborhood. Neighbors refused to believe she could be capable of such atrocious acts.

"If you believe your mother could do it, then you'd believe that she could do it. She's not a murderer. That's the craziest thing I've ever heard," stated one neighbor. Another friend said that "Ms. Rachals would be the last person one would suspect

across state lines, killing victims at random or seeking out a specific type of victim. Because of a lack of crime data correlation, this type of offender has been recognized only in the past few years. Fourteen offenders, or 23% of all female offenders, were identified as traveling. Among serial killers who have at least one partner and travel from state to state, again only a relatively small proportion involved female offenders. Twenty-eight offenders, or 45% of female killers, were classified as local killers, or serial offenders who sought out their victims within the boundaries of one state or city. The third type, the place-specific killer, repeatedly murdered her victims in the same location. Some of the common locations were nursing homes, hospitals, and private homes. Nearly one-third of all female serial murderers were identified as place-specific.

Each mobility category was examined for the number of victims killed. Those females identified as place-specific were responsible for more than one-third (42%) of the homicides. Although offenders classified as traveling

of harming anyone. They were just so nice, so average."

One month after the last victim died, Nurse Rachals confessed to the Georgia Bureau of Investigation that she had injected five of the patients, three of whom died. Later she recanted her confession, stating that she was confused at the time of her statement. Before her trial Nurse Rachals spent several months undergoing intensive psychiatric evaluation but was found competent to stand trial. The defense worked very hard to build its case around a woman who had been molested as a child by her adoptive father and subsequently experienced blackouts. The father denied the molestation charges. At age 16, after five years of his alleged sexual advances, Terri moved out. The defense stressed that there were periods when she could not account for her actions because she suffered from a mental illness that caused her to do unusual things she could not remember. She reacted to stressful events by entering fugue states in which she experienced personality changes and could not recall where she had been or what she had done, said Dr. Kuglar, the superintendent of the Georgia Regional Hospital in Augusta.

Dr. Omer L. Wagoner, a licensed psychologist appointed by the court to examine Ms. Rachals, agreed she suffered personality disorders but not a "dissociative order" and said he believed she "thoroughly knew the difference between right and wrong." Ms. Rachals, he stated, "believed she was relieving them (the patients) of their pain and misery" by causing their hearts to stop with potassium injections.

Because of the weight of circumstantial evidence and testimony that questioned Ms. Rachals's state of mind at the time of the killings, she was convicted of giving an 89-year-old patient a heart-stopping chemical. She was given 17 years for her conviction, but under the State of Georgia Board of Pardons and Parole guidelines, Ms. Rachals was eligible for parole after serving 24 months. Although she was found to be guilty and mentally ill, state psychiatrists decided she could be adequately served on an outpatient basis and was confined at the Women's Correctional Institution near Milledgeville, Georgia.

killed more victims per offender and per case than the local category (7–10 vs. 5–7), place-specific offenders murdered more victims per case and per offender. Thirty-two percent of all female offenders were categorized as place-specific, whereas only 10% of all male offenders followed this same pattern. Since 1975 the number of place-specific female offenders has dropped considerably, while their male counterparts have remained about the same (see Chapter 5).

One reason place-specific offenders killed more victims was because they went undetected for longer periods of time; because the murders occurred in one place, there was less likelihood of detection. In addition, one typically does not imagine a serial murderer as a mother, a grandmother, or the nice lady next door. The rarity of such murders compared with other types of homicides may have influenced the length of time required to apprehend female serial offenders. Profile 7.4, which describes the case of nurse Terri Rachals, illustrates this point.

Homicides in general often have victims who place themselves in precarious positions, such as domestic disputes, or who provoke the attack by striking the first blow. As mentioned earlier, many victims play a prominent role in their own demise by facilitating the encounter with the offender (see Chapter 8). Generally, victims of serial murder played little or no part in their own deaths. Female offenders almost exclusively killed victims who were categorized as low-facilitation homicides (the victims played a small role, if any, in their own deaths).

METHODS AND MOTIVES

Female offenders, as indicated in Table 7.8, were most likely to use poisons at least some of the time to kill their victims. Some of the poisons administered to induce death quickly or gradually were large doses of potassium chloride, which attacks the heart, and strychnine or arsenic. Arsenic was popular for hundreds of years as a method of murder. In the 1800s arsenic could be purchased at any chemist's shop and was commonly used in small quantities by women to improve their facial complexions. Male customers often purchased arsenic to use in their gardens to kill rats and mice. As Gerald Sparrow noted in his book *Women Who Murder* (1970), "the poison eaters" regularly ingested arsenic to improve their attractiveness. The *Chambers Journal* and *Black Woods Magazine,* published during the 1850s, carried a series of articles on the poison eaters.

> It is not generally known that eating poison is actually practiced in more countries than one. In some districts of Lower Austria and in Styria, as far

Table 7.8 Methods and Motives of Female Serial Murderers in the United States, 1821–1995

Method		Motive	
Some poison	45%	Money sometimes	47%
Poison only	35	Money only	27
Some shooting	20	Control sometimes	13
Some bludgeoning	16	Enjoyment sometimes	11
Some suffocation	16	Sex sometimes	10
Some stabbing	11	Enjoyment only	3
Suffocation only	11	Sex only	0
Shooting only	8		
Some drowning	5	Combinations of the preceding motives	15
Stabbing only	3	Other motives including: (1) drug addiction, (2) cults, (3) cover up other crimes, (4) children become a burden, feelings of being an inadequate parent, and so on	24
Combinations of the preceding methods	33		

> as the borders of Hungary, the strange habit of eating arsenic is quite common. The peasantry in particular are given to it. They obtain it under the name of Hedri from the traveling hucksters and gatherers of herbs, who get it from the glass blowers, or purchase it from cow-doctors, quacks or mountebanks. The poison eaters have a two-fold aim in their dangerous enjoyment: one of which is to obtain a fresh healthy appearance, and also to acquire a degree of sexual desire. On this account gay village lads and lasses employ the dangerous agent, that they become more attractive to each other; and it is really astonishing with what favorable results their endeavors are attended, for it is just the youthful poison eaters that are, generally speaking, distinguished by a blooming complexion and an appearance of exuberant health (Sparrow, 1970, p. 88).

Sparrow goes on to describe the "miraculous cosmetic properties" found in arsenic. Thus, we see that arsenic was readily available without suspicion to anyone wanting to use it to commit murder. Although arsenic does not mix well with cold water, it is nearly undetectable in hot food and drinks, especially coffee or cocoa. The length of time required to kill a person with arsenic varies, depending on such factors as the amount of poison administered and the general health of the intended victim. A large dose brings on death usually in a few hours, but death may be prolonged by using small amounts. In such cases the victim may live for several weeks or even months. Arsenic poisoning is a particularly gruesome manner of death because it causes severe and frequent vomiting coupled with intense pain. Naturally, fever, vomiting, and pain may be indicative of several maladies, so arsenic poisoning was seldom raised as a diagnosis. Once a killer was discovered and the bodies were exhumed, arsenic could be easily detected because it acted as a strong preserving agent after death. Today, pure arsenic is no longer readily available, but it is often found in pesticides.

We are now more likely to hear of killers, especially nurses and other health care providers, using potassium chloride, which is difficult to detect once the body has been prepared for burial. Succinylcholine, another relatively undetectable drug, is used as an anesthetic to relax muscles during surgery. An excessive dose inhibits the chest muscles from functioning, and the victim simply stops breathing (Helpern & Knight, 1977, p. 26). This drug was used by Nurse Genene Jones (see Profile 7.5).

Poisoning was so common a method for killing that nearly half of the female offenders in this study used only poison to commit their murders. Most of these women were offenders who acted alone to kill their victims. Other female offenders resorted to more violent methods, such as shooting, bludgeoning, or stabbing. Not surprisingly, most female offenders who had an accomplice(s) used violent means to kill the majority of their victims (see Chapter 6). About one-third of the female offenders used a combination of methods in their killings.

Female serial killers differed noticeably from their male counterparts in methods and motives. Males were more mobile and attracted more attention than the women. Although both groups selected the powerless as victims or at

PROFILE 7.5 Genene Jones, 1978–1982

In February 1984, Nurse Genene Jones was sentenced to a maximum term of 99 years for the murder of 15-month-old Chelsea McClellan. Testimony showed the little girl had died after injections of succinylcholine, a hard-to-detect drug that paralyzes. An expert witness stated at her trial that the drug has long been a favorite for killing because it is difficult to trace. Under Texas law, a 99-year term is equivalent to a life sentence; therefore, Ms. Jones will be eligible for parole in 20 years.

Jones was also charged with using the drug to harm six other children at a physician's office where she had worked for three weeks. It is believed her motive was a need to prove there were enough sick children to justify construction of a pediatric intensive-care unit in Kerrville, Texas. However, the scope of her criminal behavior also extended to a hospital in San Antonio, Texas, where she was charged with injuring at least one child. Investigators believe that as many as 46 babies and children were murdered at the San Antonio hospital during the time Nurse Jones worked there. It is believed that the children were given injections that stopped their hearts. A team of experts from the Centers for Disease Control in Atlanta, Georgia, found that seven children had been killed by a deliberate overdose of the heart drug digoxin. Digoxin was not ruled out in at least 21 other deaths. Ms. Jones was never tried for these homicides.

least those who were easily rendered powerless, their methods of killing usually differed. Males often selected more violent means of killing, including sexually attacking and frequently mutilating the corpse. Women in this study, with a few exceptions, generally were not sexually involved with their victims, nor did they kill them by particularly violent methods in comparison to their male counterparts. These comparisons lead us toward the inevitable question of why do these women commit multiple murders?

We must begin our discussion of motives with the premise that the reality of female crime is largely unknown. Historically, female crime has been explained in terms of a biological framework. The likelihood of a woman committing a crime was believed (and many still subscribe to such interpretation) to be linked to hormonal changes, menstruation, maternity, and other physiological explanations. Only recently have theorists begun to consider social structural influences on women and crime. Of these influences, money was found to be the most common motivator to murder. This seems to contradict motives stated for homicides in general, at least at the North Carolina Correctional Center for Women in Raleigh, where John T. Kirpatrick and John A. Humphrey conducted a study of 76 women who had killed. They noted that "in order for women to kill, it had to be perceived by them as a life-threatening situation affecting their physical or emotional well-being" ("Women Who Kill," *New York Times,* 1987). (But are women who kill under these circumstances really any different from women who are classified as serial killers? Although the list in Table 7.8 does show a ranking of motives, more involved explanations may exist that reflect social and cultural influences generally ignored in the epidemiology of homicide.)

At the turn of the nineteenth century, researchers involved in the study of criminal behavior leaned heavily toward a biological explanation for crime. Lombroso and Ferrero (1916) insisted that biological factors were the keys in understanding criminal behavior in women:

> We have seen that the normal woman is naturally less sensitive to pain than a man. . . . We also saw that women have many traits in common with children; that their moral sense is deficient; that they are revengeful, jealous, inclined to vengeances of a refined cruelty.
>
> In ordinary cases these defects are neutralized by piety, maternity, want of passion, sexual coldness, by weakness and an underdeveloped intelligence. But when a morbid activity of the physical centers intensifies the bad qualities of women, and induces them to seek relief in evil deeds . . . it is clear that the innocuous semi-criminal present in the normal woman must be transformed into a born criminal more terrible than any man. . . . The criminal woman is consequently a monster (pp. 150–152).

Sigmund Freud's influence was felt as psychobiological explanations for female crime began to emerge. Pollak (1950) argued that women appeared less often in criminal statistics because of their innate ability to deceive others. This, according to Freud, was due to the fact that they are born sans penis (Strachey, 1961). Consequently:

> Man must achieve an erection in order to perform the sex act and will not be able to hide his failure . . . and pretense of sexual response is impossible for him, if it is lacking. Woman's body, however, permits such pretense to a certain degree and lack of orgasm does not prevent her ability to participate in the sex act. It cannot be denied that this basic physiological difference may well have a great influence on the degree of confidence which the two sexes have in the possible success of concealment and thus on their character pattern in this respect (p. 10).

Gradually, other studies involving professional researchers began to make tentative connections between female criminality and alcohol, women's liberation, menstruation cycles, and hormonal imbalances. These last connections appear to have found more credence among professional researchers.

Dr. Eva Ebin, professor of psychiatry at State University of New York, noted that some women experience a postpartum syndrome that can cause them to become psychotic. She observed a shift in a woman's personality that causes her to "break" under stress. Caring for a newborn may create stresses that the mother is not emotionally prepared to handle. In Pennsylvania in 1985 a woman killed her month-old son by tossing him into a mountain stream, and in 1986 a West Virginia mother wrapped her newborn child in a plastic bag and dropped her into the Shenandoah River. In 1995, Susan Smith placed her two young sons in the back seat of her car, released the brake, and

PROFILE 7.6 Christine Falling, 1980–1982

Nineteen-year-old Christine was a high school dropout with the vocabulary of a sixth-grader. Obese, epileptic, and intellectually stifled, Christine lived in Perry, a town in southern Florida where poverty is a way of life. She had been born into an unstable family; her mother, Ann, was only 16 and already had two children, and her father, Tom, age 65, worked in the woods. Frequently her mother would leave for periods of time and Tom would have to care for the children. Eventually Christine and her sister were adopted by a couple named Falling. Conflict quickly generated between the couple and the two girls, resulting in frequent family fights. Finally at age 9, Christine and her sister were placed in a children's refuge near Orlando.

Christine's personality profile by age 9 indicated some potentially serious problems. She had been known on more than one occasion to torture animals, such as cats, by throwing them high into the air or wringing their necks. She later explained this behavior by saying she was trying to find out if cats really had nine lives. Staff members at the refuge described her as a compulsive liar and thief, a child who would break rules to gain attention. She frequently was the brunt of her peers' jokes because of her obesity and dull-wittedness. After continuing problems with the Falling family, Christine, now 12, left in search of her mother near Blountstown, Florida. She found her mother and then married a man in his mid-twenties. After six weeks of fighting, the marriage ended. A year later she began making frequent visits to the hospital, claiming an array of problems and ills. During this two-year period, the hospital recorded at least 50 visits from Christine.

Christine began babysitting and gained a reputation as one who loved children, especially babies, and was very good at caring for them. Unfortunately, no one knew what methods Christine used to quiet the infants. Two-year-old Cassidy "Muffin" Johnson became her first victim on February 25, 1980. One year later 4-year-old Jeffrey M. Davis succumbed to Chris-

walked away while the automobile rolled into a lake, drowning the boys. In all of these instances the mothers fabricated stories of their children being kidnapped. Dr. Ebin explains these concocted stories as "a trick of the mind. It's a dissociative reaction. It's wishful thinking that they hadn't done it. They need to believe it in order to go on" ("When Moms Kill Their Infants," *Washington Post,* 1988).

Resnick (1970) reported that two-thirds of the mothers who commit filicide (the killing of a child over 24 hours old) suffer from various forms of psychosis, such as severe depression, and that they make frequent suicide attempts. Resnick also found that mothers who committed filicide were motivated by altruistic reasoning—that the children were better off dead. In addition, Rosenblatt and Greenland (1974) reported that before killing their children, over 40% of the mothers intimated their fear or intent of killing to friends, physicians, or social-service-agency personnel.

We have only recently begun to connect female crime to stress-related factors and to understand how stress affects behavior. It is believed by some experts that stress is the generic cause of many diseases, both physiological and

tine's loving care. Three days later, while the funeral was being held for the boy, Christine was caring for 2-year-old Joseph, a cousin to the victim. He also died while sleeping, his parents still at the funeral. In one year, three children died strange and unexpected deaths while in the care of the young babysitter. Always distraught at the tragic deaths, Christine appeared as baffled as everyone else about the causes of death. Physicians explored a variety of medical explanations but no one was ever quite sure what had happened.

Christine decided to stay away from children for a while and became a housekeeper for 77-year-old William Swindle. The day she began caring for him, Mr. Swindle was found dead on his kitchen floor. No autopsy was performed, and it was assumed he had died of natural causes. Christine next babysat 8-month-old Jennifer Y. Daniels, the daughter of her stepsister. Mrs. Daniels had left Jennifer momentarily with Christine while she went into a store. On her return Christine announced the child had just stopped breathing. Cause of death was listed as sudden infant death syndrome.

In 1982, after moving back to Blountstown, Christine was asked to babysit 10-week-old Travis D. Coleman. He, too, died in his sleep. Five deaths and several near-death situations all with small children, all in two and one-half years, all in the care of the same person, finally caused people to start questioning Christine. To avoid the death penalty, she eventually confessed in a plea bargain to killing Muffin, Jennifer, and Travis. Christine described her method of killing as "smotheration" and stated in her confession: "I love young 'uns. I don't know why I done what I done. . . . The way I done it, I saw it done on TV shows. I had my own way, though. Simple and easy. No one would hear them scream."

Christine was given a life sentence and will not be eligible for parole until the year 2007. She is presently incarcerated in Florida's Broward Correctional Institution.

psychological. Societal factors, such as the fact that women do not earn as much as men, could be facilitating variables in homicide. But these factors should not be considered the primary cause. More likely in the Kirpatrick-Humphrey study the cause is linked to the women's life histories and to the kinds and severity of the stress they encountered. Nearly all of the women in the study came from very violent upbringings and experienced high levels of domestic violence—seeing their mothers and fathers fighting, often with weapons ("Women Who Kill," *New York Times,* 1987).

In addition to witnessing conflict, several offenders in the Kirpatrick-Humphrey study were beaten or sexually abused as children. Half of the women had lost a loved one either in childhood or adulthood. "Loss is an important source of stress because not only is it stressful in itself but it also precipitates other stress, as when they have to move in with grandparents or drop out of school due to the death of a parent. . . . These are women who feel at once overpowering aloneness and simmering resentment of others" ("Women Who Kill," *New York Times,* 1987). (Christine Falling, described in Profile 7.6, appeared to have experienced many of these stressors.)

The available biographical data on female serial murderers also indicate several instances of broken homes, displaced children, and other emotionally traumatic experiences. However, we must again proceed with caution in suggesting that stress explains all such criminal behavior. Our society includes many victims of child abuse of all varieties, as well as children who are displaced or who experience other traumas or stresses, who do not become murderers or criminals of any type. Although there are exceptions, according to the available data, female multiple murderers generally do not appear to have experienced more traumas as children than other criminals or perhaps even noncriminals. A critical factor may be their inability as children or as adults to deal constructively with their own sense of victimization. This inability may be fostered by significant others, strangers, and the various societal institutions that affect everyone to varying degrees. Simply because we ascertain that children who later become mass murderesses have been exposed to the same traumatizations that other children experience does not mean they are able to cope with those experiences in similar fashions.

If we are to accept the taxonomy of motives in Table 7.8, then women's motives for serial murder appear to center on financial security, revenge, enjoyment, and sexual stimulation. Those who murdered children seemed to display little or no psychosis. Although data are limited regarding biographical information, several cases in the present study revealed histories of child abuse—including sexual molestation, prostitution, and neglect—extreme poverty, and unstable marital relationships.

PSYCHOPATHOLOGY OF FEMALE OFFENDERS

Female serial murderers appear to exhibit traits similar to those of male serial murderers in terms of psychopathology. For example, the women tended to be insincere, amoral, impulsive, prone to exercise manipulative charisma and superficial charm, without conscience, and with little insight, because they failed to learn from their mistakes. Guze (1976) concluded from a 15-year longitudinal study of female felons in prison that psychopathology was the most frequent personality diagnosis for these offenders. Cleckley (1976), in his text *The Mask of Sanity,* describes psychopaths as irresponsible, unpredictable, pathological liars who display a flagrant disregard for truth. He concluded that psychopaths are of above-average intelligence but are self-destructive in that they frequently involve themselves in high-risk ventures, generally blame others for their failures, and have no long-range goals. They are able to mimic the behavior of others but carry no actual burden of remorse for their crimes.

It is unlikely that every psychopath possesses all of these characteristics or that he or she constantly exhibits any of these traits. Instead, psychopathic behavior may be cyclical, like the Jekyll-and-Hyde syndrome. Although fewer in numbers, female serial killers certainly can exhibit psychopathic characteristics and must be considered to be as lethal as their male counterparts. Jane Toppan, from the witness stand at her trial for murder, stated: "This is my ambition—to have killed more people—more helpless people—than any man or woman has ever killed." In the previous study female serial killers were classified as predominently stay-at-home killers who operate carefully and inconspicuously and who may avoid detection for several years. Currently we see more female offenders mimicking their male counterparts in becoming more localized in their efforts to find and kill their victims. Does psychopathology play a role in determining victim selection, or is finding victims a product of cultural filters, economic demands, and opportunities? One hopes that future research will focus more attention on exploring the psychopathology of female offenders. We have only begun to explore their motivational dynamics.

SENTENCING FEMALE OFFENDERS

To some extent our society has become increasingly desensitized to death. The media often provide a distortion of reality that is pervasive throughout much of our movie industry. The "splatter movies" with their endless sequels perpetuate bizarre images of those who kill. Some of these movies surpass our own worst nightmares. However, although male offenders have received media profiling that incites fear and paranoia in our communities, women fail to receive similar caricaturization. Even those few female killers who have received national attention do not instill the fear that male killers do. Certainly, this is not unexpected, because males do most of the killing and are usually responsible for most of the sadistic and perverted acts committed against victims. Our underestimation of the ability of women to commit murders as heinous as those that males commit may be a factor in the perceived differential treatment of women in the criminal justice system. Consider the monikers given by the media to female serial murderers (Table 7.9).

Historically, female offenders in this study received monikers that were either neutral or trivializing in their relationship to the crimes committed. The "Beautiful Blonde Killer," the "Giggling Grandma," and "Old Shoe Box Annie" are stereotypic, patronizing, and sexist. Even more recent monikers for female offenders are gender based: Black Widow, Death Angel, and Damsel of Death. Conversely, males have received some of the most fear-inducing names imaginable, such as "The Strangler," "The Ripper," "The Night Stalker," "The Moon Maniac," and so on. The distinction appears to be based on the method of killing and the degree of violence and viciousness displayed by the killer. Even in those cases in which males were accomplices to females in serial murder, the moniker seemed to be influenced by gender: for instance, "The Bloody Benders" and "The Lonely Hearts Killer." Apparently, not only are we less likely to suspect female offenders but also less likely to accord them the same degree of dangerousness as we do males. In reality some of these female offenders have killed several more victims than many of their male

Table 7.9 Monikers of Selected Female Offenders

Year Killing Began	Number of Victims	Name
1864	12–42	Queen Poisoner/Borgia of Connecticut
1872	14	The Bloody Benders/The Hell Benders
1881	8+	Borgia of Somerville
1901	27	Sister Amy
1901	16–20	Belle of Indiana/Lady Bluebeard
1913	3–5	Duchess of Death
1914	11+	Mrs. Bluebeard
1920	3+	Old Shoe Box Annie
1925	11–16	Giggling Grandma
1925	3	Borgia of America
1931	15	Beautiful Blonde Killer
1949	3–20	Lonely Hearts Killer
1964	5	Grandma
1975	2+	Black Widow
1984	9–12	Death Angel
1989	7–9	Damsel of Death

counterparts. Part of this disparity in treatment of offenders can be traced to the writings of Pollak (1950) and W. I. Thomas (1907, 1923). Women were observed to be accorded differential treatment because of the "chivalry" of a system dominated by men. Women were also treated more "humanely" because they were not considered dangerous. From these earlier writings there appears to have been some confusion about the assignation of causes. Women were viewed as being deceptive, manipulative, and devoid of emotion. Stereotyping women in general with these qualities was overkill to say the least. What is closer to the truth is that these qualities can be attributed to some women and some men as psychopathic tendencies. Regardless of gender, those people who manifest psychopathic qualities are much more likely to inflict harm on society than are members of the general population.

The perception of violence may play an important role in our treatment of female offenders. We seem to be much more uncomfortable and less willing to execute women than men. Table 7.10 indicates by percentage the adjudication of women in this study. No more than 18% of the female offenders were placed on death row, but only one has ever been executed. Sixty-nine percent received life in prison or shorter sentences or were sent to mental institutions. My intent here is not to point out a lack of punishment but to underscore the apparent preferential or discriminatory treatment experienced by female offenders.

Table 7.10 Adjudication of Female Offenders in the United States, 1826–1995

Status	Percentage
Never apprehended	6
Killed before apprehension	4
Confined to psychiatric hospital	5
Given prison time (including life)	64
Death row	18
Pending	3
	100

N = 56

SUMMARY

We have examined the cases of several females identified as serial killers. Although they appear to be increasing in absolute numbers, they still represent only a small portion of serial-murder cases. In America, this type of offender was noted even in the early nineteenth century but has only recently begun to receive media attention. Several female serial killers acted alone. Those who had male partners were much more likely to use violence in killing their victims, whereas those who acted alone often used poisons. Females in this study appear to kill approximately the same number victims on the average as their male counterparts (7–9 for females and 6–11 for males). Because of the relatively small number of female offenders, however, such findings are more likely to raise suspicions than encourage agreement. The women, on the average, tended to be slightly older than the male offenders. The most likely occupational categories for females were semiskilled, unskilled, and professionals. Some of these as well as some of the "homemakers" earned the dubious moniker of "black widow." Several offenders categorized as nurses or health care providers, were found to be "angels of death." Very few females were known to have criminal records and, with few exceptions, most were white.

Over the past few years, female offenders killed fewer family members while increasingly targeting strangers. Female offenders who acted alone were more likely to kill hospital and nursing-home patients than female offenders with accomplices. Husbands were the primary target of offenders who targeted family members. Most offenders murdered at least one teenager, and a majority also killed at least one adult. Approximately 40% killed at least one child. Regarding children, gender preference seemed to make little difference for female killers. Since 1975 female offenders have become more local in their areas for killing, a trend that increases their public visibility. Historically, poison has been the most commonly selected mode of killing for female offenders, who were less inclined to employ violent methods than male offenders were. Most females had experienced various forms of abuse as children, including sexual abuse and broken homes. Many appeared to be motivated to kill for financial gain, yet the literature suggests more complex explanations of psychopathology. Similar to their male counterparts, several of these females appeared to have developed sociopsychopathic personalities. Compared with male offenders, female serial killers in this study appeared to have been differentially treated by the media and the criminal justice system.

Chapter 9 explores serial killing through the mind of a serial murderer. The interview in this chapter shares insightful information about people who feel a need to kill. Chapter 10 also examines serial murders in other countries and the similarities they share with those in the United States. The reader will find the profile of Andrei Chikatilo, the Russian Ripper, one of the world's most brutal and destructive serial killers. Chapter 11 explores profiling issues and what appear to be the future challenges and trends in criminal justice investigations regarding the apparent increase in serial murders and the growing interest in multiple homicide.

8

Victims

Criminologists have recognized for some time the need to understand the victim and his or her involvement with the offender. Hewitt (1988) reviewed the body of literature of victim-offender relationships in homicides based on data from a large heterogeneous population. He then examined demographic characteristics of victims and offenders in the often publicized community of "Middletown, U.S.A." (Muncie, Indiana) and found the victim-offender relationships to be similar to those in larger cities. Studies in victimization assist in clarifying the victim side of the offender-victim relationship, measure in part the degree of vulnerability and culpability of certain victims, and often reveal the social dynamics of criminal acts. Case study analysis in serial murder has begun to provide researchers with insightful information, however tenuous. Elliot Leyton (1986a), for example, in his book *Hunting Humans,* provides an in-depth investigation into the lives and minds of a few contemporary serial killers and their relationships with their victims. The purpose of this chapter is to contribute to this body of knowledge by focusing on the victims of serial murderers and the demographic factors

Portions of this chapter are based on material from "Etiology of Victimization in Serial Murder," by E. W. Hickey, in S. A. Egger (Ed.), *Serial Murder: An Elusive Phenomenon* (Praeger Publishers, New York, 1989), copyright 1989 by Steven A. Egger. Used with permission. Material also used from "Responding to Missing and Murdered Children in America," by E. W. Hickey, in *Helping Crime Victims,* Albert R. Roberts (Ed.), 158–185, copyright 1990 by Sage Publications, Inc. Reprinted by permission.

associated with their victimization. Such demographic data can assist in determining variations, if any, between the victims of homicides in general and the victims of multiple murderers. Also, from a historical perspective, we are able to challenge current notions pertaining to serial murderers and their victims by drawing on this extensive database of serial-murder victims.

One of the most perplexing questions researchers are unable to answer is "How many serial murderers have killed or are presently killing in the United States?" Agents from the Federal Bureau of Investigation at one time estimated the number of offenders active in the United States at 35 but there may be as many as 100 or more. This does not mean there are 35–100 *new* offenders each year but rather that 35–100 serial killers may be active in a given year. From the 399 offenders in this present study, more than half committed their murders over a period of at least one or more years. Some of these offenders were active for several years. When controls were made for gender, female offenders often reported operating years longer than their male counterparts, a time factor that may be a function of killing method or the types of victims selected. Of the 337 cases of serial murder, 43 (13%) were exclusively female. Several of the cases involved women who were care providers.

Between 1950 and 1995 the number of identified serial killers surged compared to previous years. Since about 1975 the rise has been even more dramatic (see Figure 8.1). We should expect to see a continued increase in the numbers of cases of serial murder beyond the year 2000 but not at the same dramatic rate of increase experienced during the 1970s and 1980s. Certainly media attention has been instrumental in creating public awareness of the serial murderer. It is unlikely, however, that media attention alone is responsible for the recent "emergence" of serial killing.

According to the time frame of this study, over three-fourths of the 337 cases (399 offenders) appeared since 1975. Although we recognize that the "dark figure," or the unknown killer, will always exist, the study's data may be viewed as indicating trends in serial murder. One of the trends indicates a tremendous increase in the number of cases during the past 20 years in comparison to the previous 175 years. Although the debate continues over causal explanations for this dramatic rise in serial murder, we must not forget the victims. The dynamics of victimization will in all likelihood enable researchers to better understand the etiology of serial murder.

DEMOGRAPHICS OF VICTIMIZATION IN SERIAL MURDER

As indicated in Table 8.1, the number of known victims of serial murder has risen markedly since 1950. For those who fall prey to these offenders their plight is a deplorable one indeed, but the odds of becoming a victim are minuscule when one considers the size of the population as a whole. Of all types of crimes, homicide in general has one of the lowest victimization rates. If we

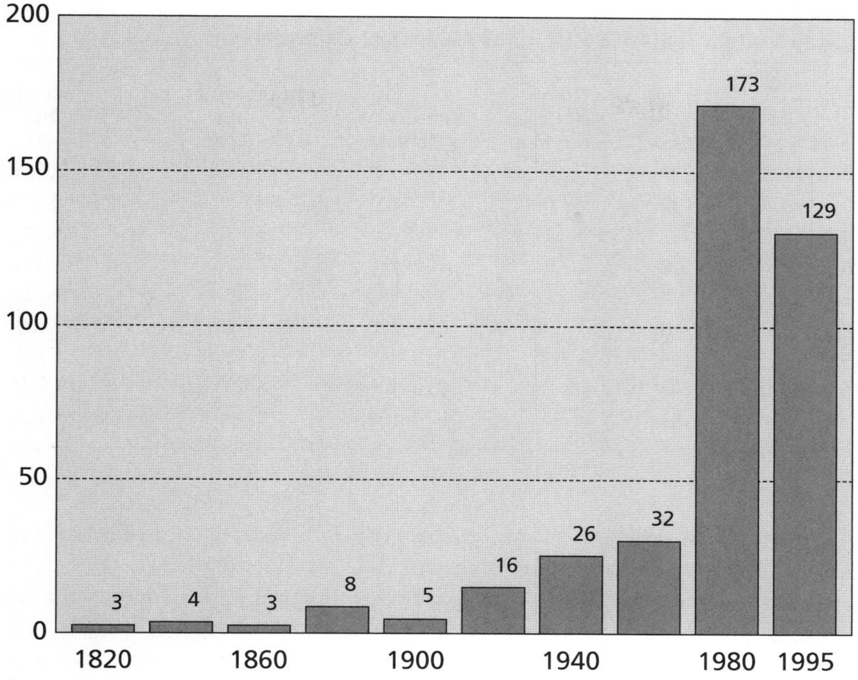

FIGURE 8.1 Number of Serial Killers in the United States by Decade, 1800–1995

N = 399 offenders

Number of Serial-Murder Cases and Offenders in the United States, 1800–1995

Years	Total Number of Cases	Number of Cases per Year	Number of Offenders	Offenders	Number of Offenders per Year
1800–1995	337	1.7	399	100%	2.0 (195 yrs)
1800–1969	132	.8	151	38	.9 (169 yrs)
1970–1995	205	8.2	248	62	9.9 (25 yrs)

were to take all of the victims in this study on serial killers between the years 1975 and 1995 and assumed for a moment these deaths occurred in 1 year instead of 20 years, the serial-murder rate would still only be approximately 0.4 per 100,000 population. Distributed evenly over the 20-year span, the rate is 0.02 per 100,000 population. The current annual rate of homicide in the United States is about 9.6 per 100,000 population. Inversely proportional to the nominal risk of falling prey to serial murderers is the amount of fear and public awareness of this phenomenon. We run a greater risk of being a victim

Table 8.1 Victims/Serial Murderer Comparisons in the United States, 1800–1995 (N = 337 Cases/399 Offenders)

Years	Total Number of Cases	Number of Cases per Year	Number of Victims	Number of Victims per Case	Number of Victims per Year
1800–1995	337	1.7	2,526–3,860	7–11	13–20 (195 yrs)
1800–1824	2	.08	104	52	4 (25 yrs)
1825–1849	3	.12	10–16	3–5	4–6 (25 yrs)
1850–1874	8	.32	86–138	11–17	3–6 (25 yrs)
1875–1899	7	.28	114–384	16–55	5–15 (25 yrs)
1900–1924	24	.96	207–286	9–12	8–11 (25 yrs)
1925–1949	33	1.32	236–416	7–13	9–17 (25 yrs)
1950–1974	107	4.3	773–1064	7–10	31–43 (25 yrs)
1975–1995	153	7.7	974–1398	6–9	49–70 (20 yrs)

of domestic homicide and an even greater risk of being a victim of other violent crimes than we do of dying at the hands of a serial killer.

Having minimized the risk the general population experiences, we must recognize that rates will vary considerably when we control for specific segments of the population. In short, some of us are at much greater risk than others. As noted in Table 8.1, the number of victims per case has declined only slightly since 1900. (This may in part be explained by greater accuracy in police investigations and efficiency in apprehension of offenders.)

Several of the states reporting between 1 and 5 cases of serial murder have small populations (Table 8.2). Generally, states with larger populations and large metropolitan areas are more likely to report cases of serial murder. Except for California, the most populous state, there does not appear to be regionality in serial killing. Instead, serial murder appears to be correlated with population density more than regional variations. Inevitably, we expect to find cases in every state. Except for New York, which reported the second highest number of cases of serial murder, California reported more than double the cases found in any other state between 1800 and 1995, and that trend appears to have continued in recent years (Table 8.2; Figure 8.2).

Three other states, one northern and two southern, reported between 16 and 25 serial-homicide cases. In group 3 we again see representation both from the North and the South. In each succeeding group of states we see representation from each region of the United States. In contrast, homicide rates in general can vary dramatically from one geographic region to another in the United States.

Gastil (1971) and, later, Doerner (1975), explaining the consistently higher murder rates in the southern states, concluded that a regional subculture of violence exists in this area. Blau and Blau (1982), controlling for income inequality, found, however, that poverty and southern location were not related to homicide rates, and the number of blacks in the community was a poor

Table 8.2 Distribution of Serial Murderers by State, 1800–1995 (*N* = 337 cases)

State	Number of Cases in Which One or More Victims Were Killed	State	Number of Cases in Which One or More Victims Were Killed
California	50+	Oregon	
		Utah	
New York	31	Colorado	
		Kansas	
Texas		Louisiana	
Florida	16–25	Tennessee	
Illinois		Idaho	
		Montana	
Ohio	11–15	North Dakota	
		Arizona	
Georgia		New Mexico	
Washington		Alaska	
Oklahoma		Wyoming	
Alabama		Nebraska	
Nevada		Minnesota	
Wisconsin		Missouri	1–5
North Carolina	6–10	Iowa	
New Jersey		Maine	
Connecticut		Kentucky	
Massachusetts		Virginia	
Pennsylvania		Arkansas	
Michigan		Maryland	
Indiana		Mississippi	
		South Carolina	
		West Virginia	
		Delaware	
		Vermont	
		Rhode Island	
		New Hampshire	
		Hawaii	
		South Dakota	

prediction of violence. This lack of consensus regarding a regional subculture of violence is pervasive among current researchers. Unlike homicide cases in general, in which, according to police records, African Americans are responsible for over 50% of the deaths, black serial murderers constitute approximately 20% of the offenders in my study.

Serial murderers are often portrayed by the media as wanton killers who travel aimlessly across the United States in search of victims. As noted earlier,

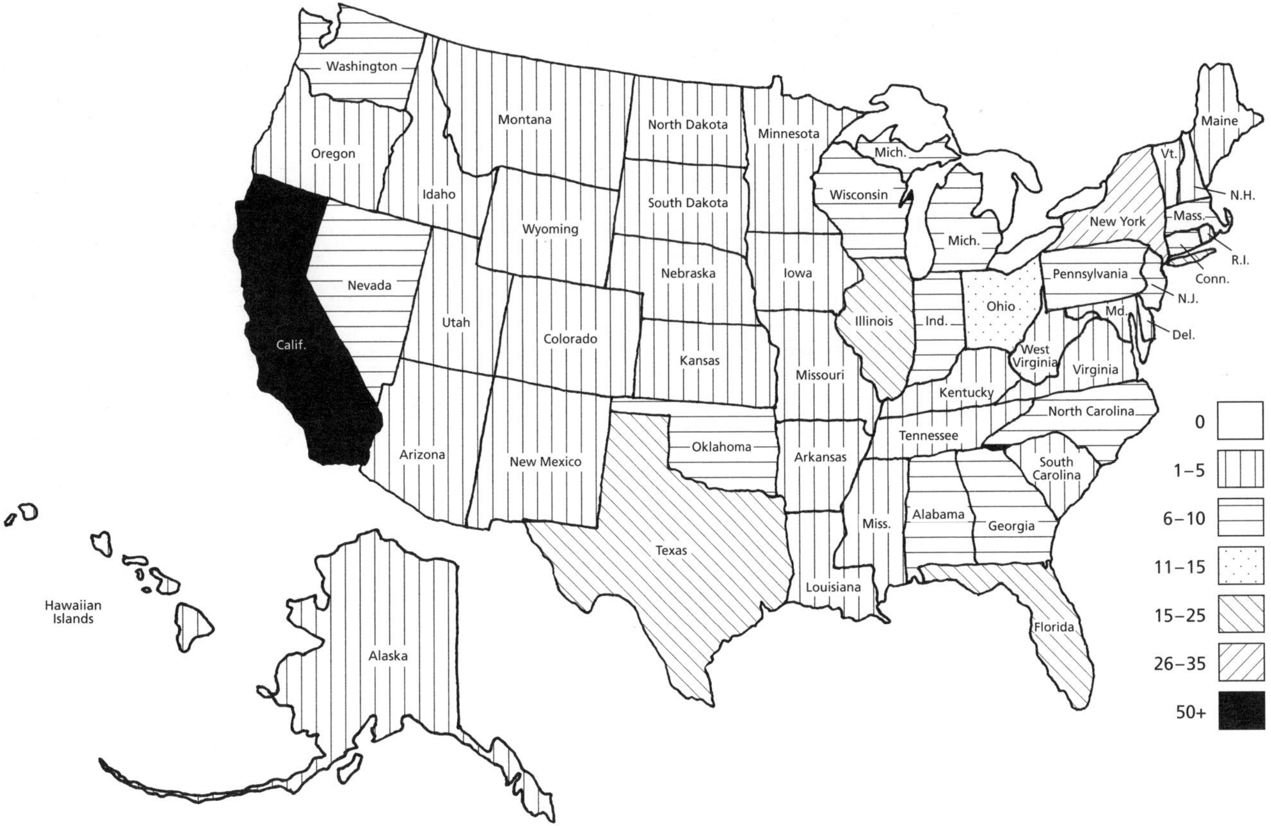

FIGURE 8.2 Frequency of Serial Murderers by State, 1795–1988 (Based on Activity of 203 Male and Female Serial Killers)

Table 8.3 Victims of Serial Murder in the United States, 1800–1995, by Mobility Classification

Mobility Classification of Killers	Percentage of Victims (N = 2,526–3,860)	Number of Cases (N = 337)	Percentage of Offenders (N = 399)	Average Number of Victims per Offender	Average Number of Victims per Case
Total	100	337	100	6–10	8–11
Traveling	36–41	114	34	7–12	9–14
Local	36–43	175	52	5–7	8–9
Place-specific	20–23	48	14	9–16	11–18

Hickey (1985, 1986) created a mobility classification for serial murderers and identified three distinct killer types (Table 8.3). First are place-specific offenders, or those who murder within their own homes, places of employment, institutions, or other specific sites. For example, John Wayne Gacy, Jr., murdered 33 young males in his home, over the course of nearly a seven-year period. Second are the local serial killers who remain within a certain state or urbanized area to seek out victims. In 1986 Michael D. Terry confessed to killing six male street prostitutes whom he had encountered, all within a 14-square-mile area of downtown Atlanta, Georgia. Third are the traveling serial murderers, distinguished by their acts of homicide while traveling through or relocating to other areas in the United States. Randall B. Woodfield, also known as "the I-5 Killer," is believed by many to have murdered as many as 13 victims while he traveled the 800-mile stretch of freeway through Washington, Oregon, and California.

In using these typologies to analyze our victim data, it was found that overall, 20–23% of victims were killed in specific places, whereas 36–43% were murdered by offenders identified as local killers. The traveling killers accounted for 36–41% of the victims. These data indicate that the majority of serial killers (68%) operated in a specific place or general urbanized area but did not travel into other states. In grouping these two mobility typologies, it was found that 59–63% of all the victims were killed by men and women who generally stayed close to home. The data indicate a shifting in mobility since 1975, with those who travel out of state declining somewhat. Conversely, those offenders classified as local killers increased in frequency. One explanation for these changes may be related to the increase in urbanization. With nearly three-fourths of the U.S. population distributed among large urban areas such as Los Angeles, New York, and Chicago, offenders are able to maintain anonymity and also have access to a large pool of victims.

Also, the number of place-specific offenders has decreased largely in part because of methods of killing. Poisons such as arsenic and cyanide, once commonly used by women killers to murder their families and friends, are now more easily detected. Consequently, between 1975 and 1995 the number of victims killed by place-specific offenders in this study declined significantly. The percentage of victims killed by local offenders between 1975 and 1995 increased noticeably. There was also a decline in the number of victims killed by traveling offenders during this time.

Two major homicide studies by Wolfgang (1958) and Pokorny (1965) found that the number of victims of homicides was divided almost equally between those killed in the home and those killed in areas outside the home. By comparison, serial-murder victims were more likely to be killed away from their homes, suggesting that they may be vulnerable in areas of the community where their assailants have easy access.

According to the numbers for the three mobility groups in Table 8.3, place-specific cases were the least common and were responsible for the smallest percentage of homicides but represented the greatest average number of victims per case. These findings contradict the general belief that serial killers are primarily offenders who travel across the United States, murdering as they go. According to these data, perhaps a greater area of concern should be focused on serial killing in hospitals, nursing homes, and private residences. Considering that by the year 2000 the population of elderly is expected to be near 35 million, more attention will be required to protect them from potential predators.

A commonly held notion about serial murder is that offenders have a tendency to operate in pairs or groups, making the abduction and/or killing of a victim an easier task. Of the 399 offenders surveyed, 28% had at least one partner in committing their homicides. Although the number of team offenders in this study is significant, the majority of offenders apprehended tended to commit their murders alone.

Another important issue concerns the types of victims serial killers single out. One of the most common beliefs concerning serial killing is that the offender often develops a pattern in his or her modus operandi. However, to a great extent the offender's behavior is directly related to the type of victim selected. For homicides in general, victimologists agree that sometimes the offender and the victim are "partners in crime"—or at least that the victim precipitates his or her own demise. Many domestic disputes that lead to fatalities are initiated by the victim. Karmen (1990) refers to this notion of shared responsibility as victim blaming. Homicides in general often include this element, especially because of the prior relationship of the victim to the offender. In Wolfgang's (1958) study and Pokorny's (1965) Cleveland study, a replication of Wolfgang's work, the findings showed a similar pattern. In both studies, those directly involved in the homicide were usually family relatives or close friends. A common assumption, however, is that victims of serial murder are killed primarily by strangers. Using the three categories of family, acquaintances, and strangers as potential victims, Figure 8.3 indicates that stranger-to-stranger serial homicides increased markedly between 1950 and 1974. According to these data, the number of offenders killing at least one stranger continued to increase until 1995.

To further illustrate this apparent rise in stranger-to-stranger serial murder, offenders were surveyed regarding preferences toward strangers, acquaintances, or family members as victims (Table 8.4). Historically, 8% of offenders were

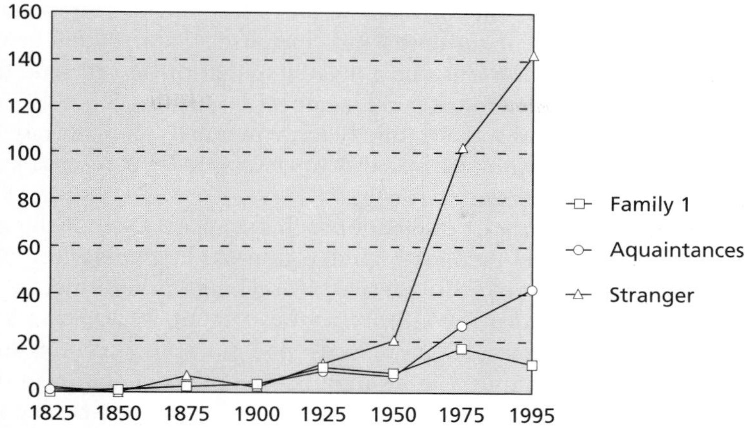

	1825	1850	1875	1900	1925	1950	1975	1995
Family	0	2	3	4	10	8	17	11
Acquaintance	1	1	3	4	8	7	27	42
Stranger	2	0	6	3	12	20	101	142

FIGURE 8.3 Serial Offenders Who Killed at Least One Family Member, Acquaintance, or Stranger

Table 8.4 Preferences of Offenders toward Murdering Family, Acquaintances, or Strangers as Victims in the United States, 1800–1995

	Percentage of Male Offenders (*N* = 326)	Percentage of Female Offenders (*N* = 62)	Percentage of Total (*N* = 388)
Family only	3	34	8
At least one family member	10	50	16
Acquaintances only	8	19	10
At least one acquaintance	25	35	26
Strangers only	70	24	61
At least one stranger	87	32	76

found to murder family members only, with female offenders 11 times more likely to do so. Only 10% of all offenders targeted acquaintances only, and these offenders were again more likely to be females. In contrast, 61% killed strangers only, with male offenders 3 times more likely to do so than female offenders. Gender differences in serial killing between female and male offenders has only recently begun to attract attention. Keeney and Heide (1994) found gender variation, including damage and torture to the victim, weapon and method used in killing, stalking versus luring behaviors, crime scene organization, motive, history of substance abuse, and psychiatric diagnosis. Similarities were found in educational level, familial dysfunction, race, history of child abuse, and occupation. These differences underscore a need to focus research efforts on examining victim-offender relationships.

At least 26% of all offenders in this study killed one or more acquaintances, whereas 16% killed one or more family members. These figures have changed very little from the previous study, suggesting that the target trend for victims continues to lean toward stranger-to-stranger homicides. Since 1975 very few offenders were found to have killed family members. By contrast, offenders murdering strangers only, increased sharply. Overall 76% of serial killers murdered at least one stranger.

Various reasons can be offered for such a dramatic trend. Killing strangers is probably perceived by most offenders as providing safety from detection. Also, the anonymity and thrill derived by seeking out unsuspecting strangers certainly must attract many killers (Leyton, 1986b). Perhaps even more important, offenders can much more easily view strangers as objects and thereby dehumanize their victims. On his capture, one offender confessed that he did not want to know his victims' names or anything about them, and if they did give a name, he would quickly forget it.

Another factor influencing victim selection is the degree of power and control the offender is able to exert. Serial killers rarely seek out those who are as physically or intellectually capable as themselves. Instead, by either randomly or carefully targeting victims, serial killers mentally and/or physically stalk their prey. Because strangers seem to be the primary target, offenders were also surveyed as to the specific type of stranger-victim they most commonly murdered (Table 8.5).

Although many of the categories under the heading of "strangers" in Table 8.5 are not mutually exclusive, they do represent the actual types of strangers reported in this study. Thus, "young women alone" in category 1 may also fit into the category of "hitchhikers" or "people walking on streets." "Young women alone, including female college students and prostitutes," was the most commonly noted stranger-victim category. The second category of "children (boys and girls)" was also frequently noted as desirable victims. Combined, these two categories accounted for most of the stranger-victim serial murders.

When offenders murdered acquaintances, friends and neighbors appeared to be the most common victims, although they were followed closely by "children (girls and boys)." With the addition of "women alone, including waitresses and prostitutes," these first three categories represent the majority of the acquaintance-victims. In the family grouping, offenders were most likely to kill their own children, husbands, or wives, although several other relatives were represented. The most salient factor among the groupings of strangers, acquaintances, and family members was that most of the victims were women and children. Whatever the specific motives of the killers were, they chose to act out their aggressions on those perceived to be weak, helpless, and without power or control. Males certainly were not exempt from victimization, but they were in the minority. These figures differ from those for homicides in general; in 1992 about 78% of approximately 22,540 murder victims were males. In addition, the typical murder victim generally is a member of a racial or an ethnic minority. Fifty percent of murder victims in the United States in 1992 were African Americans (FBI, 1993). The opposite is true of the victims

Table 8.5 Order of Types of Victims Sought Out by Serial Murderers

A. Strangers

1. Young women alone, including female college students and prostitutes
2. Children (boys and girls)
3. Travelers, including hitchhikers
4. People at home, including entire families
5. Hospital patients, including the handicapped
6. Business people, including storeowners and landlords
7. People walking on streets/in stores
8. Older women alone
9. Police officers
10. Employees
11. Derelicts/transients
12. People responding to newspaper ads
13. Racial killings

B. Acquaintances

1. Friends and neighbors
2. Children (girls and boys)
3. Women alone, including waitresses, prostitutes
4. Adult males
5. People in authority, including landlords, employers, guards
6. Members of one's own group—i.e., gangs and inmates
7. Patients

C. Family

1. Own children
2. Husbands
3. Wives
4. In-laws
5. Other relatives—i.e., nephews, nieces, uncles
6. Mother of the offender
7. Siblings
8. Grandparents

surveyed in the present study, in which the majority of the victims (and offenders) were Caucasian.

Offenders in this study did not overwhelmingly target a specific age group (Table 8.6). For example, only 6% of offenders murdered children only, and 5% specifically targeted teens. Young and middle-aged adults were the most likely targets (77%), but only one-third of all offenders killed only adults. Overall, 5% of offenders killed only elderly victims. Although we might expect a substantial percentage of offenders to kill at least one child or teenager, the number of offenders (17%) killing at least one elderly person was much higher than anticipated. Very few offenders killed victims in all age groups,

Table 8.6 Percentage of Offenders Murdering in Specific Victim-Age Categories*

Age Range of Victims	Percentage of Offenders
Only	
Children	6
Teens	5
Adults	33
Elderly	5
At Least One	
Child	23
Teen	39
Adult	77
Elderly	17
Combinations† (*N* = 124)	
Teens/children	10
Adults and children	23
Adults and teens	60
All age groups	7

* *N* = 399 offenders

†Calculated on the number of offenders who killed only in combinations.

and in respect to all combinations of victim relatedness, offenders were most likely to kill adults and teens.

Since 1975, the data indicate a shifting in some of the trends, which may be a foreboding of things to come. Offenders have been more likely to target only the elderly. Also, the overall trend in cases of serial killing involving at least one or more elderly persons has risen significantly. This noticeable rise in the serial killing of the elderly may indicate a continued increase in such crimes as the American population continues to get older. The increasing number of people in nursing homes and the rising demand for home care of the elderly may attract individuals wishing to fulfill an "angel of death" fantasy. This fantasy motivates offenders who for some reason nurture hatred for the elderly, believe in "mercy killing," derive pleasure from watching unsuspecting, powerless individuals die, or simply wish to be recognized as someone of importance. In one instance, an orderly confessed to poisoning patients so that when they stopped breathing he could be the first one on the scene to save them. Unfortunately he noted that in his quest to be a hero, several patients died. In another case, Donald Harvey, who worked as a nurse's aide in Ohio, was arrested in 1987 and pled guilty to the deaths of 54–58 people, almost all hospital patients and many of them middle age and older.

In recent years the numbers of hospital patients and those in residential care who become prey to serial killers is increasing. Orville Lynn Majors is

Table 8.7 Percentage of Offenders Murdering in Specific Victim-Gender Categories, 1800–1995

Gender of Victims	Percentage of Offenders
Only	
Females	35
Males	22
Both	42
At Least One	
Female adult	65
Male adult	50
Both	32
At Least One	
Female teen	30
Male teen	14
Both	3
At Least One	
Female child	16
Male child	16
Both	8

N = 387 offenders

linked to 110–130 murders of hospital patients between 1993 and 1995 in Vermillion, Indiana. A killer who loathed the elderly, Majors injected large doses of potassium chloride into his victims and watched them as their hearts stopped beating. In 2000, Michael Swango was linked to nearly 200 murders of hospital patients both in the United States and other countries. However Swango, like Donald Harvey, Orville Majors, and other hospital killers, are seldom convicted for most of the deaths. Prosecutors usually attempt to obtain convictions in five or six cases to avoid lengthy, expensive trials. Majors was convicted in six deaths and received a 360-year sentence while Swango received life in prison for killing four victims.

Offenders were described earlier as being more likely to target women and children than males. The data in Table 8.7 support the claim that, in general, serial killers have victimized female adults (65%) consistently more than male adults, but half of all offenders surveyed had killed at least one male adult. Nearly one in three offenders targeted at least one female teen. An equal number of offenders (16%) killed at least one female or one male child. This shift may in part be due to the increasing accessibility men have to women as they become more visible in the workplace and institutions of higher education.

VICTIM SELECTION AND PROSTITUTES

Serial murderers select victims who are easily dominated because their systemic issue is power and control. There are some victims who are also selected due to fantasy or paraphilic appeal to the offender. Karmen (1984) goes on to point out that people who appear at the "right time" or "right place," or maintain certain lifestyles, expose themselves more than others to risk of victimization. Egger and Egger (2001) suggest that in some cases of serial murder the offender is selecting victims who reflect his general lifestyle. Indeed, offenders may even be relating the victim to the killer's *previous* lifestyle or *fantasized* lifestyle. Sometimes offenders are drawn to victims who represent what they consciously or subconsciously desire for themselves. The fact that the offender is driven by deep-seated feelings of inadequacy becomes manifested in his desire to destroy that which he ultimately cannot possess. If he cannot have these attributes, then his victims will not have them either. Serial-murder cases are replete with offenders who engage in *proxy* murders. They are killing someone who reminds them or symbolizes that which they desperately want but will never have. These attributes, tangible or intangible, haunt the offender and serve as reminders of his own limitations. Ultimately he seeks to destroy persons of beauty, wealth, or assertiveness. Other offenders destroy those who symbolize what he fears or loathes including gays, the homeless, prostitutes, the elderly, and the infirm.

The dehumanization of victims renders them as objects of hatred and lust. Killing the victim carries no greater moral impact than smashing a bottle or discarding old clothes. This may help in understanding the love-hate relationship between some serial killers and their mothers. Ed Kemper was deeply attached to his mother in that he loved her because she was his mom, yet hated her for abandoning and rejecting him. After Kemper destroyed and cannibalized several college students from the University of California, Santa Cruz, where his mother was an employee, Ed butchered his mother and used her decapitated head as a dartboard.

Egger and Egger (2001) in their insightful examination of victims of serial murder note that society affords many offenders near-hero status whereas the victims serve only to enhance the killer's persona. This is manifested in movies. Egger and Egger refer to victims as the "*less dead* . . . devalued strata of humanity." According to Steve Egger, the "*less-dead,*" in reference to victims of serial murder:

> comprise most of the victims of serial killers. They are referred to as the "less-dead" because they were "less-alive" before their violent demise and now become the "never-were." These victims are the devalued and marginalized groups of society or community. They are the vulnerable and the powerless. For example, prostitutes, migrant workers, the homeless, homosexuals, institutionalized persons, and the elderly who are frequently the victims of serial killers are considered "the less-dead." These groups lack prestige and in many instances are unable to alert others to their plight. They are powerless given their situation in time, place, or their immediate surroundings (Egger, 1992).

Victims receive their "just desserts" because in American society victims of crime are often perceived as losers and no one wants to identify with losers. Thus, victims get what they deserve or what we think they deserve and the killer is admired for his intelligence, skill, and elusiveness. Egger and Egger (2001) observe:

> It is only when the "less-dead" are perceived as above the stature of prostitutes, homosexuals, street people, runaways or the elderly that our own at-risk vulnerability becomes a stark reality. Even when we begin to take on an identity with the killer's prey, we shirk such feelings and intellectualize the precipitant behavior of victims and their lifestyles as the reason for their demise (p. 2).

They go on to state that the majority of victims of serial murder are "less dead." Such assertions are supported by the disdain Americans hold for those outside our societal mainstream. Kim Egger (1999) found in her study of serial killers between 1960 and 1995 that 78% of all victims were female prostitutes. Egger also noted that between 1991 and 1993 there was a total of 198 prostitutes murdered by serial killers, an average of nine victims per case. Again, prostitutes were far more likely to be targets than any other group of victims (Egger & Egger, 2001, p. 8). These "less dead" victims are easy prey and will not draw a serious public outcry. The Green River serial murders of prostitutes produced over 50 verifiable victims yet was never solved. The Task Force eventually disbanded due to a lack of public support and dwindling leads on the case. Consider the public reaction if the 50+ victims had been respectable, middle-class, tax-paying, law-abiding citizens. Egger and Egger (2001) note that when female drug addicts and prostitutes are being murdered the residents of that community may recognize, before law enforcement, that a serial killer is in their midst. Such cases are rather common but no two cases are exactly alike (see Profile 8.1).

VICTIM FACILITATION

A final consideration regarding the etiology and demographics of serial-murder victimization focuses on the concept of *facilitation,* or the degree to which victims make themselves accessible or vulnerable to attack. Wolfgang (1958), in his noted Philadelphia study, examined the notion of "victim-precipitated" homicide. He observed that some victims are catalysts in their fatal attack by rendering either the first blow or threatening gesture. Among Wolfgang's several conclusions, he found that the victim was often the husband of the offender, had been drinking, and had a history of assaultive behavior. He concluded that the victim may be one of the critical precipitating causes of his or her own death (pp. 245, 264). In addition, Reiss (1980) studied victim-prone individuals and found they were more likely to experience the same form of victimization than to be subject to two different criminal acts. McDonald (1970) observed that victim-prone people have acquired particular

PROFILE 8.1 The Prostitute Murders, California 2000–2001

In a small town in western United States prostitutes were being murdered. There were four victims thus far. Each victim was poor and a welfare recipient. All were prostitutes or "strawberries" (women who perform sexual acts for drugs), and all except one were mid- to late-twenties; the other was a 15-year-old. All were known to be petty crime offenders, and except for the teenager, the drugs and exposure to street life had taken a toll on their physical appearance. They were all killed in the early morning hours. The killer appeared to easily lure his victims and overpower them. His attacks were brutal, utilizing several methods of subduing, torturing, and killing each victim. Most of the victims were beaten horribly, strangled, throats cut, or mutilated. The teenager had her face severely mutilated unlike the others, perhaps because the killer viewed all prostitutes as ugly. Using a ice-pick, the killer also inflicted nearly 150 stab wounds around her genitalia. Now she fit his perception. Another victim had both her arms broken, probably with a tire iron. None of the victims had been raped. Each body was left in open view outside of town. The killer was patient and waited for an opportune time. He preferred to kill when the moon was full.

In this case the other prostitutes were very much aware of the disappearances of the victims even before the bodies were discovered. Although violence is viewed as an occupational hazard, prostitutes try to "size up" a john before going off with him. In this case they each had judged him not to be the killer. Law enforcement kept the public from knowledge of the murders so as not to create "panic." Public reaction, once news of the killings was made known to the community, was typically loud and predictably short. In most cases of murdering prostitutes, the offender does not usually change his type of victim. Indeed, there are exceptions, but generally this tends to be part of the modus operandi of the serial killer. In recent years several men working in professions such as the military, transportation, and sales, which require extensive or frequent travel, have been arrested for the murders of prostitutes. We can expect that as global mobility increases so will the numbers of men who target prostitutes in other states or in overseas countries.

attitudes and lifestyles that increase their vulnerability. According to Doerner and Lab (1995), victim precipitation is a "major contributing factor" in serious violence. Wolfgang (1958) noted that in many instances the characteristics of homicide victims in general resembled those of their assailants. Who became the offender and who became the victim often was determined more by chance than any other factor. He noted that few women committed murder and that most women who did commit murder were responding to the violent behavior of males. The Philadelphia study also revealed that most murders were intraracial: blacks killing blacks and whites killing whites.

As discussed earlier, the victims of serial murder appear increasingly to fall prey to strangers. Unlike homicides in general, in which the victim often knows the offender and provocation plays an important role in the killing, involvement of the victims of serial murder in their own victimization may be best determined by the

Table 8.8 Degree of Victim Facilitation in Serial Murder Cases in the United States, 1800–1995

Facilitation	Number of Victims	Percentage of Victims	Percentage of Cases	Number of Victims per Case
High	311–396	11–13	12	9–11
Low	1,418–2,257	60–64	70	7–11
Combination	632–880	25–27	18	11–16
Total	2,361–3,533		100	

Based on 304 cases, 366 offenders.

degree of facilitation created by the victim, or the degree to which the victim placed him- or herself in a vulnerable situation (Table 8.8). For example, picking up hitchhikers can place the driver or the passenger of a vehicle in a highly facilitative position for killing. Low facilitation was defined as sharing little or no responsibility for the victimization. For example, a child is abducted by a stranger while playing in his yard, a patient is poisoned to death during a hospital stay, or a woman is abducted from a shopping mall during daytime business hours. Usually these types of victims are completely unsuspecting of any imminent danger.

Data on offenders were examined regarding the methods used to obtain victims, and, in turn, data on victims were examined as to their lifestyles, type of employment, and their location at the time of abduction and/or killing. The overall trend indicated that 11–13% of all victims in this research were highly facilitative in their own deaths. Some were hitchhiking, others worked as prostitutes, and still others placed themselves in one way or another at the mercy of strangers. Over two-thirds of all victims were generally in the right place at the wrong time and became a homicide statistic. Since the 1988 study, decreases appeared in both high and low categories, prompting a near fourfold increase in combinations of high and low facilitation. Whether this reflects a trend in offender versatility, a statistical aberration, or simply problems in consistently defining and measuring facilitation over time, will require further exploration.

Although some people argue that much of the preceding research substantiates the contention of those claiming our society has experienced a dramatic emergence of serial killing, others may argue that such claims are the product of vague definitions, variations in reporting, the omnipresence of high-tech media, or a statistical artifact. However, of greater concern than the extent of serial murder is its reality. The pervasiveness of serial murder will unlikely ever challenge that of domestic homicide. What does seem to be increasingly apparent is that we are confronted with a phenomenon for which we have had little explanation and which we have little ability to deter. The risk of victimization in our general population appears to be extremely small, yet there are those who are at greater risk as a result of their age, gender, place of residence, or lifestyle. The fact that relatively few individuals are victims of serial murderers should in no way alter our concern for the victims.

The etiology of victimization is of concern to researchers wishing to expand their explanations of criminal behavior. Victim profiling can be an effective tool in understanding causation as well as providing direction for deterrence efforts. The victims in this study, except for those from California, exhibited little regionality. Increasingly they were targets of offenders who operated locally in areas with higher populations. Unlike homicide in general, in which the victim often knows his or her attacker, serial murder usually involves stranger-to-stranger situations. Young women and children are at greatest risk of victimization, especially those who are alone or can be isolated. Males, although not as frequently targeted, are also well represented as victims. In respect to age groups, offenders appear to kill young adults in greater proportion, yet in recent years the elderly have been frequently selected as victims. Most victims do not facilitate their deaths as a result of their lifestyle, although in recent years an increasing number of victims has appeared to place themselves at risk.

MISSING AND MURDERED CHILDREN

In 1979 6-year-old Etan Patz walked along a busy New York street to await his school bus. He had walked that one block to the bus before, but today was the first time his mother felt he was capable of going alone. Etan never arrived at the bus stop and has not been seen or heard of since his disappearance 22 years ago. In 1981 6-year-old Adam Walsh was abducted from a shopping mall when he was momentarily left unattended. His head was eventually recovered by investigators.

These two cases attracted extensive media coverage and motivated the creation of the Adam Walsh Child Resource Center in Ft. Lauderdale, Florida. However, in many other instances the offender, not the victim(s), receives the national media attention. In 1981–1982, 11 children disappeared in the area of Vancouver, British Columbia. Eventually, Clifford Robert Olson was arrested in the murder of the eleventh missing child. Although Olson was a suspect in the other disappearances, no one was sure what had become of the children and teenagers, ages 12–17. Olson, a man with an extensive history of criminal behavior, offered to take investigators to the graves of several victims in return for money. Without the money there would be no names or bodies returned, and the parents might never know if their child had been one of his victims or had disappeared for some other reason. If Olson had in fact killed their children, the families wanted to know and desperately wanted the bodies returned for a proper burial. After some deliberation the British Columbia government agreed to pay Olson $10,000 for each body returned to them. The killer responded by leading them to ten gravesites. Olson's wife was given the $100,000* and has since divorced him and relocated with her son. Olson now resides in a Canadian prison in where he must serve a minimum of 25

*After extensive public outcry the money was returned to the government.

years before he will be eligible for a parole hearing (author's files; interview with offender).

These types of abductions, murders, and serial killings of children generally precipitate alarm and fear in any community. The true extent of the problem of missing and murdered children is often subject more to speculation than fact. In 1983 the U.S. Department of Health and Human Services stated that 1.5 million children are reported missing every year. The executive director of the National Center for Missing and Exploited Children (the center), a nonprofit clearing house set up by the government in 1984, indicated that strangers were responsible for the abductions of 4,000 to 20,000 children each year. In addition the Center reported that 25,000 to 500,000 are victims of parental kidnapping ("How Many," 1985). Other organizations, such as the Federal Bureau of Investigation, strongly disagree with such figures and report much smaller numbers of victims.

Part of the problem of disagreement over current data can be traced to two sources: methodological issues in data collection, and operational definitions of the categories of missing children. Only in recent years has national attention been focused on the plight of missing children. Sorely needed are more national surveys that can be compared to regional and statewide data. A need is also apparent for consistency in defining the types of missing children. Most missing children can be classified as runaways, many leaving home several times in one year. Each time they run away, however, they can be counted again as missing children. Most runaways eventually return home, whereas others can be classified as parental kidnappings (Abraham, 1984). Most abductions of children are by parents or relatives, often engaged in custody battles with their former spouse or relative. The following list expands and refines the various categories used until now to clarify missing and murdered children:

1. **Runaways**—children who voluntarily leave home without parental/guardian permission.
2. **Parental abductions**—children abducted by the noncustodial parent or the parent who does not have legal guardianship.
3. **Relative abductions**—children abducted by a relative, such as an uncle, aunt, or in-law who takes a child from the parent or legal guardian.
4. **Discarded children**—children who are forced to leave their homes by parents or guardians who reject them.
5. **Disposable children**—children who are murdered by their parent(s) or legal guardians.
6. **Stranger abductions**—children who are taken by persons who are strangers to the victim and the victim's family.
7. **Abbreviated abductions**—children who are abducted for a short period of time (minutes or hours) and then released. These children may never be recorded in police records.
8. **Aborted abductions**—children who manage to escape the attempted kidnapping.

Table 8.9 Missing and Murdered Children Reported to the National Center for Missing and Exploited Children between June 13, 1984, and January 7, 1988

	Percentage Found Alive (*N* = 8,562)	Percentage Found Dead (*N* = 117)	Percentage Still Missing (*N* = 7,832)	Percentage of Total (*N* = 16,511)
Runaways	65	13	28	50
Parental abductions	28	3	54	38
Relative abductions	5	20	15	9
Stranger abductions	2	64	3	3
Total	100	100	100	100

SOURCE: U.S. Department of Justice, 1988

The National Center for Missing and Exploited Children released the number of children reported to them as missing between June 1984 and January 1988 (Table 8.9). As expected, runaways represented the greatest percentage of children found alive, whereas stranger abductions accounted for the greatest percentage of those children found dead. Abraham (1984) found that only three out of every ten children kidnapped by a parent will ever see the other parent again and that physical and sexual abuse of the abducted child is common. Table 8.9 indicates that nearly one-fourth of the children that were abducted by a parent or a relative and later found had been murdered. These findings also challenge the generally accepted notion that 95% of missing children are runaways. According to the National Center, parental and relative abductions accounted for nearly half of all missing children reported to their agency. In contrast to their earlier findings of several thousands of children being abducted by strangers each year, their data indicated approximately 150 stranger abductions per year during the three-and-one-half-year study (FBI, 1988).

In 1987 the FBI reported that 2,398 children had been murdered. These deaths included those reported to the National Center for Missing and Exploited Children as well as children who were killed by their parents or legal guardians and those categorized as discarded children. Death tolls could be much higher if we were able to account for all the children still missing.

According to the FBI approximately one-fourth of all male children murdered in 1987 were 14 years of age or younger. By comparison, over half of all female children murdered that year were 14 years of age or younger. When controls were made for all age categories, male children were more than twice as likely to be murdered. When the 15–19 age group is excluded, the ratio nearly evens out between males and females. In other words, the percentages of male children being murdered in all age categories, with the exception of the 15–19 group, are similar to those of female children in respective age groupings. The dramatic difference between murders of males and females age 15–19 may be explained in part as a result of drug- and gang-related violence. Yet these data also reveal that nearly one-fourth of all children reported murdered in 1987 were 4 years of age or younger (FBI, 1988). This figure, of course, includes children killed by their mothers or fathers, as well as abducted and murdered child victims.

Although in 1987 blacks constituted less than 13% of the U.S. population, they represented half of all the murdered children reported to the FBI. Although males were more likely than females to be murdered between the ages of 15 and 19, blacks were more likely than whites to be murdered in the same age group (FBI, 1988). Again, this can be explained in part by the socioeconomic conditions under which the majority of blacks are forced to live. When we exclude the 15–19 age group, black children represent 41% of all children murdered (age 14 and younger). It appears that even young black children are at significantly higher risk of being murdered than their white counterparts. By 1995 the primary cause of death for young African American males in the United States was homicide. In 1994, Gary, Indiana, reported a homicide rate approximately six times that of the national rate. The majority of their homicides are young African American males caught up in drug- and gang-related activities.

In January 1989, the Office of Juvenile Justice and Delinquency Prevention published a bulletin of the preliminary estimates of stranger abduction homicides of children. The data were gathered from the FBI's Supplemental Homicide File and represent the first findings from the National Studies of the Incidence of Missing Children. It was estimated that between one and two stranger abductions per 1 million of the general population occurred per year, with teenagers between the ages of 14 and 17 exhibiting the highest rates. Such figures indicate that the risk of a child being abducted and murdered by a stranger is much lower than previous estimates (U.S. Department of Justice, 1989a, 1989b). Child murders by strangers that may have involved abduction ranged from a low of 110 in 1980 to a high of 212 in 1982, but no evidence was found to suggest that these types of homicides are on the rise. Where strangers are concerned, the preliminary data suggest that girls are at greater risk than boys; in addition, the rates for black children are three times higher than for white children. This report, along with five other major studies cited, dispels the myths that thousands of children are being abducted and murdered each year and that cases are on the rise (U.S. Department of Justice, 1989a, 1989b). As the report also observes, most of these data originate from police statistics, and the conclusions, therefore, are tentative. Nonetheless, the preliminary report is encouraging.

The fact remains, however, that some children do fall prey to strangers, some of whom are serial offenders. Based on the present study, the following section explores factors in the murders of children who were victims of serial killers.

Table 8.10 Relationship of Serial Murderers in the United States to Their Child Victims

Relationship	Percentage of Male Offenders (N = 66)	Percentage of Female Offenders (N = 22)	Percentage of Total (N = 88)
Strangers	65	9	51
Strangers/acquaintances	16	0	13
Family	1	64	17
Family/acquaintances	5	18	8
Family/stranger	5	0	3
Acquaintances	5	9	6
All	3	0	2
Total	100	100	100

Children as Victims of Serial Murderers

If we are to protect children from adults who would kill them, we must be willing to look beyond the traditional notions of victim-offender relationships. Although researchers are still attempting to measure the extent of the serial-murder phenomenon, the evidence is clear that young women and children are the prime targets of such attacks. According to the case files of 391 known serial killers in the United States, 93 (24%) had killed at least one child. The child-killer group included males (74%) and females (26%); very few of the offenders were black (author's files).

Although a consensus has not yet been reached to explain the low numbers of black offenders who kill children, it is possible that blacks have been overlooked during the emergence of the serial-murder phenomenon. Most serial offenders are white and lower-middle-class or middle-class, and their homicides tend to be intraracial. The fact that some major urban centers are now predominantly black and are politically controlled by black citizens may in part explain why increasing attention is being focused on the plight of missing and murdered black children. As mentioned earlier, in 1981 Wayne Williams, who is black, was arrested in the killings of 25–30 black youths in Atlanta, Georgia. The murders and their investigation attracted national media and government attention. In recent years a few blacks have also been involved in interracial serial killings and have received considerable publicity for their crimes. In 1985 Alton Coleman and his companion Debra Brown, both black, went on a killing spree in the Midwest, murdering several victims, including young children both black and white. One in four offenders (26%) targeted children only.

As expected, female killers of children from this group were more likely to murder victims from their own families or other relatives, whereas males were seven times more likely to be total strangers to their victims (Table 8.10). In addition, female offenders were more prone to use poisons to kill their victims; males who killed children frequently mutilated, strangled, shot, or bludgeoned their victims.

Table 8.11 Mobility Classification of Serial Murderers in the United States Who Have Killed One or More Children

Mobility	Percentage of Male Offenders (*N* = 68)	Percentage of Female Offenders (*N* = 24)	Percentage of Total (*N* = 92)
Place-specific	13	33	19
Local	41	46	42
Traveling	46	21	39
Total	100	100	100

By using the mobility classifications to analyze the child homicide data, most of the offenders were found to have stayed (local type) within one state (Table 8.11). But many of the child killers (39%) in this study were categorized as the "traveling" type. Male offenders were twice as likely to travel and hunt for child victims as female offenders. Also, females who killed children were more likely to be classified as local than place-specific or traveling. Although several women were typed as place-specific, with the murders occurring in their own homes or places of work, some of the females teamed up with males. By contrast, the largest group of male offenders operated as traveling types, followed closely by local offenders. One implication derived from these data is that children, when targeted by a serial killer, can be at risk both in and out of the home. Although the likelihood of a child being murdered by a serial offender is remote compared to the much higher risk of being the victim of domestic homicide, the fact that any risk exists underscores the need for increased education regarding the etiology of serial murder.

For male offenders the primary motive reported for the killing of children was sexual gratification (Table 8.12). In one recent case spanning several months, the offender lured several young boys into his control and then sexually molested them. He later confessed to killing the boys for fear that they would tell someone about the molestation.

The female offenders were much more likely (38%) to kill children for financial reasons. In several cases female offenders have murdered their own children, other relatives, or even neighbors in order to collect the insurance. In addition, both male and female offenders often reported deriving enjoyment (23%) from the killing of children. Overall, males were much more inclined to report a combination of motives for killing (59%) compared to their female counterparts (33%). The desire to exert control over the child victim was also a primary motivation in killing, particularly in the case of male offenders (42%).

Another important key to understanding the serial killer of children is to dispel notions of lunacy, mental illness, or psychosis. As mentioned in Chapter 3, very few offenders—whether they kill children or adults—are ever found to be insane by legal definitions. A more suitable term for such killers is *psychopaths.* This label is intended to include persons with particular personality

Table 8.12 Reported Motives of Serial Murderers in the United States Who Have Killed One or More Children

Motives	Percentage of Male Offenders (*N* = 69)	Percentage of Female Offenders (*N* = 24)	Percentage of Total (*N* = 93)
Sexual gratification	68	8	53
Control	42	17	35
Enjoyment	28	8	23
Monetary gain	14	38	20
Personal reasons*	13	0	10
Mental illness	9	4	8
Combination of motives	59	33	53

*Males generally reported an "urge to kill," whereas female offenders reported that "they were not good mothers," "children were a burden," or they were trying to hide other crimes. Sometimes the killings were reported to have been motivated by racism or hatred.

defects or disorders that often are not discernible to those around them. Such individuals often possess several or all of the following characteristics: charismatic; above-average intelligence; little or no conscience or sense of guilt or responsibility; highly manipulative; compulsive lying; devoid of feelings for others, especially their victims; and outwardly friendly.

For some offenders, killing children may represent an act of revenge on an unjust society or perhaps a desire to prevent others from experiencing the joy and happiness in life they themselves felt denied. Such reasons for murder make children prime targets for offenders. They are viewed as being more trusting, naive, and powerless than adults and are more easily abducted.

Certainly not all psychopaths are violent offenders, and possessing psychopathic characteristics does not always lead individuals to criminal behavior. However, the majority of offenders in this study do possess many psychopathic personality defects. The ability and need for these offenders to control others is tremendous. Children become prime targets because they can be easily controlled and manipulated. Placed in a conducive environment for these child-killers, abductors, and molesters, children have little resistance to their persuasive powers. Parents need to be just as concerned about where their children *go* in their unsupervised time as they are about teaching them not to "take candy from strangers."

Robert Theodore Bundy was executed in the state of Florida for the murder of 12-year-old Kimberly Leach, whom he kidnapped from the grounds of her junior high school in 1978. Bundy also lured a 15-year-old girl into his car while she was attending a youth conference at Brigham Young University in Provo, Utah, in June 1975. Because of his charisma and his ability to persuade his victims to ignore taking precautions with a total stranger, he was able to abduct, sexually torture, and murder several dozen young women. His usually fail-safe plan involved approaching potential victims in the daytime and in places where the victims felt no danger. He often feigned an arm or leg injury and simply asked an intended victim to help him carry something to his car. He was also known to have posed as a police officer and would talk victims into entering his vehicle. By the time the victims may have sensed danger, they were already under the killer's total control.

Luring Children

We have all heard horror stories about abducted children. Unfortunately, child abductors can be particularly creative in their methods of finding suitable victims. One 16-year-old offender being evaluated for a sex-offender program in a psychiatric facility in the western United States noted how simple it was for him to find child victims to molest. His favorite "hunting grounds" were shopping malls because he always found parents who were willing to leave their children, sometimes even young children, alone for a few minutes around the toy counters. The children whom he approached, escorted to the washroom, and molested inevitably seemed to trust him. Some of his victims were so young he was sure they would not understand what had occurred once he allowed them to leave. On a "good" night he claimed he could lure three to four children to the washrooms.

In another case a 15-year-old offender who had been arrested in Hawaii for sexual molestation of children was never prosecuted because his family relocated. A few months later the offender abducted a 3-year-old child while she played inside her fenced front yard. After raping and strangling the infant, he left the body in a vacant building.

In 1977 Operation Police Lure was organized in Oakland County, Michigan, by a law enforcement task force in response to a series of seven unsolved child homicides. At the time some people believed that a serial killer was responsible for several of the abductions. In the area where the children were probably lured and abducted, a survey was administered to students in 54 elementary and junior high schools in grades 4 through 9 in an effort to gather more data on child molestation and abduction. The children reported 782 incidents of attempted or actual cases of molestation that had never been reported to authorities. Police investigators also found that children aged 10–12 were the most likely targets and that males and females were victimized at about the same rates. Although victims were approached at different times of day, 3:00 to 6:00 P.M. was the time most frequently reported. Children profiled the offenders as white males, usually in their twenties or thirties, who often attempted to lure them by asking for help, such as looking for a lost puppy. When vehicles were used, the abductors and molesters also seemed to prefer two-door blue models (Wooden, 1984).

Child abductors, of course, do not come in only one mold and generally do not fit the stereotype of the peculiar-looking "dirty old man." Some very benign-looking individuals are arrested for child abductions and molestations. Creating a new typology of such offenders becomes problematic because it excludes many variations of the traditional stereotype. Some important aspects, however, can be noted about the nature of child abductions. Although coercion, bribery, and other such methods to lure victims are frequently employed, asking for help from a child is not only effective from an offender's perspective but also creates difficulty for parents in protecting their children. The thought of helping find a lost animal, such as a puppy or a kitten, can easily distract the child from paying attention to the person seeking the assistance. Similarly, the offenders may use a badge or a blue vehicle to appear as an authority figure to the intended victim. Most children are taught or have learned by experience a degree of respect for authority figures and will automatically respond to their commands.

Wooden (1984) outlines a variety of child lures used by offenders, including an appeal to a child's ego by telling the child that he or she is to be in a beauty contest or a television commercial. Some offenders tell the child that an emergency has occurred and they have come to escort the child home immediately. Wayne Williams was believed to have posted employment advertisements for young men throughout the area in which he resided. In the case of Ted Bundy and others like him similar themes are used but in a more sophisticated manner. Wearing a cast to evoke sympathy or displaying fictitious business cards initially alleviates fears of dealing with a stranger. Offenders who have become adept at manipulating can exert complete control over others, especially children. The following tragic story illustrates how devastating the control some offenders have over their victims can be.

*A Child Killer's Story**

I remember it was late fall and I was living in T———, Arizona, on the run from the law in Montana. At 24 I had already committed several violent crimes and was basically out of control. Deep into depression and frustrated, I found myself walking across a field about 4:00 P.M. one cold, dreary day. I thought I was alone when I noticed two girls also walking across the field. Immediately I knew I was going to kill them. Moving in their direction, I began to speak to them in a friendly voice. They said they were on their way to play badminton. Both were 11 years of age but one looked physically more mature than the other. It was really very easy, and I was so persuasive, the girls did not even hesitate when I suggested we go to a secluded area. They were such trusting children.

I pulled out my knife and told them to do as I said or I would hurt them. I could see the surprise and fear in their eyes as I ordered the smaller of the two to remain where she was while I moved the second child to another area. They were prevented from seeing one another. Each child was staked out on the ground "spread eagle" and their clothes torn off. They didn't dare scream for each time they tried I beat them. I systematically tortured them, going back and forth but spent more time with the smaller child. I had other plans for the prettier girl. The more

*This story was edited from a taped interview I conducted with a multiple homicide offender December 5/6, 1988. By request of the offender his identity will remain anonymous.

> they responded to the torture, the more I tried to hurt them. I burned them with cigarettes, I beat them repeatedly and hurt them sexually. After about two hours the first child was not responding very well, she was very cold, her eyes appeared glazed, and she appeared to be in shock. I took the handle of her racquet and strangled her to death.
>
> I untied the other girl and told her to get dressed and that if she did as I said we would come back for her friend. I told her not to worry that I would not hurt her anymore but she must obey me. I gave her my coat, as her blouse had been cut away in the attack. As we left, I noticed it was after 6:00 P.M. I decided to take her to my home and kill her there. We walked quickly across the field, the child trying her best to keep up with me. As we started along the sidewalk, a police car came around the corner and pulled up beside us. They had their public address system on and were looking for the two missing girls. Apparently the mother of the child walking with me had gone out looking for her daughter when she realized her child had left for the courts without her coat. When neither of the girls could be located, the concerned parents had contacted the police.
>
> Now I was walking less than five feet from the patrol car. The girl was behind me several feet and in a moment I expected the child to run to their car and give me away. I quickly walked down the street, anticipating the command to halt. After about 30 yards I suddenly heard the little girl yelling at me, "Mister, Mister, please slow down you're walking too fast!" I glanced over my shoulder and was amazed to see her still walking behind me. The police had seen us but there was nothing about our behavior that was suspicious and she was hurrying after me. I took her hand and we walked on. In a few moments we approached another street corner when suddenly she saw her father drive by in a car. "There goes my Daddy! He's looking for me," I remember her saying. She did not call out and her father drove on, oblivious to how close he had come to finding his missing child.
>
> She walked with me to my place without any struggle or protest. I again went through my ritual of removing her clothes and staking her out. She was all mine from about 7:00 P.M. till 3:00 the next morning. She never screamed because she knew I would not take her back to her friend if she failed to obey my every command. When I finished, I suffocated her to death. Later that day I borrowed a car and carried her body into the mountains. Searchers found the first child about an hour after we left the secluded area and the second child about a day after I dumped her body. They never would have caught me had I not left the sack in which I had wrapped the second child. It was an odd weave and had the child's blood on it. Police showed the sack on television and someone recognized it as mine. I was captured in another state a few days later.

The offender's initial charisma and his subsequent intimidating and brutal methods were used in succession to gain total control over the children. Even the offender admitted surprise in finding his second victim following him past the police car. In frustration we want to understand why a victim would not run from her attacker. This is reminiscent of the *Stockholm Syndrome,* in which the victim begins to identify with his or her captor. The child, concerned for her friend and mentally numbed from her ordeal, was incapable of fleeing her assailant.

PROTECTION AND PREVENTION

Many people today feel a sense of impending doom because they believe that they will inevitably fall prey to criminal victimization. A great deal of this fear is created by constant media reports that focus on the most heinous crimes committed in our society. However, we must never forget that there are many factors that play a role in the dynamics of victimization. Age, race, gender, socioeconomic status, place of residence, employment, education, lifestyles—all of which can affect the types of crimes committed in particular areas—must be considered when considering the risk factors. Even then, crimes that appear to have little or no correlation with most risk factors do occur. It becomes disconcerting for people to feel they may be at risk and yet powerless to effectively respond to such concerns. Regardless of their utility, most strategies embraced by adults to protect themselves—such as enrolling in self-defense courses, carrying a weapon, or increasing home security—are not viable for children. More important, we may delude ourselves into believing that law enforcement can provide sufficient protection for children and that school officials can always provide adequate supervision.

The perception of increasing randomness of child victimization outside the home has initiated awareness and action on the part of concerned parents and community activists. The experience of victimization often serves as a catalyst for involvement in victims' rights and victim advocacy groups. Some of these organizations function primarily as support groups, whereas others focus attention on introducing legislation aimed at addressing the rights of victims, including the handling of criminals in our judicial system. The murder of a child has effects that extend far beyond the loss of life, as is evidenced by the experiences of the parents of child victims. Although some may seek vengeance on offenders, others become involved with groups that actively work to prevent future victimizations, assist other victims being processed through the criminal justice system, and provide counseling, because after the media headlines subside, the agony may just be beginning for many of those related to a murder victim. The following statement provided by Ruth Kuzmaak and her husband, Dr. John Kuzmaak, of Portland, Oregon, describes the effect of their daughter's homicide on the Kuzmaak family and the frustrations they continue to face years later.

The Kuzmaak Story

I write the following not to enlist the reader's sympathy. I do not want sympathy. I write instead hoping that others will have a better understanding for those persons who have endured criminal victimizations.

I keep searching for the right descriptive words to convey the emotional impact our daughter's murder made on us. "Devastating" just doesn't make it—"ravaged" is closer, engulfed, overwhelmed, drowning in sadness, numb, oblivious to EVERYTHING else, totally immersed in the horror, the why, the who, what she had to go through in the closing minutes of her short life, how terrified she must have been, did she scream for help and no one came, did she fight, the pain, how it felt to be strangled, what her dying thoughts were, how she must have held out hope until the last that she would be rescued, her shock and disbelief that this was happening, and as the information unfolded itself to us in bits and pieces that first day, the anguish of hearing how badly she was beaten, then a couple of hours later crying out when I heard that she had been repeatedly stabbed. Then, the ultimate horror to learn that the cause of death was strangulation. To be deprived of breath—lungs bursting—"Oh, God, oh God," I would wail, tears streaming, hands clenched and imploring.

That is how I remember the day, March 21, 1979. A decade has passed, but the emotions go on, the anger, the sorrow, and the loss.

I wanted to go to the funeral home to see her, but everyone told me that I should remember her the way she was in life, not in death, so I didn't. I have regretted it over and over—that I didn't have the courage to look at her after she had suffered through so much. It was something I should have done.

A big, black Cadillac picked us up in the morning she was to be buried. We drove slowly to the funeral home, parking in the rear. Shortly, the back door opened and men in dark suits started carrying out her casket to the hearse.

"There she is," said our son. She had been so vibrant, so much fun to be with, so bright, and so loving, and here she was being carried out in a coffin. Gone from life. Gone from us.

I counted 75 cars winding up the hill behind us at the cemetery. Many more had mistakenly gone to the funeral home. Plainclothes police photographed the cars and the people. I asked that the poem "Thanatopsis" be read. The minister asked if she had been baptized, and I said she had.

Within six weeks I had lost 22 pounds, going from 141 to 119. My husband and I kept working at his dental office, which helped considerably during the day, but the nights were a horror. I would wake up two and three times an hour, and each time I had to face, once more, the reality. I had always been an avid reader, and so I would grab a book and start reading until I once more fell asleep. Books became my narcotic.

Relatives, friends, and our dental patients were extremely kind to us during this time. They say that sorrow needs a good support system and we had one. But, within a few months all but Ken, Janet, Aunt Lois, and Donna's girlfriend, Chris, had dropped away and out of our lives. When I did have occasion to talk to people, they avoided the subject. It was as though Donna had never existed. One night we went out with a couple we had known for years. I was describing a court hearing we had gone to.

We had heard that the defendant might be a suspect in Donna's murder, and he was being tried on another charge. Our friend, a dentist, interrupted with, "Ruth, could we talk about something else? This is so depressing." Increasingly, we became more isolated.

We could get so little information from the police that we would think up ruses in order to try to get them to say more. "Was she raped? Sodomized? No?" Then, we would wrack our brains trying to figure out why they called it a "sex crime." Ken and I had long conversations, filled with theories and speculations.

An enormous boulder had been dropped in our river of life and we all struggled to stay afloat. Within 18 months I had breast cancer. Grandma Kuzmaak developed a giant stomach ulcer from which she never recovered. I was glad that my mother had died for she just couldn't have stood it. Janet had lost her best friend, for she and Donna had been very close in both ages and affection. A 12-year-old neighborhood girlfriend of Donna's had to have psychiatric help. Nightmares were constant for me. They were filled with vicious, evil, predatory men, and in some of them I was trying to shelter Donna from them. But I had good dreams, too. In them, Donna was again a small, little girl in pigtails. She had always been such a gentle child.

About 1982, Janet talked me into going on a local television talk show. The audience was to be made up of parents of murdered children. During the program, I complained about the inaccessibility of information from the police about what had happened to her. Afterward, Dr. Larry Lewman came over to me and said that he had done Donna's autopsy and that this information was open to us. No one had told us this.

We went down to his office two days later and he went over the autopsy with us. I learned that her nose had been shattered, that she had received a violent blow on the back of her head, that she had been stabbed nine times in the chest and also in the vagina, and strangled with her pantyhose. The vaginal sexual mutilation was why the police considered it a sex crime. Now, we knew.

I started reading everything I could get my hands on about the mentality of these sexually sadistic killers. It was an ugly education. I added new words to my vocabulary, such as *necrophilia.* Although Donna's autopsy showed no semen, I learned that these killers frequently masturbated on or near the body.

We met with other victims and formed a group called "Crime Victims United." This, then, became the focus of my life. I could channel my energies, my rage, and Donna's murder into something really worthwhile.

It took us two attempts to pass a statewide victims' rights measure. No longer would surviving family members be forced to sit in the hall during the trial. We got equal peremptory challenges (before, the defendant had twice as many as the state), victims could make victim impact statements in court, prior convictions could be raised to the jury, and many other important changes.

My husband, Jack, showed gritty determination in these efforts, getting thousands of signers in order to get it on the ballot in each of the elections. Having accomplished this goal, however, I believe he feels now that "enough is enough." But I go on. We have had several arguments about it recently.

Our children have been quite supportive of our efforts, though one day Janet said to me, "Mom, we're here, too." And . . . that really hurt!

I watched Dr. Martha Gluckman of Patuxent Institute being interviewed on *Nightline*. She was being questioned about the paroles given to convicted murderers and rapists at Patuxent and also the unsupervised weekend passes.

One inmate had been convicted of murdering his girlfriend and her parents. He had been sentenced to three life sentences, to be served consecutively starting in the early 1980s. Already he had been given 12 weekend unsupervised passes.

Another inmate, Charles Wantland, had murdered a 12-year-old boy three weeks after being paroled. He had served only 6 years of a 30-year sentence for murder.

Yet another sex offender convicted in 1972 was serving a life sentence for rape, perverted practices, assault, and kidnapping. He was paroled in 1980 and within a year convicted of three more rapes.

Dr. Gluckman vigorously defended the passes and furloughs, saying, "George Bush said he wants a kinder and gentler nation, and I think it should start with Corrections." The remark left me totally outraged.

On Memorial Day and Donna's birthday we go to the cemetery. I can't keep the tears from flowing each time I stoop to arrange the flowers.

I can talk about Donna's murder with the kind of detachment I use when discussing the weather. But, I still can't really THINK about it. This statement has made me think about it, and it has been difficult. But, I truly hope that it will be of benefit in helping people understand.

Our daughter's murder remains unsolved (Hickey, 1990b).

The Kuzmaak story represents the experiences of many families affected by the murder of a loved one. In this case the homicide is believed to be the work of a serial killer.

AGENCIES FOR MISSING, MURDERED, AND EXPLOITED CHILDREN

At the national level a multitude of agencies are now beginning to organize themselves to specifically address the issues of missing, exploited, and murdered children. Established in 1984 by the U.S. Department of Justice, the National Center for Missing and Exploited Children operates as a national clearinghouse for information about missing and murdered children and sexual exploitation, including child pornography and prostitution.

National Center for Missing and Exploited Children

1835 K Street, N.W., Suite 700

Washington, DC 20006

1–800–THE–LOST

This hotline (1–800–843–5678) is available to anyone with information about missing or exploited children. The Telecommunications Device for the Deaf (TDD) hotline is 1–800–826–7653. The U.S. Department of Justice publishes a variety of brochures that address parental kidnapping, child protection, runaways, and sexually abused or exploited children; and that list whom to contact if your child is missing; and that examine a host of other topics regarding children as well. Anyone or any group interested in the safety and welfare of children would be well served to contact this agency.

The parent agency that directly coordinates the many federal agencies pertaining to children is the U.S. Department of Justice, Office of Juvenile Justice and Delinquency Prevention, Washington, DC 20531. The U.S. Department of Justice's Coordinating Council on Juvenile Justice and Delinquency Prevention includes representatives from the Department of Health and Human Services and the Department of Education. This council, working in conjunction with the Attorney General's Advisory Board on Missing Children, coordinates communications with the Federal Bureau of Investigation and the National Obscenity Enforcement Unit (both agencies of the Department of Justice), the U.S. Department of State, the U.S. Postal Service, the U.S. Customs Service, the Interstate "I SEARCH" Advisory Council on Missing and Exploited Children, and the National Center for Missing and Exploited Children. The U.S. Department of Justice is very active in collecting and disseminating information about missing and exploited children and publishes reports summarizing the progress made in the 1990s.

Another agency that now has national recognition in addressing the issues of missing, abused, and neglected children is the following:

Adam Walsh Child Resource Center, Executive Office

9176 Alternate A1A, Suite 200

West Palm Beach, FL 33403-1445

516–863–7900

Several states have created clearinghouses for missing and exploited children; these agencies usually can be contacted through the state police and are coordinated with the National Center for Missing and Exploited Children. In the state of Indiana, for example, extensive information packets are available upon request.

Missing Children Clearinghouse

Indiana State Police

State Office Building

100 N. Senate

Indianapolis, IN 46204

1–800–831–8953 (Indiana only)

(317) 232–8248 (out of state)

In 1996, California opened its Registered Sex Offender Directory, which contains the names, addresses, and photographs of the state's worst repeat sex offenders. California currently has approximately 67,000 registered sex offenders, 4,200 of whom are classified as serious and chronic offenders. In Fresno, California, alone, there are 414 registered repeat offenders. There is also a Child Molester subdirectory that allows concerned citizens 18 years of age or older with identification to sign in and use the manual. This may well prove to be a useful tool for the public to keep track of sex offenders moving into their neighborhood. Concerned citizens may, for a $10 fee, use California's Child Molester Identification Hotline by dialing 1–900–463–0400. This service has a list of over 40,000 registered, convicted child molesters.

Other states have also made strides in organizing victim advocacy groups. A sample of privately sponsored crime victim groups and organizations can be obtained from:

Citizens for Justice and Crime Victims United

P.O. Box 19480

Portland, OR 97219

(503) 246–5368

This politically active crime victims' support group, which meets regularly to discuss current legislative issues pertaining to victims' rights and to listen to various speakers dealing with the laws, courts, stress management, counseling, and so on, publishes a regular monthly newsletter.

The following nonprofit all-volunteer organization was formed in response to problems within the criminal justice system:

The Stephanie Roper Committee and Foundation, Inc.

14750 Main #1B Pratt Street

Upper Marlboro, MD 20772-3055

(301) 952–2319 (fax)

(301) 952–0063

1–877–VICTIM 1 (toll free)

e-mail: mail@stephanieroper.org

This committee addresses administrative and legislative reform in the sentencing and parole of violent offenders and the establishment of victims' rights. The foundation provides direct services to victims and their families by offering comfort, support, and assistance throughout the period of dealing with the criminal justice system. It also maintains an active court-watch program to monitor the application of victims' rights under law.

9

Interviewing Serial Murderers

Scientific researchers have developed several methodologies for data collection and analysis. Typically, data gathered from random sample surveys or aggregate data collection allows researchers to perform comparative analyses of various social phenomena, based on information gathered from a large number of subjects. Researchers can also gather information from life history analysis. Diaries, autobiographies, and personal interviews can provide particularly insightful information unavailable through more empirically oriented research. The "trade-off," which may not always be equitable, permits researchers to focus exclusively on a few cases in order to allow in-depth exploration.

Obviously, gathering data about serial killers cannot be managed by simply mailing out questionnaires or conducting telephone surveys. Serial killers are not only relatively rare in number, but they also are not easily accessible. The Federal Bureau of Investigation undoubtedly has the easiest access to serial killers once they have been incarcerated. However, even agents from the Behavioral Science Unit in Quantico, Virginia, do not receive cooperation from all multiple-homicide offenders. Some killers do confess their crimes, but some serial killers continue to claim they are innocent long after they go to prison and, thereby, refuse to cooperate with police by giving them any information about the murders. In all likelihood, many of the myths associated with serial killers could be dispelled if researchers were able to have greater access to offenders. Indeed, the interview could become a critical tool in understanding serial murder.

Interviewing multiple-homicide offenders certainly is not without its limitations and problems. Given the nature of their offenses, offenders are often eager to gain the attention of the researcher, police, or anyone else who will help publicize the crimes. Many of these offenders have led insecure and emotionally truncated lives; they are at last receiving the attention they have so desperately longed for. Sometimes, as in the case of Henry Lee Lucas (see Chapter 6), offenders will confess to many more homicides than they actually committed in order to attract public attention. This in turn brings into question the validity of multiple-homicide data. Researchers must be careful not to be drawn into the sensationalism of high victim counts in lieu of investigating the accuracy of those claims.

In addition, certain individuals who are attracted to offenders befriend and follow them through the criminal justice process. Such "groupies" have been common in cases of particular notoriety, including that of Ted Bundy. Several young women, similar in appearance to his victims, attended the court sessions and frequently corresponded with the killer. Some wanted to marry Bundy; others believed they could "help" Ted. Such "groupies" are often criticized because they contribute to the killer's notoriety. Similar criticism is sometimes leveled at researchers who spend time interviewing serial offenders, because the information can be easily manipulated and distorted.

In addition, a serial offender may tell interviewers exactly what he or she wants them to hear—or, conversely, what he or she thinks the interviewers want to hear. Some psychiatric units term such behavior "gaming." Occasionally criminals who have been sent to a psychiatric hospital for evaluation feel a need to live up to the expectation that they are indeed criminally insane. To prove their state of mind, the offenders will "bounce off the walls" for a few days, often in an isolation cell, until they calm down. Inevitably they realize that most people they see on the ward are not acting out and appear rather "normal." To some degree the serial killer, thrust under public scrutiny, may feel a need to fit the typical "mold" of such offenders.

Another criticism regarding interviews is that what offenders have to say, even if they believe it, may not reflect a realistic perspective. Hindsight can easily distort reality and mold it to the psychological needs of the offender. How objective, how truthful, can we expect serial murderers to be? One can expect a certain degree of distorted thinking in the mind of an offender who has mutilated 15 or 20 victims.

Although such criticisms certainly have merit, researchers recognize that, despite the stumbling blocks, interviews can be productive. The interview should be regarded as another source of information, another perspective into the murdering mind. Some offenders have acquired particular insight into their own distorted thinking or the mind-set of other serial killers. For example, serial killers are stereotyped as persons without or incapable of remorse. Although this appears to be true for many such offenders, there are also exceptions. One offender, the killer of five young boys in Utah, apologized to the victims' families and begged their forgiveness. On several occasions he expressed his deep regrets and sorrow. To prove sincerity and to show his willingness to do anything to help right the wrongs he committed, Arthur Gary Bishop stopped his appeals process to allow himself to be executed. Although his remorse appeared to have been sincere, Bishop recognized that what he had become had completely engulfed him. Shortly before his execution, he commented that even though he was deeply sorrowful for his deeds, he knew that if he were released he would continue to kill.

Each murderer has an explanation of what may have caused him or her to commit terrible crimes. Researchers would be remiss if they did not take every opportunity to gather such information. However, researchers must be cautious about assuming they understand the mind of the serial killer simply because they may have interviewed two or three offenders. Also, some offenders believed to be linked to many deaths may be incarcerated for only one or two homicides and emphatically deny involvement in other killings. Several appear to have embraced the "Bundy Complex," or complete denial of responsibility despite overwhelming evidence to the contrary. However, these offenders can also provide researchers with insights to their personalities and psychological characteristics.

Dr. Candice Skrapec, a criminal psychologist at California State University in Fresno, California, has, like your author, interviewed several Canadian serial killers. In her recent research (2001) Skrapec explores the method of empirical phenomenology. She believes that "learning about a murderer's personal construction of meaning in their own lives positions us to be able to identify the motivations underlying their repeated acts of killing" (p. 46). She challenges traditional methods of inquiry into motivations for serial murder and cautions researchers regarding implied meanings of their data. Indeed, she raises an excellent point: Perhaps we are so eager to interpret motives of serial killers that the processes by which we conduct our examinations and draw our conclusions are inherently flawed. Indeed, what categorically makes a serial killer different from everyone else? Skrapec (2001) observes:

> The literature on serial murder is largely the product of broad-based descriptive study of large numbers of cases of serial killers or the result of individual case studies. We have learned much useful information from, for example, the accounts of law enforcement agents (see Douglas & Olshaker, 1999; Ressler & Shachtman, 1997; Vorpagel, 1998), forensic psychiatrists and psychologists (in terms of their case experiences, e.g., Kirwin, 1997; Lewis 1998) and other social scientists (e.g., Jenkins, 1994; Leyton, 1999). Specific details about how information is collected, assessments of reliability of sources, and the like are, however, frequently lacking in published sources (Skrapec, 2001, p. 47)

Skrapec argues that mere descriptions of the offenders, their crimes, and victims fall short of where we really need to be in understanding the phenomenon. She relates the example of Ed Kemper who challenged a researcher during an interview because she was not asking the right questions. After all, if you, as a reader, could sit with Ed Kemper and ask him anything you wanted, what would you ask? He thinks you might want to know what it feels like to have sex with a corpse or sit on your living room couch and look over and see two decapitated girls' heads on the arms of the couch. Kemper says: "The first time it makes you sick to your stomach" (p. 48).

Perhaps the reason that we are asking the "wrong" questions is because we are so anxious to have answers. Answers to keep the media filled with sensational material whether there is merit in the information or not is really of little import when the bottom line is selling newspapers and magazines. Let us pause for a moment and consider three vital issues when conducting research:

1. Maintain objectivity.
2. Acknowledge other perspectives.
3. Recognize that asking the "right" questions is more important than finding quick answers.

Remember that serial murder constitutes a process, not just an act of killing. The offender certainly did not become a serial killer overnight, nor should the researchers questions be geared toward finding a quick and effortless answer. Answers will take care of themselves if we are able to ask the "right" questions. Monahan & Steadman (1984) noted several problems with researchers in conducting diagnostic work including:

Memory bias: the interview is tainted by the biases of the researcher based upon prior experience or knowledge about the offender or case. *False positives or false negatives:* the researcher predicts behavior by the subject but is wrong in his prognosis. Conversely, false negatives means that the researcher predicts that certain behaviors will not occur in a subject but they do. *Weighing current factors:* researchers need to examine the case in its entirety. The subject must be examined in his current status as well as where he has come from. Subjects are in transition and need to be viewed as dynamic not static entities. *Illusionary correlations:* researchers sometimes are quick to make comparisons in a subject's behaviors and outside events. Often such "correlations" are spurious. *Hindsight bias:* the researcher has gained some experience and therefore comes to expect certain responses from the subject. This can be very costly if the researcher begins to over guide the subject. *Overconfidence:* the researcher sometimes fails to connect with the subject because the researcher exudes a sense of superiority, or insight unavailable to the subject. Remember that prison visits are not visits to the zoo. *Overfocusing:* researchers sometimes are mesmerized by the notoriety of the killer. A Dahmer, or Bundy, or Gacy sometimes causes the researcher to focus on unusual aspects of the case including paraphilia or how victims were killed without understanding the meaning of those behaviors.

Conducting psychological research into the minds of serial killers poses problems when the researcher is not adequately trained or flexible enough to adjust to unusual subjects. Indeed, we must not only be asking the "right" questions as Kemper suggests, but also be cognizant of body language, interview settings, and efforts by subjects to control the interview process. The fact that the killer manipulates control is not the problem because in that control he/she will tell us much. The issue lies in the researcher not being able to effectively adapt to the subject thereby irritating, boring, or bringing the interview to an abrupt ending. That is the essence of phenomenology or the ability to interpret social and psychological settings without first controlling them.

Do you really think a person who has spent the past several years stalking, torturing, killing, and cannibalizing hapless victims actually cares what you want? Every person, however, does have a story to tell. So, be an observer without prejudice or bias. Of course you are not expected to agree with the killer's perspectives, but you are not there to judge him either. That has already been done. Your job is to gather information without corrupting it.

Skrapec notes that taking another's life may be understandable and acceptable, in terms of its apparent utility. Both the author and Dr. Skrapec have interviewed men who found the window to motivation was the need for intimacy. This is not the same form of intimacy normally experienced but rather an intimacy of violence where sexuality of violence becomes the tool to achieve that intimacy. There are no standard serial-murderer psychometric testing protocols or instruments finely tuned to capture the essence of their motivations. Skrapec observes that "the task is to examine systematically the serial murderer through the portrait he paints of himself and his world, being careful not to provide him with a palette but rather to allow him to choose his own" (p. 50). Such a painting must be a recounting of his own contextual cutting points, his own subjective life experience. Your author agrees with Dr. Skrapec that the sexual violation of victims, for example, may be quite secondary to the empowerment he experiences in the suffering he brings to his victims.

To achieve this level of subjectivity Skrapec proposes another method of inquiry: empirical phenomenology. She poses the dictum by Kluckhohn and Murray (1953): "Every man is in certain respects (a) like all other men, (b) like some other men, (c) like no other man" (p. 53). In understanding what the repeated acts of killing mean to the offender, we can understand the motive forces that drive the behavior. This is empirical phenomenology. It is attention to the killer's words and expressions of emotion. The researcher must then "identify the principles that organize his thinking and thus determine his perceptions and feelings and, ultimately, his behavior" (p. 53). This is accomplished through inductive reasoning that comes from understanding the stories or narratives of the offenders, even if they are all lies. Everything has context and subjective meaning. To understand serial murderers we must realize that the "underlying structures of an experience are determined by interpreting an individual's narrative about the situations in which the experience occurs" (p. 55). Skrapec (2001) suggests that researchers who are interviewing serial murderers do the following:

1. Allow each serial killer to relate his own killing experiences in his own words.
2. Analyze these descriptions to determine the structure of their experience.
3. Interviews may follow a semi-structured protocol.
4. Offenders have complete control over the content of the interview.
5. Offender may take frequent tangents relative to the protocol because he finds meaning in doing so.
6. Interviews should be audiotaped in order to preserve tone, voice, laughter, and so on, and disencumber the researcher from taking exact notes.

7. After each interview the researcher reviews the audiotapes from the most recent interview and makes notes regarding additional questions, clarification of issues, or themes to pursue.
8. All audiotapes should be transcribed and hard copies made for review.
9. Supplemental information about the offender, victims, and other aspects of the case should be integrated with information from the audiotapes. This information may come from personnel sources such as correctional officers, prison administrators, police reports, coroner's reports, psychological evaluations, court transcript summaries, parole application documents, and so on. Discrepancies can be discussed with the offender, not for verification, but for the meaning that such information carries for the offender.
10. Collection and analysis are then subject to the protocol for empirical phenomenological research as defined by von Eckartsberg (1986). This includes (a) constructing a research question understandable to others, (b) gathering a descriptive narrative where the subject is viewed as a co-researcher, and (c) scrutinize the data in terms of structure, meaning, organization, coherence, clustering, and so on. This may be considered the Cadillac of content analysis. Everything must be evaluated. This is what is meant by being close to the data. As a result, the researcher will identify the motives the offender sees as being important for himself in doing the killings as well as the meanings he attaches to each of those murders.

Skrapec also points out that terminology is very subjective and open to interpretation. Words like stranger, intimacy, anger, and hate carry different meanings for different people. The point she makes is a critical one: Researchers must clearly define or operationalize their terms and be sure that the offender's subjective interpretation is understood by the researcher. Traditional psychometric testing cannot differentiate the nuances and semantics as can empirical phenomenological research. Such an approach will provide insights unattainable through traditional research protocols. Indeed, such an approach can be applied to other types of violent repetitive offenders including rapists, stalkers, child molesters, and arsonists. Your author has interviewed several serial killers while writing this book and has encountered difficulties in data collection and interpretation. Anyone who plans on conducting such research must realize that far beyond that first interview that fills the interviewer with anticipation, excitement, fear, or awe lies a wealth of information and understanding. Trying to understand what makes serial killers "tick" is no easy task. The key is being able to develop research skills that will enable the offender to provide that information.

The following is an unedited portion of an interview your author (H) conducted with a male serial offender (O). The interview was audiotaped, reviewed, and then new lines of questioning were developed. Generally your author followed a rather serendipitous line of questioning based upon the offender's responses. The interview is published anonymously as part of the agreement in exchange for the interview. The offender, in this instance, does not wish to have any publicity regarding his crimes. He claims 12 victims. Read the interview carefully. Does the interviewer allow the subject to speak freely about his experiences? Does the researcher guide the interview or is the subject free to go on tangents? This was the first face-to-face interview of a serial killer conducted by your author. How could the interview be improved?

AN INTERVIEW WITH A MALE SERIAL MURDERER

H: How long have you been in the prison?

O: I've been here eight years now. It took about a year and a half to get me here, convicted, through the trial process.

H: You were convicted in what area?

O: Southern Arizona.

H: Are you in isolation?

O: No, I'm not—general population.

H: You've murdered children. Don't you find that to be a problem?

O: Absolutely. Not as much as when I first came here. I had a tremendous amount of publicity. It was that first six months to a year that was pure hell. But since then it's tapered off. It never stops completely. There is always somebody whispering and pointing and trying to stir some of the other convicts and make a name for themselves.

H: Have you ever been attacked?

O: Yes, I have.

H: By somebody who didn't like you because you were a child-killer?

O: I think it was about six months after I got here, I was struck in the head from behind. Put me right out, and I'd say that was one of the turning points for me in here in terms of my own outlook. That did a lot.

H: I bet it did.

O: I was walking to work one day, and all of a sudden I see this big arm coming at me. I thought, here it comes again, and I wheeled around and swung at the arm and crouched like a karate stance, but inside I almost fainted. I almost died right there, and prior to all of this, I had read about rape victims and how they live in . . . they have tremendous psychological problems, fear, afraid to get close to anybody, especially strangers, afraid of being alone, and I always thought that was hogwash. It was always just a small thing to me. Their reaction was, I always thought, cowardly. But now here I am, that arm. That arm coming at me and thinking I've had it, and that was the first time that I started really looking at what I've done to others, the trauma, particularly to those whom I didn't kill and the first time I could experience firsthand just how really black that was. I guess in a sense it was the first time I ever saw the truth.

H: As a serial killer, do you perceive that you will ever get out of here? Do you believe that if you do what is right, play the game they play here, follow the rules, do good time, that you'll get out with some life left?

O: Probably that'll never happen. The people in this state have pretty much made it clear that I am a state hazard.

H: If they abide by the sentencing structure you'll leave here 30 years from now . . . 30 years from the time you came in.

H: If you can't pay for it now, do you think that you'll ever be able to pay for it? Do you feel you'll be in damnation for the rest of your life or eternity?

O: No, because I also believe that God is an understanding God. There's no way in the world when I started when I was a kid and started a lying lifestyle and thinking perversely, reading things that I should never have touched . . . there's no way in the world that I could have ever have known I was gonna kill at the end of the road, and I think that God knows that too, and that He knows it started in anger. Now that doesn't lessen my responsibility at all because I'm the one who made the choices all the way down the road even though I was blind where it would end. But I think He understands that. I mean He's aware of that, and I think that I can stand before Him and say:

God, you know that I didn't plan it this way, you know when I was more or less swept up.

H: But you feel responsible for what you did?

O: Sure, sure. You're still making the decisions. There were times when I could have stopped. There was one case in point. My father . . . I went and took his credit card one time and this is all again, living this distorted existence of extravagance. I'm Number One. I can do anything I want. I want to appear like I'm really somebody so I get my father's credit cards, and I ran them up, and I used to take care of the bills so he didn't know what was going on for a while. Well, pretty soon I couldn't hide the bills anymore, you know. I used to just write the checks out for him and he'd sign them. Now this had gone on for months. They called him at work, and they asked him what had happened with the payments. When I say I ran them up, probably ten or fifteen, thousands of dollars, and my father, when he confronted me, at first he was upset, then he said you're gonna pay for this. And he says later, just tell me, tell me how many more there are, how many more I can expect, get them all together, I'll pay for it. You won't pay a cent. Just start your life over today. It was very attractive. That moment stands out. It was so full of meaning, so full of possibility. It wasn't just the bills, but it was the whole lying existence that was on the line. The whole distorted thought line. I didn't have the guts, even though I was going to get caught anyway. I told him, "That's all of it." And, the next ones, naturally, when another would show up at work, he was disgusted.

H: Let's explore a little bit with your support system. You have Susan. Now, Susan has been coming to see you for four years?

O: Six years I think, five or six years, maybe seven. I believe that if she felt that, God felt that, this was not the right thing, she would walk away in an instant. I've told her this and it kind of gets her upset at times. Susan, I am really convinced that you really believe that you feel you're doing the right thing. At times I really think you're wrong. At times I think you're wasting your life. At times I feel that you should get on with your life, I'm going to be here forever. At least I believe I will be and it certainly looks that way. It's not an easy relationship.

H: She supports you in some way; she said she used to write letters. Now she comes to see you all the time.

O: Yeah, they changed the rules here and they allow a lot more visits.

H: You earn your own money. What do you do in here?

O: I work as an orderly inside. It's not an hourly job. Most prisons will only permit you to spend so much per month. That's to curtail the drug traffic, and here it's $120 per month. I make $95, right around there. They're paying for your job and your skills.

H: Do you have other people come and visit you?

O: Mike comes in once about every three to four months—when he can. I used to have another friend that used to come in fairly regularly every other month or so—she just died last month. She was an older lady. She was the only person I knew that started coming in that knew me before.

H: And your dad is?

O: Deceased.

H: And your mom?

O: She's living in a large city right now. I call her every other week.

H: So you are still close with your mom?

O: Yes. She is not aware—she is aware of these two murders. I had an assault with a deadly weapon, drunk driving, she's aware that this wasn't the only crime I committed. It started from youth and it was cumulative. It wasn't something that happened overnight—it wasn't something that was like a man who woke up one day and said I'm gonna go out and do this. My brothers, when I was taken down to my hometown, they all came and visited me. And I talked to another brother for the first time in a few years just a couple weeks ago. Now, my younger sister, we get along real fine. The oldest girl I get along with just fine. We don't talk much—I think that has to do with out of sight, out of mind. I could call them regularly if I wanted—I think it's just easier that way not to hate me, but they're embarrassed. And I think they feel enough for me that it is painful when we talk. Now for my older sister she won't have it—I have to call her and talk with her once in a while. And my mom insists on my calling every other week, and Henry I haven't spoken with him for five years.

H: Do you go to the college program?

O: I was for about a year and a half—then I became very discouraged. I have a life sentence in another state as well for kidnapping concurrent with what I'm doing up here. I went to that hearing—it was an especially long hearing and I talked to them just as I talked to you, and when I was all done, they just blasted me. You're nothing but a con, you vicious killer. I went back to my cell, I went back, and just sat there, crushed. I was devastated. Not because I expected anything, because I told them, I don't feel like I have anything coming, so I can live with whatever you folks say. I fully expected nothing but I didn't expect that. They'd ask why did you do this and what were you thinking? And I told them, there's no way to make the truth look pretty. And they took that and threw it back in my face.

H: Tell me about your education.

O: I flirted with it, you might say. I was there, I had a scholarship to go to a private university, and I dropped out. I was drunk most of the time—in fact I didn't finish out the year, the first semester.

H: What were you thinking about majoring in?

O: Psychology. I think that had more to do with my father's work. Working with mentally retarded and emotionally disturbed. I was basically living a double life. I was one thing to this person and another thing to that person, all lies. And the reason for that is just a low self-image. You're not happy with who you are. You're not comfortable with who you are. You don't have any self-confidence. I wasn't out committing crimes all the time. One day I'd be fine, and the next time I'd be out, I'd have this compulsion to go out and kill somebody, and so I started looking back at each instance, what was I thinking, and this is what I came up with, and it's kind of a higher stage process. The first stage is what I call distorted thinking. It's a distorted thought line, and I found that I was God's gift to earth, I'm the center of the universe. I'm perfect. I'm the smartest guy that ever lived. Nobody's as perceptive as I am. So long as nothing came against that self-image, I was fine. But the problem with that was that it, as I mentioned earlier, was all lies. Everything was a lie, and you know a lot of times the money that I had was my father's credit cards and it was a lie. I'd go on a date, and be living it up like this was mine. So long as I was living it out, I was all pumped up. I felt very important, just this immense personality, and that couldn't last because it was always based on lies. There was always going to be some challenge to this grandiose self-image. Sometimes it would be a lot of little things, sometimes it would just be the stress of having to live these little lies, having to always be looking over your back, and other times it would be a very definite event, a girlfriend leaves you or something like that. Whenever that happened, then there would be a fall. I was always way up here, and I think that's true of most serial types, serial offenders like I was, arrogant, maybe not outwardly, but at least internally. We're arrogant people, perceiving ourselves as almost godlike beings. All of a sudden we have this fall, psychological fall, and it's very debilitating, very disorienting, confusing, harrowing. It's a very scary feeling. I'm used to being perfect.

I'm not about to put up with anything that tarnishes my own sense of perfection, so that would lead to internal negative response, and that's what I was saying to myself. I'm not gonna have this, and instead of being scared, frightened, knocked off balance, I wheeled into a retaliatory mode. I'm gonna fight this. I'm gonna stand up for my self-importance. The way to deal with that was simply to prove it. You're going to be a somebody, and my means of being a somebody was violence. To me violence had already been reinforced through time as a means of being the star, center stage in this drama. Up to this point I've had a fall, and I felt like I'm not in control. I'm not top dog.

H: The fall comes as a result of what?

O: Of any challenge to the feelings of superiority. If you live out in the real world, you're going to get them, at work, your relationships and so forth. That's why it's repetitive. That's why it always continues, and violence to me had been reinforced as a means of taking control, as a means of getting even, getting even with the world. It's reaffirming that I was all those things, and the actual deed, the victimizing, the brutalizing of another human being, was my proof, a seal, a seal of approval, self-approval, my evidence that I'm really a somebody, and the result of that would be a triumph, a restoration, I'm restored. I'm doing not what other people will, but what I will, and that would restore all those feelings of largeness, power, self-importance that strengthened the overloaded ego that I had in the first stage, and I'd be fine. The act done, it wasn't done so much for fun as it was for restorative gain. As long as I was back in that first stage, there really wasn't any desire to go out and kill. It wasn't like I had an ongoing insatiable lust for murder, and it really wasn't a lust for murder. It was a lust for self-importance at the expense of others, and that's basically the cycle. Sometimes it wouldn't take very much at all. I had a friend who owned a body shop, and I was working for him, and had no car and I get on a bus and I'm just filthy. I was just as filthy as can be, and I'm in distorted thinking. This gal gets on the bus, dressed up real nice and the seat next to me is the only one empty and she comes over and she looks at that seat and then she looks at me—all covered with dust and smelly—and she just turns her nose up in the air, spins around, and walks up and grabs a bar. How can you sit there? Right away I become very conscious of all this. I'm on the run at this time.

H: You had committed some crimes?

O: Yes, I had committed a kidnapping.

H: Had you killed anybody at that time?

O: Yes. All these images of what I used to do which I always thought was so great and the cars—all those flashed alongside the image of this gal going oomph. And boom, I'm in the fall real quick and I just wanted to hide, okay? Wanted to hide and there's that confusion of the fall and then quickly into a negative response. That bitch, who does she think she is? . . . and so on. That wouldn't have mattered to me if that happened to me today. I'm a lot more confident in my own self now. That kind of thing doesn't bother me. I've gotten used to it.

H: Did you have a desire to kill her?

O: Yes I did. And I did—not her.

H: But you acted on somebody else?

O: Yes—shortly thereafter. And I hope you can see the cycle here . . . being way up here and then crashing down, sudden rejection, lonely, the retaliatory mode—the determination to set things straight.

H: To gain control?

O: Right, and then restoration. Yes, it's a very distinct cycle, very distinct.

H: So, what you're telling me . . . it means imbalance. In your case and other serial cases, you chose to go the very destructive path.

O: Right, because of what had been reinforced over the years as a means of coping with stress. From a young age you start imagining yourself as being special, beyond all other people in the world. You're going to have stress; you're going to have all these things because the world isn't going to cooperate with you. And that's what happens. I think from the time I was a youth, somehow or another I got it into my head that I was immortal, even from the time I was five years old, and smarter than anybody.

H: Where do you think you got that notion?

O: The banana incident, this one time in the middle of the night; I think one of my brothers got up—I'm 4 so they gotta be 3 and 2—and took a banana out of the fruit bowl. My father loved bananas, grapes, and when he got up in the morning, the banana's gone. Well, it so happened that during the night I got up to use the restroom and they heard me and said, "Who is that?" I said, "———" and they said okay, so I went back to bed. Well, my father called me on the carpet in the morning. Now he's already told me honesty is the best policy and he asks me if I took it. I said no and he called me a liar. He told me I don't believe you. You were up in the middle of the night. He put me up against the wall with my nose to the wall, kept me there all morning until I copped it, till I told him I took this banana. To this day I can remember how long that was. It was like an eternity, and I remember from that age thinking, feeling a real contempt for truth, honesty. Honesty isn't going to save my butt—then the hell with you. I'll lie at every opportunity I get.

H: Did you hate your father for it?

O: No—as a matter of fact I didn't even remember it all that much. I just remembered the results.

H: What kind of victims did you select?

O: It was people like kids, usually attractive, just like the ones I was in high school with, and I had felt rejected [by].

H: Your victims, you say, were primarily white female teenagers.

O: Yes.

H: Did you ever attack males?

O: Only in one instance. I think the serial murder by virtue of the nature of the compulsion . . . If they don't find somebody in a reasonable amount of time, they will take anybody. Incidentally, the two here were the only children. All the rest were at least in their teens or older.

H: I'm sure 10-year-olds are not going to be too much aware of what's going on.

O: And I think that's the reason. I've also heard the term "compartmentalization." I like kids. I always did. Back then it was perhaps self-serving. I used to take kids out to the ballpark. I got the praise and adulation of the parents. I enjoyed it, and here I killed two kids because I was in a frenzy—at that time I was in a fall and had been there for long enough and had failed to find somebody that fit the model. And there were these two victims of opportunity, like a wolf stalking.

H: Hunting humans?

O: Yes.

H: You say you killed approximately 12 victims. When you first began, until you were caught or until you did your last two, was there a greater space, time frame, between the first and second victim? Did they progressively get closer together? Did you notice you were escalating toward the end?

O: It was erratic. I mean, I just killed somebody and I'm infuriated because I didn't get done what I had to do, couldn't act out this ritual that accidentally killed this body, and within a matter of hours I had someone else. With this second victim it involved brutalizing, rape, and then killing. Actually rape ended the episode, killing was just getting rid of the witness. The first killing was not done that way. The first killing, the victim died before I had acted out even. . . .

H: Were you erratic in your methods you used in killing? Did you have a pattern you used each time?

O: No. It was very specific, and yes I did have a pattern and most serial killers do.

H: By the time you got to the two girls you had killed several people. In some serial cases by the time they get to the last few victims they are really in a frenzy as you said you were, so to kill them is much more brutal, much more vicious.

O: Yes. I strangled one and I suffocated another with a pillow. It was a ritual. From the time I was a kid I used to go down to the garage and read these books. My father had a rather extensive library. In a room with all these books and reading about violence, and I'm already a liar, I'm already living this imaginary existence. I'm already a manipulator. The violence that I read was a means of getting even with people, you know, people who got in my way, who challenged me. You know, I'm reading all these books because they're the kind of things that turn me on, that I'm interested in, fascinated with, and I think when I entered puberty, that's when the switch overcame. That's when you have a natural enemy in females. You have perceived them as a natural enemy since the first time they challenge you. You call it rejected, but I, in my mind-set, would call it the challenge against my sense of superiority.

H: You killed sometimes for what other people would perceive as trivial issues.

O: Yes. Very trivial. You're living on such a high plane, such a distorted plane, that trivial is very big.

H: How did you feel after you did a killing? What were your physical and psychological responses to it?

O: Relief. Kind of a mixture. It's a very intense feeling. Self-magnification is a very intense feeling, and sex is power, so was the assault.

H: There was a sexual component to most of the killings?

O: Yes. Sex was sort of a vehicle. So when that was done, climax was reached. You've already terrorized this person. You've already hurt them, beat them, whatever. But there would be a feeling of letdown. You're excited, and then all of a sudden you come down. Kind of like a ball game. All this had been acted out for years and in particular, it always involved stripping the victim, forcing them to strip themselves, cutting them, making them believe that they were going to be set free if they cooperated, tying them down and then the real viciousness started. The victim's terror and the fact I could cause it to rise at will . . . their pain didn't register. All I could relate to was the ritual and the sounds. All this was proof to me that, I'm in control, I am playing the star role here, this person is nothing but a prop. I'm growing and they're becoming smaller. Once both the violence and the sexual aspect were completed, then that was it. That was the end of an episode.

H: Do you think if you were out that you would kill again?

O: I don't know. I don't think so because the kind of mind-set that was required for that is based on many lies. I sit in that cell and sometimes I just feel I'm so filled with frustration and rage toward myself because I didn't con anybody. I didn't con anybody at all. I conned myself.

H: Have you ever thought about suicide? Have you tried suicide?

O: No.

H: Do you feel some guilt that your father is dead?

O: Yeah, absolutely. I'll tell you why, because my father was the best friend I ever had but I didn't recognize that. On the very night he died, I wished he'd die. I hoped for him to die. I said boy, if he dies, he'll not be around to bother me anymore. I felt that right from Day One. There's no way that I can erase the fact that in his last week of life I was hoping and hoping, die on me, die on me 'cause he was a strict disciplinarian. He was blunt. He was straightforward, and I didn't like that.

H: Were you ever abused as a child?

O: No I wasn't. Growing up, I saw myself as abused, hated my father, and he was Public Enemy Number One to me. He did no more than what I had coming. The discipline I received was for things I did, and I just didn't want to accept it as such. The thing is that there are people who are psychologically less ready for failure than others. And I feel that when my father disciplined me, I was not ready for that, unwilling to accept that rather than take blame for what I did and accept my just desserts; instead I would just freeze up and deal with that by saying, no I'm not wrong, he's wrong. I'm right, and that became a pattern, a way of dealing with anything, any failure, any challenge, anything that might indicate imperfection in my life, and that's typical of the serialistic mind-set, . . . they are totally incapable of accepting anything that would tarnish their self-image of perfection.

H: You hated your father?

O: Yes, I did.

H: Did you hate your mother?

O: No, I didn't. I always felt I could manipulate her.

H: Some serial killers abuse animals, or have abused animals when they were younger, or they wet the bed, or enjoyed setting fires. Did you have any of those types of things in your past?

O: I can only think of one instance where I abused an animal, and I didn't find it particularly satisfying. I think every child at one time or another has wet the bed, but I didn't. As a small child I had a little problem, and as for the fire-setting, there was something. I kind of enjoyed it because it was destroying. It was model airplanes, you know, set them on fire in the backyard. It looked like a crashing plane, but there was a kind of reveling in it, seeing this whole being reduced to smoldering ashes.

H: Did you set fires later?

O: No.

H: You recognize what you've done, and you believe you wouldn't do it again. I've interviewed many people, and if they didn't comply, didn't say the right things, they were never going to get out.

O: I hear what you're saying and that's certainly possible. One never knows until it hits. I would think that certainly there is no way of knowing, absolutely no way of knowing. But, one, I've done this on my own. I've never seen a shrink as long as I've been in here, and aside from a 15-minute psychological evaluation that was done before my parole board hearing for my crime in another state, aside from that I've talked to no one. This is something that I chose to do on my own and it was not fun and it was not easy and it's taking years to reach the point where I can admit these things let alone talk to you about them. In talking about maturing I think that's probably part of it. In some respects serial killers are nothing more than children in men's bodies.

The following interview statements reflect the thoughts and feelings of a select number of other serial killers. Each of these offenders was markedly distinct in personality, emotional stability, IQ, attitudes, and types of victims selected.

A. Offender has killed over 50 victims, many by poison or suffocation. He considers himself to be a nice, compassionate, caring person and is mean or cruel only when provoked. A homosexual, he remembers (since the age of 5) a semihappy childhood during which he was the victim of sexual abuse. The abuse lasted 13 years and involved a male neighbor and an uncle. As a child he was told his mother would be harmed if he did not submit to the sexual advances. Fearing for her safety, he complied. The sexual abuse, he feels, had nothing to do with the killings or his later involvement with homosexuality. He claims a strong belief in a forgiving God and expresses interest in the occult, although he denies that Satan influenced his actions. Some victims he killed as "acts of mercy," others died at his hands as a result of vengeance, fear, "justice," or anger. The offender claims remorse for some of the murders but would definitely repeat some of them again. He claims that although he was mentally disturbed during some of the killings, he no longer suffers from psychological problems. He portrays himself as a caring person who is at peace with himself and wants to help others avoid becoming murderers. If he can do this, he feels he will have accomplished something.

B. Offender has killed at least ten victims brutally, with extreme mutilation and trophy collecting. He portrays himself living a Jekyll-and-Hyde existence. He also describes a deep love-hate relationship with his mother. He killed out of frustration and his inability to communicate socially or sexually. The offender deeply feared failing in relationships with women. He felt that if he could just kill his mother, the need for murder would stop. He claims regret for not having sought out help earlier and thereby sparing several innocent lives. He feels that if he had had the courage, he could have sought help. He believes that if he were now free from prison, he would get married and have children.

C. Offender has killed 40–50 victims. Some of his victims were killed to cover up other crimes, but many were women who hitched a ride with him. He believed that women who hitchhiked were prostitutes. He carries a deep aversion to prostitutes because his mother was one. As a child he was subject to sexual exploitation and constant rejection by his mother. He finally killed her. After he killed several dozen victims, he claimed God helped him have a change of heart. For him, the best way to avoid capture was to be constantly traveling. Now that he is on death row, he expresses remorse for the plight of his victims, including their families. He feels that his home life is primarily to blame for his criminal behavior. Both of his parents were usually drunk and showed no interest in him or the other siblings. He feels that a serial killer is someone who bases his or her life on that activity and that is exactly what he feels he did. A Christian, he firmly believes that he has been saved in God's eyes.

D. Offender has killed at least three victims and now resides in an institution for the criminally insane. He claims to have been under the influence of hallucinations that led to the murders. He claims remorse for killing his victims, especially his son, but says that he forgot about the killing after it was done. For this offender it did not matter who his victims were. Inevitably he knew he was going to kill three million people, so it really did not matter where he started. In addition, the offender has a fascination with mutilating sexual organs and claims he will do so again if he ever gets an opportunity. He explains that his hallucinations continue to encourage him to kill. He believes the voice in his hallucinations is that of the devil, which possesses him.

10

Serial Murder from a Global Perspective

Just like in America, mass murder is common globally. Serial murder tends to be overshadowed by accounts of mass murder that occur with amazing regularity (see Profile 10.1). Offenders seem to bear common traits regardless of their race, ethnicity, or nationality. Most suffer from various forms of mental disorder or have experienced severe psychological stress and are unable to cope. Their capacity for violence is accelerated by fantasy, access to guns, and alienation. They finally arrive at a point where they are so disconnected from society, family, and friends that violence becomes a viable option.

BEYOND JACK THE RIPPER

Serial murder also finds its roots in stressors such as rejection, abandonment, loss, humiliation, and hatred. The offenders are rarely considered under law to be insane or deranged as they often are in the cases of mass murder. These observations, however, are from an American perspective, examining American serial killers using American criminal profiles. Most Americans have frequently heard of Jack the Ripper (see Profile 10.2) because he is considered by many to have ushered in the concept of serial murder even though such a form of killing has been on the earth for hundreds of years. The Ripper's twisted sense of humor and his brutal method of killing and dismemberment brought to bear the attention of the world. To this day visitors can go to Whitechapel and retrace the footsteps of Jack the Ripper.

PROFILE 10.1 The Port Arthur Massacre, 1996

Martin Bryant, a 28-year-old man carrying sports bags full of hand guns and automatic rifles entered a café in Port Arthur, Tasmania, on April 28, 1996, and after having lunch, began shooting customers. As people fled the building he walked outside and shot several more tourists as they ran, hid under buses or behind trees. Leaving the area in his car, with surfboard on top, Martin came upon a woman walking alongside the road with her young daughter and carrying a baby. Martin exited the car and shot and killed all three. He proceeded to drive along the road shooting at oncoming vehicles. After killing several more victims in their cars he took a hostage and barricaded himself in a cottage. He would eventually kill the hostage before setting fire to the building, nearly killing himself. Except for the owners of the burned cottage who he had killed several hours earlier in an effort to secure more guns, the massacre took just under 9 minutes. The final count was 35 men, women, and children dead along with 18 others seriously wounded. Witnesses reported that Bryant was laughing during the shooting and seemed indifferent to the human suffering he was creating. Like many mass murderers, Martin was a loner who exhibited many antisocial characteristics. As a child he displayed cruelty toward animals as well as toward other children. He was indifferent to the suffering of others and was often inappropriate in his language when speaking to females. His father had committed suicide and the woman Martin lived with—a wealthy, eccentric widow—had recently been killed in an auto accident. With low IQ, emotionally void, antisocial, and completely disconnected from intimacy, Martin's life was for him a surrealistic experience. He carefully planned the attack by securing weapons and purchasing items that he would later use. He calmly executed his victims, very similar to other mass murderers. Sometimes a person under incredible stress and unable to find manageable or acceptable solutions to his demise might decide to kill himself. Often, once that decision is made, the person becomes very calm as he prepares to carry out his plan. For the mass murderer, the attack is in many ways a form of suicide. He has thought through the attack many times in rage fantasy and now he finally creates the opportunity to carry out his death wish. For Martin, the actual killing may have been anticlimactic to the fantasy and preparation stages of his death plan. He currently is serving a life sentence, no parole, in Hobart, Tasmania. (Readers are encouraged to use the Internet to more closely examine the Port Arthur massacre and the mindset of Martin Bryant.)

PROFILE 10.2 Jack the Ripper, 1888

By comparison to other serial killers, Jack the Ripper was not prolific in his murders, but, like Ted Bundy, the Ripper has become a criminal icon and a name used to measure other serial killers. The Ripper killed at least five London prostitutes and more likely his death toll was closer to ten or fifteen. No one knows for sure, but the Ripper promised through missives to the British media that he would not stop until he had killed twenty victims. His interest in postmutilation of the corpse set him apart from others who, at the time, preyed on prostitutes. The Ripper was very adept at eviscerating the victim and removing her organs. His first victim was murdered on Easter Monday in London's Whitechapel. The Ripper clearly derived sexual gratification from her dismemberment. Once the victim was killed according to his sexual fantasy, the Ripper proceeded to examine body parts. If he was not pressed for time as in the case of Jeanette Kelly, the Ripper had at least two hours to thoroughly complete his task. She had her throat cut to the spinal column, nearly severing the head. Her ears had been removed as was the nose and placed on a severed breast in an effort to create a face. The other severed breast lay on the nightstand covered with her kidneys and heart. Close by was the right thigh upon which rested the liver. Her sexual organs were never recovered. This practice was common among most of his victims. The Ripper seemed to take delight in excising the uterus. Jack enjoyed taunting police and newspapers and would send letters written in victim's blood vowing death to all prostitutes. Jack even sent a victim's kidney to a citizen's vigilante committee formed to catch him. Jack the Ripper was never caught and many theories currently abound as to the actual identity of the killer.

What many Americans do not know, however, is that since Jack's debut, there have been other "Rippers" in England. European countries have also had their share of multiple killers. For example, Harold Smith (1987) identified several noted serial killers in Europe, and Jenkins (1988) chronicled the activities of multiple killers in England between 1940 and 1985. Indeed, serial killings have appeared and been documented in most countries. Even Russia, which used to underreport crime, has reported cases. In one instance a Soviet newspaper, *Sovetsky Sport,* reported that the director of a teenage sports club murdered several children and photographed their hanging corpses. The offender, Slivko of Nevinnomyssk, was executed for his crimes. The paper also noted that the crimes had occurred over a span of several years. Another Soviet publication reported the execution of a locksmith in Byelorussia for the murders of 33 female victims. France has experienced "Bluebeards" and "Rippers"; England, "Vampire Killers" and "Rippers"; Germany, "The Monster of Düsseldorf" and "The Ruhr Hunter"; Ecuador, "The Monster of the Andes."

GLOBAL ISSUES IN SERIAL MURDER

Three key issues surface as we explore serial murder from a global perspective—(1) that serial murder is defined or viewed differently in other cultures, (2) that cultural differences influence the methods and motives for serial murder, and (3) serial-murderer profiles constructed in the United States are often contradicted by profiles created by law enforcement agencies in other countries. One of the contentions about serial killers in the United States as viewed by the FBI is that nearly all serial killers are lust killers, men who are sexually motivated to murder. This, in part, helps the reader understand why the FBI has always exhibited reluctance to accept the fact that females can be serial murderers too. Is it possible that simple greed and not lust can motivate serial killers? We now know that women can kill serially and not be sexually motivated. Can the same be said of some male serial killers?

Andreas Ulrich (2000) in his article *Mörderisches Mirakel* (*Murderous Miracle*) explains the behavioral attributes of German serial killers. Ulrich notes that in the case of Ulrich Schmidt, a German serial killer convicted of four murders and a suspect in others, did not appear to have the same motive for each murder. German police also found that nearly 10% of all homicides resulting from robberies and sexual offenses are committed by serial killers. They examined all cases of serial murder between 1945 and 1995 in Germany that included three or more victims and found 54 male serial killers and 7 women. According to this study, sexual motives as profiled by the FBI were not substantiated in the German cases. Homicides resulting from robberies were equally as frequent as those with sexual motivation. In the case of Gerhard Schroeder from Bremen, who murdered three prostitutes during the late 1980s, investigators sought a sexually motivated offender only to discover after his capture that the killer selected the victims primarily because he believed that they would have substantial money in their possession. This incorrect profile had police searching in the wrong areas, which afforded Schroeder more time to kill (Ulrich, 2000).

Investigators at the Bundeskriminalamt (BKA) are now utilizing "VICLAS" (Violent Crime Linkage Analysis System) developed in Canada (see Chapter 11). Investigators use a questionnaire comprised of 168 checklist items focusing on evidence and offender characteristics. The investigators now look for killers based upon patterns that often do not fit typical criminal profiles, especially in cases once thought to be sexually motivated. In the Harbort (2000) study of German serial killers, he found that the typical killer possessed minimal to average intelligence, is emotionally void, and has a history of criminal behavior. Similar to those in the USA, German serial killers report abusive childhoods marked by rejection, alcoholism, and violence. Many of the offenders were found with various brain abnormalities. The study also notes that German serial killers do not rearrange the crime scene, rarely leave behind signatures, and seldom take gruesome trophies. In support of Hickey's 1997 findings of American serial killers, German offenders do not travel widely to find victims. Most of the offenders found their victims within

30 kilometers of their residence. Sometimes the killers would rob the victims as in the case of the "Choker of Ricklingen" (Wuerger von Ricklingen). Another offender suffocated five victims between 1986 and 1993, all in his own neighborhood in Hannover, Germany. In addition, they also found that the higher the intelligence level of the offender the faster the arrest of the killer. High-IQ German serial killers averaged 4½ years until arrest following their first murder whereas less-intelligent offenders took twice as long to be apprehended. Harbort notes that the less-intelligent offenders were harder to catch because they did not fit criminal profiles utilized by investigators. Joachim Georg Kroll, known as the "Laundry Room Killer" from Duisburg, with a 76 IQ, could barely add or subtract or carry on a conversation but was able to kill eight people over twenty years and is believed to have killed many more (Ulrich, 2000). Consider the case of Dr. Harold Shipman (see Profile 10.3), a British medical doctor who is now considered to be the most prolific serial killer ever in all of Europe. Note who he killed, his methods, his motivations, and his general characteristics, which all helped him elude typical criminal profiles.

Consider also that in some societies serial murder may have strong political or economic overtones that little resembles anything in our criminal profiles and yet is distinctly serial murder (see Profile 10.4)

PROFILE 10.3 Dr. Harold F. Shipman, "The Jekyll of Hyde," 1976–1998

Harold Frederick Shipman came from a blue-collar background. His father was a lorry driver and they lived in a small house in Nottingham. At 17 his mother passed away from cancer. Harold had been very close to his mother and often watched while doctors would inject her with morphine to ease her suffering. One day, while sitting in her armchair, fully clothed, she died. Harold developed an interest in medicine and eventually graduated in 1970 from Leeds University. Along the course of studies he also became addicted to pethidine, an opiate, and wrote illegal prescriptions for himself. He was caught and was removed from his position. In 1977 he returned to work in a Hyde medical practice telling them that he was rehabilitated from his addiction. After 15 years of employment he left and began his own family practice, a one-doctor show. He was what one expects in a good doctor: caring, concerned, competent, and available. His popularity gained him over 3,000 patients. He worked alone and without regulation. No one was there to notice that Shipman's death rates and prescription rates were extremely high. During the course of his 24-year career Dr. Death, as the media refers to him, killed regularly using the painkiller diamorphine or better known as heroin. His patients were all females between the ages of 49 and 81. Most were over 65. He would visit them and treat his patients as if he were an old friend. He often patted their hands as he injected them with large doses of heroin, telling them that

(continued)

PROFILE 10.3 Continued

their pain would soon be over. Many of his victims were left sitting in their armchairs while Dr. Death went back to his office to falsify their death certificates. During the latter part of his career over half of his patients died within an hour of his home visit. In the end he signed the financial assets of a wealthy victim over to himself and was caught when the daughter, an attorney, examined her mother's estate. Dr. Shipman denied everything but was convicted in January 1999 of murdering 15 women. He is linked to 23 other deaths and is believed to have killed between 200 and 300. One of the problems faced by investigators was that several victims had been cremated, making death certification impossible. Dr. Shipman currently is housed in England's highest security level prison in Durham, in northern England.

What about motivation? Was Dr. Shipman merely trying to ease the suffering of the elderly as doctors had done for his own mother? Did he simply get a bit greedy when he had the opportunity to cash in on a wealthy victim? There is little evidence to indicate that he was killing for money, except his last victim. One plausible explanation is that Dr. Shipman enjoyed the control and being able to play God. He enjoyed controlling when a person would die and how they were to die. He is not the first British doctor to feed poison to his victims and then leave while they died. In the United States, Donald Harvey, a hospital orderly, also killed dozens of patients for no material gain. What then would drive a doctor, who vows to care for the ill, to kill them methodically? Certainly the issue of control must be considered as part of the puzzle but there is more. Consider the possibility of abandonment. Harold was his mother's favorite child. He knew that she was dying and knew that she could go at anytime. There was absolutely nothing he could do to alter that inevitability. When she was gone, Harold, now Dr. Shipman, knew that no one he cared for would ever leave him again without his permission. By killing his female patients he controlled the when and how, two issues that he had no control over when his mother died. Remember that many died just as his mother did, sitting in their armchairs. None of them suffered from the injection, just like his mother, because he used large doses of heroin. He never had to wonder when one of his female patients might suddenly die because he was in control, always.

Another issue centers on the fact that Dr. Shipman did not fit typical serial-killer profiles. As one investigator said: "He is the dullest serial killer I have ever met." He was not sealing up his victims in the walls of his home, taking body parts as souvenirs, nor was he a necrophile or some psychotic killer using a hammer and screwdriver to dispatch his victims as Britain has seen in other serial-murder cases. He was benign in appearance and affable in demeanor. He certainly did not fit any operational profile created by the FBI. His killings were dutiful, regular, and methodical. These are the trademarks of place-specific killers. Those who work in the health care industry seldom are lust killers. Their motivations may systemically have similar origins but how those motivations are expressed are a result of various filters including gender (many place-specific killers are female), age, intelligence, employment, location, and so on.

PROFILE 10.4 Am Spiegelgrund Klinik, Lebensunwertes Leben, 1940–1945

The Steinhof psychiatric hospital in Vienna, Austria, or more commonly referred to as Spiegelgrund hospital was one of 31 centers established by the Nazis for euthanasia. Unlike the death camps designed by Hitler for his Final Solution, these centers were primarily for German children who were considered physically or mentally defective. During the time of operation of these centers, over 6,000 children were euthanized. The death toll at Spiegelgrund was estimated at over 1,000, making it one of the top killing hospitals. The Third Reich viewed the children as an insult to the Aryan race because they possessed defective genes and were "useless eaters." The children, referred to as *Lebensunwertes Leben* or life unworthy of life, were housed in one of four pavilions, depending on whether they were deaf, blind, retarded, or disabled. Most of the children were in pavilion 15 where the majority of deaths occurred. Antisocial children were housed in pavilion 18 and the mentally disturbed in pavilion 17. Most of the wartime staff were Nazi party members who enthusiastically supported the concept of a pure race. Parents, encouraged by the Third Reich, brought their children to Spiegelgrund believing they would receive special care for their offspring. The hospital was peaceful and well kept, and had a staff who offered assurances that the children would be well cared for by qualified doctors. The care they received was monstrous.

Staff selected children with harelips, children with eyes too far apart, or children who stuttered. Lethal injections or sleeping pills quickly euthanized selected children. Others were not so fortunate and were starved to death or placed outdoors to freeze as part of the experiments in testing human endurance. Some children, including babies, were dipped in ice water and then placed on balconies completely naked in the middle of winter. The children were timed to see how long before pneumonia developed and killed the child. Still others died from beatings or disease. Children who were considered antisocial were beaten into submission until they willingly conformed to the Nazi's scheme or they were euthanized. There were daily torturing and denunciations of children by staff. The children, many of whom were 7–8 years of age, were starved and regularly told how useless they were to their country. They were beaten and had their heads placed in toilets.

One doctor is well remembered by survivors of Spiegelgrund. Dr. Heinrich Gross, whom the children referred to as Doktor Speiberl or Doctor Vomit, was known for his administrations of poisons. He was also known as Dr. Scythe because he wore polished boots and a Nazi colonel's uniform while he selected children to be euthanized. After the war some of the staff were hanged or given prison sentences for their part in euthanizing the children. Dr. Gross managed to avoid punishment and was even awarded prestigious honors for his research into the minds of defective children. Gross's interest in hereditary biology made him perfect for working at Spiegelgrund where he had access to the brains of hundreds of children. He became an expert on the pathology of mental illness and, after the war, lectured and became an expert court witness in thousands of criminal cases. He was one of the highest paid forensic experts in all of Austria. Dr. Gross's downfall was the discovery of hundreds of jars of formaldehyde containing the brains of children whom Dr. Gross used for his experiments. He had kept the

(continued)

PROFILE 10.4 Continued

jars hidden in a vault at the same hospital where the children were euthanized. Dr. Gross had also taken photographs of the children he treated. Of the 772 children known to have died in the clinic, Dr. Gross signed the death certificates of 238. Investigators found, through examination of the brains, that Luminal, a powerful sleep-inducing drug, had been administered to many of the children. The death certificates signed by Dr. Gross listed pneumonia as the cause of death. Even with such compelling evidence Dr. Gross eluded conviction (Silvers and Hagler, 1997). In 2000, at age 84 and while standing trial for Nazi war crimes, the judge declared Gross unfit to stand trial due to the onset of dementia.

ASSESSING GLOBAL DATA ON SERIAL MURDER

The chronological lists in Tables 10.1 and 10.2 of non-U.S. serial killers are only partial listings of such offenders in other countries. They essentially comprise some of the more sensational and publicized cases. We are hampered by differential reporting patterns, definitional problems, and impediments to accessing pertinent data. Some general comparisons can be made between serial killers in the United States and in 22 other countries researched by the author.

1. Many countries appear to have a similar problem of certain cases being defined as "superkillers." This means that some offenders have claimed or have been accused of hundreds of murders. The problem with these numbers is that they are usually not verifiable. Many of the "superkillers" lived in earlier centuries when documentation was practically nonexistent. In all likelihood, the large numbers are a product of sensationalism and exaggeration. For example, in the United States during the 1800s, Charles Gibb, John Murrell, H. H. Holmes, and Jane Toppan allegedly murdered collectively more than 900 people. In other countries, dating back as early as the 1400s and as late as the 1970s, 11 offenders, including Thuggee Buhram of India; Susi Olah of Hungary; Gilles de Rais of France; Teofilo Rojas of Colombia; Pedro Lopez of Ecuador; Countess Elizabeth Bathory of Hungary; and Abbe Guibourg, Madame de Montespan, Catherine la Voisin, and Marie de BrinVilliers of France supposedly murdered over 6,400 victims!
2. Well-publicized cases in which females are the offenders appear to be much more common in foreign countries. Similar to female offenders in the United States, there does not appear to be a "Jack the Ripper" type of female offender in other countries. In cases where physical violence was used, women usually had at least one accomplice. Also, most female

Table 10.1 A Sampling of Non-U.S. Male Serial Killers

Year(s)	Name	Number of Victims	Country
1430	Gilles de Rais	800+	France
1600	Sawney Beane	1500+	Scotland
1785–1808	Andreas Bichel	50+	Bavaria
1790–1840	Thuggee Buhram	931	India
1820	William Burke	32	Scotland
1840	Billy Palmer	14	England
1861–1864	Joseph Phillipe	8–18	France
1865	Pierre Voirbo	11	France
1869	Jean Baptise Troppmann	8	France
1871–1872	Vincent Verzeni	12	Italy
1890	Alfred Deeming	20	Australia, England
1894–1897	Joseph Vacher	10–20	France
1898–1901	Ludwig Tessnow	30+	Germany
1901–1903	George Chapman	3+	England
1908–1936	Adolf Seefeld	12	Germany
1911–1915	George J. Smith	3	England
1913–1930	Peter Kurten	15+	Germany
1913–1920	George Karl Grossman	50+	Germany
1915–1922	Henri Desire Landru	11+	France
1918–1922	Fritz Haarman	30–40	England
1920–1923	Albert Edward Burrows	4	England
1924	Carl Denke	30+	Poland
1941–1946	Dr. Marcel Petiot	63	France
1942	Gordon F. Cummins	3	England
1942	Edward Joseph Leonski	?	Australia
1943	Bruno Ludke	85	Germany
1943–1953	John R. H. Christie	6+	England
1944–1949	John George Haigh	9	England
1945–1963	Teofilo Rojas	592+	Colombia
1946	Neville Heath	5+	England
1953–1963	Efrain Gonzales	117	Colombia
1958	Peter Manuel	9	Canada
1959	Wendell Lightborne	3+	England
1959–1976	Joachim Kroll	14+	W. Germany
1960–1964	Klaus Gossman	7	Germany
1960–1961	Michael Copeland	3	Germany, England
1961–1963	William MacDonald	?	Australia
1962	Lucian Staniak	20	Poland
1962–1966	Jurgen Bartsch	4	W. Germany
1962–1971	Graham Young	?	England
1963–1964	Ian Brady	3+	England

(continued)

Table 10.1 Continued

Year(s)	Name	Number of Victims	Country
1964	Hans Van Zon	5	Holland
1965–1967	Raymond L. Morris	1+	England
1966–1976	Charles Sobhraj	10	England
1969–1984	Daniel Camargo Barbosa	71	Brazil
1971	Sjef Rijke	2+	Holland
1971	Fran Hooijaijers	5–250	Europe
1971–1983	Peter Sutcliffe	13	England
1973	Bruce Lee	26	England
1973–1975	Patrick David Mackay	5–7	England
1973–1981	Clifford Olson	11+	Canada
1974–1981	James Odo	3+	Canada
1976–1998	Dr. Harold Shipman	200–300	England
1977–1983	Dennis Nilsen	15–17	England
1977	Pedro Lopez	300+	Ecuador
1977	Al Marjek	3	Syria
1977–1980	Arn Finn Nesset	22–25	Norway
1978–1990	Andrei Chikatilo	53	Russia
1980–1981	Robert E. Brown	9	Canada
1982	Barry Peter Prudom	?	England
1984–1985	Pawel Alojzy Tuchlin	9+	Poland
1984–1986	Thierry Paulin	14	France
1985	Angel Piaz Balbin	8	Peru
1986	Sohrab Aslam Khan	13	Pakistan
1987	"Locksmith"	33	Russia
1990–1991	Scott Cox	20+	Canada
1991	Marcelo Costa de Andre	14	Brazil
1992–1999	Luis Alfredo Garavito	140+	Columbia
1993–1995	Andonis Daglis	3	Greece
1993–1995	John Brown	5	South Africa
1993–1995	Samuel Coetzee	5	South Africa
1995–1996	Andre Cassimiro	5	Brazil
1996	Giovanni Faggi	6	Italy
1996	Leszek Pekalski	12+	Poland
1997	Roman Burtsev	6+	Russia
1997	Gerd Wenzinger	12+	Brazil

Table 10.2 A Sampling of Non-U.S. Female Serial Killers

Year(s)	Name	Number of Victims	Country
1610–1614	Countess Elizabeth Bathory	600	Hungary
c. 1660s	Catherine la Voisin	1500+	France
c. 1660s	Madame de Montespan	1400+	France
1676	Marie de BrinVilliers	100+	France
1809	Anna Marie Zwanziger	3+	Bavaria
1811	Anna Marie Schonleben	3+	Germany
1828	Gesina Gottfried	20+	Germany
1830–1850	Helena Jegado	60+	England
1852–1871	Mary Ann Cotton	14–21	England
1890	Greta Beier	4	Germany
1908	Jeanne Weber	9+	France
1909–1929	Susi Olah	100+	Hungary
1924–1926	Antoinette Scieri	6	France
1927–1947	Lily Young	100+	Canada
1936	Dorthea Waddingham	?	England
1953–1963	Maria de Jesus Gonzales	91+	Mexico
1953–1963	Delfina de Jesus Gonzales	91+	Mexico
1963–1964	Myra Hindley	3	England
1968	Mary Flora Bell	2	England
1971–1987	Rosemary West	12+	England
1977	Cecile Bombeek	3–30	Belgium
1977–1983	Dahlia Allam	4	Austria
1981	Phoolan Devi	20	India
1983	Maria Velten	5	W. Germany
1983–1989	Maria Gruber	49–300	Austria
	Irene Leidof		
	Stephanija Mayer		
1990	Karla Homolka	3	Canada
1990–1992	Karla Teale	3–6+	Canada
1991	Anna Villeda	8	Mexico
1991–1997	Kathleen Atkinson	4+	England
1992	Beverly Allit	4	England

offenders who lived during earlier times resorted to poisons, as their female counterparts in the United States did.

3. Team killers, or those who killed with accomplices, appear to be much more common in the United States than in other countries. However, in-depth examination of cases in other countries may yet reveal many more team killer cases. For the present, those designated as team killers in other countries appear to kill twice as many victims each as their U.S. counterparts.

4. Team killers and solo killers, regardless of whether they were American or foreign, murdered approximately the same percentages of all victims.
5. U.S. killers appear to be much more mobile and travel more than foreign offenders do; those in other countries are much more likely to be classified as "local" killers. This may in part be due to proximity to population centers, language barriers, cultural diversities, or availability of transportation.
6. In the majority of cases, both U.S. and foreign offenders were strangers to their victims. Foreign killers also appear to target acquaintances as victims.
7. Torture, strangling, and stabbing/chopping as modes of death seem to be used in similar percentages of cases. Americans sometimes use guns to kill or torture their victims; however, foreign offenders appear to rarely use firearms.

Empirical study of serial killers worldwide has been limited. Although many countries have recorded cases of serial killing, the majority of cases appear to come from industrialized nations. Philip Jenkins (1988) conducted his study of serial killers in England between 1940 and 1985. He also conducted a historical-comparative study of serial murder in relation to social issues occurring in England, Germany, and the United States between 1900 and 1940. Only recently did Canter, Missen, and Hodge (1997) identify 164 serial killers in the United Kingdom since 1860. They were able to conclude that Britain probably has about five active serial killers at any given time and that they account for more victims proportionately than American serial killers. Your author met with serial-murder investigators from South Africa. One such investigator, Micki Pistorius, whose sole job was to track down serial killers in South Africa, indicated that most cases of serial murder in her country are relatively new. In the past several years, white farmers have become the targets of blacks who wish to take over lands controlled by whites. As Gorby (2000) notes, serial murder has been hidden from the public in some countries. Iran executed a man, now referred to as the Tehran Vampire, for raping and murdering nine women. The Soviet Union would not allow information about serial killers to become public knowledge either and yet Russia has seen many serial-killing cases. As a result many victims have died because the public was not aware that predators were in their midst. The horrific case of Andrei Chikatilo is an excellent example of what can happen when the presses and law enforcement are silent (see Profile 10.5)

Chikatilo represents one of Europe's most prolific serial killers. He was a man consumed with the destruction of children and adolescents. He could have and should have been stopped very early on in his killing career, but like so many other serial murderers, he was able to evade law enforcement. If cultural filters play any role in serial murder, distinguishing the murders, the offender, or victims in certain characteristic ways, they do not seem to differentiate this Russian serial killer in any significant respect from those roaming the streets of the United States. Andrei Chikatilo was a man of low self-esteem and much anger and hatred who acted out his paraphilic fantasies upon vulnerable youth. We would be naive to think this killer is an anomaly in the Russian social landscape.

PROFILE 10.5 Andrei Chikatilo, 1978–1990

Also known as the "Russian Ripper" who brutally killed 14 young girls, 21 boys, and 18 women, Chikatilo continued his stalking, murdering, and cannibalizing for 12 years. Born in the Ukraine in 1936, Chikatilo was known as an intelligent man of modesty who enjoyed playing chess. His education from Rostov University included degrees in Russian language and literature, engineering, and Marxist-Leninism. During his career of killing, Chikatilo was married with two children, a boy and a girl, about the same ages of many of his victims. He was considered a steady wage earner and one who never was forceful or beat his children. By the time he was arrested for the "Forest Strip Murders" in the town of Novocherkassk, Chikatilo was a gray-haired grandfather living a reclusive lifestyle. Yet he was far from being a recluse.

Life had been hard for Chikatilo. His older brother Stepan had been abducted and cannibalized during the Ukrainian famine of the 1930s. He grew up fearful, insecure, and envious of a more successful career. Everything he did, including his military experience, he perceived as inconsequential. He harbored a hero fantasy to compensate for his sense of failure. A successful career had been thwarted in part by his father, who, after the war, had been sent to a prison camp for allowing himself to be taken prisoner by the Germans. Chikatilo had a disturbing employment record. He first worked as a dorm monitor at a local mining school. His history of peeping through keyholes and wandering into girl's toilets eventually expedited his termination.

His forced relocation to Shakhty in the south of Russia meant a reduction in job status and quality of life for his family. A man of low self-esteem and a pronounced sense of inferiority around groups of people, Chikatilo became a master at manipulating and molesting children of all ages. His increased attraction to children gradually stifled any desire he might have had for his wife. As a manifestation of his own self-hate, he admitted his "sexual weakness" to the police. He explained to them that his interest in children was something of his distant past. Now that he was married with children, Chikatilo reasoned, he had overcome such urges. To the police, the explanation seemed plausible enough. Unfortunately for dozens of children, Chikatilo's pedophilia would not be examined closely enough to see through his deception.

By this time he had murdered two children. His first victim in 1978 was 9-year-old Lena Zakotnova. He had lured her to a dilapidated shack he used for his private retreat. Lena was bound, choked, and stabbed three times in the abdomen and sustained vaginal injuries before she was tossed in a nearby river to die. He had tied a scarf around her eyes so she could not see him. Considering the amount of evidence Chikatilo left behind, his capture should have been inevitable. A bungled investigation and a desire by investigators to close the case led to the confession and conviction of another man.

His progressively violent fantasies fueled his next murder of 17-year-old Larisa Tkachenko. After strangling her into unconsciousness, he stuffed her mouth with dirt. She too sustained vaginal injuries. Chikatilo then, with his teeth, tore off her nipples and swallowed them.

Chikatilo was promoted to senior engineer in 1981. This promotion would require that he travel within the region. He relished the opportunity to meet young people traveling alone. Chikatilo hunted his victims in and

(continued)

PROFILE 10.5 Continued

around train and bus stations on his way to and from work. He kindly offered them candy, money, and comfort as an enticement to take a little walk with him over to the forest strips where they could be alone. He became adept at targeting naive, trusting victims who perceived him as a nice man.

Chikatilo's escalation in brutality was incredible. His own sense of inferiority would not allow his victims to look at him during the attacks. The victim's stare, even in death, disturbed the killer's paraphilic fantasies. He soon resolved the problem. His third victim was a 12-year-girl whom he had picked up at a bus stop and then escorted into some nearby bushes. He stabbed her 41 times, several of them into her eyes. Victims would look no more upon him during his rage. By July he had killed three more victims—two girls, ages 14 and 16, and a 9-year-old boy. After subduing the little boy, he had the child stick out his tongue. Chikatilo then, with his own teeth, ripped it off.

Sexually inadequate, Chikatilo could never use his own genitals to actually penetrate his victims. Methodically, after ejaculating externally onto his victims, he used a twig to place his sperm into their vagina or anus. His desire for viscera was increasing. In December 1982 he murdered 10-year-old Olya Stalmach by stabbing her in the eyes, torso, and vagina over 50 times. He then eviscerated her. His appetite for removing internal body parts earned him the name of "Ripper."

For the next eight years Chikatilo killed in ernest. He hunted runaways, intellectually slower children, and young women who thought him to be just another man looking for a sexual encounter. His established methods he seldom varied. He stabbed his victims between 30 and 50 times. One boy he stabbed over 70 times. He nearly always mutilated their eyes. Older girls had their breasts or nipples severed or chewed off and their uteruses removed. He found distinct pleasure in eating the uterus as he walked home after a kill. With boys, he would cut off their penises and/or remove their testicles. Victims were often still alive during the taking of his trophies. His monstrous acts never abated. He began removing the upper lip and nose of his victims then placing them into the victim's stomach or mouth.

In 1984 he was faced with a criminal complaint for theft, was dismissed from his job, and lost his membership in the Communist party. His anger and fantasies continued to escalate his attacks. One of Chikatilo's later victims, 11-year-old Yaroslav Makarov, was killed shortly before his capture in 1990. Chikatilo tore out his intestines and heart with his bare hands.

Initially, the murders were investigated by local police. With the frequency of new victims the Russian attorney general's office took control of the investigation. The case had been bungled from the start and was rife with incompetence. Police had decided that they were looking for a dishonorably discharged police officer. Chikatilo was no police officer but he did harbor a sincere interest in police work. By 1984 police had arrested, detained, and interrogated dozens of men who were known pedophiles, several mentally disordered youth, and hundreds of homosexuals. In 1985, Inspector Kostov joined the manhunt. Other law enforcement agencies, including the FBI, consulted with Kostov. The persistence of Kostov ultimately led to Chikatilo's capture and his confession to all the murders. One month after his confession Andrei Chikatilo was executed with a bullet in the back of his head (Lourie, 1993; Cullen, 1993). International interest in this case led to the making of the video *Citizen X* and the writing of at least three books.

THE GORBY STUDY*

Much closer empirical examination of serial homicide data in other countries was recently conducted by Gorby (2000). He compiled an impressive data set of 300 serial killers representing 241 cases of serial murder identified in 43 different countries, excluding the United States between the years 1800 and 1995. About half of the cases were found in four nations: United Kingdom (20%), Germany (15%), South Africa (8%), and Australia (7%). European countries represented 57% of the cases, Asian countries 14%. North American (excluding the United States), African, and Oceana countries each accounted for 8% whereas only 6% were found in South America, Central America, and the Middle East combined. About 9% of cases were transnational where the offender killed in more than one country (p. 54). Gorby explores the emergence of serial murder by comparing European and non-European countries. Table 10.3 indicates that since 1900 the percentage of European cases has decreased steadily while just the opposite is occurring in non-European countries.

He noted that the length of serial-murder cases ranged from less than one year to 37 years. About a third of all cases were one year or less, about 33% more than five years, and nearly one in five cases lasted over ten years. Gorby also found that females comprised about 25% of his serial killers, whereas in the United States, Hickey (1997) found only 17% of his data to be females. Gorby noted that offenders ranged in age between 13 and 60 at the onset of their killings, the average age being 30. By the time offenders finished their killing careers (last murder) the age range was 16–70 and the average age of 35 (see Table 10.4).

Similar to Hickey (1997), Gorby found that about 33% of offenders had at least one accomplice compared to 28% found in the United States. Nearly

*The author wishes to express his appreciation to Brad Gorby for his permission in using some of his findings from his 2000 study of foreign serial killers.

Table 10.3 Year of First Murder by Geography of Serial-Murder Case

Year	European	Non-European	Total
1800–1824	5 (100%)	0 (00.0%)	5 (2.1%)
1825–1849	5 (100)	0 (00.0)	5 (2.1)
1850–1874	7 (100)	0 (00.0)	7 (2.9)
1875–1899	10 (71.4)	4 (28.6)	14 (5.8)
1900–1924	22 (75.9)	7 (24.1)	29 (12.0)
1925–1949	19 (63.3)	11 (36.7)	30 (12.4)
1950–1974	27 (54.0)	23 (46.0)	0 (20.7)
1975–1995	42 (41.6)	59 (58.4)	101 (41.9)
Total	137 (56.8)	104 (43.2)	241 (100)

Table 10.4 Age of Offender at Time of First Murder by Gender of Offender

Age	Males	Females	Total
13–20	33 (20.4%)	11 (26.8%)	44 (21.7%)
21–25	35 (21.6)	6 (14.6)	41 (20.2)
26–30	33 (20.4)	5 (12.2)	38 (18.7)
31–35	20 (12.3)	6 (14.6)	26 (12.8)
36–40	16 (9.9)	3 (7.3)	23 (11.3)
41–50	33 (20.4)	4 (9.8)	22 (10.8)
51+	5 (3.1)	7 (17.1)	9 (4.4)
Total	162 (100)	41 (100)	203 (100)

Table 10.5 Age/Gender of Victim and by Gender of Primary Offender (*N* = 241)

Victims	Male Cases	Female Cases	Total
At least one female adult	132 (67.7%)	20 (43.5%)	152 (63.1%)
At least one male adult	85 (43.6)	29 (63.0)	114 (47.3)
At least one female child	61 (31.3)	20 (43.5)	81 (33.6)
At least one male child	49 (25.1)	21 (45.7)	70 (29.0)
Only female adults	44 (22.6)	0 (0.0)	44 (18.3)
At least one female elderly	26 (13.3)	17 (37.0)	43 (17.8)
At least one male elderly	16 (8.2)	16 (34.8)	32 (13.3)
Only male adults	19 (9.7)	3 (6.5)	22 (9.1)
Only female children	9 (4.6)	1 (2.2)	10 (4.1)
Only male children	10 (5.1)	0 (0.0)	10 (4.1)
Only female elderly	6 (3.1)	0 (0.0)	6 (2.5)
Only male elderly	0 (0.0)	1 (2.2)	1 (0.4)
Some victims unknown	19 (9.7)	12 (26.1)	31 (12.9)

80% of the team killer cases consisted of only two offenders. One team had eight offenders. However, although a third of the cases were team killers, they only accounted for 13% of the total murders. About half the teams were comprised of both male and female offenders, whereas 38% were all male teams and 10% were all female teams. He also found that one-third of the teams were made up of family members.

Gorby (2000) also noted that offenders in his study killed an average of 12 victims per case, similar to the Hickey study. Nearly 80% killed nonfamily members and 5% killed only family members. Females were also far more likely to murder family members (60%) compared to males (12%) (see Table 10.5).

Gorby also examined the issue of mobility among his serial killers and found that 85% kill in a local area with only 15% traveling to other cities,

Table 10.6 Case Mobility by Gender of Offender

Mobility	Male Offenders	Female Offenders	Total
Place-Specific	7 (3.6%)	14 (30.4%)	21 (8.7%)
Local	154 (79.0)	29 (63.0)	183 (75.9)
Traveling	14 (7.2)	1 (2.2)	15 (6.2)
Transnational	20 (10.3)	2 (4.3)	22 (9.1)
Total	195 (100)	46 (100)	241 (100)

Table 10.7 Methods of Murder by Gender of Offender (*N* = 241)

Method	Male Cases	Female Cases	Total Cases
Some strangled/asphyxiated	96 (49.2%)	8 (17.4%)	104 (43.2%)
Some stabbed/cut	72 (36.9)	0 (0.0)	72 (29.8)
Some poison/withheld T_x	25 (12.8)	34 (73.9)	59 (24.4)
Some beat/bludgeoned	46 (23.6)	1 (2.2)	47 (19.5)
Only poison/ withheld T_x	17 (8.7)	28 (60.9)	45 (18.7)
Some firearms	40 (20.5)	3 (6.5)	43 (17.8)
Only strangled/asphyxiated	38 (19.5)	4 (8.7)	42 (17.4)
Some unknown methods	22 (11.3)	8 (17.4)	30 (12.4)
Only stabbed/cut	24 (12.3)	0 (0)	24 (10.0)
Only firearms	19 (9.7)	1 (2.2)	20 (8.3)
Only beat/bludgeoned	7 (3.6)	0 (0.0)	8 (3.3)
All unknown methods	4 (2.1)	3 (6.5)	7 (2.9)
Some burned/fire	6 (3)	0 (0.0)	6 (2.5)
Some other methods	3 (1.5)	3 (6.5)	6 (2.5)
Only other methods	1 (0.5)	2 (4.3)	3 (1.2)
Only burned/fire	1 (0.5)	0 (0.0)	1 (0.4)

states, or countries. As in the United States, women were far more likely to kill at home or at work than male offenders. Rarely did they ever travel to other cities or countries to continue their killings (see Table 10.6).

Finally Gorby examined methods of killing (see Table 10.7). Males overall preferred to strangle or asphyxiate their victims compared to 37% in the Hickey study. As the only method of killing the Gorby study found that 20% of males chose this method compared to just 11% in the Hickey study. American serial killers, not surprisingly, were twice as likely to use firearms (41%) sometimes to murder as compared to 21% in the Gorby study. Most females in the Gorby study used poisons or withheld medical assistance. A few others strangled their victims but in only one case was a gun used or a victim was bludgeoned to death.

11

Profiling, Apprehension, and Disposition of Serial Killers

Robert Keppel, a former detective investigating the Ted Bundy case, once remarked that apprehending serial killers is very difficult. "Police departments generally are not equipped or trained to apprehend serial killers. They are organized to catch burglars and robbers and to intervene in family fights" (Lindsey, 1984, p. 1). Several factors set the serial offender apart from typical domestic killers and other violent criminals. Serial killers can be highly mobile and traverse many law enforcement jurisdictions while still remaining in a relatively small area geographically. Offenders generally prefer strangers as victims and are usually careful to minimize the amount of evidence left at the crime scene. Consequently, months may go by before there is sufficient interagency communication to recognize a common pattern of homicides. Coordination of information can be even more difficult when offenders cross several state lines, committing murders along the way. Although there has been considerable criticism of law enforcement in tracking down serial killers, police have made concerted efforts in some cases to join forces and conduct multiagency investigations. In several cases task forces have been organized, including:

1. **The Michigan Murders**—The Wastenow County prosecutor's office that included five different police agencies set up a multiagency task force. Eventually the Michigan State Police assumed the coordination efforts, and on August 1, 1969, John Norman Collins was arrested in the murders of seven young females.

2. **The Atlanta Child Killings**—In July 1980, under the direction of then-commissioner Lee Brown, a task force of local police agencies was formed. In November, the FBI was ordered into the investigation and eventually assumed direction of the investigation. On June 21, 1981, Wayne B. Williams was arrested in the murder of Nathaniel Cater and suspected to be involved in the disappearances and deaths of 27 other victims.
3. **The Green River Killings**—In 1982, a task force of police investigators was organized to track down the killer(s) of young female prostitutes, hitchhikers, and transients in the Seattle, Washington, area. Having learned a great deal from mistakes made in an Atlanta investigation, the Green River task force was thought to be the best investigative team ever organized. However, even with sophisticated techniques for investigating, it was not until July 1989, seven years later, that a suspect was arrested. He was eventually released for lack of evidence. The task force was later disbanded and as of this writing the Green River killer remains free.

Public anxieties demand quick apprehension of a serial offender; however, conducting investigations requires an enormous amount of resources and agency coordination. Montgomery (1992, 1993) notes that nearly 20,000 suspect names were collected in the Green River killer case at a cost to taxpayers of over $20 million. Police also examined data on 185,000 persons in England's Staffordshire case of serial murder (Canter, 1994) and the Yorkshire Ripper case where 268,000 names of possible leads were collected using over 5 million man-hours of police work and $6–7 million in costs (Doney, 1990). Considering the increasing costs of task force investigations, the Unabomber case (see Profile 11.2), which spanned 18 years and three task forces, cost approximately $75 million including the costs of prosecution. Glover and Witham (1989) identified four issues in managing major cases:

1. **Media Impact**—Long-term media coverage creates immense pressure on law enforcement. Police must nevertheless establish an acceptable working relationship with the press.
2. **Management of Departmental Resources**—Who will take charge of the investigation and maintain a coordinated flow of command?
3. **Multiagency Jurisdiction**—Coordinated investigations, reporting, and expenditure of resources need to be addressed.
4. **Unusual Complexity of the Case**—Numerous victims, locations, and modes of death can create problems in sorting out evidence, investigative leads, and so on (pp. 2–16).

Doney (1990, p. 102) adds to this list by noting that some serial killers improve in their ability to select and kill victims and thus avoid detection. Also, false confessions, copycat murders, and political pressures for an arrest to be made all contribute to the complexity of serial-murder investigations.

FORENSIC SCIENCE

Part of the aftermath of the O. J. Simpson trial is the reassessment of the role of forensics and forensic experts in criminal trials. Although some may feel that forensics now stands on weaker ground as a result of the 1993 Supreme Court decision changing the rules by which scientific information is to be used in courtrooms, others view it as a blessing. In *Frye* v. *United States* (1923) the courts followed a "general acceptance standard" that requires new information be examined by the court prior to presenting it to a jury. Under Frye, scientific evidence must be based on a technique accepted in a field to which it pertains. In *Daubert* v. *Merrill Dow* (1993) the courts gave more discretionary power to trial courts in determining the probative value of scientific evidence. The *Daubert* decision gave what appeared to be much more flexibility and power regarding admissibility of evidence. However, because *Daubert* was based upon statutory grounds and not constitutional grounds, the courts are much more inclined to follow the more restrictive Frye standard (Wint, 1998). Physical evidence is critical to cases, and pressure is being applied to find the most qualified experts who can withstand courtroom scrutiny. But forensics means much more today than simply working with physical evidence, creating even more challenges to what actually constitutes acceptable scientific evidence and who can be considered as an expert. In 1998 the author was asked to consult as an expert witness in a federal case of stalking. Psychiatrists for both the defense and prosecution were quickly accepted by the courts as experts in their fields. Your author, although a recognized criminologist with considerable expertise in the area of stalking, was forced to undergo nearly two hours of examination by a most adept defense attorney. The judge finally ruled that your author qualified as an expert. This was not only an issue of having a new type of expert (in this case a criminologist) but an unlicensed expert asked to testify in a case that drew its experts primarily from licensed psychiatrists. (The offender did receive a 3½-year sentence.)

The term *forensics* means belonging to or used in courts of law. This has given rise to forensic medicine or the use of medical expertise in legal or criminal investigations. In turn, forensic psychology has begun to offer insights into criminal behavior and the criminal mind. Criminology and psychology join forces to create criminal profiling, or the creation of criminal portraits that assist those in law, law enforcement, mental health, or academics to better understand crime and criminals.

Increasingly, pressure is being placed on law enforcement, social scientists, and biologically oriented researchers to identify which individuals will become involved with criminal behavior, who their victims will be, and which appropriate criminal justice measures should be used to deal with the offending. Predicting criminal behavior accurately has never been an exact science, but more than ever a demand for accuracy exists. The movement today is toward integrating sciences and technology into an interdisciplinary approach to criminality. This approach encompasses behavioral, psychological, and biological explorations of criminal behavior and their legal applications. This exploration must incorporate various academic and applied disciplines such as those related to the courts, corrections, law enforcement, and victimology. Disciplines such as criminology, criminal justice, psychology, psychiatry, sociology, law and jurisprudence, mathematics, statistics, geography, and behavioral medicine, to name but a few, need to be integrated into the field of forensic science.

We might envision forensics as a hub of a wheel with the spokes representing the sciences. For example, geography is now becoming a tool to address issues of crime and victimization. This approach is referred to as *spatial mapping* or *environmental criminology* and is used to generate geographic profiles of offenders, victims, and crime scenes. Computers are now being used to identify crime locations in urban and suburban areas by plotting where they have occurred over time. This geo-mapping approach to crime prediction has tremendous implications for future urban development, police administration, and policy development. Spatial mapping can also be applied to understanding criminal victimization, victim profiling, and promotion of victim protection. David Canter of Liverpool, England, established a program in Investigative Psychology in which computer models are used to predict criminal offending.

Criminalists work in crime labs conducting tests and analyses in ballistics, serology, toxicology, hair-fiber evidence, DNA, latent prints, and other areas relevant to determining the nature of collected physical evidence. Physical forensics is often critical to the outcome of criminal cases. In addition, physical evidence frequently helps investigators explain the psychology of the crime and that of its perpetrator(s). Thus enlightened, criminal psychologists promote greater understanding of criminal personalities among researchers, the courts, and law enforcement. Forensics is also of practical value to correctional and law enforcement administrators interested in the classification of prisoners or in the provision of training for personnel who investigate and manage offenders and offender populations.

Academically based institutions are beginning to find their role in forensics and have begun implementing programs that are broadly based in the sciences. John Jay College in New York City now offers a program in criminal forensics. California State University, Fresno and University of California, Davis are expected to soon begin a joint doctoral program in criminology that will offer courses in victimology, forensic psychology as well as foundational courses in criminal justice, and criminology. Psychologists are also in great demand with the movement in health care going toward managed care and greater emphasis on classification of prisoners. Psychologists need exposure to and understanding of criminal behaviors and personalities. Integration of the sciences is not a simple matter, but progress is being made, albeit slowly.

With the victims' movement having become firmly entrenched in the American court system, the voices of victims are being heard at long last. California State University–Fresno is the first (and only) university to offer a four-year program in victimology and victim services as part of our general criminology program. Victimology is an integral part of forensics as we learn more about victims' rights and victim-offender relationships. This author is very fortunate to be part of this program, to teach criminal psychology, and to consult in various cases of homicide, sex crimes, arson, and other violent crimes. Several of my graduate students have embraced such topics as serial murder, mass murder, serial bombing, serial arson, sex crimes, and stalking. Like me, they have come to share the passion for understanding, as Gwynn Nettler (1982) often referred to the many roads, the many whys, and the many contingencies of criminality. It is particularly enjoyable to work with students who have a desire to explore the changing parameters of forensics and to shape the role they will one day play in helping to harness the sciences into an exact forensic tool.

PROFILING

The term *profiling* refers to many areas of forensics. For example, Owen (1998), noted author of *In the Mix,* develops inmate profiles by examining the lives and crimes of incarcerated women at Central California Women's Facility in Chowchilla, California. Her work has provided clarity and insight into life behind bars for female felons. Jackson (1996) explored the world of credit card fraud and the types of people who repeatedly engaged in such crimes. Wallace (2001), an expert in domestic violence, profiles the types of criminals who target the elderly. Today profiling has become a tool used widely in criminal investigations. Profiling is developing as a science but continues to receive mixed reviews. Some professionals, such as Canter (2000), Godwin (1999), and Levin and Fox (1985), have been skeptical of the utility of profiling, particularly the psychologically based approach. Other researchers express varying degrees of support for the success of psychological profiling development, including Egger (1985), Geberth (1983), Holmes (1990), and Ressler and his colleagues (1988). Psychological profiling has yet to function as a "magic wand" to solve serial killings, but it is still too early in its development to be considered a failure. Programs such as those developed around profiling often require several years of testing and refinement before we are able to evaluate them. For profiling to fulfill its potential, law enforcement personnel must be willing to collaborate with those in the academic and medical professions. For example, psychiatrists can be of particular value in profiling, provided law enforcement people are willing to accept and use their profiles. The problem in dealing with lust killers, for example, is that as offenders they present a very complex set of behavioral and psychological characteristics. Psychologists Purcell and Arrigo (2000) illustrate the complexities of such killers by proposing an integrated model of lust killing and paraphilia. Liebert (1985), in evaluating the contributions of psychiatry to the investigation of serial murders, such as lust killings, stated:

> Acceptance that the Borderline or Narcissistic Personality Disorder, with severe sociopathic and sadistic trends, can commit murder as a substitute for normal erotic pleasure or even non-violent perversion is the foundation for exploration of motivation in serial murders. With a mutually

> respectful desire to learn about the bizarre world of the lust murderer, the investigator and psychiatric consultant can enhance their sense of "type" for a suspect. The investigator is less likely to make a mistake in judging the grandiosity of pathological narcissism and the manipulativeness of sociopathy with "normalcy." The lust murderer can present a facade of relationships and effective, perhaps even superior, performance. Not infrequently, he will be in the bright-superior intelligence range and, therefore, potentially a skilled impostor (p. 197).

Wilson and Soothill (1996) state that profiling needs a framework that has some flexibility. They argue that profiling can be useful:

- As an investigative tool where leads are limited
- Providing direction to a lagging investigation
- Giving psychological insights in conducting interviews
- Offering psychological advice for witnesses or juries
- Developing systematic computer tracking of unsolved serial-murder cases
- Facilitating communication among jurisdictions dealing with serial offenses
- Offering critique of investigative procedures, forensic evidence collection, and sampling
- Providing insights for the application of theories used to explain crime and criminal behavior
- In evidence corroboration

Types of Profiling

The term *typology* has lent itself to the development of various forms of profiling that are now used as criminal investigative techniques from white-collar crimes to serial murder. The following forms of profiling will help to illustrate the emerging issues involved in criminal investigations. Geographical profiling and the scientific, empirically based offender profiling by David Canter and colleagues are both becoming leading approaches in criminal investigations. They both can offer tremendous assistance to investigators in making profiling a more scientific and precise science. Investigative profiling today can be viewed from several perspectives:

1. **Offender Profiling—**Law enforcement agencies collect data, often using case studies or anecdotal information, which then is transformed into general descriptions of the types of persons most commonly associated with a certain type of criminal activity. This stereotyping is common in seeking out drug couriers and terrorists. This form of profiling can often be invasive and legally tenuous. Civil rights advocates quickly point out the flaws in using physical characteristics to profile criminals. Dodd (1998) also found that such profiling could be very misleading. For example, one might consider that people involved in fraudulent insurance claims usually are in need of money. The opposite was reported in Dodd's study of fraudulent insurance claimants. Of

the 209 false claims, only 13% were in need of the money, whereas 57% earned a regular income. David Canter along with Gabriella Salfati and S. Hodge from England have made significant progress in elevating offender profiling from a street-level operation to a sophisticated approach to criminal investigation. Indeed, Canter (2000) takes umbrage with American profiling stating that profiling was originally the purview of psychologists, not the FBI. He rejects the detective deductions of profiling as being "anecdotal, deductive, fictional hero" approaches to solving crimes through "gut-feeling" investigations. Clinical observations alone are insufficient in making decisions about criminal behavior. Indeed, criminologists, psychologists, and psychiatrists have been ineffectual in accurately predicting criminal behavior. Our predictive capabilities are replete with *false positives,* or incorrectly predicting that someone will behave in a certain criminal manner. Canter (2000) believes that many profilers today operate under the guise of informed speculation. Like psychic detectives and astrologers, such profilers are shrouded in ambiguity and therefore can shift their explanations to fit the situation. In addition, Copson (1995) found that in only 3% of his study of criminal cases where profilers were consulted did they help to identify the offender.

Canter (1999, 2000) and Farrington (1998) also remind us that psychology is germane to explaining a variety of crimes and that there are many differences *between* offenders and nonoffenders. Salfati and Canter (1999) established a scientific classification system of homicide crime scenes, offenders, and themes associated with those crime scenes. Canter promotes his *radex model* (Canter & Alison, 2000) as a powerful tool in differentiating criminals. Using his circle theory approach, Canter (2000) explains that mathematically, using a computer, criminal behavior can be examined and measured at a very general level (center of the circle) to more specific "styles of offending." As we move conceptually away from the circle center, we see more differentiation between offenders. The power of the radex model is that it identifies the salient aspects of a crime (Canter, Hughes, & Kirby, 1998). Richard Kocsis, Ray Cooksey, and Harvey Irwin (2000) in their study of offender characteristics in Australian sexual murders examined 85 cases using the statistical tool of multidimensional scaling (MDS). The technique produced a five-cluster model of sexual murder behavior. The central cluster represented typical behaviors to all patterns of sexual murder. Outlying patterns revealed "rape," "fury," "predator," and "perversion" zones, each with distinct offense styles. This empirical model of sexual murder underscores the complexity in understanding the dynamics in the relationship between sexual activity and violence. Approaching criminal profiling from a scientific, actuarial model is having a very impressive influence on proactive investigators. American law enforcement will benefit greatly by integrating their profiling techniques with the computer modeling espoused by the Canter school.

2. **Victim Profiling—**Profilers identify the personality and behavioral characteristics of crime victims who tend to fall prey to certain types of offenders. Information can be gathered through personal records; interviews with

witnesses, victims, family, and friends; crime scene examination; and autopsies. Investigators will enhance their effectiveness in murder investigations as victim-offender relationships are more closely scrutinized. Victims, even in death, are often storybooks about the offender and the circumstances of the crime.

3. **Equivocal Death Profiling—**Also referred to sometimes as psychological autopsy, investigators apply nonscientific information to explain the motivations of a person or group engaged in suicide pacts or difficult-to-explain deaths.

4. **DNA Profiling—**In recent years several cases of murder have been solved as a result of the advent of DNA profiling or genetic science. This includes gathering DNA from crime scenes, victims, and offenders in efforts to match up perpetrators to specific crimes. Between 1979 and 1986 a serial killer stalked, raped, and murdered at least six victims in southern California. Newly found DNA evidence from rape kits found in archived cases conclusively linked these murders. Investigators then used other profiling techniques by examining the predator's stalking and killing habits to link the killer to four more murders.

5. **Crime Scene Profiling—**Also referred to as criminal investigation analysis this form of profiling is based upon the FBI model developed by their Behavioral Science Unit. Investigators focus on crime scene descriptions, photographs, offender behavior pre- and post-criminal act(s), traffic patterns, physical evidence, and victim information and place less credence on psychological data. Psychosocial data are compared to other similar cases and investigators engage in an experiential-informational guessing technique to reconstruct the offenders' personality. From the FBI's 1988 study of 36 serial sexual murderers a dichotomy of offender characteristics was developed. The "organized" offender is methodical, premeditated, mature, resourceful, and usually involved sexual perversion. The "disorganized" type of killer was found to act much more randomly, opportunistically—opposite characteristics of the organized offender—and often with some form of mental disorder (Ressler et al., 1988). Their dichotomous profile includes the following characteristics:

Organized	*Disorganized*
Good intelligence	Average or low intelligence
Socially/sexually competent	Socially/sexually incompetent
Stable work history	Lack of stable work history
Controlled during crime	Anxious during crime
Living with someone	Living alone
Very mobile	Lives near crime scene
Follows investigation in media	Little interest in media
May leave town/change job	Little change in lifestyle
Uses alcohol prior to crime	Little alcohol use

Organized	*Disorganized*
Premeditated offense	Spontaneous offense
Victim a stranger	Victim or location unknown
Conversation with victim	Little conversation with victim
Demands submission	Sudden violence to victim
Uses restraints	Little use of restraints
Violent acts prior to death	Postmortem sexual acts
Body hidden	Body left in view
Weapon/evidence absent	Weapon/evidence often present
Transports body	Body left at scene

The problem with this dichotomous model is the lack of rigorous reliability and validity testing. Even though the model has been used extensively by investigators, the model may not have the utility previously thought. Kocsis, Irwin, and Hayes (1998) found that, although there is some merit to the dichotomy, a more useful evaluation of criminal behaviors is necessary. Kocsis, Cooksey, and Irwin (1999) noted that

> this conceptual failing of the organized/disorganized dichotomy is more apparent when it is recognized that it makes no distinction between behaviors that commonly occur in all offenses and those that discriminate aspects of a specific offender. For example if an offender uses a knife in a sexual murder, this may not actually be a behavioral clue about the specific offender, but rather, simply a common behavior pattern observed in most sexual murders. . . . some incorrect offender characteristics could be concluded from the use of a knife when it truly just represents a common behavior amongst most sexual murders. This failing to empirically distinguish between common behaviors and those which are discriminatory of a specific individual is a flaw that prevails throughout much of the literature on profiling in general (p. 5).

6. **Psychological Profiling—**Tracking the serial killer and the multitude of problems posed by such a task has led, in the past few years, to the development of psychological profiling, a tool used to prioritize a variety of homicides and other serious crimes. Psychological profiling, also known as criminal personality assessment, is applied to criminal behavior profiling, offender profiling, victim profiling, and crime scene profiling. It is used by law enforcement agencies in the United States, Canada, and Britain. Swanson, Chamelin, and Territo (1984) define the intent and purpose of this type of profiling:

> The purpose of the psychological assessment of a crime scene is to produce a profile, that is, to identify and interpret certain items of evidence at the crime scene that would be indicative of the personality type of the individual or individuals committing the crime. The goal of the profiler is to provide enough information to investigators to enable them to limit or better direct their investigations (pp. 700–701).

Profilers match the personality characteristics of a certain type of offender with those of a suspect. Investigators use batteries of interviews and testing to establish their base of information. Experts are frequently called upon to predict future behavior of an offender including pedophiles, child molesters, rapists, and other sexual deviants. The investigator usually has a particular offender that he is profiling. In efforts to improve the effectiveness and credibility of psychological, crime scene, and criminal profiling, organizations such as the *Academy of Behavioral Profiling,* founded by Brent Turvey, attract investigators and researchers interested in both the forensic and investigative criminal analysis.

7. **Geographical Profiling—**While investigators have been working to improve both crime scene profiling and psychological profiling, other researchers and investigators like former Detective Kim Rossmo from Canada have been actively developing a geographical approach to criminal investigations. Also referred to as spatial mapping, this technique combines geography and environmental criminology to connect crime scenes to offender habitats and hunting grounds. Such profiling is empirically based and has not placed much value on motivation or personality. It does help law enforcement in deciding where to begin knocking on doors and setting up stakeouts. In the case of the "Railroad Killer," the offender had stayed near trains and therefore was likely a drifter or transient. The geographic similarities linked him to many killings and he was eventually identified, arrested, and sent to prison. A geographical profile includes the elements of *distance, mobility, mental maps,* and *locality demographics.* Offenders are profiled by the amount of distance covered by a serial offender. Some may travel because they have access to transportation whereas others are limited in their access. This can create problems because some serial offenders like Ted Kaczynski, the Unabomber, used buses to transport his bombs or mailed them. Mental maps refer to an offender's cognitive images of his or her surroundings. As offenders become more comfortable with his tools and surroundings, the more likely he will be to expand those boundaries. Offender travel routes can be critical to a serial-murder investigation. Kim Rossmo (1999), one of the noted pioneers of geographic profiling, identifies four offender styles in hunting for victims:

1. **Hunter—**identifies a specific victim in his home area.
2. **Poacher—**prefers to travel away from home area for hunting victims.
3. **Troller—**an opportunistic killer, he attacks victims while carrying out his regular activities.
4. **Trapper—**a spider-and-fly scenario where an offender enjoys laying a trap for a victim.

Rossmo (1995) conducted an impressive, critical examination of serial-murder cases using data sets from the FBI and your author. His eclectic approach to geographic profiling utilizes not only empirical data but also psychological information. A geographical profile includes a study of area maps, examination of crime scenes, interviews of witnesses and investigators, and knowledge of abduction and body dumpsites where serial murder is involved. Rossmo's Criminal Geographic Targeting, a computerized program, produces a topographical map based on crime scene information. The more crime scenes, the greater the predictability of the program. Using the eleven crime scenes of serial killer Clifford R. Olson who raped, sodomized, and hammered boys and girls to death, Rossmo was able to pinpoint the killer's area of residence to within a four-block radius. In another case of serial rape, Rossmo used 79 crime scenes to pinpoint the actual basement of the offender's home as the location of the attacks. Scotland Yard, Dutch police, the FBI Behavioral Science Unit, and many other law enforcement agencies in need of better science to solve their cases frequently use Rossmo. Godwin (1999), in his work, *Hunting Serial Predators,* prefers geographic profiling to the methods employed by the FBI because he feels that there is greater predictive value. Godwin, author of the computer program *Predator,* used for geographic profiling, believes that using both body dumpsites and locations of victim abductions or where they were last seen will provide the best results in locating the offender. Godwin refers to "landscape layouts" that include bars, nightclubs, red-light districts, depressed, poverty-ridden areas of a community, parking lots, jogging paths, rest stops, and college campuses as preying grounds for serial killers. Killers tend to hunt for victims in relation to where the offender works, lives, and carries out his routine daily activities. This geographic comfort zone becomes the hunting grounds for a serial offender. Geography is fast becoming a tool in offender profiling that law enforcement can use with increasing accuracy.

The following are two examples of profiling in action: In New York a police department submitted an unsolved case after months of intensive but futile investigation. A woman had been strangled and brutally beaten, her mutilated body left on the roof of the Bronx housing project where she had lived. FBI profilers suggested to police that they look for a white male, 25–35 years of age, who lived or worked in the area, a high school dropout, and living by himself or with one parent; very likely police had already interviewed him. A few months later police arrested a 32-year-old white male, a high school dropout, living with his father on the fourth floor of the victim's building. Police had interviewed the son but then removed him from their suspect list because he had been confined to a mental hospital at the time of the murder. Further investigation revealed that patients at the hospital were able to come and go as they wished (Barnes, 1986).

In a second case, several young women had been killed in various states. As police began to gather data, agents began to notice similarities in the modus operandi. Victims tended to be found along major interstate highways and trucking routes. Eventually a truck driver was arrested in the murders.

Problems in Profiling

Profiling can be very useful, but caution must be exercised to avoid constructing hasty or poorly grounded profiles that may lead investigators in wrong directions. This inevitably places a strain on resources, and, most important, additional lives may be lost. Errors in the information transmitted to NCAVC (National Center for the Analysis of Violent Crime), mistaken assessments by the evaluation team, and other potential glitches mean profiles can and do go wrong. In one case, for example, a profile on a criminal suspect told investigators the man they were looking for came from a broken home, was a high school dropout, held a marginal job, hung out in "honky tonk" bars, and lived far from the scene of the crime. When the attacker was finally caught, it was learned the psychological assessment was 100% wrong. He had not come from a broken home; he had a college degree, held an executive position with a respected financial institution, did not use alcohol, and lived near the scene of the crime. With this possibility for error, the bureau warns investigators not to become so dependent on the evaluation that they neglect other leads or become biased to the point where they blindly follow only the clues that match the scenario described in the profile's report (Goodroe, 1987, p. 31). In 1996, Richard Jewell, a security guard at the Olympic Games in Atlanta, Georgia, noticed an unattended knapsack. Concerned that it might contain a bomb, he immediately reported his findings to his superiors. While Olympic visitors were being evacuated, the sack exploded, killing one woman and injuring over 100 others. Jewell quickly became a suspect because he "fit" the profile of someone who would set a bomb and then become a hero for saving others. He seemed to be enjoying the sudden notoriety of the event and being recognized as a public hero. Investigators also noted that he had mentioned to the media how he hoped to land a permanent job with law enforcement after the Games. Jewell became a prime suspect and quickly became subject to an intensive investigation. The media harassed him for several months before investigators were forced to admit that they had the wrong man. Indeed, not until November 2000 was Eric Robert Rudolph indicted, in absentia, for several bombings of abortion clinics and three Atlanta bombings, including the explosion at the Olympic Games.

Sometimes investigators ignore or fail to understand offender profiles and are quick to rush to conclusions based upon a piece of physical evidence. In the case of Cary Stayner, the Yosemite Park killer who had abducted and murdered a woman, her daughter, and her teenage friend, four suspects were arrested. The suspects had some physical evidence that linked them to the murders. The FBI was adamant that the killers were behind bars. Your author, when interviewed by local media, explained that the probability of these murders being committed by several people was very low. Given the facts of the case at that point, the profile, given the manner in which the victims were killed, strongly suggested that this was the work of a lone predator. The suspects were also petty criminals and drug dealers, hardly the types of offenders who suddenly carry out such sadistic sexual murders. Months passed and your author continued to maintain that the real offender was still free to kill while these common criminals sat in jail. Then another brutal murder occurred involving a Yosemite Park worker, Joie Armstrong. She had been decapitated. Some investigators still maintained that the men in custody were the killers of the three park tourists. Much of that line of thinking was discarded when Cary

PROFILE 11.1 Efren Saldivar, "Angel of Death," 1988–1998

In 1998 Efren Saldivar, 28, a respiratory therapist for nine years at Glendale Adventist Medical Center in California, confessed to killing dozens of terminally ill patients over a ten-year period. He claimed to be an "angel of death" who had killed as many as 200 victims from several hospitals where he had worked part-time. Because there was no independent corroborating evidence, police released Saldivar who later recanted his confession stating that he was depressed and wanted to be executed. An investigation continued into the possibility that Saldivar was telling the truth, but it was not until three years after his confession that he was arrested and charged with six murders. Saldivar admitted injecting fatal doses of pavulon, a muscle relaxer that suppresses natural breathing, and succinylcholine chloride, a drug that also stops natural breathing, into 40–50 victims. Later, investigators realized that Saldivar probably had murdered closer to 200. Typical in such cases, hospitals terminate employees who may have been suspicious but seldom report the suspect. In the case of Saldivar, five respiratory therapists were fired in 1998 following an internal investigation.

Stayner not only confessed to the Armstrong murder, but also to the other three killings. It was the manner in which the victims were killed that linked the cases. These were sexual killings where decapitation becomes part of the sexual experience. Certainly this was not the work of petty criminals. Your author drew his conclusions based upon information about how the victims died and, using a psychological profile, determined that the killings were the work of a lone sexual predator. Stayner was sentenced to life in prison, no parole, for the Joie Armstrong case and is now being tried in the three tourists' murders (author's files). The profile can be a useful tool but, like any tool, it can be misused. Profiles can complement crime scene investigations and strengthen interagency and interdisciplinary cooperation.

Care Providers and Serial Murder

One area that geographic profiling is not designed to address is murder described by your author as *place-specific.* These are the stay-at-home or at-work killers who have no dumpsites for bodies. Dr. Harold Shipman (see Chapter 10) whose victims died in their homes, fit no particular geographic pattern. Donald Harvey, another "angel of death," killed primarily in hospitals, again leaving no geographic pattern. Unfortunately, even utilizing psychological profiling fails to identify these types of serial killers until the body counts are often very high (see Profile 11.1).

As discussed earlier, there does appear to be an increase in the number of people being killed in nursing homes and hospitals. Sophisticated drugs such as digoxin, pavulon, and potassium chloride are either difficult to detect or the procedures for testing for such drugs are not well established or too costly to check for routinely. At the Toronto Hospital for Sick Children in Ontario, Canada, dozens of infants were believed to have been killed with overdoses of the heart drug digoxin between 1980 and 1981. Authorities were never told until it was too late. By then evidence had been discarded, exhibits misplaced, bodies cremated, and files "cleaned up." One nurse, arrested for the crimes, was released because of lack of evidence. To date that case has yet to be resolved.

Murders are increasing in nursing homes and hospitals because of some of the following reasons:

1. Victims are accessible and vulnerable.
2. An offender can easily operate without detection because no one expects such crimes would or could ever occur in such a setting.
3. An offender has access to a variety of murder weapons that are then easily disposed of without detection.
4. Often autopsies are not performed when a death occurs under the care of an attending physician. People routinely die in hospitals, especially in critical-care units. Consequently, there is rarely a need to be suspicious. Doctors can misdiagnose the actual cause of death. Congestive heart failure, for example, may be induced through a variety of causes.
5. Supervisors or administrators sometimes minimize reports that somebody is acting suspiciously or could be harming patients. Scandals of purported murders inevitably can adversely affect admission rates. Negative publicity in the minds of some administrators is to be avoided at all costs.
6. Finally, prosecuting those who are believed to be involved in the deaths of patients can be very difficult as a result of lost evidence, sensationalism, and legal procedures. For example, in August 1975, FBI agents were called to the Ann Arbor Veterans Hospital to investigate 50 breathing failures spanning a six-week period. On June 16, 1976, a Detroit grand jury indicted nurses Filipina Narcisco and Lenora Perez with mass poisoning. In July 1977, the two women were found guilty of injecting five patients with pavulon, a drug that freezes the muscles necessary for breathing. A federal judge granted the pair another trial, citing misconduct by federal prosecutors that had denied the women a fair trial. Federal prosecutors then dropped the charges (*Detroit Free Press,* December 6, 1988).

Investigators need to realize that, with an aging population, the elderly are extremely vulnerable to serial murderers. Although other crimes against the elderly and others requiring health care have remained fairly constant over the past 25 years, there has been a significant increase in serial murders involving the elderly. Certainly these offenders who kill in hospitals and nursing homes do not fit the stereotype of the typical lust murderers who stalk and viciously attack young women nor are they usually killing for profit. They are the quiet killers, who go about dutifully performing their assigned tasks and, when the urge or opportunity arises, silently and dispassionately take the life of some unsuspecting, trusting patient. These offenders are usually not "Jack the Ripper" types nor do they attract media attention as do traveling serial killers.

Instead, these are murders by people who enjoy, at some psychological level, the power of controlling life and death. Such persons are difficult to identify because they can be such friendly and outwardly compassionate persons. Unlike typical serial killers, place-specific murderers, especially those providing care for the elderly and infirm, have access to potentially lethal weapons (medications) as part of their work routine. Hospital personnel in general are ill prepared to cope with their suspicions and the consequences of homicides. Sometimes, as in the case of Donald Harvey or Jane Toppan, the offender is simply asked to resign when suspicions surface, and the police are not involved. In turn, such offenders inevitably find other hospitals or nursing homes in which to work and kill again. Hospital workers are in demand, especially anyone with some skills or experience. References are seldom checked, and even then there generally is no formal documentation of the reasons for which a person left his or her previous employment. In the future, more attention will be needed in exploring these types of offenders if we are going to develop effective tools for profiling and apprehension.

NCAVC AND VICAP

In 1984, the U.S. Department of Justice, composed of the Office of Justice Programs, the National Institute of Justice, and the Office of Juvenile Justice and Delinquency Prevention, along with the Federal Bureau of Investigation in conjunction with the Criminal Justice Center at Sam Houston State University in Huntsville, Texas, established the National Center for the Analysis of Violent Crime (NCAVC). This center serves as a clearinghouse and resource for law enforcement agencies involved in "unusual, bizarre and/or particularly vicious or repetitive violent crime" (Brooks et al., 1987). The NCAVC was composed of four core programs: Research and Development; Training; Profiling and Consultation; and the Violent Criminal Apprehension Program (VICAP).

VICAP was located in the Behavioral Science Unit in Quantico, Virginia, and served as a national clearinghouse for reports involving solved or unsolved homicides, attempted homicides, abductions, missing persons where violence is suspected, and unidentified dead bodies involving homicides. In turn, VICAP provided law enforcement agencies "reporting similar pattern violent crimes with the information necessary to initiate a coordinated multiagency investigation so that they might expeditiously identify and apprehend the offender(s) responsible for the crimes" (Brooks et al., 1987, p. 41). Once patterns were established by VICAP staff involving victimization, physical evidence, information about the suspect(s), modus operandi, and so on, then the multiagency coordination is set into motion. Cavanagh and MacKay (1991, pp. 5–6) point out that criminal profiles are compiled in a variety of cases including those involving postmortem mutilations, torture, child molestations and abductions, bank robberies, serial arson, lust murders, as well as serial murder. Ressler and his colleagues (1988) summarized the actual step-by-step process provided by VICAP:

When a new case is entered, the VICAP computer system simultaneously compared and contrasted over 100 selected modus operandi (MO) categories of that case with all other cases stored in the database. After overnight processing, a printed computer report was returned to the VICAP crime analyst handling the case. This report listed, in rank order, the top ten "matches" in the violent crime databank; that is, the ten cases that were most similar to the new case. This crime pattern analysis technique called *template pattern matching,* was specifically designed for VICAP and programmed by the FBI Technical Services Division. The VICAP computer system also produced selected management information system reports that monitored case activity geographically, with hope that it would eventually trace the travels of serial violent criminals across the United States (p. 113).

In June 1985, VICAP became operational, and within the first year several problems were recognized with the system. More sophisticated computer programs had to be installed to sufficiently manipulate and analyze the large amounts of data and properly develop case matching. In addition, VICAP received fewer cases than expected, and a good understanding of cases from reported data was more difficult to achieve than anticipated (p. 118).

Certainly NCAVC and VICAP had the potential to move forward in the battle against violent and nonviolent criminals. Even though tracking serial killers was a top priority, other offender data were also being collected and analyzed. For example, Hazelwood and Burgess (1989) conducted research into serial rapists. However, VICAP was sharply criticized by the media as not having caught any criminals (Allen, 1988). One of the problems lies in the limited cooperation of other local and state police agencies. Considering there are over 17,000 law enforcement agencies in the United States, many of which operate on shoestring budgets, it is not surprising that the flow of information to the federally operated control center has been less than overwhelming. VICAP was viewed as a program that eventually could not meet agency expectations. Lack of concern for validity, reliability, and constructing theoretical basis in BSU's research brought into question the utility of profiling as articulated by the FBI (Rossmo 1995).

By 1995 the FBI's Behavioral Science Unit in Quantico, Virginia, had faced severe funding cuts and reorganization. Today, the BSU is now known as the Investigative Support Unit (ISU), part of the Critical Incident Response Group at the FBI Academy. Much of its functions are the same but are more streamlined, more effective.

Fox and Levin (1995) remind us that the ISU becomes involved primarily in the most difficult cases requiring additional investigative techniques and insight. Ressler and his colleagues (1988) also noted, "VICAP's purpose was not to investigate cases but to analyze them" (p. 119). Ressler is correct in his observation. Jackson and associates (1993, 1994) observed that profiles do not directly apprehend offenders because it is a management instrument in assisting specific criminal investigations. During the next several years NCAVC and the Investigative Support Unit will continue to improve the quality and sophistication of computer programs, reporting methods, and analytical procedures. One hopes that, in years to come, those who operate the unit will continue to refine definitions of serial killing, which generally has focused on lust killers who move about the country. Serial killers who are place-specific, those who do not become sexually involved with victims, and female serial offenders all warrant recognition and appropriate inclusion in NCAVC files. We may never have female lust killers in our society, but, as has been presented in this research, women simply choose other methods of murder and have proven they are capable of mass murders and serial killings. The NCAVC program is a developing tool that law enforcement can use to assist them in their investigations.

They are not alone as agencies such as those in Washington develop their Homicide Investigation Tracking System (HITS), in New York the Homicide Assessment and Lead Tracking (HALT), Homicide Evaluation and Assessment Tracking (HEAT) in New Jersey, in Indiana the Criminal Apprehension Assistance Program (ICAAP), in Canada the RCMP Violent Crime Linkage Analysis System (ViCLAS), and in England the Police Research Group (PRG) of the British Home Office (Rossmo, 1995). Important advances are being made to merge the sciences into a cohesive investigative tool. Rossmo (1995), in his seminal work using geographic profiling, applied geographic concepts in the analysis of criminal target patterns. He analyzed relationships between offender residence and crime site locations. This applied science of profiling merges both theoretical and structural frameworks into an increasingly useful investigative tool. Additional tools such as DNA profiling should play a significant role in connecting samples of semen and blood from crime scenes to offenders. Currently, a national DNA identification index merging federal, state, and local data into the Combined DNA Index System (CODIS) provides a forensic index for unsolved crimes and a convicted offender index for known felons. Other indices such as those for missing persons and unidentified bodies are also in the planning stages. The Automated Fingerprint Identification System (AFIS) used to identify Richard Ramirez, the Night Stalker of Los Angeles, has also become more useful in police investigations (Rossmo, 1995, pp. 83–85). However, we must not forget that tools are for assisting investigations. In the final analysis, it is the police or agents in the cities and towns throughout America who, using the available tools, must track down and apprehend the serial killers.

At the investigation level, Keppel (1989) examined the *solvability factors* involved in serial murder and found the most important ones to be:

1. Quality of police interviews with eyewitnesses
2. Circumstances that led to the initial stop of the murderer
3. Circumstances that established probable cause to search and seize physical evidence
4. Quality of the investigations at the crime scene(s)
5. Quality of the scientific analysis of the physical evidence (p. 4)

This last solvability factor often becomes critical in multiple homicide investigations because they can include an enormous amount of physical evidence taken from the crime scene(s), from the offender(s) and his or her possessions, and from victims and their possessions. Forensic science has become a valuable tool in linking suspects to the crime scenes and in identifying evidence. Regional labs, such as the Atlanta Crime Laboratory, are used to analyze physical evidence from crime scenes in many states. For example, in the Atlanta child murders, a great deal of hair fiber evidence was catalogued and eventually used to convict Wayne Williams. Other types of forensic evidence inspection and analysis now performed in crime labs include:

1. Glass and soil fragments
2. Organic analysis such as elements, compounds, chromatography, spectrophotometry, and mass spectrometry
3. Inorganic analysis such as atomic absorption spectrophotometry and neutron activation analysis
4. Hair, fibers, and paint analysis including typing and identification
5. Drug analysis such as narcotics, stimulants, depressants, and hallucinogens
6. Toxicological analysis such as alcohol, drugs, poisons
7. Arson analysis including flammable residues and explosives
8. Serological analysis including blood, bloodstains, and semen
9. Fingerprinting analysis including classification, detection, and preservation of prints
10. Firearms and toolmarks including analysis of bullets, gunpowder residue, primer residue, serial number restoration, and so forth
11. Document and voice analysis such as handwriting comparisons, typewriting, alterations, erasures, obliterations, and voice examinations
12. DNA testing, typing, and using the combined DNA Index System (Saferstein, 2001)

Homicide detectives know that their tools for murder investigations are changing with technology. Fingerprinting is now computerized, eliminating the inability to find matches of prints to offenders. The system, Automated Fingerprint Identification System or AFIS, codes specific points from crime scene fingerprints and stores them in a memory bank that can be compared to millions of other prints in just moments. Some officers are now resorting to voice-stress analysis in looking for deception when a suspect refuses to answer questions. Others are learning the art of kinetic interviewing, which is the science of reading body language to measure deception. Even though "hunches" will always find a place in law enforcement, those "gut feelings" will increasingly find their origins in forensic science. This fact has never been clearer than in the case of Ted Kaczynski, the Unabomber, America's serial bomber who had eluded capture for 18 years. During the course of this investigation three consecutive Unabom Task Forces were organized to coordinate interagency cooperation. Some agents spent half of their careers hunting for this one offender. Using every available tool, this task force assembled some of the nation's most skilled and insightful investigators. Profile 11.2 is a brief synopsis of the case, including the author's profile of the man referred to as the Unabomber.

PROFILE 11.2 Theodore Kaczynski, the Unabomber, 1978–1996

Starting out as an apparent terrorist bombing nearly 18 years ago, the Unabomber case became the largest and most expensive manhunt in American history. The subject of radio talk shows, television documentaries, and hundreds of newspaper articles, the Unabomber attracted worldwide attention. A one-million-dollar reward was offered for information leading to the arrest of the elusive killer. Code-named UNABOMBER because of the universities and airlines he targeted in his earlier bombings, the Unabomber rose from a relatively obscure criminal status to someone of national recognition. The Unabomber killed three persons (two in California and one in New Jersey) and injured 23 others, his attacks spanning nine states. Several victims have been university professors or people directly related to technology.

By 1996, over 100 agents from the Federal Bureau of Investigation, the U.S. Postal Service, and the Bureau of Alcohol, Tobacco, and Firearms were working together as the Unabom Task Force along with the assistance of local and state law enforcement. Since the first bombing in 1978, this was the third and largest such task force to be assembled. Agent Tony Muljat, working full time on this case for 11 years, waived his retirement in hopes of bringing the case to closure. Staging his first attack in Chicago, the Unabomber appeared to relocate and was thought to be living in northern California, possibly near Sacramento or San Francisco. Eight of the 16 bombings either occurred in northern California or bombs were mailed from that area. Since 1993 all his letters and bombs were mailed from the San Francisco Bay area. The following list chronicles the Unabomber attacks.

Unabomber Attacks

PLACE	DATE	NUMBER OF VICTIMS
1. University of Illinois at Chicago, IL	5/25/78	1 injured
2. Northwestern University, Evanston, IL	5/9/79	1 injured
3. American Airlines Flight 444, Chicago, IL	11/15/79	12 injured
4. President, United Airlines, Chicago, IL	6/10/80	1 injured
5. University of Utah, Salt Lake City, UT	10/8/81	
6. Vanderbilt University, Nashville, TN	5/5/82	1 injured
7. University of California, Berkeley, CA	7/2/82	1 injured
8. Boeing Aircraft, Auburn, WA	5/8/85	
9. University of California, Berkeley, CA	5/15/85	1 injured
10. University of Michigan, Ann Arbor, MI	11/15/85	2 injured
11. Rentech Company, Sacramento, CA	12/11/85	1 death
12. CAAM's Inc., Salt Lake City, UT	2/20/87	1 injured
13. Physician/researcher, Tiburon, CA	6/22/93	1 injured
14. Yale University, New Haven, CT	6/24/93	1 injured
15. Advertising executive, North Caldwell, NJ	12/9/94	1 death
16. Timber lobbyist, Sacramento, CA	4/24/95	1 death

Several physical and psychological profiles were constructed around the Unabomber. The task force believed, for example, that the he was a white male probably in his early to mid to late forties. He was seen once in 1987 by a secretary as he hand-delivered a bomb. Only in recent years did the Unabomber begin to communicate with the public. He increasingly expressed his disdain for law enforcement, while at the same time he appeared to enjoy taunting and challenging them. Although such occurrences are rare, some serial killers, such as the Unabomber and the Zodiac killer from San Francisco, have enjoyed matching wits with law enforcement. The Unabomber had a history of sending bombs and then remaining silent for periods of time. One hiatus was six years. His bomb-making skills improved markedly in sophistication. The devices were pipe bombs with antimovement or antiopening firing switches. He evolved from using smokeless powders to a mixture of ammonium nitrate and aluminum powder. He took time to handcraft his devices, using wood and metal components.

He claimed to be part of a clandestine organization named the Freedom Club. The Unabomber signed his letters with the initials "FC" and also carefully inscribed "FC" on his bombs. In 1995 he mailed a 35,000-word "Manifesto" to the *Washington Post* and *New York Times,* demanding that his work be published or the bombings would continue. The Manifesto was a redundant diatribe of denunciations against technology, advocating the dismantling of industrial technology and the redistribution of human society. The Unabomber stated that the evils of technology would eventually destroy our society, and he felt it was his role to bring public attention to pending societal doom. The Unabomber viewed killing a few people in order to get the public's attention as completely justifiable. The task force, along with the media, faced a difficult dilemma: Do we choose not to be held hostage by this killer and run the risk of another attack or submit to his demands in order to save a life and perhaps forestall a near inevitable bombing? In order to spare another attack and in hopes that someone in the community might recognize the writing, the *Washington Post* published the Manifesto. The Manifesto was also made available on the Internet's World Wide Web.

Investigations focused on several individuals, including a sailor, a handyman, and a career criminal, but they all were eliminated as suspects. Some investigators speculated that James William Kilgore, a fugitive with ties to the Symbionese Liberation Army who went underground after a bombing incident in 1976, could have been the Unabomber. Other investigators dismissed Kilgore as a viable suspect and looked for new leads in the investigation. For example, investigators looked at possible religious connections and the Unabomber's frequent usage of biblical names. Investigators also examined commonalties between the bombings and specific people involved in the technology of developing prosthetic devices.

The final suspect (there were many) in this profile was Theodore Kaczynski. Federal agents near Lincoln, Montana, arrested him in 1996. His brother had read the Manifesto and noticed striking similarities between some letters written by his brother and the manuscript. Ted Kaczynski was living a hermit's life in

(continued)

PROFILE 11.2 Continued

a 10′ by 12′ shack without electricity or plumbing. Inside, investigators found letters and diaries connected to the bombings, various materials used in bomb construction, several detailed blueprints for bomb making, a partially completed bomb, a completed bomb that had been packaged and partially addressed, a list of potential victims, typewriters (one of which appeared to be the one on which the Manifesto was typed), clothing similar to that worn when the Unabomber was seen delivering a bomb in Salt Lake City, and possibly the original Manifesto manuscript.

Born in 1942, Ted proved to be very intelligent, graduating two years early from high school. At age 16 he started his university studies at Harvard on a scholarship. Throughout his formal education Ted was perceived by others to be a loner who shunned potential friends. In 1967 he earned a doctorate in math from the University of Michigan and began teaching that same year as an assistant professor at the University of California, Berkeley. Three semesters later he suddenly resigned from his position and began living a transient lifestyle. He relocated to Montana and also spent time working at odd jobs in Utah. In 1978, and shortly after the first attack by the Unabomber, his brother David hired him to work in a foam rubber manufacturing company. He tried dating a female coworker but after two dates she ended the relationship. Ted retaliated by posting limericks about her around the office. When confronted by his brother, Ted became angry. The harassment incidents resulted in Ted being fired by his brother. Ted returned to Montana and became more reclusive. In 1990 his father, dying of cancer, committed suicide. Ted did not attend the funeral.

Ted appeared to have harbored much resentment against his family and society in general. He sent a letter to his mother referring to her as a "dog" because of his inability to form lasting relationships. His brother David, with whom he had been close in younger years, married and began a career. In many respects Ted appeared to have perceived himself rejected or abandoned by those supposedly closest to him. His reclusive lifestyle may well have exacerbated a growing sense of paranoia about people and society.

Your author served as a consultant to the Unabomb Task Force and profiled the Unabomber to be a man of low self-esteem who thrived on the notoriety he has achieved. The Unabomber did not impress me as a true believer in the evils of technology. His desire to return to a pristine lifestyle appeared to cover a more systemic motivation. He used the issue of technology to promote his own self-interests, frustrations, sense of rejec-

Unsolved Murder Cases

At the time of this writing serial killers roam the streets of Los Angeles, Chicago, and New York. The killers are going after "strawberries," or prostitutes who sell sex for drugs. Several women will be murdered. Regardless of the motive, offenders who want to kill young women can find easy targets among prostitutes. Dealing with strangers is their trade, and someone who decides to start killing prostitutes can go undetected for years.

tion, and anger. He reconstructed history to justify his behavior. He did not want people to see him as a terrorist but as one who cared for the welfare of his society. The Unabomber appeared to have cared for no one but himself. An intelligent man, the Unabomber probably engaged in jobs requiring little of his intellect. He was more of a thinker than a doer. The only things he ever completed were his bombs and they are all about him. Ted Kaczynski, a man of rationalization and unconscious pretense, appears to "fit" the Unabomber profile.

His need to validate his life may have driven him to seek the limelight. Ted did not appreciate being "upstaged" by other criminals. For example, at the time of the World Trade Center explosion in February 1993, he had been inactive for over six years. Just over four months after the blast Ted struck again twice. His message was very clear: You may be able to catch those amateurs but I am still here, after all these years. Then, on April 19, 1995, terrorists struck the Federal Building in Oklahoma City, Oklahoma, killing nearly 168 people. Turning to an associate, your author commented that the Unabomber would strike soon because once again he had been upstaged and would no longer be getting the media attention he craved. A few days later a timber lobbyist in Sacramento, California, became the third murder victim of the Unabomber.

Ted Kaczynski, the Unabomber, is a walking facade. His self-pity has driven him to envy. Besides his drive for recognition, Ted also found pleasure in depriving others of their talents, skills, and livelihoods by sending devices that would blow off their fingers, hands, faces, or destroy eyesight. Unable to achieve the successes and attention earned by real scientists and scholars, he did not want them to have the rewards either. He rejected technology because he perceived that technology had rejected him. In truth, Kaczynski appears to be a man of many contradictions, frustrations, and self-deceptions. Ultimately, he is nothing more than other serial killers who rear their ugly heads; he just found an innovative way to do it.

The trial was relatively brief. Kaczynski was found to be guilty but a paranoid schizophrenic. He was sent to federal prison with no possibility of parole. Ted Kaczynski continues his reclusiveness in the confines of his small prison cell where he continues to vehemently insist that he is neither schizophrenic nor insane in any way. His notoriety has influenced a few living on the fringes of our society to emulate him. Regardless of the eccentric nature of the messenger, the message that Kaczynski was sending appeals to many who feel they cannot compete or be comfortable in a society that is so dominated by fast-paced technology.

In July 1982, a cyclist found the strangled body of 16-year-old Wendy Coffield. Seven years later, Wendy was joined by nearly 50 other female hitchhikers, transients, and prostitutes from the Seattle, Washington, area. These killings were dubbed the "Green River Killings," because most of the victims were located in or around the Green River area. A task force was created to focus specifically on apprehending the Green River killer. At times as many as 60 agents were investigating the case on any given day. Bodies kept surfacing, and police maintained their intense manhunt. The killings appeared to have stopped, and, with no leads, police came to a standstill in the investigation. Possibly the killer moved to another killing site or is in prison for other offenses. Perhaps he became ill or died. Unless the killer chooses to come forward, it is unlikely the case will ever be solved.

Another serial-murder case occurred in the Boston area, where at least eight prostitutes were found dumped in woods along the interstate highways. Similar stories can be related about missing and murdered young women in Kansas City, Missouri (1988), and the Washington, D.C., area (1987). A small sampling of other unsolved cases includes: the 1983 Joliet, Illinois, murders, 15 victims; the 1976 killings in the Detroit area, 7 victims; the 1974 "Los Angeles Slasher" case, involving 8 victims; the "Texas Strangler" case of 1968–1971, involving 11 victims; the 1967 Kenosha, Wisconsin, murders of 7 victims; the 1956 Chicago serial killings of 5 people; the 1935 "Mad Butcher of Cleveland" case that yielded 12 victims; and the 1906 Chicago, Illinois, murders of at least 20 victims.

Women, of course, are not the only targets. The "Executioner" in Los Angeles (1986) killed at least nine male transients. Vagrants, like prostitutes, are accessible and vulnerable. Occasionally homosexuals, usually males, become the target of someone who has decided it is time to cleanse the earth of people they perceive as wicked. More often it becomes evident that such killers are themselves homosexuals. (However, this does not mean that homosexuals are given any more to violent pathologies than heterosexuals. Although there have been a number of homosexually related serial killings, those figures do not appear to be disproportionate to other types of serial killings.)

When we take into account the fact that serial killers operate in nursing homes, hospitals, and private homes as well as in and around cities and in different states, it is not surprising that we are faced with what appears to be an increasing number of unsolved cases. According to media reports, the United States is being "inundated" with serial killers, most of whom are extremely difficult, if not impossible, to apprehend, and law enforcement and the criminal justice system is unable to effectively stop serial killers. However, such criticism of law enforcement may be premature, if not inappropriate. Law enforcement may be doing a much better job than anyone realizes. For example, it is quite plausible that law enforcement personnel actually apprehend many would-be multiple-homicide offenders for one or two murders, thus stopping them before they can commit more. On what can we base this assumption? We know that prison populations comprise an estimated 20–30% of psychopathic or antisocial personality types. These types of offenders are considered to be the most dangerous because they are more prone to violent behavior. Certainly not all psychopaths are prone to violent behavior, nor do all those in prison have the propensity to harm others, but many do. We also know that such offenders have the highest rates of recidivism for criminal behavior and time in prison. An argument could then be made that many psychopaths who have been apprehended would have killed if they had not been arrested. Most of them are caught as a result of their own blunders and the good investigative skills of the police.

Serial killers are not indestructible nor do they have special mystical powers. They are not Hannibal Lecters. Your author has interviewed and researched enough serial killers to debunk such a myth. They are offenders with grotesquely distorted fantasy systems. They are humans who have acquired certain skills and certain patterns of deviousness that permit some of them to elude police. Making an accurate determination of the number of active serial killers is virtually impossible. As discussed in this final chapter, police agencies have only recently begun to allocate resources specifically for the detection and apprehension of serial murderers. And when these murderers are apprehended, the courts are faced with the determination of appropriate sentencing of these offenders. Sentencing often fails to meet the demands of public outrage or provide necessary treatment facilities and programs for these violent offenders.

DISPOSITION

Once a serial killer is apprehended, the disposition of the offender is often very time-consuming. Some of the most notorious cases receive extended hearings and go through a morass of legal proceedings. In part, this specialized treatment is due to the complexity of the case as well as to the tendency of such crimes to attract prominent legal figures. Most of these cases end up costing the taxpayers millions of dollars, and many communities are becoming impatient with lengthy legal proceedings. Meanwhile the offender often assumes celebrity status, attracting reporters and television and radio stations throughout the country.

Sentencing

Many Americans are apprehensive about giving serial killers anything but a death sentence. However, not all states carry the death penalty, and sometimes (as in the case of Donald Harvey) offenders will enter into a plea bargain to avoid the sentence of death. Indeterminate sentencing, whereby the offender receives a range of years in prison, is occasionally passed down by the judge. In some cases offenders will serve their multiple convictions concurrently, which means, for example, that 180 years in prison for six murders actually becomes 30 years plus time off for good behavior. Some offenders are given life in prison with no possibility of parole. It is unlikely that a serial or mass murderer, once convicted and incarcerated, will ever be free again. Some offenders, such as Edmund Kemper and Charles Manson, do receive periodic parole hearings, but these hearings become little more than a legal formality. No parole board is likely to take the risk of releasing a convicted mass killer back into society.

Although offenders convicted of serial murders are not paroled, some other types of murderers are. Those offenders presently in prison for violent crimes who, if paroled, will eventually go on to become serial offenders are often impossible to identify. We generally cannot incarcerate people for crimes they have yet to commit. The closest we have come to this is through the habitual-offender classification, which involves a person who has been convicted of three or more felonies. Such offenders are considered to be likely candidates for committing future crimes and are given extended sentences in some states. Selective incapacitation (incarcerating chronic offenders for longer periods of time than other offenders) may affect serial-murder rates by unknowingly containing potential offenders. Court records are replete with the names of offenders incarcerated for murder(s) who served time and were then released into the community, where they killed again and again.

In 1939, Louise Peete, convicted of murder, was paroled only to become involved in the murders of several more victims. A similar situation occurred with George Fitzsimmons, who was institutionalized for killing his parents. Upon his early release to his aunt and uncle, he took out insurance policies on them and then stabbed them to death. Frederick Wood had served 17 years in Clinton State Prison for second-degree murder. Following his release, he went on a killing spree, and, upon his next arrest, confessed to five more murders. Another killer, Richard Marquette, was paroled after 12 years for the mutilation murder of a woman. He went on to decapitate and mutilate at least two more women before he was apprehended a second time (Brian, 1986).

This does not mean that most people who commit murder and serve time in prison are likely to kill again after their release. It does suggest, however, that some violent offenders never should be released.

Capital Punishment

Many proponents of the death penalty argue that punishment for crimes should be gauged according to the seriousness of the criminal offense. The harshest penalty then should be reserved for the worst crimes. Modern classical thinkers also point out that capital punishment stands as the last resort to deter people from committing particularly heinous crimes. Obviously someone who is already serving a life sentence with no chance of parole has little to lose by killing a correctional officer or another inmate. However, certain offenders might be less inclined to kill witnesses if they knew a death sentence would likely be imposed. In addition, supporters of the death penalty believe that offenders such as serial killers are so dangerous to other human beings that executing them presents the safest way of protecting society. Others argue, from an economic perspective, that maintaining offenders in prison for life is inevitably much more expensive than executing them.

Victims' rights groups have flourished in the past several years. Some have become particularly outspoken regarding the demise of the usually forgotten victim. The courts are asked to consider, in several states, victim impact statements outlining the devastation of physical, emotional, and financial hardships the victim has suffered. Victims seek restitution, compensation, and a sense of justice. Frank Carrington (1978) observed in the introduction of his book, *Neither Cruel nor Unusual:*

> This book is written from the point of the proponents. It is not objective. It is a defense of the death penalty. In a prior book, *The Victims,* I took the position that it is high time that the rights of the victims of crime were recognized in our criminal justice system. No where is this more true than in the area of capital punishment. Richard Franklin Speck is today contentedly watching television in an Illinois penitentiary at the taxpayers' expense. The eight students whom he murdered have been in their graves for ten years, all but forgotten (p. 14). [Author's note: Speck has since died in prison.]

Efforts are being made by victim coalitions to strike a blow for victims' rights. It seems that the criminal has been afforded all the rights; these groups say that now it is time to create a sense of legal and moral balance. People experience a myriad of emotions once they become victims of crime or their families become victims, especially murdered victims. Revenge, hatred, anger, depression, and anxiety become moving forces in victims' lives and have made stalwart retributionists out of some formerly indifferent people.

Opponents to the death penalty are just as vocal and adamant that state-sponsored executions must never be accepted as a course of punitive action. Indeed, it is argued that adopting capital punishment as a method of expressing social vengeance unalterably impedes our moral progress. Legal scholars, such as Charles Black (1974), argue that arbitrary discretion is found in every case that leads to the chair. In other words, given the same crime of murder, not all offenders sentenced to death will stand the same chance of being executed. Such discretionary factors include race, gender, age, and IQ of the offender.

In the case of Paula Cooper, a black 15-year-old girl in Gary, Indiana, who stabbed an elderly white Bible teacher 33 times, great debates began, and national attention was focused on her death sentence. Even Pope Paul VI sent a message from Rome to intercede on her behalf. Eventually, in 1989, the Indiana Supreme Court removed her from death row. We have decided that people are just too young to be executed for crimes committed at 15. "When a nation does violence to human beings, by conducting wars or executing criminals, it incites its citizens to more criminal violence than they would otherwise commit . . . the state can make violence the coin of its own realm" (Wilkes, 1987, pp. 27–28).

Brian (1986) conducted interviews with some of the country's most outspoken and respected opponents to the death penalty. Psychiatrist Karl Menninger, philosopher Hugo Bedau, and sociologist Michael L. Radalet each point out various problems with a pro-capital-punishment stance: For example, it discriminates against minorities; innocent people are sometimes mistakenly executed; in our current "pick and choose" mentality there appears no rational reasoning in selecting those who should be put to death and those who should be allowed to live; and executions constitute cruel and unusual punishment (Ch. 22). Jeffrey J. Daughtery, 33, was electrocuted in Florida State Prison in November 1988. In his final statement he criticized the legal system by stating, "I hope with all my heart I will be the last sacrificial lamb of a system that is not just, and all these people know it is not just. The executions serve no purpose." Daughtery had been involved in the serial murders of four young women. In 1996, Utah executed a murderer by firing squad. The last time Utah had used the firing squad was approximately 20 years ago, when it brought back capital punishment by executing Gary Gilmore. In the 1996 execution the condemned man had hoped that by choosing the firing squad over lethal injection people around the nation would be reminded again of the brutality of the death penalty.

Black (1974) expounded on cruelty in capital punishment:

> When we turn from the two usual arguments in favor of capital punishment—retribution and deterrence—to the other side, we find, above all, that the cruelty of it is what its opponents hate—the cruelty of death, the cruelty of the manner of death, the cruelty of waiting for death, and the cruelty to the innocent persons attached by affection to the condemned—unless of course, he has no relatives and no friends, a fairly common condition on death row (p. 27).

In the matter of serial killers, it seems that people are overwhelmingly in favor of execution. In a sense, it has become a numbers game: The more victims an offender kills, the more people are willing to accept execution as the "best" choice in sentencing. The more victims involved, the more intense is the media coverage. It is not surprising, then, that since the early sixties, when serial killers began to appear in larger numbers, the general public has been increasingly turning a deaf ear to objections regarding capital punishment. California, for example, which has experienced a proliferation of mass murders, has a special provision for such offenders: In cases of multiple homicides, offenders can be sentenced to death or life in prison without eligibility of parole. Most states appear to use both of these sentences to handle special cases of multiple killings. Consequently, most serial killers in prison today will never have the opportunity to be free again.

Because of the relative rarity of serial-murder cases and the accompanying publicity, there exists a much smaller risk of racial discrimination involving cases of capital punishment. Similarly, it would be extremely unlikely for an innocent person to be executed for seven or eight murders. The issue of intelligence and competency is negated by the fact that most serial offenders are of at least normal, if not above-average, intelligence. Rarely are they found to be insane or incompetent. Consequently, when we are faced with the serial killings of dozens of children, even some people who generally oppose capital punishment agree that exceptions are necessary.

Few people have many qualms about executing an offender who has murdered 30 young women. However, one seldom finds such a display of revelry as occurred when Ted Bundy was electrocuted. One anonymous proponent of capital punishment for mass killers wrote the following verse:

to a mass murderer

You know the Judge can send you up
for your remaining years,
And so I send this card to you
to banish all your fears;
No life in prison awaits you, pal.
You won't be rotting there;
The legislators changed the law—
They're bringing back the Chair.

We execute in the name of justice, for revenge, for punishment, for protection, to reduce recidivism, and a host of other often-emotional reasons. These reasons seem to become clearer when we are faced with a case of multiple homicide. Aside from the moral and philosophical issues surrounding the death sentence, if American society is going to use capital punishment, then serial offenders, who are by far the most dangerous offenders, should be first to qualify for execution. If capital punishment is not to be used, then we must ensure that serial killers remain securely confined.

The following statements were made by inmates of Pendleton, a maximum-security prison in Indiana. Some of the offenders were serving time for single homicides, robberies, or drug-related crimes. They were asked the question: What should we do with serial killers? The inmates responded:

1. "I feel that a counseling and treatment program could be established if necessary. If this does not help, then maybe we should go back to electroshock treatments and start from the beginning."
2. "The question was raised, are serial murderers treatable? I believe that more experience is needed in both medical and psychology fields before the question can be truthfully answered. As it stands now, I am not in favor of capital punishment, but I don't believe in keeping a person locked up for life either. Maybe, just maybe, there is some way to make use of these people that will please both society and the trade unions. Maybe there are certain kinds of people, certain environments that they can safely be useful to. We should also answer the questions brought about by serial killing. Can [serial killers'] thoughts and feelings be changed? When the questions are asked, we must stay away from socially acceptable answers and deal only with the realistic answers and act on them."
3. "I think the serial killers should be given the opportunity to live, but they should be given this opportunity in a cell locked up for the rest of their life. What I am saying is, lock them up and put the key in the river."

4. "A serial killer is a person with strong emotional instabilities. I am not saying they're not intelligent, but deranged in the sense of perception of rights and wrongs."
5. "These people perform the most hideous acts on human beings possible. I don't think they should ever be released back into society. A person that ever possesses or has possessed such behaviors, can never be trusted. I know you should try, but is it worth the expense of possibly more victims? I say, hell no."
6. "As far as what to do with them goes, I feel they should be studied. Researched for as long as it is deemed helpful to resolving the problems. Do you kill them after this? I should say no, but what good are they to society? I don't believe in capital punishment, but I am leery of these types of persons. As long as it's affordable and feasible, they should be housed in institutions. But one day we will have to discover the way to cure them or in the end kill them."
7. "They are a menace to society. A touchy decision to make on what should be done. But research is my main idea through dealing with these types of individuals . . . study rather than execute."

There is much we could learn about serial killers by studying those now incarcerated. We have already grouped some sex offenders into special programs, often in state hospitals, where they can receive treatment and be studied at the same time.

By creating regional centers designed to accommodate limited numbers of serial offenders, both researchers and law enforcement alike could benefit. Such an arrangement, however, would require federal funding, the consent of offenders, and extensive planning and interagency coordination. In the meantime, serial offenders can almost routinely expect a death sentence or life in prison without parole.

Treatment

In seeking to interview a serial offender who had murdered between 10 and 12 teenagers and children, your author received a personal letter from the warden attempting to explain why such a visit would be unwise. In part, the letter stated: "To permit such a visit would reinforce the inmate's notoriety. It does not assist nor encourage him to become a law-abiding individual and countermands our desire to ultimately integrate him into an open population setting within an institution" (author's files, November 1988).

Implicit in this statement is the assertion that a serial killer can be viewed as a candidate for some form of rehabilitation, even if it is enough to allow him or her to integrate with other inmates. Also implicit is the notion that some form of therapy can assist the offender by increasing his or her willingness to be law-abiding. One usually does not think of serial killers in these terms. Rather, it generally becomes the aim of many to have the offender executed or permanently incarcerated. No treatment strategies are discussed as part of the sentence. Once the offender enters prison, he or she is, for all intents and purposes, forever removed from normal society. Prisons are not managed or operated in such a manner that they are able to provide specialized services.

Dr. Samuel Yochelson, a psychiatrist, served as project director for the Program for the Investigation of Criminal Behavior, funded by the National Institutes of Health. Half of his subjects were psychiatric patients, and the remainder came from the courts and other agencies:

> To his consternation, he found that after several years of intensive treatment, in which they gained many insights, his criminal patients were still committing crimes. However, the crimes were now more sophisticated, and the insights they gained were being used to excuse what they did. Insight became "incite." In following the lead of the therapists, the criminal discovered even more people against whom he was incited. The criminal became skillful in seizing upon any adversity in his life and blaming it for his criminality. Traditional therapy became just one more criminal enterprise. The efforts to help him were exploited by the criminal to make himself look good and to substantiate his view of himself and of the outside world (Samenow, 1978, p. 17).

Treatment, however, may provide researchers opportunities to explore facets of the murdering mind that have yet to be examined. Certainly the prognosis for rehabilitation is not good. It is unrealistic to believe that the psychological complexity of a repetitive killer might ever be completely dismantled.

Considerable work has been conducted in the area of sex-offender research, providing some insight into "lust" killers and the prognosis of treatability. Dr. Liebert (1985), who served as a consulting psychiatrist on the Green River task force, the Atlanta children's murder task force, and the "Ted" (Bundy) task force, Washington, noted:

> The lust murderer has primitive personality abnormalities making him incapable of normal intimacy. . . . Lust murderers may be able to maintain effective facades as impostors, imitating normal people, but they are not normal enough to tolerate the intensive bonding demands for meaningful psychotherapy. . . . Lust murder represents the extreme sadomasochistic and sociopathic end of the Borderline-Narcissistic Personality Disorder Spectrum—consequently, the least treatable part of the spectrum (1985, p. 197).

Our society's continued frustration in dealing with dangerous sex offenders has led to a growing ostracism of these people. In one case, a convicted child molester with an extended history of sexual assaults was ordered by the courts to post a large sign on his door that read "Dangerous Sex Offender—No Children Allowed." Unfortunately, although the intent may be good, such an approach will do little to deter someone who wishes to act out his or her deviant sexual fantasies.

Future Issues and Research

Several issues, focal concerns, and areas of research currently need attention as we explore the phenomenon of serial murder. Some specific needs are:

1. Increased interaction and involvement between academicians and law enforcement in the form of seminars and workshops.
2. Increased cooperation between law enforcement agencies to improve the circulation of data regarding violent offenders.
3. Increased training of local and state law enforcement personnel in respect to serial murder and scientific profiling.
4. Increased empirical research into all facets of serial murder to further our understanding of the offenders and victims.
5. To debunk and challenge many of the myths and stereotypes that surround serial murderers and their victims.
6. To generate an acceptable operational definition of serial murder that will inevitably reduce confusion among governmental and private agencies.
7. To explore improving methodological issues in data collection and analysis of multiple-homicide offenders.
8. To examine prevention strategies using a team of experts, including law enforcement; social services; and medical, psychiatric, and academic personnel.
9. To create public-awareness programs that filter information in a rational and responsible manner.
10. To allow for greater accessibility to incarcerated serial killers through the establishment of special research programs and projects.
11. To establish projects funded by the federal government specifically for the advancement of multiple-homicide research.

CLOSING THOUGHTS

Maxfield (1989), in his examination of homicide categories, stated: "Certain types of homicides are as amenable to prevention as are the events and circumstances with which they are associated. . . . If propensity to commit violent crimes follows certain patterns, intervention at early stages may truncate a criminal career" (p. 29). His conclusions are based on drug-related homicides, street gangs, and conflict-related murders—but is it possible to create a prevention strategy for serial murder? Currently, we see little hope either of deterring the adult serial offender or of protecting the potential victim. However, members of various communities are singling out what they feel facilitates and stimulates serial offenders. Some groups have increased their war on pornography, alcohol, and drugs, believing that curtailing such vices will inevitably reduce violent criminal behavior. Others are beginning to realize the vulnerability of certain people identified as potential victims. For example, the United States has over 15,000 nursing homes that provide a wide range of quality care. Patient care and safety are growing concerns as more cases of "mercy killing" and angel-of-death attacks begin to surface. Much improved legislation is necessary if we are to protect the elderly and sick.

We must also become more aware of people who create emergencies in order to be rescuers, such as those who work as firefighters and set fires or work as nurses and poison patients. Such people create the opportunities to live out their hero fantasies. One glaring example is the case of the fire investigator in California connected to a string of arson fires throughout the state. Whenever the offender attended an arson investigation conference, he would take advantage of the opportunity to set fires. He became legendary in his uncanny ability to assist in the investigations and quickly ascertain the fires' points of origin. California suffered millions of dollars lost in property damage and dozens of injuries. At the time of this writing he has been convicted of several counts of homicide connected to arson fires. These offenders feel so inadequate that they are willing to jeopardize lives in order to be recognized. Although such people are relatively rare in professions like fire fighting and nursing, it would seem advisable for such professions to implement and adhere to sound psychological testing and screening of potential employees.

Of course, every person should use general caution in dealing with strangers and reduce his or her own vulnerability by decreasing unnecessary risk-taking. Walking or jogging alone, hitchhiking, or giving rides to total strangers, allowing strangers into one's home—all these activities increase risk potential.

The issue of prevention is really twofold. On one hand, we are trying to detect, apprehend, and incarcerate serial offenders and figure out ways to protect ourselves; on the other hand, we want to identify strategies to prevent individuals from becoming serial killers. People sometimes ask: What is the single most important recommendation that should be made from what we currently know about serial murder and our efforts to deter the phenomenon? Our knowledge is limited, but from the available data, *reducing violence in the home appears to be the most significant action we can take to affect the circle of violence outside our homes.* This would include reduction/eradication of all forms of child abuse, including neglect, both physical and emotional. It would include reduction/eradication of spouse abuse and a restabilization of the family unit. It would require less divorce and increased bonding between parents and children. It would require parents taking parenting much more seriously. Someone once said that no success can compensate for failure in the home and that the greatest work we will ever do will be within the walls of our own homes. There is more truth to this statement than we realize. Parenting by instinct simply does not work. Just because people are able to reproduce does not make them fit parents. Effective parenting requires time, commitment, and patience. Your author's wish list would include a requirement that students in junior high school, high school, and in colleges and universities all be required to take parenting classes whether or not they plan on becoming parents. We all deal with children and as the old African saying goes: "It takes a village to raise a child." Our society requires a driver's license in order to drive motorized vehicles. So too, we should be required to achieve a certain level of understanding of the requisites of fundamental parenting.

However, a solid, happy home does not guarantee the absence of later violence. Nor does your author suggest that parents are wholly responsible for the behavior of their children, but, indeed, parents represent a vital part of the puzzle. *We must remember, however, that children may often forget what we, as adults, say or do to them, but children never forget how we make them feel.* If we can alter how people feel about themselves—increase their self-esteem—we might be able to alter how they will feel and respond to others. These recommendations have no particular novelty or originality and may appear idealistic, but they are nonetheless timely. It appears much easier to build hospitals to care for the tens of thousands who die every year of alcoholism, tobacco-related diseases, and diseases caused by pollutants than it does to address the more chronic social ills of our society.

The need for more prisons is also a harbinger of things to come. For example, California's largest growth industry is criminal justice. Billions of dollars are allocated every fiscal year. California has the largest number of persons incarcerated in the entire world. California also has the world's largest population of female offenders (Chowchilla) as well as the largest institution (Atascadero) for the criminally insane. Although society cannot excuse those who willfully commit crimes, we must also be cognizant of the fact that many offenders have been victims too. The cycle of violence becomes perpetual. The roots of victimization run deeply into our social structure and will only go deeper if we continue to ignore the needs of the family.

References

Abraham, S. (1984). *Children in the Cross-Fire: The Tragedy of Parental Kidnapping.* New York: Atheneum.

Abrahamsen, D. (1973). *The Murdering Mind.* New York: Harper and Row.

———. (1985). *Confessions of Son of Sam.* New York: Columbia University Press.

Adler, F. (1975). *Sisters in Crime: The Rise of the New Female Criminal.* New York: McGraw-Hill.

Aichorn, A. (1934). *Wayward Youth.* New York: Viking Press.

Alexander, S. (1983). *Nutcracker: Money, Madness, Murder: A Family Album.* New York: Dell.

Allen, T. (1988, November 13). Portrait of a serial killer. *Statesman Journal.*

Allen, W. (1976). *Starkweather.* Boston: Houghton Mifflin.

American Psychiatric Association. (1988). *Diagnostic and Statistical Manual of Mental Disorders* (3rd ed., revised). Washington, D.C.

———. (1994). *Diagnostic and Statistical Manual of Mental Disorders* (4th ed.). Washington, DC.

Associated Press. (1989). Mass grave found in Mexico. New York. April 11, 1989.

Athens, L. H. (1980). *Violent Criminal Acts and Actors.* Cambridge, MA: Routledge and Kegan Paul.

Bandura, A. (1973). *Aggression.* Englewood Cliffs, NJ: Prentice-Hall.

———. (1974). Behavior theory and the models of man. *American Psychologist,* 29, 861–862.

Bandura, A., and R. H. Walters. (1963). *Social Learning and Personality Development.* New York: Holt, Rinehart and Winston.

Bard, M., and D. Sangrey. (1986). *The Crime Victim's Book* (2nd ed.). New York: Brunner Mazel.

Barnes, B. (1986). FBI specialist. *Atlanta Journal and Constitution,* pp. 1, 7a.

Bartol, C. R., and A. M. Bartol. (1986). *Criminal Behavior: A Psychosocial Approach*. Englewood Cliffs, NJ: Prentice-Hall.

———. (1995). *Criminal Behavior: A Psychosocial Approach* (4th ed.). Englewood Cliffs, NJ: Prentice-Hall.

Baumann, E. (1987, October 12). When demons preyed. *Chicago Tribune*, pp. 1–2.

Becker, H. (1963). *Outsiders: Studies in the Sociology of Deviance*. New York: Macmillan, p. 9.

Bensing, R. C., and O. Schroeder, Jr. (1960). *Homicide in an Urban Community*. Springfield, IL: Charles C Thomas.

Berkow, R. (1977). *The Merck Manual* (13th ed.). Rahway, NJ: Merck, Sharp and Dohme Research Laboratories.

Berkowitz, L., and J. Macaulay (1971, June). The contagion of criminal violence. *Sociometry*, 34, 238–260.

Bierer, J. (1976). Love-making—An act of murder. *International Journal of Social Psychiatry*, 22(3), 197–199.

Black, C. (1974). Capital punishment. In *The Inevitability of Caprice and Mistake*. New York: Norton.

———. (1980). Objections to S. 1382, a bill to establish rational criteria for the imposition of capital punishment. *Crime and Delinquency*, 26, 441–453.

Blackburn, R. (1971). Personality types among abnormal homicides. *British Journal of Criminology*, 11.

Blau, J. R., and P. M. Blau. (1982, February). The cost of inequality: Metropolitan structure and violent crime. *American Sociological Review*, 47, 114–129.

Boar, R., and N. Blundell. (1983). *The World's Most Infamous Murders*. New York: Simon and Schuster.

Brian, D. (1986). *Murderers Die*. New York: St. Martin's Press.

Briar, S., and I. Piliavin. (1965). Delinquency, situational inducements and commitment to conformity. *Social Problems*, 13, 35–45.

Brodsky, S. L. (Ed.). (1973). *Psychologists in the Criminal Justice System*. Urbana, IL: University of Illinois Press.

Brooks, P. R., M. J. Devine, T. J. Green, B. L. Hart, and M. D. Moore. (1987, June). Serial murder: A criminal justice response. *Police Chief*, 40–44.

Brophy, J. (1966). *The Meaning of Murder*. New York: Thomas Y. Crowell.

Brown, S. E. (1984). Social class, child maltreatment, and delinquent behavior. *Criminology*, 22(2), 259–278.

Brownmiller, S. (1975). *Against Our Will: Men, Women and Rape*. New York: Simon and Schuster.

Bruch, H. (1967). Mass murder: The Wagner case. *American Journal of Psychiatry*, 124(5), 693–698.

Bugliosi, V. (1974). *Helter Skelter*. New York: Norton.

Cameron, D., and E. Frazer. (1987). *The Lust to Kill*. New York: New York University Press.

Canter, D. (1994). *Criminal Shadows*. London: Harper Collins.

———. (2000). Offender profiling and criminal differentiation. *Legal and Criminological Psychology*, 5, 23–46.

Canter, D., C. Missen, and S. Hodge. (1997). Are serial killers special? *Policing Today*.

Canter, D., D. Hughes, and S. Kirby. (1998). Pedophilia: Pathology, criminality, or both? The development of a multivariate model of offence behavior in child sexual abuse. *Journal of Forensic Psychiatry*, 9, 532–555.

Canter D. V., and L. J. Alison. (2000). Profiling rape and murder. (*Offender Profiling* series, Vol. V). Aldershot: Dartmouth.

Capote, T. (1965). *In Cold Blood*. New York: Random House.

Caputi, J. (1987). *The Age of Sex Crime*. Bowling Green, OH: Bowling Green State University, Popular Press.

———. (1989). The sexual politics of murder. *Gender and Society*, 3(4), 437–456.

———. (1990). The new founding fathers: The lure and lore of the serial killer in contemporary culture. *Journal of American Culture,* 13(3), 1–12.

Carr, C. (1994). *The Alienist.* New York: Random House.

Carrington, F. (1978). *Neither Cruel nor Unusual.* Westport, CT: Arlington House.

Cavanagh, K., and R. E. MacKay. (1991). Violent crime analysis section. *RCMP Gazette,* 53(1), 5–7.

Chapman, J. (1980). *Economic Realities and the Female Offender.* Lexington, MA: Lexington Books.

Charny, I. W. (1980). A contribution to the psychology of genocide: Sacrificing others to the death we fear ourselves. *Israel Yearbook on Human Rights,* 90, 90–108.

———. (1982). *How Can We Commit The Unthinkable?* Boulder, CO: Westview Press.

Cheney, M. (1976). *The Co-Ed Killer.* New York: Walker.

Cleary, S., and J. Luxenburg. (1993, October). Serial murderers: Common background characteristics and their contribution to causation. Paper presented at the annual meeting of the American Society of Criminology, Miami, FL.

Cleckley, H. (1976). *The Mask of Sanity* (5th ed.). St. Louis, MO: Mosby.

Clinard, M. B., and R. Quinney. (1986). *Criminal Behavior Systems: A Typology* (2nd ed.). Cincinnati, OH: Anderson.

Cline, V. (1990). Privately published monograph, Department of Psychology, University of Utah, Salt Lake City.

CNN. (1993). *Murder by Number.* Two-hour documentary on the phenomenon of serial murder.

Cole, R. (1998). Prosecutors say women seduced, poisoned elderly men for money. Associated Press. January 10.

Coons, P. M. (1988, January 5). LaRue D. Carter Memorial Hospital, personal memo to author.

Copson, G. (1995). Coals to newcastle? Part 1: A study of offender profiling (paper 7). London: Police Research Group Special Interest Series, Home Office.

Corder, B. F., B. C. Ball, T. M. Haizlip, et al. (1976). Adolescent parricide: A comparison with other adolescent murder. *American Journal of Psychiatry,* 133, 957–961.

Cormier, B. M., C. C. J. Boyer, R. Boyer, and G. Mersereau. (1972). The psychodynamics of homicide committed in a semispecific relationship. *Canadian Journal of Criminology and Corrections,* 14, 335–344.

Cullen, R. (1993). *The Killer Department.* New York: Pantheon Books.

Cullen, T. (1977). *The Mild Murderer.* Boston: Houghton Mifflin.

Dahmer, L. (1994). *A Father's Story.* London: Little, Brown.

Daly, M., and M. Wilson. (1988). *Homicide.* New York: Aldine de Gruyter.

Daniels, S. (1989). Satanic beliefs, criminal actions. *The Training Key,* International Association of Chiefs of Police, 390.

Danto, B. (1982). A psychiatric view of those who kill. In J. Bruhns, K. Bruhns, and H. Austin (Eds.), *The Human Side of Homicide.* New York: Columbia University Press, pp. 3–20.

Daubert v. *Merrill Dow Pharmaceuticals, Inc.,* 113 S. Ct. 2786 (1993).

Dean, A. L., M. M. Malik, W. Richards, and S. A. Stringer. (1986). Effects of parental maltreatment on children's conceptions of interpersonal relationships. *Developmental Psychology,* 22(5), 617–626.

Deming, R. (1977). *Women: The New Criminals.* Nashville, TN: Thomas Nelson.

De River, J. P. (1949). *The Sexual Criminal.* Springfield, IL: Charles C Thomas.

Dettlinger, C. (1983). *The List.* Atlanta, GA: Philmay Enterprises.

De Young, M. (1982). *The Sexual Victimization of Children*. Jefferson, NC: McFarland, p. 125.

Dietz, P. (1986). Mass, serial and sensational homicide. *Bulletin of the New England Medical Society,* 62, 477–491.

———. (1994). To Kill and Kill Again. Optomen Television: London, England.

Dodd, N. J. (1998). Applying psychology to the reduction of insurance claim fraud. *Insurance Trends,* 18, 11–16.

Doerner, W. G. (1975, May). A regional analysis of homicide rates in the United States. *Criminology,* 13, 90–101.

Doerner W. G., and S. Lab. (1995). *Victimology.* Cincinnati, OH: Anderson.

Doney, R. H. (1990). The aftermath of the Yorkshire Ripper: The response of the United Kingdom police service. In S. A. Egger (Ed.), *Serial Murder: An Elusive Phenomenon*. New York: Praeger, pp. 95–112.

Dostoyevsky, F. (1962). *The House of the Dead*. London: Dent.

Douglas, J., and Olshaker, M. (1999). *The Anatomy of Motive.* New York: Scribner.

Drukteinis, A. M. (1992). Serial murder: The heart of darkness. *Psychiatric Annals,* 22, 532–538.

Dugdale, R. (1910). *The Jukes.* New York: Putnam.

Durham v. *United States,* 214 F. 2d 862 (D.C. Cir. 1954).

Dutton, D. G., and S. D. Hart. (1992). Evidence for long-term, specific effects of childhood abuse and neglect on criminal behavior in men. *International Journal of Offender Therapy and Comparative Criminology,* 36(2).

Egger, K. (1999). Preliminary database on serial killers from 1900–1999. In S. Egger (2001), *The Killers Among Us: An Examination of Serial Murder and Its Investigation* (2nd. ed.). Upper Saddle River, NJ: Prentice-Hall.

Egger, S. A. (1984). A working definition of serial murder and the reduction of linkage blindness. *Journal of Police Science and Administration,* 12, 348–357.

———. (1985). Serial murder and the law enforcement response. Unpublished dissertation, College of Criminal Justice, Sam Houston State University, Huntsville, TX.

———. (1986). Utility of the case study approach to serial murder research. Paper presented at the 1986 annual meetings of the American Society of Criminology, Atlanta, GA.

———. (1990). *Serial Murder: An Elusive Phenomenon*. New York: Praeger.

———. (2001). *The Killers Among Us: An Examination of Serial Murder and Its Investigation*. Upper Saddle River, NJ: Prentice-Hall.

Eisler, R. (1951). *Man into Wolf.* New York: Greenwood Press.

Eitzen, D. S., and D. A. Timmer. (1985). *Criminology.* New York: Wiley.

Ellis, A., and J. Gullo. (1971). *Murder and Assassination*. New York: Lyle Stuart.

Ellis, B. E. (1991). *American Psycho.* New York: Vintage Books.

Epstein, S. (1995). The new mythic monster. In J. Ferrell and C. Sanders (Eds.), *Cultural Criminology.* Boston, MA: Northeastern Press, pp. 66–79.

Estabrook, A. (1916). *The Jukes in 1915*. Washington, DC: Carnegie Institute of Washington.

Eth, S., and R. S. Pynoos. (1985). Developmental perspective on psychic trauma in childhood. In C. R. Figley (Ed.), *Trauma and Its Wake: The Study and Treatment of Post-Traumatic Stress Disorder.* New York: Brunner and Mazel, pp. 36–52.

Eysenck, H. J. (1973). *The Inequality of Man*. San Diego, CA: Edits Publishers.

———. (1977). *Crime and Personality* (2nd ed.). London: Routledge and Kegan Paul.

Farrington, D.P. (Ed.). (1998). *Psychological Explanations of Crime.* Aldershot: Ashgate.

Federal Bureau of Investigation (2000). *Crime in the U.S., Uniform Crime Reports.* Washington, DC: U.S. Department of Justice, U.S. Government Printing Office.

———. (1984a). *Crime in the U.S., Uniform Crime Reports.* Washington, DC: U.S. Department of Justice, U.S. Government Printing Office.

———. (1984b). *Report to the Nation on Crime and Justice.* Washington, DC: FBI Statistical Department, United States Department of Justice.

———. (1985). *FBI Law Enforcement Bulletin Crime Scene and Profile Characteristics of Organized and Disorganized Murderers,* Vol. 54, pp. 18–25.

———. (1988). *Crime in the U.S. Adapted from the Uniform Crime Reports.* Washington, DC: U.S. Department of Justice, U.S. Government Printing Office.

———. (1993). *Crime in the U.S. Adapted from the Uniform Crime Reports.* Washington, DC: U.S. Department of Justice, U.S. Government Printing Office.

———. (1995). *Crime in the U.S. Adapted from Uniform Crime Reports.* Washington, DC: U.S. Department of Justice, U.S. Government Printing Office.

Felthous, A. (1980). Aggression against cats, dogs and people. *Child Psychiatry and Human Development,* 10(3), 169–177.

Felthous, A., and S. Kellert. (1985). In America's abuse problem. *ASPCA Animal Watch,* Fall/Winter 1992, p. 10.

Fessenden, F. (2000, April 10). Seething anger has deadly aim. *New York Times,* p. 1.

Fineman, K. R. (1995). A model for the qualitative analysis of child and adult fire deviant behavior. *American Journal of Forensic Psychology,* 13(1).

Finkelhor, D. (1979). *Sexually Victimized Children.* New York: Free Press.

———. (1988). *Nursery Crimes.* Newbury Park, CA: Sage.

Fortune, J. (1934). *The Story of Clyde Barrow and Bonnie Parker.* Dallas, TX: Ranger Press.

Fox, J. A., and J. Levin. (1989). Satanism and mass murders. *Celebrity Plus,* 49–51.

———. (1994). *Overkill: Mass Murder and Serial Killing Exposed.* New York: Plenum Press.

———. (1995). Serial murder: A survey. In T. O'Reilly-Fleming (Ed.), *Serial and Mass Murder: Theory, Research and Policy.* Toronto: Canadian Scholar's Press.

Frank, G. (1966). *The Boston Strangler.* New York: The New American Library.

Franke, D. (1975). *The Torture Doctor.* New York: Hawthorn Books.

Frederick, C. (1981). Violence and disasters: Immediate and long-term consequences. Paper presented at Psychosocial Consequences of Violence Conference, The Hague, April 6–10.

Freeman, L. (1955). *Before I Kill More.* New York: Crown.

Freiberger, K. (1997). Application of prominent typologies to the female serial murderer phenomenon. Master's thesis. Virginia Commonwealth University, Richmond, VA.

Freud, S. (1936). *The Problem of Anxiety.* New York: Norton.

Fromm, E. (1973). *The Anatomy of Human Destructiveness.* New York: Holt, Rinehart and Winston.

Frye v. *United States,* 293 F. (D.C. Cir. 1923).

Gaddis, T. E., and J. O. Long. (1970). *Killer: A Journal of Murder.* New York: Macmillan.

Gallagher, B. J., III. (1987). *The Sociology of Mental Illness* (2nd ed.). Englewood Cliffs, NJ: Prentice-Hall.

Gastil, R. D. (1971, June). Homicide and a regional culture of violence. *American Sociological Review,* 36, 412–427.

Gaute, J. H. H., and R. O'Dell. (1979). *The Murderer's Who's.* New York: Methuen.

Geberth, V. J. (1983). *Practical Homicide Investigation.* New York: Elsevier.

Gebhard, P. H. (1965). *Sex Offenders.* New York: Harper and Row, p. 856.

Gibbs, W. W. (1995, March). Seeking the criminal element. *Scientific American,* 101–107.

Gibson, W. B. (1965). *Murder, The Fine Art.* New York: Grosset and Dunlap.

Gill, E. (1994). Children and animals: A clinician's view. *The Animal's Agenda,* March/April, 20–21.

Glaser, B. G., and A. Strauss. (1967). *The Discovery of Grounded Theory: Strategies for Qualitative Research.* Chicago: Aldine.

Glover, J. D., and D. C. Witham. (1989). The Atlanta serial murders. *Policing,* 5(1), 2–6.

Godwin, J. (1978). *Murder U.S.A.* New York: Random House.

Godwin, G. M. (1999). *Hunting Serial Predators.* CRC Press.

Goffman, E. (1961). *Asylums.* Garden City, NY: Doubleday.

Golden, C., J. Moses Jr., J. Coffman, W. Miller, and F. Strider. (1983). *Clinical Neuropsychology.* New York: Grune and Stratton.

Goodroe, C. (1987, July). Tracking the serial offender. *Law and Order,* 29–33.

Gorby, B. (2000). Serial murder: A cross-national descriptive study. Master's thesis. California State University, Fresno. Fresno, CA.

Gray, G. (1986). Diet, crime and delinquency: A critique. *Nutrition Reviews,* 44, 89–94.

Graysmith, R. (1976). *Zodiac.* New York: Berkeley Books.

Greswell, D. M., and C. Hollin. (1994 Winter). Multiple murder: A review. *The British Journal of Criminology,* 34(1), 1–14.

Grombach, J. V. (1980). *The Great Liquidator.* New York: Doubleday.

Gunn, L. (2000). Serial killers and their victims: An examination of social class. Master's thesis. California State University, Fresno. Fresno, CA.

Guttmacher, M. (1973). *The Mind of the Murderer* (Selected Libraries Reprint Series). New York: Arno Press.

Guze, S. B. (1976). *Criminality and Psychiatric Disorders.* New York: Oxford University Press.

Hafner, H., and W. Boker. (1973). Mentally disordered violent offenders. *Social Psychiatry,* 8, 220–229.

Hagan, F. E. (1986). *Introduction to Criminology: Theories, Methods, and Criminal Behavior.* Chicago: Nelson-Hall.

Hahn, J. K., and H. C. McKenney. (1972). *Legally Sane.* Chicago: Henry Regnery.

Haizlip T., B. F. Corder, and B. C. Ball. (1964). The adolescent murderer. In C. R. Keith (Ed.), *The Violent Adolescent.* New York: Free Press.

Hale, E. (1983, April 18). Startling discoveries shed new light on enigma of multiple personality, *Chicago Tribune,* pp. 1, 5.

Harbort. (2000). In *A. Ulrich Morderisches Mirakel* (Murderous Miracle). Der Spiegl: Germany.

Hare, R., and J. Jutai. (1959/1983). Criminal history of the male psychopath: Some preliminary data. In K. T. Van Dusen and S. A. Mednick (Eds.), *Perspective Studies of Crime and Delinquency.* Boston, MA: Kluwer-Nijhoff, pp. 225–236.

Hare, R. D. (1991). *The Hare Psychopathy Checklist—Revised.* Toronto: Multi-Health Systems.

Harris, T. (1987). *Red Dragon.* New York: Bantam.

———. (1989). *The Silence of the Lambs.* New York: St. Martin's Press.

Hazelwood, R. R., and A. W. Burgess. (1987, September). An introduction to the serial rapist. *FBI Law Enforcement Bulletin,* pp. 16–24.

———. (1989, February). The serial rapist: His characteristics and victims. *FBI Law Enforcement Bulletin,* pp. 18–25.

Hazelwood, R. R., and J. Warren. (1989, January). The serial rapist: His characteristics and victims. *FBI Law Enforcement Bulletin,* pp. 10–17.

Heath, L. (1984, August). Impact of newspaper crime on fear of crime: A multimethodological investigation. *Journal of Personality and Social Psychology.*

Heide, K. (1995). *Why Kids Kill Parents: Child Abuse and Adolescent Homicide.* Thousand Oaks: Sage Publications.

Hellman, D. S., and N. Blackman. (1966). Enuresis, firesetting and cruelty to animals: A triad predictive of adult crime. *The American Journal of Psychiatry,* 122, 1431–1435.

Helpern, M., and B. Knight. (1977). *Autopsy: The Memoirs of Milton Helpern, the World's Greatest Medical Detective.* New York: St. Martin's Press.

Henderson, S. K. (1939). *Psychopathic States.* New York: Norton.

Henn, F. A., M. Herjanic, and R. H. Vanderpearl. (1976). Forensic psychiatry: Diagnosis of criminal responsibility. *Journal of Nervous and Mental Disease,* 162, 423–429.

Hewitt, J. D. (1988). The victim-offender relationship in homicide cases: 1960–1984. *Journal of Criminal Justice,* 16(1), 27–38.

Hickey, E. (1985, March). Serial murderers: Profiles in psychopathology. Paper presented at the annual meeting of the Academy of Criminal Justice Sciences, Las Vegas, NV.

Heckert, D. M., and M. Ferraiolo. (1996). Social constructions of female serial murderers. Paper presented at the annual meeting of the American Society of Criminology, Chicago, IL.

———. (1986, October). The female serial murderer. *Journal of Police and Criminal Psychology,* 2(2), 72–81.

———. (1990a). The etiology of victimization in serial murder. In *Serial Murder: An Elusive Phenomenon.* New York: Praeger, pp. 53–71. Copyright by Steven A. Egger.

———. (1990b). Missing and murdered children in America. In *Helping Crime Victims: Research, Policy, and Practice.* Newbury Park, CA: Sage, pp. 158–185. Copyright by Albert R. Roberts.

———. (1996, January). Preliminary findings in profiling juvenile firesetters. Paper presented at the annual meeting of the California Association of Arson Investigators, Fresno, CA.

———. (1997). *Serial Murderers and Their Victims.* Belmont, CA: Wadsworth.

———. (2000). Application of domestic and stranger stalker-victim profiles. International Security Academy, Tel Aviv, Israel.

Hickey, E., D. Margulies, and J. Oddie. (1999, February). Victim profiling in cases of stalking and obsessional harassment. Paper presented at the American Academy of Forensic Sciences Annual Meeting, Orlando, FL.

Hill, D., and W. Sargent. (1943). A case of matricide. *Lancet,* 244, 526–527.

Hill, D., and P. Williams. (1967). *The Supernatural.* New York: Signet Books.

Hirschi, T. (1969). *Causes of Delinquency.* Berkeley: University of California Press.

Hirst, W. (1982). The amnesic syndrome: Descriptions and explanations. *Psychological Bulletin,* 91, 435–460.

Hoffer, P. C., and N. E. H. Hull. (1981). *Murdering Mothers: Infanticide in England and New England, 1558–1803.* New York: New York University Press.

Hoffman-Bustamante, D. (1973). The nature of female criminality. *Issues in Criminology,* 8, 117–136.

Hollandsworth, S. (1993, May). See no evil. *Texas Monthly,* pp. 92–140.

Holmes, R. M. and Holmes, S. T. (2000). *Mass Murder in the United States.* Upper Saddle River, NJ:Prentice Hall.

Holmes, R. M. (1990). *Profiling Violent Crimes.* Newbury Park, CA: Sage.

Holmes, R. M., and J. DeBurger (1988). *Serial Murder.* Newbury Park, CA: Sage.

Holmes, R., and J. DeBurger. (1985). Profiles in terror: The serial murderer. *Federal Probation.* U.S. Department of Justice.

The Holy Bible. (1979). King James Version, Church of Jesus Christ of Latter-Day Saints, Salt Lake City, UT, pp. 1241–1271.

HBO (1984). *Murder: No Apparent Motive.* Stamford, CT: Vestron Video.

Horney, J. (1978). Menstrual cycles and criminal responsibility. *Law and Human Nature,* 2, 25–36.

Houts, A. C., J. S. Berman, and H. Abramson. (1994). The effectiveness of psychological and pharmacological treatments for nocturnal enuresis. *Journal of Consulting and Clinical Psychology,* 62, 737–745.

Howard, C. (1979). *Zebra: The True Account of the 179 Days of Terror in San Francisco.* New York: Richard Marek.

How many missing kids? (1985, October 7). *Newsweek,* pp. 30–35.

Inciardi, J. A., and A. E. Pottieger (Eds.). (1978). *Violent Crime: Historical and Contemporary Issues* (Vol. 5). Newbury Park, CA: Sage.

Inglis, R. (1978). *Sins of Fathers: A Study of the Physical and Emotional Abuse of Children.* New York: St. Martin's Press.

Jackson, J. (1996 Winter). Computer crimes and criminals. *American Criminal Justice Association Journal,* 57 (1&2), 32–36.

Jackson, J. L., P. van den Eshof, and E. E. de Kleuver. (1994). *Offender Profiling in the Netherlands* (Report NSCR WD94-03). Leiden, The Netherlands: The Netherlands Institute for the Study of Criminality and Law Enforcement.

Jackson, J. L., P. J. van Koppen, and J. C. M. Herbrink. (1993). *Does the Service Meet the Needs? An evaluation of consumer satisfaction with specific profile analysis and investigative advice as offered by the Scientific Research Advisory Unit of the National Criminal Intelligence Division (CRI), The Netherlands* (Report NSCR 93-05). Leiden, The Netherlands: The Netherlands Institute for the Study of Criminality and Law Enforcement.

Jaffe, P., D. Wolfe, S. Wilson, and L. Zak. (1986). Similarities in behavior and social maladjustment among child victims and witnesses to family violence. *American Journal of Orthopsychiatry,* 56, 142–146.

James, P. D., and T. A. Critchley. (1986). *The Maul and the Pear Tree.* New York: Mysterious Press.

Jeffery, C. R. (1993, Spring). *Journal of Criminal Justice Education.* New York: John Jay College.

Jeffery, C. R. (1995, March). Seeking the criminal element, by W. W. Gibbs. *Scientific American,* 101–107.

Jenkins, P. (1988). Myth and murder: The serial killer panic of 1983–85, *Criminal Justice Research Bulletin,* 3(11), 1–7.

———. (1994). *Using Murder: The Social Construction of Serial Homicide.* New York: Aldine de Gruyter.

Jones, A. (1980). *Women Who Kill.* New York: Holt, Rinehart and Winston.

Jones v. *United States,* 103 S. Ct. 3043 1983.

Justice, B., R. Justice, and I. Kraft. (1974). Early warning signs of violence: Is a triad enough? *American Journal of Psychiatry,* 131, 457–459.

Kadish, S. H., and M. G. Paulsen. (1981). *Criminal Law and Its Processes.* pp. 215–216.

Kahaner, L. (1988). *Cults That Kill: Probing the Underworld of Occult Crime.* New York: Warner Books.

Kahn, M. (1971). Murderers who plead insanity: A descriptive factor-analytic study of personality, social, and history variables. *Genetic Psychology Monographs,* 84.

Karmen, A. (1990). *Crime Victims* (2nd ed.). Pacific Grove, CA: Brooks-Cole.

Karmen, A. (1984). *Crime Victims.* Pacific Grove, CA: Brooks-Cole.

Karpman, B. (1954). *The Sexual Offender and His Offenses.* New York: Julian Press.

Katz, J. (1988). *Seductions of Crime: Moral and Sensual Attractions in Doing Evil.* New York: Basic Books.

Keeney B., and K. Heide. (1994). Gender differences in serial murderers: A preliminary analysis. *Journal of Interpersonal Violence,* 9(3), 383–398.

———. (1995). Serial murder: A more accurate and inclusive definition. *International Journal of Offender Therapy and Comparative Criminology,* 39(4).

Keppel, R. D. (1989). *Serial Murder: Future Implications for Police Investigations.* Cincinnati, OH: Anderson.

Kerman, S. L. (1962). *The Newgate Calendar.* New York: Capricorn Books.

Keyes, D. (1986). *Unveiling Claudia: A True Story of Serial Murder.* New York: Bantam Books.

Keyes, E. (1976). *The Michigan Murders.* New York: Simon and Schuster.

King, B. (1996). *Lustmord, The Writings and Artifacts of Murderers.* Burbank, CA: Bloat Publisher.

Kirby, P. (1998). The feminization of serial killing: A gender identity study of male and female serialists in female dominated occupations. Doctoral dissertation. The American University, Washington, DC.

Kirshner, L. (1973). Dissociative reactions: A historical review and clinical study. *Acta Psychiatrica Scandanavica,* 49, 698–711.

Kirwin, B.R. (1997). *The Mad the Bad and the Innocent: The Criminal Mind on Trial.* New York: Little, Brown.

Kluckhohn, C., and H. A. Murray. (1953). Personality formation: The determinants. In C. Kluckhohn, H. Murray, and D. Schneider (Eds.)., *Personality in Nature, Society and Culture.* New York: Knopf, pp. 53–67.

Kocsis, R. N., H. J. Irwin, and A. F. Hayes. (1998). Organized and disorganized behavior syndromes in arsonists: A validation study of a psychological profiling concept. *Psychiatry, Psychology and Law,* 5, 117–130.

Kocsis, R., R. Cooksey, and H. Irwin. (1999). Criminal profiling of offender characteristics from crime behaviors in serial rape offences. (In press).

———. (2000). Criminal profiling of offender characteristics from crime behaviors in australian sexual murders. (In press).

Kramer, E., and A. Iager. (1984). The use of art in assessment of psychotic disorders: Changing perspectives. *Arts in Psychotherapy,* 11(3), 197–201.

Lange, J. E. T., and K. DeWitt, Jr. (1990, February). What the FBI doesn't know about serial killers and why. Paper presented at the Metropolitan Washington Mensa Regional Gathering, Arlington, VA.

Langlois, J. L. (1985). *Belle Gunnes.* Bloomington, IN: Indiana University Press.

Larson, O. N. (Ed.). (1968). *Violence and the Mass Media.* New York: Harper and Row.

LaVey, A. (1969). *The Satanic Bible.* New York: Avon.

Lee, R. A. (1988, July–August). A motive for murder. *Police Times,* 6.

Leibman, F. H. (1989). Serial Murderers: Four case histories. *Federal Probation,* 53, 41–45.

Leith, R. (1983). *The Prostitute Murders.* New York: Pinnacle Books.

Lemert, E. (1951). *Social Pathology.* New York: McGraw–Hill.

Lester, D. (1979). The violent offender. In Hans Touch (Ed.), *Psychology of Crime and Criminal Justice.* New York: Holt, Rinehart and Winston, p. 301. (Citing the National Commission on the Causes and Prevention of Violence, to Establish Justice, to Ensure Domestic Tranquility.) Washington, DC: U.S. Government Printing Office, 1969.

———. (1986). *The Murderer and His Murder.* New York: Ams Press.

Lester, D., and G. Lester. (1975). *Crimes of Passion: Murder and the Murderer.* Chicago: Nelson Hall.

Levin, J., and J. A. Fox (1985). *Mass Murder: The Growing Menace.* New York: Plenum Press.

Lewis, D. O., B. S. Moy, L. D. Jackson, R. Aaronson, N. Restifo, S. Serra, and A. Simos. (1985, October). Biopsychosocial characteristics of children who later murder: A prospective study. American Journal of Psychiatry, 142, 10.

Lewis, D. O. (1998). *Guilty by Reason of Insanity: A Psychiatrist Explores the Minds of Killers.* New York: Fawcett Columbine.

Leyton, E. (1986a). *Hunting Humans.* Toronto: McClelland and Stewart.

———. (1986b). *Compulsive Killers: The Story of Modern Multiple Murder.* New York: New York University Press.

———. (1993). *Sole Survivor.* Toronto: McClelland-Bantam.

———. (1999). In Lester Kurtz (Ed.), *The Encyclopedia of Violence, Peace and Conflict.* Three volumes. New York: Academic Press, 1999.

Liebert, J. A. (1985, December). Contributions of psychiatric consultation in the investigation of serial murder. *International Journal of Offender Therapy and Cooperative Criminology,* 29(3), 187–200.

Lifton, R. (1982, November). Medicalized killing in Auschwitz. *Psychiatry,* 45(4), 283–297.

Lindsey, R. (1984, January 21). Killers who roam the U.S. *New York Times,* pp. 1, 7.

Linedecker, C. L. (1980). *The Man Who Killed Boys.* New York: St. Martin's Press.

———. (1987). *Thrill Killers.* New York: Paperjacks.

Linnoila, M., M. Virkkunen, M. Scheinin, A. Nuutila, R. Rimon, and F. K. Goodwin. (1983). Low cerebrospinal fluid 5-hydroxyindole acetic acid concentration differentiates impulsive from non-impulsive violent behavior. *Life Sciences,* 33, 2609–2614.

Livsey, C. (1980). *The Manson Women.* New York: Richard Marek.

Locke, J. (1705). Some thoughts concerning education. In *The Works of John Locke in Nine Volumes* (12th ed.). London: C & J Rivington, 1968, 112–114.

Lockwood, R., and G. R. Hodge. (1986). The tangled web of animal abuse: The links between cruelty to animals and human violence. *The Humane Society News* (Summer).

Lockwood, R., and A. Church. (1996). Deadly serious: An FBI perspective on animal cruelty. *Humane Society of the United States* (Fall).

Lockwood, R., and F. Ascione (Eds.). (1998). *Cruelty to Animals and Interpersonal Violence.* West Lafayette, IN: Purdue University Press.

Lombroso, C., and G. Ferrero. (1916). *The Female Offender.* New York: Appleton.

———. (1972). *Criminal Man According to the Classification of Cesare Lombroso.* Montclair, NJ: Patterson Smith, p. 100.

Lourie, R. (1993). *Hunting the Devil.* London: Grafton.

Lunde, D. T. (1976). *Murder and Madness.* San Francisco, CA: San Francisco Book Company.

Maas. P. (1975). *King of the Gypsies.* New York: Viking Press.

MacDonald, J. (1963). The threat to kill. *American Journal of Psychiatry,* 120, 125–130.

Main, V. (1997). The changing image of serial killers in film: A reflection of attitudes toward crime from 1929–1995. Master's thesis. California State University, Fresno, Fresno, California.

Malmquist, C. P. (1971). Premonitory signs of homicidal aggression in juveniles. *American Journal of Psychiatry,* 128, 461–465.

———. (1996). *Homicide: A Psychiatric Perspective.* Washington, DC: American Psychiatric Press.

Marron, K. (1988). *Ritual Abuse.* Toronto: McClelland-Bantam.

Marsh, F. H., and J. Katz (Eds.). (1985). *Biology, Crime, and Ethics: A Study of Biological Explanations for Criminal Behavior.* Cincinnati, OH: Anderson.

Marwick, M. (1970). *Witchcraft and Sorcery.* Baltimore, MD: Penguin Books.

Masters, B. (1986). *Killing for Company.* London: Coronet.

Masters, R. E. L., and E. Lea (1963). *Sex Crimes in History.* New York: Matrix House.

Matthews, J. (1996). *The Eyeball Killer.* New York: Zebra Publishers.

Matza, D. (1964). *Delinquency and Drift.* New York: Wiley.

Maxfield, M. G. (1989, November). Circumstances in supplementary homicide reports: Variety and validity. *Criminology,* 27(4), 671–695.

May, R. (1980). *Sex and Fantasy.* New York: Norton, p. 140.

McCarthy, J. B. (1978). Narcissism and the self in homicidal adolescents. *American Journal of Psychoanalysis,* 38, 19–29.

McDonald, R. R. (1986). *Black Widow.* New York: St. Martin's Press.

McDonald, W. (1970). The victim: A social psychological study of criminal victimization. Unpublished doctoral dissertation. Ann Arbor, MI: University Microfilms.

McLeod, M. (1984). Women against men: An examination of domestic violence based on an analysis of official data and national victimization data. *Justice Quarterly,* 1, 171–193.

Mead, M. (1964). Cultural factors in the cause of pathological homicide. *Bulletin of Menninger Clinic,* 28, 11–22.

Mednick, S., and J. Volavka. (1980). Biology and crime. In N. Morris and M. Tonry (Eds.), *Crime and Justice.* Chicago: University of Chicago Press, pp. 85–159.

Mednick, S., G. William, and B. Hutchings. (1983). Genetic influences in criminal behavior: Evidence from an adoption cohort. In K. Teilmann, V. Dusen, and S. Mednick (Eds.), *Perspective Studies of Crime and Delinquency.* Boston: Kluwer–Nijhoff, pp. 39–57.

Megargee, E. I., and M. J. Bohn, Jr. (1979). *Classifying Criminal Offenders.* Newbury Park, CA: Sage.

Meloy, R. (1988). *The Psychopathic Mind: Origins, Dynamics and Treatment.* London: Jason Aronson.

———. (1993). *Violent Attachments.* New Jersey: Login Bros.

Messner, S., and K. Tardiff. (1986). Economic inequality and levels of homicide: An analysis of urban neighborhoods. *Criminology,* 24, 297–317.

Michaud, S. G., and H. Aynesworth. (1983). *The Only Living Witness: A True Account of Homicidal Insanity.* New York: Linden Press, Simon and Schuster.

Miller, A. (1984). *For Your Own Good.* New York: Farrar, Straus, and Giroux.

Miller, D., and J. Looney. (1974). The prediction of adolescent homicide: Episodic dyscontrol and dehumanization. *American Journal of Psychoanalysis,* 34(3):187–198.

M'Naughten. (1843). 10 Clark and Fin. 200, 210, 8 Eng. Rep 718, 722.

Monahan, J., and G. Geis. (1976). Controlling "dangerous people." *Annals of the American Academy of Political and Social Science,* 423, 142–151.

Monahan, J., and H. Steadman. (1984, September). *Crime and Mental Disorder.* Washington, DC: National Institute of Justice Research in Brief.

Money, J. (1976). Influence of hormones on psychosexual differentiation. *Medical Aspects of Nutrition,* 30, 165.

Money, J., and J. Werlas. (1982). Paraphiliac sexuality and child abuse: The parents. *Journal of Sex and Marital Therapy,* 8, 57–64.

Montgomery, J. E. (1992, February). Organizational survival: Continuity or crisis? Paper presented at the Police Studies Series, Simon Fraser University, Vancouver, British Columbia.

———. (1993). Organizational survival: Continuity or crisis? In M. Layton (Ed.), *Policing in the Global Community: The Challenge of Leadership.* Burnaby, British Columbia: Simon Fraser University, pp. 133–142.

Moser, D., and J. Cohen. (1967). *The Pied Piper of Tucson.* New York: The New American Library.

Mother faces trial in child's death. (1987, June 7). *Atlanta Journal and Constitution.*

Murder: No Apparent Motive. (1980). Home Box Office Undercover Series.

Nash, J. R. (1973). *Bloodletters and Badmen.* New York: M. Evans and Company.

———. (1980). *Murder America.* New York: Simon and Schuster.

———. (1981a). *Almanac of World Crime.* New York: Anchor Press-Doubleday.

———. (1981b). *Look for the Woman.* New York: M. Evans and Company.

———. (1984). *Crime Chronology.* New York: Facts on File.

Nettler, G. (1982). *Killing One Another.* Cincinnati, OH: Anderson.

Neustatter, L. W. (1957). *The Mind of the Murderer.* London: Christopher Johnson.

Newsweek. (1985). The hunt for the emotional rapist. December 16, p. 30.

Ninety-eighth Congress. (1984). Hearing Before the Subcommittee on the Judiciary United States Senate, First Session on Patterns of Murders Committed by One Person, in Large Numbers with No Apparent Rhyme, Reason or Motivation, July 12, 1983. Washington, DC: U.S. Government Printing Office. Serial No. J-98-52.

Norris, J. (1988). *Serial Killers.* New York: Doubleday.

Nunberg, H. (1955). *Principles of Psychoanalysis.* New York: International Universities Press.

O'Brien, D. (1985). *Two of a Kind: The Hillside Stranglers.* New York: New American Library.

Oddie, J. (2000). The prediction of violence in stalkers. Doctoral dissertation. California School of Professional Psychology. Fresno, CA.

Olsen, J. (1972). *Son: A Psychopath and His Victims.* New York: Dell.

———. (1974). *The Man with the Candy.* New York: Simon and Schuster.

Ondrovik, J., and D. Hamilton. (1991). Credibility of victims diagnosed as multiple personality: A case study. *American Journal of Forensic Psychology,* 9, 13–17.

Optomen Television (1994). *To Kill and Kill Again.* A British Television documentary on serial murder broadcast by the Public Broadcasting Service in the United States and internationally.

Orne, M. T., D. F. Dinges, and E. C. Orne. (1984). On the differential diagnosis of multiple personality in the forensic context. *International Journal of Clinical and Experimental Hypnosis,* 32, 118–169.

Ott, J. (1984). The effects of light and radiation on human health and behavior. In L. J. Hippchen (Ed.), *Ecologic-Biochemical Approaches.* New York: Van Nostrand Reinhold, pp. 105–183.

Owen, B. (1998). *In The Mix.* Albany: State University of New York.

Patterson, G. R., B. D. DeBaryshe, and E. Ramsey. (1989). A developmental perspective on antisocial behavior. *American Psychologist,* 44, 329–335.

Pearson, E. (1936). *More Studies in Murder.* London: Arco.

Pearson, P. (1995, October). Behind every successful psychopath, *Saturday Night.* Pp. 50–59.

———. (1997). *When She Was Bad: Violent Women and the Myth of Innocence.* Toronto: Random House Canada.

Peck, M. S. (1983). *People of the Lie.* New York: Simon and Schuster.

Perdue, W., and D. Lester. (1974). Temperamentally suited to kill: The personality of murderers. *Corrective and Social Psychiatry and Journal of Behavioral Technology, Methods, and Theory,* 20.

Peyton, D. (1984, December 16). Henry Lucas was a killer at age 14. *West Virginia Herald-Dispatch,* A5.

Pfeffer, C. (1980). Psychiatric hospital treatment of assaultive homicidal children. *American Journal of Psychotherapy,* 2, 197–207.

Piers, M. W. (1978). *Infanticide.* New York: Norton.

Podolsky, E. (1964). The chemistry of murder. *Pakistan Medical Journal,* 15, 9–14.

Pokorny, A. D. (1965, December). A comparison of homicides in two cities. *Journal of Criminal Law, Criminology and Police Science,* 56, 479–487.

Pollak, O. (1950). *The Criminality of Women.* Philadelphia: University of Pennsylvania Press.

Pollock, P. H. (1995). A case of spree serial murder with suggested diagnostic opinions. *International Journal of Offender Therapy and Comparative Criminology,* 39(3).

Posner, G. L., and J. Ware. (1986). *Mengele.* New York: Dell.

Prentky, R. W., A. W. Burgess, and D. L. Carter. (1986). Victim responses by rapist type: An empirical and clinical analysis. *Journal of Interpersonal Violence,* 1, 73–98.

Price, J. M. and K. A. Dodge. (1989). Peers' contributions to children's social maladjustment. In T. J. Berndt and G. W. Ladd (Eds.), *Peer Relationships in Child Development.* New York: Wiley Press, pp. 341–370.

Prince, M. (1908). *Dissociation of Personality.* New York: Longman, Green.

Purcell, C. (2000). An investigation of paraphilias, lust murder and the case of Jeffrey Dahmer: An integrative theoretical model. Doctoral dissertation. California School of Professional Psychology, Fresno, California.

Purcell, C., and Arrigo, B. (2001). Explaining paraphilias and lust murder: Toward an integrated model. *International Journal of Offender Therapy and Comparative Criminology,* 45(1), 6–31.

Quimby, M. J. (1969). *The Devil's Emissaries.* New York: Barnes.

Rada, R. (1983). Plasma androgens in violent and non-violent sex offenders. *Bulletin of the American Academy of Psychiatry and the Law,* 11, 149–158.

Rada, R. T., D. R. Laws, and R. Kellner. (1976). Plasma testosterone levels in the rapist. *Psychosomatic Medicine,* 38, 257–268.

Raine, A. (1993). *The Psychopathy of Crime.* San Diego, CA: Academic Press.

Rappaport, D. (1988). *Inside Terrorist Organizations.* New York: Columbia University Press.

Reckless, W. (1967). *The Crime Problem.* New York: Appleton Century Crofts.

Reinhardt, J. M. (1960). *The Murderer's Trail of Charles Starkweather.* Springfield, IL: Charles C Thomas.

———. (1962). *The Psychology of Strange Killers.* Springfield, IL: Charles C Thomas.

Reiss, A., Jr. (1980). Victim proneness in repeat victimization by type of crime. In S. Fineberg and A. Reiss, Jr. (Eds.), *Indicators of Crime and Criminal Justice: Quantitative Studies.* Washington, DC: U.S. Department of Justice, pp. 41–54.

Reiss, A. J., and J. A. Roth (Eds.). (1993). *Understanding and Preventing Violence.* Washington, DC: National Academy Press.

Rennie, Y. (1978). *The Search for Criminal Man: A Conceptual History of the Dangerous Offender.* Toronto: Lexington Books.

Resnick, P. (1969). Child murders by parents. *American Journal of Psychiatry,* 126, 325–334.

———.(1970). Murder of the newborn: A psychiatric view of neonaticide. *American Journal of Psychiatry,* 126, 58–63.

Ressler, R. K., et al. (1985). *FBI Law Enforcement Bulletin,* 54, 1–43.

Ressler, R. K., A. W. Burgess, and J. E. Douglas. (1988). *Sexual Homicide.* Lexington, MA: Lexington Books.

Ressler, R. K., and T. Shachtman. (1997). *I Have Lived in the Monster.* New York: St. Martin's.

Revitch, E. (1965). Sex murderer and the potential sex murderer. *Diseases of the Nervous System,* 26, 640–648.

Revitch, E., and L. B. Schlesinger. (1981). *Psychopathology of Homicide.* Springfield, IL: Charles C Thomas.

Ritzer, G. (1992). *Contemporary Sociological Theory.* New York: McGraw-Hill Publishers.

Robins, L. N. (1966). *Deviant Children Grow Up.* Baltimore, MD: Williams and Wilkins.

Rosen, I., J. Satten, K. Menninger, and M. Mayman. (1960). Murder without apparent motive. *American Journal of Psychiatry,* 117, 48–53.

Rosenblatt, E., and C. Greenland. (1974). Female crimes of violence. *Canadian Journal of Criminology and Corrections,* 16, 173–180.

Rossmo, D. K. (1995). Geographic profiling: Target patterns of serial murderers. Doctoral dissertation, Simon Fraser University, Burnaby, British Columbia.

———. (1999). Geographic profiling. In J. Jackson and D. Bekerian (Eds.), *Offender Profiling: Theory, Practice and Research*. New York: Wiley.

Rowe, D. (1986). Genetic and environmental components of antisocial behavior: A study of 265 twin pairs. *Criminology,* 24, 513–532.

Rowe, D., and D. W. Osgood. (1984). Heredity and sociological theories of delinquency: A reconsideration. *American Sociological Review,* 49, 526–540.

Rubin, R. (1987). The neuroendocrinology and neurochemistry of antisocial behavior. In S. Mednick, T. Moffitt, and S. Stack (Eds.), *The Causes of Crime: New Biological Approaches.* Cambridge, England: Cambridge University Press, pp. 239–262.

Rule, A. (1980). *The Stranger Beside Me.* New York: New American Library.

———. (Stack, A.) (1983). *Lust Killer.* New York: New American Library.

———. (Stack, A.) (1984). *The I-5 Killer.* New York: New American Library.

———. (1988). *The Want-Ad Killer.* New York: New American Library.

Rumblelow, D. (1979). *The Complete Jack The Ripper.* Bungay, England: Chaucer Press.

Saferstein, R. (2001). *Criminalistics: An Introduction to Forensic Science* (7th ed.). Englewood Cliffs, NJ: Prentice-Hall.

Salfati, C. G., and D. Canter. (1999). Differentiating stranger murders: Profiling offender characteristics from behavioral styles. *Journal of Behavioral Sciences and the Law,* 17, 391–406.

Samenow, S. E. (1978, September–October). The criminal personality: New concepts and new procedures for change. *The Humanist,* 16–19.

———. (1984). *Inside the Criminal Mind.* New York: Time Books.

Sampson, R. (1987). Personal violence by strangers: An extension and test of the opportunity model of predatory victimization. *Journal of Criminal Law and Criminology,* 78, 327–356.

Satten, J., K. Menninger, I. Rosen, and M. Mayman. (1960). Murder without apparent motive. *American Journal of Psychiatry,* 117, 48–53.

Schacht, T. E. (1985). DSM-III and the politics of truth. *American Psychologist,* 40, 513–521.

Schreiber, F. R. (1973). *Sybil.* New York: Warner Books.

———. (1983). *The Shoemaker.* New York: Simon and Schuster.

Schur, E. M. (1972). *Labeling Deviant Behavior.* New York: Harper and Row, p. 21.

———. (1984). *Labeling Women Deviant: Gender, Stigma, and Social Control.* New York: Random House.

Schwarz, T. (1981). *The Hillside Strangler: A Murderer's Mind.* New York: Doubleday.

Scully, D., and J. Marolla. (1985). Riding the bull at Gilley's: Convicted rapists describe the rewards of rape. *Social Problems,* 32, 251–263.

Seagrave, K. (1992). *Women Serial and Mass Murderers.* North Carolina: McFarland & Company, Inc., Publishers.

Sendi, I. B., and P. G. Blomgren. (1975). A comparative study of predictive criteria in the predisposition of homicidal adolescents. *American Journal of Psychiatry,* 132, 423–427.

Sifakis, C. (1982). *The Encyclopedia of American Crime.* New York: Facts on File.

Silvers, J., and T. Hagler. (1997). In the name of the fuhrer. London: *Sunday Times Magazine,* pp. 32–42.

Simons, R. (1983, March). No ghosts for killer Gacy. *Toronto Star.*

Sizemore, C. (1982, August 25). Conversation hour. Annual meeting of the American Psychological Association, Washington, DC.

Skrapec, C. (2001). Phenomenology and serial murder. *Homicide Studies,* 5(1), 46–63.

Slovenko, R. (1989). The multiple personality: A challenge to legal concepts. *Journal of Psychiatry and Law,* 17, 681–719.

Smith, H. E. (1987, January). Serial killers. *C.J. International,* 3(1), 1–2.

Smith, S. (1965). The adolescent murderer: A psychodynamic interpretation. *Archives of General Psychiatry,* 13, 310–319.

Sparrow, G. (1970). *Women Who Murder.* New York: Abelard-Schuman.

Spitzer, R. L. (1985). DSM-III and the politics-science dichotomy syndrome. *American Psychologist,* 40, 522–526.

Stanley, A. (1983, November 14). Catching a new breed of killer. *Time Magazine;* reported by David S. Jackson.

Steffensmeier, D. J., and M. J. Cobb. (1981, October). Sex differences in urban arrest patterns, 1934–1979. *Social Problems,* 29, 37–50.

Stoller, R. F. (1975). *Perversion.* New York: Pantheon Books, p. 128.

Strachey, J. (Ed.). (1961). *The Standard Edition of the Complete Psychological Works of Sigmund Freud* (Vols. 1–20). London: Hogarth.

Strauss, M. A. (1994). *Beating the Devil Out of Them.* New York: Lexington Books.

Strauss, M. A., and L. Baron. (1983). *Sexual Stratification, Pornography, and Rape.* Durham, NH: Family Research Laboratory, University of New Hampshire.

Study belies reports of satanic network. (1994, October 31). *New York Times.*

Suinn, R. M. (1984). *Fundamentals of Abnormal Psychology.* Chicago: Nelson-Hall.

Swanson, C. R., N. C. Chamelin, and L. Territo. (1984). *Criminal Investigation.* New York: Random House.

Sykes, G. (1976). *The Concise Oxford Dictionary* (6th ed.). Oxford: Clarendon Press.

Sykes, G., and D. Matza. (1957). Techniques of neutralization: A theory of delinquency. *American Sociological Review,* 22, 664–770.

Tanay, E. (1976). *The Murderers.* Indianapolis, IN: Bobbs-Merrill.

Terry, G., and M. Malone. (1987). The Bobby Joe Long serial murder case: A study in cooperation. *F.B.I. Law Enforcement Bulletin,* November, pp. 12–18; December, pp. 7–13.

Thigpen, C., and H. Cleckley. (1957). *The Three Faces of Eve.* New York: McGraw-Hill.

Thomas, W. I. (1907). *Sex and Society.* Boston: Little, Brown.

———. (1923). *The Unadjusted Girl.* New York: Harper and Row.

Thompson, G. N. (1953). *The Psychopathic Delinquent and Criminal.* Springfield, IL: Charles C Thomas.

Thompson, T. (1979). *Serpentine.* New York: Dell.

Time. (1999, May 3). The monsters next door, pp. 20–52.

Turner, F. J. (Ed.). (1984). *Adult Psychopathology.* New York: Free Press Winston.

Turvey, B. (1999). *Criminal Profiling; An Introduction to Behavioral Evidence Analysis.* Academic Press.

Ulrich, A. (2000). *Morderisches Mirakel (Murderous Miracle).* Der Spiegl: Germany.

Underwood, R.C. (2000). My brother's keeper or my brother's killer: An in-depth investigation into the phenomenon of sibling homicide. Doctoral dissertation. California School of Professional Psychology, Fresno, California.

United States v. *Brawner,* 471 F.2d 969 (D.C. Cir. 1972).

U.S.: One in four children had a single parent. (1988, January 21). *Boston Globe,* p. 11.

U.S. Department of Justice. (1988). National Center for Missing and Exploited Children, Office of Juvenile Justice and Delinquency Prevention, Washington, DC.

———. (1989a, January). Stranger abduction homicides of children. Juvenile Justice Bulletin. Washington, DC: Office of Juvenile Justice and Delinquency Prevention, Government Printing Office.

———. (1989b). Missing and Exploited Children: Progress in the 80s. Washington, DC: Office of Juvenile Justice and Delinquency Prevention, Government Printing Office.

Vetter, H. (1990). Dissociation, psychopathy, and the serial murderer. In S. A. Egger (Ed.), *Serial Murder: An Elusive Phenomenon*. New York: Praeger, pp. 73–92.

Virkkunen, M. (1986). Reactive hypoglycemic tendency among habitually violent offenders. *Nutrition Reviews Supplement,* 44, 94–103.

Virkkunen, M., A. Nuutila, F. K. Goodwin, and M. Linnoila. (1987). Cerebrospinal fluid monoamine metabolites in male arsonists. *Archives of General Psychiatry,* 44, 241–247.

Vitek v. *Jones,* 445 U.S. 480, 100 S. Ct. 1254 (1980).

Volavka, J., D. Martell, and A. Convit. (1991). Psychobiology of the violent offender. *Journal of Forensic Sciences,* 37, 237–251.

Von Eckartsberg, R. (1986). Lifeworld experience: Existential-phenomenological research approaches to psychology. Washington, DC: Center for Advanced Research in Phenomenology and University Press of America.

Vorpagel, R. (1998). *Profiles in Murder: An FBI Legend Dissects Killers and Their Crimes.* New York: Plenum.

Wallace, H. (2001). *Family Violence: Legal, Medical, and Social Perspectives.* Boston: Allyn and Bacon.

Wasserman, A. (2000). Exploring "normal" adolescent sexual offenders: An investigation into moral rigidity. Doctoral dissertation. California School of Professional Psychology, Fresno, California.

Webster-Stratton, C. (1985). Comparison of abusive and nonabusive families with conduct-disordered children. *American Journal of Orthopsychiatry,* 55, 59–69.

Weisheit, R. A. (1984a). Female homicide offenders: Trends over time in an institutionalized population. *Justice Quarterly,* 1(4), 471–489.

———. (1984b). Women and crime: Issues and perspectives. *Sex Roles,* 11, 7–8.

———. (1986). When mothers kill their children. *Social Science Journal,* 23(4), 439–448.

When moms kill their infants. (1988, May 26). *The Washington Post,* B17.

White, L. (2000). Mass murder and attempted mass murder: An examination of the perpetrator and an empirical analysis of typologies. Doctoral dissertation. California School of Professional Psychology, Fresno, California.

Wilbur, C. (1978). Clinical considerations in the evaluation and treatment of multiple personality. Lecture delivered at Multiple Personality Conference, Friends Hospital, Philadelphia.

Wilkes, J. (1987, June). Murder in mind. *Psychology Today,* pp. 27–32.

Wille, W. (1974). *Citizens Who Commit Murder.* St. Louis, MO: Warren Greene.

Wilson, C., and D. Seaman. (1985). *Encyclopedia of Modern Murder 1962–1982.* New York: Putnam.

Wilson, J. Q., and R. J. Herrnstein. (1985). *Crime and Human Nature.* New York: Simon and Schuster.

Wilson, P., and K. Soothill. (1996). Psychological profiling: Red, green or amber? *The Police Journal* (January), 12–20.

Winn, S., and D. Merrill. (1980). *Ted Bundy: The Killer Next Door.* New York: Bantam Books.

Wint. A. V. N. (1998). There is power in the blood. *Journal of Criminal Justice Education,* 9(1) Spring, 169–175.

Wolfe, D. A., P. Jaffe, S. K. Wilson, and L. Zak. (1985). Children of battered women: The relation of child behavior to family violence and maternal stress. *Journal of Consulting and Clinical Psychology,* 53(5), 657–665.

Wolfgang, M. E. (1958). *Patterns in Criminal Homicide.* Philadelphia, PA: University of Pennsylvania Press.

———. (1967). *Criminal Homicide and the Subculture of Violence: Studies in Homicide.* New York: Harper and Row.

Women who kill. (1987). *New York Times,* March 22.

Wooden, K. (1984). *Child Lures.* Shelburne, VT: National Coalition for Children's Justice, Child Lures, Inc.

Yallop, D. (1982). *Deliver Us from Evil.* New York: Coward, McCann and Geoghegan.

Zitrin, A., A. Hardesty, E. Burdock, and A. Drossman. (1975). Crime and violence among mental patients. *Scientific Proceedings of the 128th Annual Meeting of the American Psychiatric Association, Abstracts,* 142, 140–141.

Index

A

B

C